W9-BZF-391

ESSAYS ON GUPTA CULTURE

Essays on Gupta Culture

Edited by
Bardwell L. Smith

South Asia Books

SOUTH ASIA BOOKS
Box 502, Columbia, Missouri, 65205

ISBN : 0 8364 08713

First Edition : Delhi, 1983

Printed in India
By Shantilal Jain, at Shri Jainendra Press,
A-45, Phase-I, Naraina, New Delhi-110 028
Published by Narendra Prakash Jain, for Motilal Banarsidass, Delhi-110 007

TABLE OF CONTENTS

LIST OF ILLUSTRATIONS

above crowned bodhisattva, *c.* 469 A.D.; copyright ASI.

Plate 23. Ajantā Cave 9, facade, right rear, standing Buddha, added *c.* 479 A.D.; AAAUM TH 24.

Plate 24. Kaṇherī Cave 3, porch, left end, standing Buddha, added *c.* 494 A.D.; AAAUM 577/66.

Plate 25. Ellora Cave 29 (Dhumar Lena), ground plan. Based on J. Fergusson and J. Burgess, *Cave Temples of India* (London, 1880) Plate LXXIX. Date of cave *c.* 465-475 A.D. (identifications and photo-angles added).

Plate 25a. Ellora Cave 29 (Dhumar Lena), section, showing light well above left court, at left of plan; total height about eighty feet. From J. Burgess, *Report on the Elura Cave Temples* (London, 1882), Plate LLLVII.

Plate 26. Ellora, Cave 29, left court, showing deep light well (about eighly feet from top to floor of court); AAAUM 11, 021.

Plate 27. Ellora Cave 29, left court, from left rear; view into main hall; AAAUM 16, 065.

Plate 28. Ellora Cave 29, Shrine, from front right, showing rear wall niche (presumably for Gaṅgādhara) at right of photograph; AAAUM WR 6.

Plate 29. Ellora Cave 29, interior, rear wall with niches (presumably for Mahādeva and Ardhanārīśvara, the latter at the left); AAAUM 15, 023.

Plate 30. Ellora Cave 29, wall at right of front portal, Rāvaṇa Shaking Kailāsa; AAAUM 15, 008.

Plate 31. Ellora Cave 16, (Kailāsa Temple), Rāvaṇa Shaking Kailāsa, below south porch; AAAUM WR 18.

Plate 32. Kaṇherī Cave 3, stambha at right of court, showing early Buddha and attendants; AAAUM 409/73.

Plate 33. Kaṇherī Cave 3, stambha at right of court, general view, showing standing Buddha at base and seated Buddha above, both second century A.D.; AAAUM 547/72.

ACKNOWLEDGEMENTS

The editor wishes to thank a number of persons who helped to make possible this volume of essays on the Gupta period of Indian history which originated with a seminar held at Carleton College during the winter and spring terms of 1977. To begin with, this seminar would not have taken place without the participation of Eleanor Zelliot, who conceived of the topic, jointly taught the course with me, and was involved in all the plans and arrangements from start to finish. Secondly, it is a pleasure to thank Mr. and Mrs. John W. Musser for their gift to Carleton in behalf of Asian Studies which enables the college to hold symposia and seminars of this kind, of which the one on Gupta India was the third. Selected papers from the first seminar on the T'ang dynasty were published under the title *Essays on T'ang Society : The Interplay of Social, Political and Economic Forces* (Leiden : E. J. Brill, 1976) and from the second seminar on sixteenth century Japan, entitled *Warlords, Artists and Commoners : Japan in the Sixteenth Century* (Honolulu : University Press of Hawaii, 1981).

Besides those who contributed to the present volume I would like to express my appreciation especially to Professors Frederick Asher, A. L. Basham, A. K. Ramanujan, Holly Reynolds and Eleanor Zelliot, whose lectures and courses at Carleton College during the academic year 1976-77 on a variety of subjects in Indian history and culture enriched the general context in which the symposium and seminar were held. I am also indebted to Professor Walter Spink for making possible an exhibition of magnificent photographs of Gupta period sculpture at Ajantā from the Asian Art Archives of the University of Michigan; to the University of Chicago Press for permission to include an adapted version of a map on the Gupta period, originally published in *Historical Atlas of South Asia*, edited by Joseph Schwartzberg; to Joseph Schwartzberg and Robert Hyde for their work on the adaptation of this map; and to Hendrika Umbanhowar for the two indices.

Furthermore, it is appropriate that the student members of the seminar be named, since they were not only sounding boards but also thoughtful critics in this process : Liz Bailey, Mark Brown, Jeffrey Coryell, Janet Eimon, Cynthia Ferguson, Christopher Garcia, Michael Humphrey, Doris Karlisch, James Matson, Mona Meers, Michael Noble, and Jean Unzicker.

PREFACE

The papers in this collection, aside from the two bibliographical essays, were written for and discussed at a 1977 symposium on the Gupta period of Indian history (*c*. 320-550 A.D.), held in conjunction with a seminar on this period conducted at Carleton College in Northfield, Minnesota. Since the fifteen-week seminar dealt with the principal historical, social and cultural features of India's "golden age", the papers written for the symposium approached specific topics with this background taken for granted. This volume, therefore, does not purport to be a synoptic coverage of Gupta history and culture, but a collection of essays which focuses on a limited number of particular areas of importance arising out of or in relationship to this classical period. The intent for the collection is thus twofold : that it contribute to the non-specialist's understanding of certain aspects of the Gupta age which are not frequently discussed in standard works on the subject, and that it raise a number of questions and formulate new positions which would also be of interest to those who are already familiar with this period of time and its culture.

As the Table of Contents suggests, the ten principal papers may be put into three broad categories, though three or four of the essays might easily have been placed in another of these categories. While only suggestive, the groupings indicate major areas of Gupta life and expression. The first of these has to do with the various ways in which political power and authority seek to establish and preserve legitimacy. After discussing at some length the relationship between religion and the state in pre-Gupta India, A. K. Narain examines numismatic and epigraphic sources of the Gupta period and shows how official political policy both recognized and protected forms of religious belief and practice at the same time as Gupta kings and chiefs used "the mystique of the Vedic rituals and symbolism" to enhance their authority. The policy of toleration was political in nature, for frequently those in authority subscribed to one or another of the popular faiths, usually Brāhmaṇic, in a personal sense. Professor Asher shows how religious symbolism serves as a visual metaphor conveying the analogous relationship between the ideal monarch and divine power and authority. His examples are both Vaiṣṇavite and Śaivite, and are drawn from South India as well as the core area of Gupta rule. The essay by Burton Stein is primarily about the importance of public ritual in sustaining the monarchical institution. In discussing this, he looks both at the role of ritual in pre-Gupta and Gupta India, seeing a transition from "sacred kings" to "sacred kingship", and shows how royal sacrifices such as the *aśvamedha* and the *rājasūya* were regenerative rituals whose purpose was to replenish the sacred power of kings so they might fulfill their obligation of protecting and nourishing all within their realm. While these particular sacrifices were both revived in and tended to fade with the Gupta, their place was taken by other rituals, especially in South India, whose inspiration included ancient *yajña*, Purāṇic festivals, Rāmāyaṇa motifs, and particularly the symbolic universe of South Indian temples. Thus, while Stein goes far beyond the Gupta in time and dwells at length on South India, he provides insight into the relationship between kingship and ritual generally and shows how the Gupta stress on sacred kingship had a persisting influence in medieval and even modern times.

The second category of essays provides further evidence into the well known fact of religious pluralism during the Gupta age. In part because these three essays approach this subject from very different directions, we are given some sense of the diversity and vitality of religious expression during these times. But it is also true that the picture we currently have of this phenomenon is fragmentary and inconclusive, suggesting the need for further research. The essay by Professor Basham examines the fifth century inscription by Vatsabhaṭṭi, a local Brāhmaṇa, who was commissioned by the guild of silk-weavers at Daśapura (now Mandasor) to honor with *kāvya* or courtly verse their gift of a temple to Sūrya, the sun-god. While one learns little about this cult, one learns much about the social history of this era and in the process gains a richer sense of how religious devotion (bhakti) and "love of the good things of this world" could co-exist. Wendy O'Flaherty, in her discussion of Gupta Purāṇic literature, gives a view of religious intolerance arising out of a period of reaction against heterodoxy which adds a note of realism alongside the ideal Gupta image. While Gupta kings patronized Buddhism, texts such as the fifth century *Viṣṇu Purāṇa* were composed by Brāhmaṇas who excoriated the Buddhists and who often lumped them together with Jains as heretics and *nāstikas,* or atheists. Professor Gokhale provides a broad picture of the state of Buddhism in the principal monastic centers against the socio-economic background of the times, looking at both the Theravāda and Mahāyāna traditions. As the Gupta period progresses it is clear that the fortunes of Buddhism were affected by resurgent forms of Brāhmaṇism both within court circles which received ancient Vedic rituals and among the masses who were increasingly drawn to the richness of Purāṇic Hinduism. While the primary consequences for Buddhism were after the Gupta age, the stage was set earlier.

The third category of papers in this collection deals with various literary and artistic expressions emerging from the Gupta period. Barbara Stoler Miller sees classical drama as an exposition of "the conflict and complementarity of order and spontaneity", one which is "rooted in the ancient Indian concern with reconciling life's multiple possibilities". Whether in lyric or epic or dramatic form the courts of Gupta India produced works which sought to "create verbal bridges to the divine as a means of glorifying and strengthening the kings they served". The notion of correspondences between the world of mankind and the world of the gods, strongly present in early Vedic tradition, is given even more elegant expression in Gupta literary language. Throughout there was the belief that life's multiple possibilities could be reconciled and that disharmonies of a social or psychological or physical nature could be resolved. The essay by A. K. Ramanujan and Norman Cutler is towards a chapter in the history of Indian poetry. It explores and illustrates the continuities and contrasts one finds as one examines the transformation of a classical tradition within the context of South India and especially within the context of Tamil bhakti poetry. In one sense, Professor Miller's depiction of classical drama is parallel to Frederick Asher's notion of historical and political allegory in Gupta art, both citing the relationship between microcosm and macrocosm. Likewise, the examination by Ramanujan and Cutler of the movement from classicism to bhakti is somewhat analogous to what Joanna Williams sees in the relationship between Vākāṭaka art and the Gupta mainstream, the former being a counterforce to, if at times being related to, the classical Gupta *koine*. Both essays stress the non-Gupta elements and the strongly independent nature of what emerged from the Vidarbha Vākāṭaka idiom in art and the Pallava tradition in bhakti poetry in their respective and very different ways. The chapter by Walter Spink, on the great cave at Elephanta, makes the case that this is a mid-sixth century Early Kalacuri monument sponsored by the great king Kṛṣṇarāja and is one of a number of monuments in the Konkan arising out of the Pāśupata sect of Śaivism. Professor Spink's thesis is that Elephanta's monumental scale attests to its royal benefaction and represents a culminating example of what could be loosely called the Gupta style in Western India. At the same time, it is near the beginning of the sequence of major Hindu cave temples in India, ones which include Bādāmī, Aihole, Māmallapuram, and Ellora. Spink sees esthetic links between the late fifth century images from the Vākāṭaka caves (Bāgh and Ajantā) and the Sārnāth of roughly the same time with the somewhat later carvings at Elephanta. He discusses at length the seventh century historically-based work of Daṇḍin, the *Daśakumāracarita*, an instructive tale about princely virtues, which helps to supplement the various literary, epigraphic, and art-historical evidence and provide clues as to the relationship between the Mahāyāna caves at Ajantā and the early sixth century Śaivite caves in the Bombay area. A century later the Early Kalacuri house is on the decline and with this "some of the last and most luminous reflections of India's earlier 'Gupta' age are extinguished."

The final two chapters are bibliographical essays on various aspects of Gupta history and culture. As with the Introduction, they were included with the non-specialist in mind and their focus is entirely on materials available in English. To assist in the process of selecting what books and articles to mention several criteria were kept in mind. Except for material of obviously classical status, works whose scholarship had been superseded were omitted. So too were a large number of summary treatments, many of which tend to duplicate each other. Also not included were works of such a highly technical or specialized nature that they were virtually inaccessible to all but a few specialists. Finally, some consideration was given to the availability of materials, though here only the most fugitive of items was not included. More important, there are obviously very important areas within India and in countries influenced by Gupta culture where the bibliographical references had to be curtailed because of the sheer immensity of materials.

In the essays of this volume the transcriptions of words from Sanskrit, Pāli, Tamil, and other Indian languages have followed the customary scholarly conventions. In general, the system used by A. L. Basham in *The Wonder That Was India* has been employed, but for various reasons consistency was not always possible or even desirable. No diacritical system suits all readers; the above merely identifies the system employed for the most part throughout this volume.

B. L. S.

INTRODUCTION

A. L. BASHAM

THE history of civilization is marked by certain periods when, in one or other region of the world, human culture reached a peak, from which it afterwards in some measure declined. As examples, we may suggest Periclean Greece, T'ang China, Elizabethan England. Such times were never wholly happy; but they were periods of comparative peace within the borders of the land concerned, when a benevolent government gave a reasonably comfortable and secure life to a large section of the population, and made it possible for artists and writers, assimilating the thought and experience of previous generations, to produce works of art and literature of exceptional merit, and for craftsmen and scholars to develop their techniques and sciences beyond all earlier skill and learning.

In India probably the most outstanding of such periods was that of the Gupta Empire, covering approximately two hundred years, from the fourth to the sixth centuries A.D. In this period India was the most highly civilized land in the world, for this was a time when in other parts of the Eurasian land-mass the nomads of Central Asia were on the move, and in both east and west stable empires were shattered by waves of barbarians.

When in 320 A.D., Candra Gupta I assumed imperial titles, hordes of nomads were attacking both the Roman and the Chinese empires, and Western Europe had entered a period of decline from which it only began to recover in the eighth century. In Eastern Europe and Western Asia, and in China, recovery was quicker, and when the Gupta Empire faded away in the middle of the sixth century the Byzantine Empire under Justinian had restored the glory of Rome in the Eastern Mediterranean and the T'ang dynasty was about to emerge in China, to reconsolidate the Empire and raise Chinese civilization to new cultural levels.

Thus the 'classical' age of Indian civilization occurred at a time when much of the rest of the civilized world was reeling under barbarian attacks and suffering a severe decline in cultural standards.

The background to the rise of the Guptas is an obscure one, but it is clear enough that over the previous centuries India had been preparing for a 'great leap forward'. Indeed most of the cultural features which give the Gupta period its special character were already in existence when the empire began, and the peace of the Gupta period merely assimilated these features fully, in a complex civilization of unexampled urbanity, to produce works of art, literature and learning which are among the greatest products of any early civilization anywhere.

The organic view of civilizations, associated with the names of Spengler and Toynbee, is hard to accept. Civilizations are not living organisms, to be born, grow, decline and die. No civilization, not even the civilizations of the Incas, Mayas and Aztecs, was completely isolated from others, and no civilization has ever been born or has ever died. The word civilization is merely a convenient label to attach to a certain complex of beliefs and actions which blurs on both its spatial and temporal edges, so to speak, into other similar complexes. On final analysis, there has never been more than one world civilization, with nuclear centres (of which the Gangetic plain was one) from which elements of culture have radiated to other parts of the world.

Nevertheless, it is worth noting that Toynbee, in his classification, made a sharp distinction between the earlier Indian civilization down to the Maurya dynasty, which he called 'Indic', and the following one, which he termed 'Indian' civilization proper, and which has survived to the present day. There is something to be said in favour of this division, though most Indologists would agree that it is rather too drastic. Mauryan civilization, as far as we can reconstruct its main features, was regimented by a state which interfered in almost every aspect of the life of the ordinary man. Its emperors erected monolithic columns, and its intellectuals favoured monolithic philosophical systems which explain away the individual as a temporary or even an illusory phenomenon. Almost the only significant surviving art of the Mauryan period is the highly polished statuary of the so-called 'Aśokan' pillars. Only with the end of the Mauryas did India witness the bursting forth of a more popular art form, no doubt already long practised on a small scale in wood, ivory and terracotta, into the ebullient and luxuriant carvings on the *stūpa* railings of Bhārhut, Sāñchī and elsewhere. Moreover, the post-Mauryan period saw the spread of new ways in religion—notably the devotional Vaiṣṇavism of the Bhāgavata sect, of whicht he chief early record is the *Bhagavad Gītā*, and the theistic and soteriological popular Buddhism of the Mahāyāna.

The process of change was encouraged by the appearance in northwestern India of waves of invaders. The successors of Alexander of Macedon, in the mid-third century B.C., established an independent kingdom in Bactria (the area of the upper Oxus, which divides Afghanistan from Soviet Central Asia). Very early in the second century, probably before the Mauryan empire had completely disappeared, Greco-Bactrian armies crossed the Hindūkush and led great raids into India proper. Soon they controlled most of what is now Pakistan, as well as parts of Kashmīr. They were followed in the first century B.C. by Scythians, called in India Śakas, and these in turn were followed by another Central Asian people, the Kuṣāṇas, whose power under the greatest of their rulers, Kaniṣka, reached at least as far east as Vārāṇasī. The Kuṣāṇas slowly withdrew from the Gangetic India, but, when the Gupta Empire began, their heirs were still in control of much of Pakistan.

The Kuṣāṇas rose to prominence in the politics of Asia at a time when another great power, that of Rome, was advancing from the West. India was not, however, directly affected politically by the Roman Empire, which extended its power at one time as far eastwards as northern Mesopotamia, but no further. Culturally, however, the effect of this expansion was considerable. Traders from Egypt visited India in great numbers from the mid-first century A.D. onwards, in search of spices, jewels, textiles and other luxuries, which were by now much in demand throughout the prosperous Roman Empire. These merchants brought wealth to India, and also many new ideas.

Contact with the West had been increasing, from the days when the Achaemenids of Iran occupied the Panjāb under Darius I (521-485? B.C.). It had been intensified as a result of Alexander's invasion, which resulted in colonies of Greek speakers settling in Afghanistan. Later, the Greco-Bactrian kings, no doubt, formed the medium of cultural influence in both directions. But in the first and second centuries A.D., contact between India and the Mediterranean was closer than ever before, indeed closerth an it was to become until the sixteenth century. Through this contact art motifs entered India from Antioch and elsewhere in the eastern provinces of Rome; the indigenous system of astronomy was strengthened and developed by Greco-Roman contacts; practical inventions, such as the 'Persian wheel' for irrigation, came to India. South Indian kings employed mercenaries and slave-girls from the West. The land grew rich at the expense of the Roman Empire, whose moralists complained of the heavy drain of wealth to the East, to satisfy the whims of the luxury-loving Romans and their women.

Simultaneously, the doors began to open to the East. From Indonesia, probably some time before the beginning of the Christian Era, India derived new crops, including the coconut, the areca-nut, and the betel vine, which are commonplaces in India nowadays. Buddhism, according to tradition, was first brought to China from Central Asia in the latter part of the first century A.D., and in the third century A.D. we hear of the first Chinese pilgrims visiting Buddhist sacred places in India. The learned brāhmaṇas deplored the evil forces which had been let loose on the sacred soil of Āryāvarta. Barbarian hordes plundered and slew, and incidentally endangered the sacred norms of the Āryans, bringing about confusion of class and caste and the break-up of the family system, while shaven heretics (mostly Buddhist monks) persuaded men and women to reject all that had traditionally been held sacred, especially the holy Vedas and the priests who memorized and expounded them. It seemed that the world was out of joint and learned men prophesied that the end of the aeon was near, when the universe would be purified by fire, water and wind (killing most of its inhabitants in the process), to usher in a new golden age.

They were not completely wrong about the new golden age, though the cataclysm they prophesied did not take place. Instead, the conquerors, the Śakas and the Kuṣāṇas, settled down and gained the acceptance of the conquered. Far away from their original homeland, from which they were cut off by new arrivals, the Śakas in Ujjain (now Madhya Pradesh) flourished from the trade with the West, and patronized the Sanskrit language. And in the western part of the Gangetic plain, and the whole of the Indus basin, the Kuṣāṇas built a great international empire.

Their greatest emperor, Kaniṣka I, ruled a state with an eastern frontier somewhere beyond Vārāṇasī and including on the west Afghanistan and regions far into Central Asia. He was a great patron of Buddhism and is remembered as such even in Chinese Buddhist texts, but a hundred years after his accession his descendant, fifth in succession, took as his throne-name that of one of the most popular Hindu deities of the time, Vāsudeva, better known nowadays as Kṛṣṇa. The chronology of these Kuṣāṇa kings, incidentally, is still one of the most disputed problems of Indian history. Estimates for the date of Kaniṣka vary from 78 to 144 A.D., and a few scholars would even place him well into the third century. After Vāsudeva, small Hindu dynasties, about which we know very little, reasserted themselves in the Gangetic area, and pushed the Kuṣāṇas out. The latter survived in the Panjāb, where in the third century they became tributaries of the new Iranian empire to the west, that of the Sāsānians.

In this period of about five hundred years, between the end of the Mauryan dynasty and the rise of the Guptas, the theologians, learned men, authors and artists had not been idle. The religious life of India underwent great changes. The gods Viṣṇu (chiefly in his incarnation Kṛṣṇa-Vāsudeva) and Śiva, not so important in earlier days, steadily gained strength at the expense of the older gods of the Vedas, such as Indra and Brahmā. Learned brāhmaṇas took over the old martial poem about a great battle in olden time, and by inserting lengthy didactic and theological passages, including the *Bhagavad Gītā*, and incorporating other stories as interpolations produced the enormous epic of India, the *Mahābhārata*. A great genius calling himself Vālmīki took up an old story about the righteous prince Rāma exiled as a hermit, incorporated themes from other legendary stories into this main plot, and produced the second of India's great epics, the *Rāmāyaṇa*. The norms of orthodox life were collated in the earliest of the versified *dharmaśāstras*, the so-called Law-book of Manu. The oldest surviving Indian medical text is ascribed to Caraka, traditionally the court physician of Kaniṣka.

The Buddhists, too, responded to the challenge of changing times by developing their system, perhaps encouraged by influences from Iran brought in by the invaders, to become a soteriological theistic religion, very different from the rather austere system of earlier days. Aśvaghoṣa, a famous Buddhist philosopher and theologian, also by tradition the contemporary of Kaniṣka, produced the earliest surviving *kāvya* or courtly poem (if we exclude the *Rāmāyaṇa*, which is in some respects to be classed in that category), and the oldest remaining fragments of Sanskrit drama. Flourishing schools of Buddhist sculpture existed in Gandhāra (the Kābul Valley) and Mathurā. The former showed particularly strong Western influence, while the latter, through which the main-stream of Indian art passed, developed a distinctive indigenous character. In both these schools it became customary to represent the Buddha in human form, but experts disagree as to which school started the practice.

In the Gupta period all these developments, which first appeared in earlier centuries, came to fruition. The new forms of Buddhism and Hinduism flourished side by side. In their service arose schools of sculpture and painting, of which the surviving works are few, but are enough to show the supreme beauty and inspiration of their best productions and the graceful competence of their more commonplace work, such as the delightful terracottas turned out by the thousand for the popular market. In literature, the period saw the most sensitive and masterly poetry and drama of Kālidāsa, whom most critics, ancient and modern, consider the greatest author in the whole literature of Sanskrit. The learned men of India perfected the system of mathematics and astronomy with the work of Āryabhaṭa and Varāhamihira. By this time mathematicians appear to have been using a numeral system with place notation, one of India's greatest gifts to the world, and had developed early forms of algebra and trigonometry. Metallurgists had learnt how to fashion objects of rust-resistant iron larger than anything known elsewhere until many centuries later. In medicine the work of Suśruta was in many respects in advance of Galen and of contemporary Chinese medical texts. The urbane *Kāmasūtra* of Vātsyāyana, a simple handbook and in no sense a scientific text, reflects the pleasures of the small class of sophisticated dilettanti with time to spare and wealth to spend on their pleasures. In this text there is nothing gross, orgiastic or sadistic—the sexuality of the *Kāmasūtra* is that of cultured men and women, with sympathy and respect for the personalities of others.

In Hinduism the earliest *Purāṇas* in their surviving form, notably the *Vāyu Purāṇa* and the *Viṣṇu Purāṇa*, were compiled about this time, on the basis of earlier legends and traditions. Of the two sacred epics, the *Mahābhārata* certainly received its finishing touches towards the end of the Gupta period and the original *Rāmāyaṇa* of Vālmīki was probably also expanded by the addition of its first and last books, which are certainly later than the main body of the poem. Schools of lawyers produced new *dharmaśāstras*, of which the most important is the pseudepigraphion ascribed to the Upaniṣadic sage Yājñavalkya, which formed the basis of the Hindu family law in most of India until it was supplanted by legislation in the 1950s. In Buddhism, the Yogācāra school emerged, the starting point of many developments in the Buddhism of later times in India, Tibet and China. It seems that no period in the earlier history of India was so productive in the fields of science, religion, literature and art.

The great achievements of the Gupta period were promoted by a government which maintained peace over most of northern India for two hundred years and which, by the standards of most early empires, was remarkably mild. We must not look on the Gupta emperors as providing a Utopia, however. In their realm there was no question of democracy, the welfare state, or the equality of all men before the law—brāhmaṇas had privileges and the lowest castes had serious disabilities. The Chinese pilgrim Fa-Hsien, reporting on his visit to the holy places of Buddhism around 400 A.D., was rather shocked by the fact that the *caṇḍālas*, or untouchables, were compelled to strike a wooden clapper when they entered a city, for fear of polluting their betters. Yet he noted that the legal system was exceptionally mild, and the death penalty was not imposed even for the most serious crime, and that subjects of the empire could move freely about the country without the need of passports or permits. The general benevolence of the norms of government, as distinct from actual practice, is very clear from the numerous royal inscriptions of the period, which form our main source of knowledge of its political history.

There is no certain evidence that in India at this time any history was written at all. The past, for the ancient Indian, was the legendary past, when men were more righteous than they are now and when the wise and brave kings of the epics and the *Purāṇas* provided paradigms for rulers of the dark age, the *kali-yuga*, which now enveloped the world. For our knowledge of the political events of the time we have to rely mainly on inscriptions recording the power and glory of a given king, often incorporating his genealogy. These panegyrics were engraved on copper plates or on the stone of temple walls, usually to record a gift of land or some other donation to a temple or monastery. Thus, our knowledge of the history of the Guptas is full of gaps, and much of our data is susceptible to various interpretations. When India was opened to the west, even the most learned men in the land were hardly aware that a Gupta dynasty had existed at all. Many of the greatest events of the period are still unknown to us, and are likely to remain so forever. If this volume were dealing with a comparable period of the history of early Europe or China, say the first twelve Caesars or the T'ang dynasty, it would be full of information on what actually happened in the political world of the time. For the Guptas, only a tenuous outline of the rise and decline of the great empire can be given.

Something important happened in the year 320 A.D., the first year of the Gupta time-reckoning. We do not know for certain what it was, but the generally accepted view is that it marks the accession of the first emperor of the line, Candra Gupta I. The official genealogies of later emperors record two of his predecessors, his grandfather Śrī Gupta and his father Ghaṭotkaca. We know nothing about their reigns, except that a much later Chinese source records the fact that a king of India whose name seems to be Śrī Gupta (*Che-li-ki-to*) endowed a Buddhist monastery and temple for Chinese pilgrims. Even this datum is less explicit than it might be, for the location of the monastery is not clearly stated, and thus we do not know with certainty the location of Śrī Gupta's kingdom, the original home of the imperial line; but it seems to have been along the Gaṅgā river, in either eastern Uttar Pradesh or Bihār.

Candra Gupta I greatly added to his patrimony and in commemoration of his triumphs took imperial titles. In place of the simple *mahārāja*, the only title given to his two predecessors, he is referred to as 'great king over kings, the supreme lord' (*mahārājādhirāja-paramabhaṭṭāraka*). His success seems to be largely dependent on a diplomatic marriage with a princess of the

Licchavis, an ancient tribe whose influence extended from the Gaṅgā, through northern Bihār and into Nepāl. The marriage is commemorated by special gold coins (probably issued by his son Samudra Gupta) and in the official genealogies of his successors. When Candra Gupta I died, he probably controlled the eastern Gangetic plain from modern Allāhābād to the borders of Bengal.

His successor, Samudra Gupta, whose accession is generally dated, without much positive evidence, in or about 335 A.D., was a great conqueror. An inscription from Allāhābād records the names of the kings he 'violently uprooted', those he defeated and restored to their thrones as his vassals, the tribal people of western India who gave him tribute, and the remoter lands which he also claimed as his tributaries, though in fact they were only in diplomatic contact with him. Much of the northern plain came directly under his control. This was surrounded by a circle of small subordinate states from the Brahmaputra valley to the borders of the Panjāb. The kings of the eastern seaboard, as far south as the Pallavas of Kāñchīpuram, had been defeated by him and were technically his subordinates; while he claimed to have received missions bearing tribute from Śrī Laṅkā, Nepāl, the Kuṣāṇa rulers of the Panjāb, and 'the dwellers in all the islands', which seems to refer to small semi-indianized kingdoms in Indonesia, Malaysia and Burma.

In the whole of India there was now only one power which could hope to resist the Guptas successfully. This was the kingdom of the Śakas of Ujjain. These invaders had now occupied the region of Mālwā from nearly three hundred years and were, as far as we can see, thoroughly indianized. Though they still called themselves 'great satraps' (*mahākṣatrapa*), looking back to long vanished overlords in the Northwest, they were completely independent and had grown rich from their control of the lucrative maritime trade with the West from the ports of Gujarāt. There is evidence that, after Samudra Gupta's death, there was fighting on the frontier between the Śakas and the Guptas, and Rāma Gupta, the successor of Samudra Gupta, got the worst of it. In the court tradition of India, a legend was transmitted for centuries of how the cowardly Rāma Gupta was replaced by his heroic brother Candra Gupta, who had saved the Guptas from a humiliating defeat by the Śakas. The story as it stands is incredible, and seems to have been invented in justification of a palace coup. For long, most historians disbelieved it entirely, but the discovery of coins and inscriptions of Rāma Gupta, who is not mentioned in the official genealogy of the Guptae mperors, give reason to believe that it has some basis.

Candra Gupta II came to the throne about 376 A.D., the heir to a great empire built by his two predecessors. His main military achievement was the defeat and elimination of the Śakas, who were finally conquered around the end of the century. Now the Gupta Empire extended over the whole of North India, from Gujarāt to Bengal and Assam. The long reign of Candra Gupta II (*c.* 376-*c.* 415 A.D.) and his successor Kumāra Gupta I (*c.* 415-*c.* 454 A.D.) marked the high watermark of the Gupta power. A matrimonial alliance with the Vākāṭaka kings of Central India (under whom the best murals of Ajantā were painted) effectively spread Candra Gupta II's influence towards the south. As far as we know, except for his campaign in Mālwā against the Śakas, there was no warfare of importance during the two reigns, and the kings, enriched by the tribute of their vassals, found time to patronize many authors, artists and learned men.

Candra Gupta II is one of the few kings of ancient India whose memory is preserved in both the literary and the folk tradition. Later Sanskrit literature preserves many tales about a great king called Vikramāditya, who expelled the Śakas from Ujjain and ruled there in great splendour. Though the traditional date is about four hundred and fifty years too early, there is no doubt that these stories are based on the memory of Candra Gupta, for on his coins he takes the secondary name or title Vikramāditya ('Sun of Valour'). His fame and stories of his adventures have penetrated the folk-culture, and mothers all over northern India still tell their children the tales of the great and good 'Rājā Bikram'

Towards the end of the reign of Kumāra Gupta I, the first real threat to the Gupta Empire appeared. A powerful band of Central Asian nomads, a branch of the people known to late classical writers as White Huns, called Hephthalites, had established themselves in the mountains of eastern Afghanistan in the latter part of the fourth century. While Candra Gupta II was conquering the Śakas and raising the Gupta Empire to its apogee, the Hephthalites were consolidating their power in the Northwest. Around 453 A.D. they launched a massive attack on the Guptas. The empire, which had not experienced a major war for over fifty years, staggered under the blow, and the old emperor Kumāra Gupta I died while things were at their worst.

The invaders, in India called Hūṇas, were expelled by Skanda Gupta, a younger son of Kumāra Gupta I, who was effectively in control of the whole empire by the middle of 455 A.D. His death, after a reign of about twelve years, marks the end of the high period of the Gupta power. It seems that Skanda Gupta was not the normal heir to the throne, and there is evidence of dynastic disputes on his death. Two or three insignificant Gupta kings appear in quick succession or perhaps simultaneously. Brief inscriptions, coins, and official sealings merely record their presence, and we know nothing about their achievements.

In 476 A.D. or earlier, Budha Gupta began to reign, and held the throne for about twenty years, but the evidence of inscriptions shows that his empire was very different from that of his greater predecessors. He was still titular overlord of the whole of northern India from Gujarāt to Bengal, but his effective power was confined to the eastern part of the Gangetic plain. His subordinates in the west merely referred to him cursorily at the beginning of their inscriptions and then proclaimed their own power and glory. Governors, originally holding authority at the Emperor's pleasure, took royal titles and set themselves up as hereditary vassal kings.

The process of disintegration was greatly furthered by new incursions of the Hūṇas. Two very powerful chieftains, Toramāṇa and his son Mihirakula, attacked the weakened empire. For thirty years from the beginning of the sixth century most of the western half of northern India was in their power, and the Guptas were for a while pushed back as far as Bengal. The Hūṇas appear in all references to them as ruthless barbarians. They were ultimately expelled, but the main credit for the expulsion is claimed not by a Gupta emperor but by a ruler of Mandasor in northwest Madhya Pradesh, Yaśodharman, who, in an inscription dated 532 A.D., claims to have subdued Mihirakula, and makes no admission of Gupta overlordship.

Confined to parts of Bihār and Bengal, in an area probably smaller than when Candra Gupta I began to build the empire two hundred years earlier, the Gupta empire survived a few decades longer, under insignificant kings of whom we know one or two of the names, but virtually nothing else. As the old empire faded away a new dynasty calling itself Gupta appeared in Magadha (south Bihar), and survived for a further two hundred years. These later Guptas claimed no relationship to the old imperial family, and they never controlled more than a fairly small area of the Gangetic plain.

BIBLIOGRAPHICAL NOTE

Since most of the statements in this Introduction are common knowledge to specialists, I have not deemed it necessary to give footnotes. The following volumes may be helpful, however, to those who wish to study Gupta history at greater depth. Facsimiles, texts, and translations of the inscriptions of the period are contained in :

Fleet, J. F. *Corpus Inscriptionum Indicarum.* Vol. III. *Inscriptions of the Early Gupta Kings and their Successors.* Calcutta : Government Printer, 1888 (rpt. Varanasi : Indological Book House, 1963). (The Mandasor Inscription of the Silk-weavers will be found on pp. 79-88).

Fleet's pioneering work needs to be supplemented by reference to numerous other inscriptions which were not known when he edited his *Corpus*. Most of these were published in the first instance in the periodical *Epigraphia Indica*, but all those of any importance, together with those edited by Fleet, will be found in :

Sircar, D. C. *Select Inscriptions bearing on Indian History and Civilization*, Vol. I. 2nd ed. Calcutta : University of Calcutta Press, 1965.

Unfortunately, the above book does not include translations, and thus the reader with no knowledge of Sanskrit will not find it very helpful.

Coins form an important source of Gupta history. The following two volumes discuss these fully and contain important introductions :

Allan, John. *Catalogue of the Coins of the Gupta Dynasties and of Śaśāṅka, King of Gauḍa.* London : Oxford University Press, 1914.

Altekar, A. S. *The Coinage of the Gupta Empire* (*Corpus of Indian Coins*, Vol. IV). Varanasi : The Numismatic Society of India, Banaras Hindu University, 1957.

The most thorough and up-to-date monograph on the Guptas is in Hindi :

Gupta. Parameśvarī Lāl. *Gupta Sāmrājya.* Varanasi: Visvavidyalaya Prakashan, 1970.

This volume runs into 666 pages, and contains not only a very detailed analysis of the data on political history, but also lengthy chapters on the religion, economic life, social life, literature and art of the period. Its first part has been translated into English by the author :

Gupta, Parameśvarī Lāl. *The Imperial Guptas.* Vol. I. *Sources, Historiography and Political History.* Varanasi: Visvavidyalaya Prakashan, 1974.

Other monographs on the period are :

Agrawala, Prithvi Kumar. *Gupta Temple Architecture.* Varanasi :
Prithivi Prakashan, 1968.

Biswas, Atreyi *The Political History of the Hūṇas in India.* New Delhi : Munshiram Manoharlal, 1973.

Goyal, S. R. *A History of the Imperial Guptas.* Allahabad : Central Book Depot, 1967.

Harle, J. C. *Gupta Sculpture : Indian Sculpture of the Fourth to the Sixth Centuries* A.D. Oxford : Clarendon Press, 1974.

Maity, S. K. *The Imperial Guptas and their Times.* New Delhi : Munshiram Manoharlal, 1975.

Maity, S. K. *Economic Life in Northern India in the Gupta Period.* 2nd ed. Delhi : Motilal Banarsidass, 1970.

Majumdar, R. C. ed. *The History and Culture of the Indian People : The Classical Age.* Bombay: Bharatiya Vidya Bhavan, 1954. (This third volume of an important series covers all aspects of the history and culture of South Asia from A.D. *c.* 320 to 800.)

Upadhyaya, B. S. *India in Kālidāsa.* 2nd ed. New Delhi : S. Chand, 1968.

PART I

POLITICAL POWER AND ITS LEGITIMATION

1

RELIGIOUS POLICY AND TOLERATION IN ANCIENT INDIA WITH PARTICULAR REFERENCE TO THE GUPTA AGE[1]

A. K. NARAIN

I. INTRODUCTION

THE role of religion in the history and civilization of India has been overstated time and again. Yet, we hardly find much discussion of the religious policy of the kings of ancient India, perhaps with the notable exception of Aśoka. It is partly because of the lack of written sources—histories and biographies and the like—and partly because of the built-in features of the Indian religions and Indian political theory, that what could be studied as king's behavior, or policy in its own right, got lost in the all-absorbing system of values as propounded by the religious systems and the political theorists.

Though it cannot be said that there was no religious persecution whatever at any time in ancient India, the fact remains that the evidence for persecution is very limited indeed, and the nature of it is such that it pales into insignificance when compared to examples in the history of some other parts of the world, or when compared with examples in the later history of India itself. In the entire history of ancient India, there are so few alleged or authenticated cases of persecution by kings that one hardly gives importance to them. There are some who almost take for granted that great religious tolerance prevailed in ancient India. They believe that the phenomenon of tolerance is an integral part of 'Hindu' thought. Radhakrishnan wrote:

1. This is a revised version of a paper presented at a symposium on the Gupta period at Carleton College, Northfield, Minnesota, in May, 1977.

"The Hindu view is not motivated by any consideration of political expediency. It is bound up with its religion and not its policy."[1] The modern concept of the secular state is supposed to derive from the West. But it has been stated that :

> "The religious liberty which prevailed in ancient India, however, does represent one essential aspect of the secular state. Government never sought to impose a particular creed upon the people. Various schools of thought propounded the doctrines of agnosticism, atheism, and materialism. Jainism, Buddhism, and, later, Judaism, Christianity, Zoroastrianism, and Islam were permitted to propagate their teachings, build their places of worship and establish their respective ways of life. The struggle for freedom of conscience in Europe and America, stretching over many centuries, has no counterpart in Indian history. From the earliest days this right seems never to have been denied. As Max Weber put it : 'It is an undoubted fact that in India, religious and philosophical thinkers were able to enjoy perfect, nearly absolute, freedom for a long period. The freedom of thought in ancient India was so considerable as to find no parallel in the West before the most recent age.' "[2]

The picture may be more mixed than Weber implies, and we are not concerned with the issue of the secularity of the state of India. Our purpose here is to examine whether these phenomena of religious liberty and tolerance were bound up with the religious systems and political theories of ancient India or were the results of a consciously followed policy by the king or the state. We should also note at the outset that here we are not discussing a situation in which religions born of diverse cultural roots, e.g., Hinduism, Islam and Christianity, were involved at one and the same time, but one in which the religions or sects have cultural roots in South Asia itself, e.g., Vedism or Brāhmaṇism, Vaiṣṇavism, Śaivism, Śāktism, Buddhism, Jainism, etc. Against a general background of the theory and practice in earlier times, we propose to deal specifically with the relationship

1. S. Radhakrishnan, *Eastern Religions and Western Thought*, 2nd ed. (London : Oxford University Press, 1940), p. 316.

2. Donald Eugene Smith, *India as a Secular State* (Princeton : Princeton University Press, 1963), pp. 61-62.

between religion and state in the Gupta period, which extended from about 300 to 600 A.D. During most of this span of time, the Guptas ruled over one of the three largest empires of ancient India, the two others being those of the Mauryas and the Kuṣāṇas, who preceded them. The peace and security, the material prosperity, the intellectual excellence, the moral stability, and the artistic splendour of the Gupta Age can be favorably compared with the best ages of the world history. The impact of the age was felt even outside the limits of the Gupta empire in South and Southeast Asia and lasted longer than their own rule. It is generally recognized that one of the most remarkable features of this age, which is known as the "golden age" or the "classical age" of South Asian history, is the religious liberty and harmony which marked the classical expression of Indian culture as a whole. Our sources consist mainly of inscriptions and coins, art and architecture, and some indirectly relevant literary works.

II. RELIGION AND STATE : BACKGROUND OF THEORY AND PRACTICE IN PRE-GUPTA TIMES

State policy in ancient India can hardly be considered free of religious considerations. But it operated in the much wider framework of the concept of *Dharma*, which is one of the most continuing ideas in ancient Indian polity. The Sanskrit word *Dharma* (Pāli—*Dhamma*) connotes, or involves, so much that a famous Western scholar has rightly observed that the word "has given and will always give great trouble to the translators."[1] In the narrowest sense of common usage now, this means 'religion', but the further back we go in the past the less we find it used for 'religion' as an organized social system. It is indeed one of those most inclusive concepts, albeit vague, which everyone in the past seemed to understand and felt free to interpret, but none defined it in concrete terms. It included natural law as well as that made by man, and it characterized the whole order of things. This larger principle transcended all modes of conduct. All the derived *dharmas*, including practice of religion as well as of state (*rājadharma*), were subsumed under it. This great *Dharma* sustained everything and this was the very basis of the state. We

1. T. W. Rhys Davids, *Buddhist India* (1903; rpt. Calcutta : 1959), p. 132.

are told in the *Bṛhadāraṇyaka Upaniṣad* that after the creation of the four classes (the Brāhmaṇa, the Kṣatriya, the Vaiśya and the Śūdra) Brahmā the creator realized that he was not strong enough, and, therefore, he created still further the most excellent *Dharma* :

> "*Dharma* is the *Kṣatra* of *Kṣatra* : ... therefore, even a weak man rules the stronger with the help of *Dharma* as with the help of a king : thus the *Dharma* is called the True : and if a man declares what is True, they say he declares the *Dharma* : and if he declares the *Dharma*, they say he declares what is True : thus both are the same."[1]

It is clear from the context that *Dharma*, identified with Truth, was created to strengthen the god Brahmā in the maintenance of Vedic Brāhmaṇical social order. The king had to be the protector of *Dharma* (*Dharmasya goptā*) in his own interest, for this was the *Kṣatra* of *Kṣatra*. It was part of king's own *dharma*, his *svadharma*, (i.e., *rājadharma*) to see that this larger principle of *Dharma* worked by making sure that people followed their own *dharmas* properly. In this manner, it was sought to maintain the stability of society in favor of the Vedic Brāhmaṇical system.

Later, with the growing interaction between religious ideas and social organizations of diverse origins, and resultant confrontation, an opportunity was provided for the king to take advantage of the widening horizon and liberate himself from the clutches of Brāhmaṇa elitism and of Vedic ritualism. With the second urban growth in Indian civilization in the seventh-sixth centuries B.C., and with the emergence of Buddhism and Jainism, the authority of the Vedas and the primacy of the Brāhmaṇa priesthood, and for that matter the *Varṇāśrama* system itself, received a serious challenge. The responsibility of the state and the role of the king acquired new dimensions. The king had options now. And, among the earliest territorial empire builders of ancient India, it so happened that there were kings who were neither Brāhmaṇas nor Kṣatriyas, the two uppermost classes. Some of them were even Śūdras. Vedic Brāhmaṇism had no alternative but to slowly become more inclusive and incorporate non-Vedic beliefs, cus-

1. *Bṛhadāraṇyaka Upaniṣad*, Ed. and Tr. Swāmī Mādhavānanda with an Introduction by S. Kuppuswāmi Śāstrī. 3rd ed. (Almora : Advaita Ashram, 1950), I, 4, 14.

toms, and rituals in its fold, and thereby also peoples outside of Vedic society; in the process, those who became kings became Kṣatriyas *post facto.* Kṣatriya kings followed a policy of balancing the orthodox and heterodox, not only by tolerating diverse new ideas but, at times, by extending their patronage to them. Bimbisāra, Ajātaśatru, Prasenajit, and the Nandas are well known examples. Some of these rulers consulted such non-Vedic leaders as Gautama Buddha even on political matters.

Political thinkers had begun breaking away from the old moorings of Vedism and, in the process of founding an independent science of polity, the Arthaśāstra, were in favor of its separation from theology; some went even to the length of denying the Vedas a place in the list of sciences. The very source of *Dharma* was in danger. Toward the closing quarter of the fourth century B.C. an eminent Brāhmaṇa, Cāṇakya, known as Kauṭilya, was openly insulted, as no one before, by the last of the Nanda kings. This erosion in the status of the Brāhmaṇa was an indication of the changing relations between the king and Vedic Brāhmaṇism.

The insulted Brāhmaṇa was not going to take things lying down. Kauṭilya resolved the controversy brewing in the minds of the political theorists of rival camps by restoring the prestige of the Vedas as well as making the king strong. He increased the authority of the state by including royal edict (*rājaśāsana*) as one of the sources of law. But he bound the state with the Vedic ideas of *Dharma* and *Adharma* and with the Vedic system of *Varṇāśrama*, which did not cut the Brāhmaṇa to size. If there took place a mixture of *varṇa* (*varṇasaṅkara*) and the system was destroyed, Kauṭilya expected the king to revive it and be a *dharmapravartaka*, or one who sets *dharma* in motion.[1]

Although there is no independent section on religion and the state in the *Arthaśāstra* there are statements throughout the work, in various contexts, which indicate Kauṭilya's mind. In regard to internal policy, he is unequivocal in holding that the state should support the cause of the Brāhmaṇical religion and society. In regard to external policy, however, the king is required to

1. *Kauṭilīya Arthaśāstra.* Ed. R. P. Kangle, (Bombay : University of Bombay, Part I, Text, 1969; Part II, English Translation 1972; Part III, A Study, 1965), 3.1.38. *caturvarṇāśramasyāyaṃ lokasyācārarakṣaṇāt naśyatāṃ sarvadharmāṇāṃ rājā dharmapravartakaḥ.* It must be said that recent statistical analysis proposes this text is a later compilation.

respect the religious sentiments of the conquered people by "showing the same devotion in festivals in honor of deities of the country, festive gatherings and sportive amusements," and "he should cause the honoring of all deities and hermitages, and make grants of land, money and exemptions to men distinguished in learning, speech and piety."[1] Evidently, Kauṭilya viewed his king as the supporter of *his* 'religion', Brāhmaṇism, and the *rājadharma* of his prescription was essentially a charter for the freedom and security of Brāhmaṇical faiths. He made the Brāhmaṇas godly on earth and gave them special concessions with respect to taxation and torture, and the right to honor and gifts. He provided for the state patronage of several gods of the Brāhmaṇic pantheon and their worship. According to him the king "should cause to be built in the center of the city shrines for Aparājita, Apratihata, Jayanta, Vaijayanta as well as temples of Śiva, Vaiśravaṇa, Aśvins, Śrī and Madirā", and "the city gates should be presided over by Brahmā, Indra, Yama and Senāpati.'[2]

Deities mentioned by name in Kauṭilya are from the Brāhmaṇic pantheon. The temples owned large properties, such as cattle, images, servants or slaves, lands, buildings, cash, gold and grains. The highest fine, or even capital punishment, was prescribed for their theft. It is laid down that the village elders were to look after temple property and see that it went on augmenting. The disputes over temple property were to be taken up by the king before all other cases that were brought to him for decision. An officer called *Devatādhyakṣa*, who apparently looked after temples and their property, saw to it that they were properly managed by the temple trustees. He could, if necessary, take possession of the temple property on behalf of the state.[3]

As against this, we hardly find any information about the state's responsibility toward or involvement in the welf are of sectsother than Brāhmaṇic. No mention is made of the monastic establishments and religious practices and mode of life followed by the heterodox sects or of the role of state regarding them. Not even the folk deities mentioned with approval in the Buddhist texts are included in the list of *deśadevatā*. On the other hand, the monks

1. *Ibid.*, 13.5.8, 11.
2. *Ibid.*, 2.4.17, 19.
3. *Ibid.*, 5.2.

belonging to these sects were looked upon with suspicion, and Kauṭilya asks the spies to check the dwellings of these monks for agents of the enemy and to confiscate their property. The administrators were supposed to bring to the treasury the property of heretical corporations or the property of temples not intended for use by a Brāhmaṇa learned in the Vedas. A suggestion is made to a prince to rob secretly the wealth, except that to be used by Brāhmaṇas learned in the Vedas, of heretical corporations or temples.[1] Kauṭilya calls the followers of heretical or non-Vedic sects *Vṛṣala* or *Pāṣaṇḍa*; some are mentioned by name, like the Śākyas and the Ājīvikas. He prescribes a heavy fine for inviting these monks to dinners in honor of the deities and the *pitṛs*. Most *Pāṣaṇḍas* are assigned a place of residence at the end of or near the cremation ground along with the *Cāṇḍālas*.[2]

Even though there are provisions here and there to indicate that the heretical sects were tolerated, it is the Vedic way of life that alone was declared beneficial to the people and the state. It is in consonance with this that the Vedic *saṃskāras* of *caulakarma*, *upanayana*, *godāna*, etc., were prescribed for the prince. The kins was to have an *agnyagāra* and a *ṛtvij* in his service which implies that he was expected to perform the Vedic sacrifices.[3] The Kauṭilyan state thus appears to have been influenced by Brāhmaṇical religious considerations requiring preferential treatment of the Brāhmaṇas and their gods and temples, and for all practical purposes it followed an intolerant religious policy. On the other hand, the text urges, without the pretence of an apology, the exploitation of religion for political ends. Among the nine classes of spies were included the false hermit, "whose shameless methods of exploiting popular superstitions in the king's interest" were explained in detail. In a financialem ergency, the Superintendent of Temples was asked to exploit popular superstitions for replenishing the royal treasury; even the Brāhmaṇical temples could conceivably be plundered by the king's officers on flimsy pretexts.[4] Kauṭilya's attitude toward religion is not without double-talk : one has only to go through his list

1. *Ibid.*, 5.2.37.
2. *Ibid.*, 2.4.23; 3.20.16.
3. *Ibid.*, 1.5.7-10; 1.19.23, 31; 5.3.3.
4. *Ibid.*, 5.2.39.

of concrete suggestions for implementing various policies and plans of internal administration and foreign relations.[1] In any case, nowhere does Kauṭilya allow his state to subordinate its interests to religion, and the non-religious character of the state can be noted in his emphasis on the unquestioned loyalty of the officials to the head of the state and not to religious practices.

In the Buddhist and Jaina texts, the *Dharma*, which the king was supposed to uphold was not based on the Vedas, did not require the agency of the Brāhmaṇa, and did not include the hierarchical social order. It was nothing more than 'the good old law', a classless social order, and a total application of the principle of righteousness to the king's administration. The good king, according to the Buddhist canon, ruled in righteousness, shunned the four wrong courses of life (*agatigamana*)—comprising excitement, malice, delusion and fear—and practiced the key royal duties (*Rājadhamma*), namely, alms-giving, morality, liberality, straightforwardness, refraining from anger and from injury, forbearance, and refraining from opposition. He won over the people by the four elements of popularity (*saṅghavatthu*), namely, liberality, affability, beneficient rule, and impartiality.[2] This definition of *Dharma*, and its approach to royal duties and behavior, is exemplified at its best in the Aśokan edicts.

But it was the Kauṭilyan guidelines which were restated, with or without modification, by later standard Brāhmaṇical works on polity and society. For all practical purposes, Kauṭilya seems to have set the norm, which meant that even the non-Brāhmaṇical texts seem to accept the structural framework provided by him. They seek to adjust their own needs and goals, sometimes by providing new interpretations of the same basic concepts and terms used by the Brāhmaṇas, such as that of *Dharma*; and sometimes by devising ways and means to avoid the rigors of a kingly behavior following the Kauṭilyan precepts. For example, the Jains prohibited their monks and nuns from wandering about in the country when it was in a politically critical condition because they could be mistaken for spies. The Jain monks sometimes hid themselves during the day and travelled by night, and in critical

1. *Ibid.*, 2.36.28; 4.13.41; 5.2.39-44; 11.1.25; 12.5.1-8; 13.2.15, 25-35.
2. *Jatakas*. Ed. V. Fausböll; Tr. E. B. Cowell, V., pp. 98, 510 (four *agatigamana*); V., pp. 176, 352 (four *saṅghavatthu*).

times it was difficult for them to get food and clothing.[1] In fact, the idea and practice of the king's religious policy and toleration were put to the test first in the time of Aśoka. Before him, the question did not arise, because, firstly, the non-Vedic heterodox sects had not grown sufficiently strong to pose a threat to the Vedic tradition. Secondly, the Brāhmaṇic social order, though challenged in principle, by then was not disturbed and the kings were concerned only with establishing their own prime position and rank.

Aśoka's conversion to, and patronage of, Buddhism created for the first time in the mind of an Indian king a conflict within his 'Duties'. The guidelines said to have been provided by Kauṭilya for Aśoka's grandfather were based upon Vedic traditions and a social order which gave undue importance to birth and ranking. In promoting an over-centralized administrative structure, Kauṭilya's callous pragmatism had created suspicion and hatred among people. The 'good old law', marked by common sense, simplicity and inherent flexibility, was to be replaced by a law which was tinged with Vedic Brāhmaṇism. Aśoka's Buddhism and Kauṭilya's *Rājadharma* were thus incompatible. It was therefore imperative for Aśoka to redefine the *Dharma* in a manner in which he could be faithful to Buddhism and yet follow the kingly duties in a righteous way. In Pillar Edict II, Aśoka asks, therefore, what is (this) *Dharma*? (*Kiyaṃ cu dhamme ti*), and answers himself that "this is : few blemishes, many good deeds, compassion, liberality, truthfulness and purity (*apāsinave bahu kayāne dayā dāne sace socaye*)".[2] The Brāhmaṇic conception of *Dharma*, connoting the comprehensive law of the social order of which the king himself was the unit, was transformed into a principle of pure righteousness. *Dharma*, which was considered transcendental, thus became also immanent. Aśoka exhorted his people to base their actions upon this new form of *Dhamma*, and his epigraphs are full of expressions prefixed by the word *Dhamma*, e.g., *Dhammavijaya*, *Dhammamaṅgala*, etc.[3]

1. *Āyāraṅgasuttaṃ*. Tr. H. Jacobi (London : Oxford University Press, 1884-95). (Sacred Books of the East, XXII, II. 3.1.10).

2. D. C. Sircar, *Select Inscriptions on Indian History and Civilization*, 2nd ed. (Calcutta, University of Calcutta, 1965), Vol. I, p. 54.

3. Also, note Aśoka's statement in Pillar Edict I : "This is the rule, namely, that which is called supporting by Dhamma, providing by Dhamma,

Aśoka's *Dhamma* has generally been understood either in the narrow sense of Buddhism or in the much wider sense of a new religion, an eclectic collection of views from various groups for public consumption in order to offset his personal faith in Buddhism, or as a cementing factor in the society. But what has been missed is that Aśoka's *Dhamma* was at once an effort to redefine the Vedic Brāhmaṇic concept of *Dharma* in such a subtle manner so as to dissociate the state's relationship to the Vedic Brāhmaṇic system, and outwardly to make it a universal idea to be shared by all for their common good rather than only for the maintenance of the *Varṇāśrama dharma*. And, having made toleration an integral part of his interpretation of *Dhamma*, he was in effect not only enlarging its scope in favor of heterodoxy but also justifying his own religious activities in favor of Buddhism. Of course, toleration, as part of his religious policy, was not a license for permissiveness but for engendering a feeling of harmony and discipline. This is why, if he wanted his people not to over-praise their own sect and decry that of the other, he also saw to it that those who were found guilty of schism in the Buddhist Saṅgha were expelled from the Order. He certainly did not persecute those who did not follow Buddhism. He brought the Śramaṇa up but did not put the Brāhmaṇa down; they were both put on the same level.

This religious policy of Aśoka, no doubt, led to the prosperity and spread of Buddhism. It did not put an end to Brāhmaṇism, but it weakened the Vedic roots of it. Surely, this gave a shock to the Brāhmaṇical theorists. Luckily for them, this new framework of Aśokan *Dhamma* disintegrated, as did Aśoka's empire soon after his death. Aśoka had introduced a great change after acquisition of authority and after winning a war, and was strong enough to pursue his policy. Shorn of its Vedic contents, Aśoka's *Dhamma* could not provide a strong enough source to sustain the legitimation of the authority and power of his weak successors against a new Brāhmaṇa leadership determined to seize the political base from the Kṣatriyas and neo-Kṣatriyas for the perpetuation of the Vedic tradition. This was their oppor-

making happy by Dhamma, guarding by Dhamma" (*dhammena pālanā dhammena Vidhāne*, *dhammena sukhīyana*, *dhammena goti*).

tunity. Puṣyamitra, a Brāhmaṇa general, killed the last Mauryan king Bṛhadratha and became the first Brāhmaṇa king of early Indian history.

An almost unprecedented phenomenon, which even Kauṭilya could not anticipate, took place. In various parts of India, from the north to the south, several dynasties of Brāhmaṇa and neo-Brāhmaṇa kings wielded political power for several hundred years, fulfilling as it were the vow of Paraśurāma to destroy the Kṣatriyas. To name only the important ones, they are the Śuṅgas (*c*.187-75 B.C.) and the Kaṇvas (*c*.75-30 B.C.) in the North, the Sātavāhanas (*c*. 30 B.C. to *c*. 225 A.D.) and the Vākāṭakas (*c*. 255-550 A.D.) in the Deccan, and the Kadambas (*c*. 345-565 A.D.)in the South. The Talaguṇḍa pillar inscription gives expression to the feeling of these Brāhmaṇa kings from Puṣyamitra to Mayūraśarman when the latter records the statement :

> "Alas ! in the age of Kali, Brāhmaṇahood is helpless against the *kṣatra*; for what can be more pitiful than this, that even after I have given full satisfaction to my *gurus* and studied my *śākhā* with great effort, the realization of my spiritual aim should depend on the king ?"[1]

No wonder these kings revived Kauṭilya's Brāhmaṇic affiliation of state with avengeance, and with more pronounced Vedism th?n what he had envisaged. The potency of the great *Dharma* created by Brahmā was sought to be strengthened by repeated performance of Vedic sacrifices. Their example was followed by some of the Kṣatriya kings also, for they found it imperative in the wake of the new awareness which took advantage of the accident of the post-Mauryan foreign incursions too.

The Ayodhyā inscription states that Puṣyamitra Śuṅga performed two *Aśvamedha*[2] and the Nānāghāt speaks of the Sātavāhana princes, and of their mother Nāyanikā, having celebrated numerous Vedic sacrifices, some of which were long forgotten.[3] This Vedic enthusiasm of a queen is, perhaps, a rare example indicating the unlimited process of acculturation, because the patriarchal Vedic tradition did not permit women in their own right

1. D. C. Sircar, "Talaguṇḍa Pillar Inscription", *op. cit.*, pp. 475-79.
2. D. C. Sircar, *op. cit.*, pp. 94-95.
3. *Ibid.*, pp. 192-97.

to perform sacrifices. The epithets *Ekabamhaṇa* (the unique Brāhmaṇa) and *khatiya-dapa-māna-madana* (destroyer of the pride and conceit of the Kṣatriyas) were applied to the Sātavāhana king Gautamīputra Sātakarṇī who was also compared in prowess and valor to Vedic and epic heroes like Nābhāga, Nahuṣa, Janamejaya, Yayāti, Rāma, Keśava, Bhīma, and others.[1]

In this 'counter-revolution', it is not unlikely that some violent persecution also took place. If the reference in the Buddhist text, *Divyāvadāna*,[2] is given credence, Puṣyamitra put a price of one hundred *dīnāra* (gold coins) for every head of a Śramaṇa, the class of people who were equated with the Brāhmaṇas by Aśoka as deserving of equal honor. But this seems to have happened, if at all, in the first flush of reaction, or, if Tarn is right, on account of their sedition in the Panjāb. Certainly, Buddhists and their activities as a whole did not suffer. It is in the period of the Śuṅgas that the famous Buddhist monuments of Bhārhut and Sāñchī came into being. And, it is the same Nasik inscription which describes the exploits of the 'unique Brāhmaṇa', Gautamīputra Sātakarṇī, which announces the gift of a cave to the Buddhist sect of the Bhadāvanīyas by the queen-mother Gotami Bala Śrī.

With the political power in their hands, it was not difficult for the Brāhmaṇas to contain the tide of Aśoka's *Dhamma*. Their main target was the new idea of *Dhamma*, and not Buddhism. They were more concerned in restoring the idea of Vedic *Dharma* which meant the re-establishment of the *Varṇāśrama* system with Brāhmaṇa primacy. Once having succeeded in this, it was not necessary for them to be violent against Buddhism and other heterodoxies. In fact, the Vedic *Dharma* also required that people should be allowed to follow, their own requisite *dharmas*, which included not only social but also religious divisions. There were other reasons too for not resorting to violence. One was the resistance which they might have encountered from the Vaiśyas, who formed the bulk of the mercantile class and rich farmers and who were the mainstay of the economy. Secondly,

1. D. C. Sircar, "Nasik Cave Inscription of Vāśisthīputra Pulumavi", *op. cit.*, pp. 203-05.
2. *Divyāvadāna*. Ed. E. B. Cowell and R. A. Neil (Cambridge University Press; 1886), pp. 433-34.

the presence of successively new foreign ethnic groups in the West and Northwest, who had entered to stay there for good, was a constant source of danger, for violence could alienate and force the persecuted to fall into enemy hands. In order to sustain the Brāhmaṇic socio-religious order, the Brāhmaṇas renewed their wise policy of compromise and assimilation with new vigor and avoided violent confrontation and alienation in all spheres except the political. In fact, what perhaps started as a counter-revolution soon turned into a counter-reformation.

The survey of pre-Gupta religion and politics cannot be complete without taking into account the role of the foreign ethnic groups known to Indian sources as Yavanas, Śakas, Pahlavas, and Tushāras, who ruled over considerable parts of India by right of conquest. The Purāṇas refer to the Yavanas as the 'Evil of the Kali Age' and we are told that they would be :

> "here by reason of religious feeling, ambition and plunder. They will not be kings solemnly anointed, but will follow evil customs by reason of the corruption of the age. Massacring women and children and killing one another, kings will enjoy the earth at the end of the Kali age. Kings of continual upstart races, falling as soon as they arise, will exist in succession through Fate. They will be destitute of righteousness, affection and wealth. Mingled with them will be Ārya and Mleccha folks everywhere : they will prevail in town; the population will perish."[1]

It is interesting to note that Pargiter has translated *Dharma*, *Kāma* and *Artha* in the above passage first as 'religious feeling, ambition and plunder' and a second time as 'righteousness, affection and wealth'. No doubt, the two uses of the word *dharma* in this passage are intriguing. If they mean the same thing they are contradictory, for if the Yavanas came to India for reasons of *dharma* how could they be devoid of the same *dharma* ? By translating the words differently, Pargiter has indicated at once his awareness of the problem and his solution of it. But history does not substantiate his understanding of the reasons for the Yavanas' coming to India.

One may grant that the Yavanas had 'ambition' and 'plunder' in mind, but I doubt if their action was prompted by 'religious

1. F. E. Pargiter, *The Purāṇa Text of the Dynasties of Kali Age*, p. 56 of the text and p. 74 of the translation.

feeling'. For the Yavana invasion, or for that matter the later Śaka and Kuṣāṇa ones, were inspired neither by anti-Buddhist nor by anti-Brāhmaṇic feelings; nor were they meant to foist a new religion upon the acquired domain. Aśoka's area of Dharmavijaya extended to the four provinces of Aria, Arachosia, Gedrosia and Paropamisadae.[1] One could argue that the Yavana invasion was directed against Aśoka's policy of *Dhamma* in Afghanistan. But Bactria was not part of Mauryan dominion (*vijita*) in Afghanistan; the Yavanas had become independent even before Aśoka's death, and Antiochus III had renewed his family's friendship treaty with the Mauryan Subhagasena in Kābul.[2] Moreover, there was no strongly entrenched and politically conscious socio-religious group in Afghanistan at that time like that of the Brāhmaṇas in northern India to raise the banner of revolt againt Aśoka's policy; on the contrary, that area for centuries to come continued to be influenced by and remained a strong center of Buddhist activities as a result of Aśoka's action.

Furthermore, the subtle suggestion made by Tarn that the Greeks came as saviours of the Buddhists against Puṣyamitra is at most only a weak speculation. But if Tarn is right in observing that Buddhist and Brāhmaṇa groups were not in a state of war, the question of saving one against the other should not arise. In fact, the Greeks were already there even before Puṣyamitra entered the scene. Again on Tarn's own testimony, "no Hellenistic King would ever have supported one religion against another, for one of the cardinal tenets of Greeks in the Hellenistic centuries was that no man's religion was any one's business but his own."[3] If the Yavanas were indeed guided by the Hellenistic tenets as stated by Tarn, the idea of foisting their own religion on the newly acquired territories did not arise. It may be noted that Kauṭilya, too, as we have pointed out earlier, required the king to respect the religious sentiments of the conquered

1. These provinces were ceded to Aśoka's grandfather Candragupta Maurya by Seleucus I. The discovery of Greek inscriptions of Aśoka in Afghanistan confirms this fact, known from the Western classical sources.

2. A. K. Narain, *The Indo-Greeks* (Oxford : Clarendon Press, 1962), p. 21.

3. W. W. Tarn, *Greeks in Bactria and India* (Cambridge University Press : 1951), p. 176.

people by all means. The Yavanas and their successors have left no indication of a religious motivation of their actions.

In fact, when the Purāṇas say that the Yavanas were here 'for reasons of *dharma*', they only mean by it such natural laws according to them as the cyclic time and corruption of age, the *paryāya-kāla* and the *yuga-doṣa*, expressions which have been used to elaborate the situation in the passage under discussion.[1] And when it is stated that they were 'devoid of the *dharma*', it meant 'righteousness', as translated by Pargiter, but in the Brāhmaṇic sense of values, pointing to the *Varṇāśrama dharma*. The *yuga-doṣa* idea is intimately connected with the cry of *Varṇasaṅkara* so loudly made in the Brāhmaṇical sources.[2] If the Brāhmaṇa was 'the natural enemy of the Yavanas'[3] and of other foreign people, he was so not on religious but on socio-political grounds, because his leadership and authority seemed exposed to danger. Once the Brāhmaṇas became assured of non-interference from these foreign groups, they found ways and means to accommodate them and this suited both the parties. They were indeed pastmasters in this art of assimilation and compromise.

After all, the Yavanas and all the other Mlecchas who followed them had come to stay. They were peoples thrown out of their homelands, to which they could not return even if they had wanted to. They were small in number. They were naturally interested neither in religious antagonisms nor in disturbing the social order. They were more concerned with establishing the legitimation of their political power and authority which they had acquired through force. It is interesting to note that while the Yavanas, the Śakas, and the Kuṣāṇas belonged to the Indo-European linguistic group, and subscribed to violence, they did not adopt the Vedic cult of sacrifice for this purpose but introduced a new amalgam, one ingredient of which was from their own home tradition and the other was based on non-Vedic ideas as a counterpoise to the post-Mauryan Brāhmaṇa leadership. Thus the Indo-Greeks took the epithets like *Theos*

1. F. E. Pargiter, *op. cit.*, p. 56.

2. "Yuga-Purāṇa," *Journal of Bihar and Orissa Research Society*, XIV, (1928); D. R. Mankad, "A Critically Edited Text of the *Yuga-Purāṇa*". *Journal of U.P. Historical Society*, XX (1947), pp. 32 ff. See lines 94-110 of the text on pp. 54-55.

3. W. W. Tarn, *op. cit.*, p. 173.

and *Epiphanos* (God-manifest) as well as those of *Dhramika* (Dikaios) and *Kalanakrama* (Eurgetos). The Kuṣāṇas adopted such epithets as *Sacadhramathida* (steadfast in the true or noble *dharma*) as well as *Devaputra* (son of the gods). The matter of legitimation was thus strengthened by making the person of the king more divine than hitherto allowed by the Vedic Brāhmaṇic tradition. The coercive force became thus endowed with a divine element on the one hand, and tempered by *dharma* in the Aśokan sense of universal righteousness on the other. The Kuṣāṇas discovered that the Brāhmaṇa cry of *Varṇasaṅkara* as a destablizing factor in society was a sham. The mystique of Vedic ritualism only strengthened the hold of the Brāhmaṇas on state and society for a time, but it did not provide a sense of participation to the common people. Its import of social discrimination and economic wastefulness must have alienated people at large for whom Vedic ritualism was a meaningless jargon. These were issues of common interest also to the Yavanas, the Śakas, the Pahlavas, and the Kuṣāṇas. Their religious policy was therefore marked by a peculiar eclecticism and they supported the popular religious sects and beliefs which reduced the importance of the role of the Brāhmaṇas, and of the Vedic rites. They not only freely selected their cults and gods, but they also became instrumental in making combinations of, and compromises between, them. If one Yavana King, Menander, was a Buddhist, another, Heliodoros, was a Bhāgavata. On the one hand, the Yavanas did not dispose of the aniconic symbols like wheel and *caitya* and, on the other hand, they gave the prototypes and the first experimental images of gods like Vāsudeva, Saṅkarṣaṇa, Śiva and Buddha, and even such syncretic ones as Gaṇeśa.[1]

While in this manner they took advantage of their authority to give a sense of direction to the rise and growth of new religious ideas, cults, and institutions, they did not prohibit the performance of the Vedic sacrifices by the Brāhmaṇas, as is clear from the various Yūpa inscriptions from Mathurā, Rājasthān and Central India in the time of the Kuṣāṇas.[2] They

1. A. K. Narain, "On the Earliest Gaṇesha", *in Senarat Paranavitana Commemorative Volume* (Leiden : E. J. Brill, 1978), pp. 142-44.

2. "Isapur Yūpa Inscription", in D. C. Sircar, *op. cit.*, pp. 149-50; "Badvā Stone Pillar (*Yūpa*) Inscriptions", in D. C. Sircar, *op. cit.*, p. 91.

thus became part of the Indian systems, and an unparalleled interaction took place, which is evident from the numismatic and epigraphic materials, as well as from the artistic productions of the age. Their creative role in transforming indigenous religious ideas and institutions, artistic expressions and iconographic forms, is manifest, to name only some, from contributions to the growth of the Bhakti movement, Mahāyāna Buddhism, and Gandhāran art. So, their religious policy was born not only out of political expediency but also out of genuinely personal, social and religious concern. Otherwise, it would be difficult to explain their initiative and active patronage, and the resultant productivity which indirectly led the Guptas later to synthesize ideas and institutions.

But before we discuss the Guptas we should note that there were several small regional and local monarchies and republics of indigenous origin before and after the Kuṣāṇas. It is interesting to find that hardly any of them patronized Buddhism or Jainism at the state level; on the contrary, their allegiance was mostly to the Brāhmaṇic cults. But what is remarkable about at least some of them is that they were symbolically headed by their local patron deities in whose name they issued their coins, e.g., the Kuṇindas, the Audumbaras, the Yaudheyas, the Nāgas, the Mitras, etc.[1]

A seal from Bhitā refers to the offer of a kingdom to the god Mahāsena.[2] But it would be incorrect to take these states as theocratic ones, because there were no priests to interpret these patron deities of the state as they were in Egypt. Be that as it may, two things are worth noting about them. First, there is no evidence of intolerance shown in these states, and, second, a large number of minor gods and goddesses of local importance as well as belonging to folk cults attained such respectability, status, and pervasiveness that they could not be ignored. The Brāhmaṇas in the wake of the Śramaṇic challenge and foreign incursions were only too eager to assimilate these local deities. In return,

1. P. L. Gupta, "Bearing of the Numismatics on the History of the Tribal Republics in Ancient India", *Indian Historial Quarterly*, XXVII (1951), pp. 197-209. P. L. Gupta refers only to the cases of the Audumbaras, Kuṇindas and Yaudheyas, but we may add to this list such monarchical states as those of the Nāgas and Mitras.

2. John Marshall, *Archaeological Survey of India, Annual Report*, 1911-12, p. 51.

the religious policy of these states became amenable to Brāhmaṇism. But some of the local and folk deities were also gradually admitted into the Buddhist and Jaina pantheons. In various particulars the several religious systems thus showed points of contact and an agreement to coexist.

The syncretism and eclecticism introduced by the foreign element and the particularistic diffusion and accommodative expansion, on account of the rise of centres of local authority in the centuries preceding the Guptas, had made the religious scene so full of options that only an assimilationist approach could contain them. And the Guptas very wisely oriented their state policy in that direction.

III. RELIGIOUS AFFILIATION AND POLICY OF TOLERATION IN THE GUPTA AGE : FACTS AS KNOWN FROM SOURCES MAINLY NUMISMATIC AND EPIGRAPHIC.

The Gupta age presents a religious canvas of complex vertical and horizontal relationships. One segment of this shows the Vedic rituals and gods standing at the vertex of diverse Brāhmaṇical religious systems which run in horizontal relationship with one another. The non-Brāhmaṇical systems are similarly shown in horizontal relationship with one another, but devoid of the Vedic vertex, and running competitively parallel to the Brāhmaṇical ones sharing in the new options provided by the popular elements of folk and local cults involving the Yakṣas, the worship of sacred trees and rivers, etc. In the hands of the Gupta kings this confusing material portrayed a picture of peculiar harmony on the canvas.

The kings and the chiefs of the Gupta age, by and large, acted on three levels. For legitimation of their authority they used the mystique of the Vedic rituals and symbolism on the one hand and appropriated some elements of divinity to their person on the other. But for their personal goals, they subscribed to one or the other of popular faiths, mostly of Brāhmaṇic origin. In their public role, they assumed a liberal disposition, allowing freedom as well as, at times, promotion of religious beliefs and practices other than their own. We will first examine the evidence pertaining to the Gupta kings and then add the information we have about their important contemporary kings and chiefs.

The first of the Gupta kings, Gupta or Śrī Gupta, is known from I-tsing's account to have built a temple for the Chinese Buddhist pilgrims at Mṛgaśikhāvana, east of Nālandā, and endowed it with the revenue from forty villages. In the absence of any positive information about this king's personal religious affiliation, it could be speculated that either he was a Buddhist himself, or, if he was a Vaiṣṇava like his successors, he did permit major Buddhist religious activity.[1] Nothing is known of his son, Ghaṭotkaca, whose name is reminiscent of one in the Mahābhārata. Also, there is little information about the personal leanings of the third king of the dynasty, Candra Gupta I, except that he is represented on his coins holding a crescent-topped standard, perhaps in allusion to his name Candra (moon), and that on the reverse of his coin there is a figure of Lakṣmī (or Durgā or Annapūrṇā) seated on a couchant lion. Certainly he was not a Buddhist. But his marriage to a Licchavi princess was one of the contributing factors in the rise of the Guptas as a major power in northern India. We do not know for certain if the Licchavis continued to be Buddhist (or were they followers of Jainism ?) in the fourth century A.D., but it is known that the Brāhmaṇa orthodoxy never accepted them into their fold, even later, without qualification.[2]

The next king, Samudra Gupta, was one of the two (the other being his son, Candra Gupta II) makers of the Gupta empire and glory. He is referred to in the Allahabad pillar inscription[3] as one "who was equal to (the gods) Dhanada, Varuṇa, Indra and Antaka, who was the very axe of (the god) Kṛtānta, who was the giver of (many) millions of lawfully-acquired cows and gold, who was the restorer of the Aśvamedha sacrifice that had long been in abeyance."[4] He is called "the supporter of the real truth of the Scriptures" (*śāstra-tattvārthabhartuḥ*) and "the

1. John Allan, *Catalogue of the Coins of the Gupta Dynasties and of Sasanka, King of Gauḍa* (London : Oxford University Press, 1914), p. xv. A. S. Altekar, in *The Vākāṭaka-Gupta Age*, pp. 129-31.

2. *Mānava dharmaśāstra*, X, 20, 22. See also A. S. Altekar, in *The Vākāṭaka-Gupta Age* (Delhi : Motilal Banarsidass, 1960), p. 217. H. N. Jha, *The Licchavis (of Vaiśālī)* (Varanasi : Chowkhamba Publication, 1970), pp. 3-14. But if the reverse device on the Candra Gupta-Kumāradevi type of coin is related to the Licchavis their Brāhmaṇic affiliation may have to be accepted.

3. D. C. Sircar, *op. cit.*, pp. 262 ff.

4. D. C. Sircar, *op. cit.*, pp. 270-71.

builder of the *dharma*-fencing" (*dharma-prācīra-bandhaḥ*) itself. He is shown on his coins dropping incense upon an altar.[1] There is a Garuḍa standard on the obverse and the figure of Lakṣmī or Gaṅgā on the reverse.[2] On one of his coin-types, we find a sacrificial horse for the Aśvamedha standing before a *Yūpa* with the epithet *Aśvamedhaparākramaḥ*.[3] His coin-legends include *kṛtāntaparaśurjayatyājitarājajetājitaḥ* ("wielder of the axe of Kṛtānta, the unconquered conqueror of unconquered kings is victorious").[4] The symbol of Garuḍa (*garutmadaṅka*), the *vāhana* of Viṣṇu, was adopted on his official seal.[5] This *vāhana* is represented in relief on his Gayā copper plate, which records the grant of a village as an *agrahāra* to a Brāhmaṇa Gopasvāmin, of the Bhāradvāja gotra and of the Bahvṛca Śākhā, for the religious merit of his parents and himself.[6] Another similar copper plate inscription[7] from Nālandā records the gift of another village to a Brāhmaṇa. While there is every indication of personal Vaiṣṇava leaning, a reference to Paśupati in the Allahabad pillar inscription and depiction of Gaṅgā on his coins shows his respect for Śaivism and such popular cults as the worship of sacred rivers.[8] In the Eran stone inscription, he claims to have superseded such Brāhmaṇical heroes as Pṛthu and Rāghava in giving gold.[9] Thus, in his religious beliefs and practices, ideals and models, symbols and attributes, Samudra Gupta personally belonged to the Brāhmaṇical fold. But, according to one source, he appointed the noted and erudite Buddhist scholar from Peshawar, Vasubandhu, to teach his son.[10] A

1. John Allan, *op. cit.*, p. 1, Pl. I.1.
2. E. g., on the 'Standard' and 'Archer' types of coins for Garuḍa and Lakṣmī, and 'Tiger-slayer' type for Gaṅgā, see John Allan, *op. cit.*, Pls. I, II, IV.
3. *Ibid.*, p. 21, Pl. V. 9.
4. *Ibid.*, p. 12, Pl. IV. 8.
5. Note the reference to this seal in the Allahabad pillar inscription, line 24 (*garutmadaṅka śvaviṣayabhuktiśāsana yācanād*·····).
6. D. C. Sircar, *op. cit.*, pp. 272-74. These plates may be later forgeries.
7. D. C. Sircar, *op. cit.*, pp. 270-71.
8. D. C. Sircar, *op. cit.*, p. 267, line 31; (*punāti bhuvanatrayaṃ paśupaterjjaṭāntarguhānirodha-parimokṣa śīghramiva pāṇḍu gāṅgam* [*payaḥ*]).
9. D. C. Sircar, *op. cit.*, pp. 268-69, lines 7-8 of the epigraph.
10. V. A. Smith, *Early History of India*, 4th ed. (Oxford : Clarendon Press, 1924), pp. 320, 325, 346-7; Takakusu, *Journal of the Royal Asiatic Society of Great Britain and Ireland* (1905), pp. 44-53; See also A. S. Altekar, *op. cit.*, p. 155.

Chinese source informs us that he was pleased to give permission to the reigning king of Śrī Laṅkā, Meghavaṇṇa (352-79 A.D.), to construct a vihāra and a rest house near the Bodhi Tree at Gayā, for the accommodation of monks and visitors from the island kingdom.[1]

Two ephemeral Gupta kings of doubtful historicity, Kāca Gupta and Rāma Gupta,[2] also seem to have been the votaries of Viṣṇu. On Kāca coins the surmounting feature of the standard is the wheel of Viṣṇu (Cakrapuruṣa).[3] The second great Gupta king, Candra Gupta II (376-414 A.D.), a son of Samudra Gupta, took the epithet of *Paramabhāgavata* and continued the use of Garuḍa and Lakṣmī on his coins.[4] He introduced a new coin-type known as Cakravikrama type,[5] with the figure of Cakra-puruṣa,[6] a personification of Viṣṇu's Cakra, identified with Viṣṇu himself in the *Ahirbudhnyasaṃhitā*.[7] It was the concept used by the Pāñcarātra Bhāgavatas to influence the political thought and ideals of kingly power.[8] If the Candra of the Mehraulī

1. Sylvain Lévi, "Les Missions de Wang Hiuen-tśe dans l'Inde", *Journal Asiatique* (1900), pp. 297-341, 401-68, esp., pp. 316 ff, 401 ff; *Journal Asiatique* (1902), p. 194. See also A. S. Altekar, *op. cit.*, p. 149. The date of Meghavaṇṇa is uncertain. Geiger (*Mahāvaṃsa*, English translation, p. xxxix) places him between 353-79 A.D., but according to Paranavitana (in Ch. XIII of A. S. Altekar, *op. cit.*) he ruled from 304-332 A.D.

2. Some scholars identify Kāca with Samudra Gupta, and some do not believe in the historical existence of Rāma Gupta as an Imperial Gupta king.

3. John Allan, *op. cit.*, p. 15, Pl. II. 6 for Kāca. For Rāma Gupta, see *Journal of the Numismatic Society of India*, XII, pp. 103-111; XIII, pp. 128-36; XVIII, pp. 108-09; XXIII, pp. 340-44; XXV, Pt. II, pp. 165 ff. One of his coin-types bears Garuḍa.

4. John Allan, *op. cit.*, pp. 24-60, Pls. VI-XI, *passim*.

5. *Journal of the Numismatic Society of India*, X, pp. 95-118, Pl. VII, 1.

6. A. S. Altekar, *Catalogue of the Gupta Gold Coins in Bayana Hoard* (Bombay : *The Numismatic Society of India*, 1954), pp. 208-09, Pl. XVIII, 14. See also A. S. Altekar, *The Coinage of the Gupta Empire*, (Corpus of Indian Coins, Vol. IV), Varanasi : The Numismatic Society of India, 1957, p. 146.

7. *Ahirbudhnyasaṃhitā*. Ed. by M. D. Rāmānujācārya under the supervision of F. Otto Schräder (Madras: Adyar Library, 1916), Vol. II, 36.63-65; 41.37.

8. C. Sivaramamurti, *Journal of the Numismatic Society of India*, XIII, pp. 180-82; V. S. Agrawala, *Journal of the Numismatic Society of India*, XVI, pp. 97-101.

iron pillar is identified with Candra Gupta II, he installed a *dhvaja* (pillar) in honor of Viṣṇu on Viṣṇupada hill. The legends on his coins also affirm his Vaiṣṇava affiliations. But the Mathurā pillar inscription mentions the installation of a couple of Śiva-liṅgas, styled Kapileśvara and Upamiteśvara after the names of two teachers of the Lakuliśa sect.[1] Whereas one Udayagiri cave inscription refers to the religious gift (*deyadharma*) of a Sanakānika vassal of Candra Gupta II, and was engraved in honor of Viṣṇu and a twelve-armed goddess (Lakṣmī ?), another inscription there records the excavation of a cave sanctuary of Śambhu, under the orders of Sāba Vīrasena, his Minister of Peace and War.[2]

In the neighborhood of Sāñchī, another epigraph[3] reports the grant, by Āmrakārdava, of twenty-five dīnāras and a village to the Ārya-saṅgha of the vihāra of Kākanādabota, for feeding Buddhist monks and for burning lamps in the *ratnagṛha* (the jewel-house), and for the increase of his own merit and that of Candra Gupta II. It is interesting to note, however, that this record ends with an imprecation that anybody who disturbs the endowment will be nvested with the guilt of the slaughter of a cow or a Brāhmaṇa, besides incurring other sins.[4] It is also significant that Āmrakārdava, probably a Buddhist, had an exalted military rank under Candra Gupta II. The Chinese traveller Fa-Hsien, who visited India during his reign, speaks enthusiastically about Buddhism and the ramification of the Saṅgha.[5] According to him, Buddhism was flourishing in the Panjāb and Bengal and was gaining ground in Mathurā, where he noticed twenty monasteries. In Pāṭaliputra there were two Saṅghārāmas, one Hīnayāna and the other Mahāyāna, tenanted by six to seven hundred monks. He describes magnificent processions of the decorated images of the Buddha and the Bodhisattvas, organized every year in the capital on the eighth day of the

1. D. C. Sircar, *op. cit.*, pp. 277-79.
2. *Ibid.*, pp. 279-80.
3. *Ibid.*, pp. 280-82.
4. [*Ta*] *detatpravṛttaṃ ya uccindyātsa gobrahma-hatyayā saṃyukto bhavetpañchabhiśchānantaryyairiti.*
5. *The Travels of Fa-hsien* (399-414 A.D.) or *Record of the Buddhistic Kingdoms,* re-translated by H. A. Giles (London : Cambridge University press, 1923), *passim.*

second moon.[1] It is interesting to note that in the epigraphs recording non-Brāhmaṇical gifts, even those issued by the officers of the king, the sectarian title of Candra Gupta II, *Paramabhāgavata*, is omitted.[2] This indicates that people did not consider it obligatory to refer to the religious affiliation of the king, and that such omissions did not incur the displeasure of the king.

Kumāra Gupta I (415-455 A.D.), calling himself *Paramabhāgavata,* continues using the Garuḍa standard and the figure of seated Lakṣmī on his coins.[3] He also repeats Samudra Gupta's Aśvamedha type and takes the epithet of *Aśvamedhamahendraḥ*.[4] Kumāra Gupta was the greatest innovator of coin-types among the Guptas.[5] It seems that at some period of his life he switched his leanings to Kārttikeya; his name, Kumāra, is in allusion to this deity. In the Śaiva pantheon, Kārttikeya—under various names—was becoming an independent cult object.[6] Kumāra Gupta issues some coins with Kārttikeya riding his *vāhana*, the peacock, on the reverse and with himself feeding this sacred *vāhana* on the obverse.[7] On his new silver coins, Garuḍa is replaced by a peacock.[8] But, whereas 'in the augmenting victorious reign' of Kumāra Gupta, Dhruvaśarman established a *sattra* or hall for distribution of charity at the shrine of Kārttikeya,[9] a Mayūrākṣaka, the minister of a feudatory of Kumāra Gupta, caused a lofty temple of Viṣṇu to be built by his sons.[10]

1. *Ibid.*, p. 47.
2. D. C. Sircar, "Sanchi Stone Inscription", *op. cit.*, pp. 280-82.
3. John Allan, *op. cit.*, pp. 61-113, Pls. XII-XVIII.
4. *Ibid.*, pp. 68-69, Pl. XII 13, 14.
5. For a complete list of his types and innovations, see A. S. Altekar, *The Coinage of the Gupta Empire.*
6. R. G. Bhandarkar, *Vaishnavism, Śaivism and Minor Religious Systems* (Poona : Bhandarkar Oriental Research Institute, 1928), pp. 214-15; see also, for example, Kuṣāṇa and Yaudheya coins.
7. John Allan, *op. cit.*, p. 84, Pl. XV. 5-11.
8. *Ibid.*, pp. 107-110, Pl. XVIII, 1.-15. This is the northern variety, also known as "The Central Provinces" type, of the silver coins of Kumāra Gupta.
9. "Bilsad Stone Pillar Inscription", in J. F. Fleet, *Corpus Inscriptionum Indicarum*, Vol. III, *Inscriptions of the Early Gupta Kings and their Successors.* (1888; rpt. Varanasi : Indological Book House, 1963), pp. 42-44; D. C. Sircar, *op cit.*, pp. 285-87.
10. "The Gaṅgdhar Stone Inscription", in J. F. Fleet, *op. cit.*, pp. 74 ff.

There are references to the temple of the divine mothers, full of Ḍākinīs, later in the same inscription.[1] At Mandasor, in Central India, we have evidence of a guild of silk weavers erecting a noble edifice to the Sun God while Kumāra Gupta "was reigning over the earth."[2] A Karamdaṇḍā inscription records the gifts made to some Brāhmaṇas of Ayodhyā for the worship of Mahādeva, locally known as Pṛthvīśvara, by a Mahābalādhikṛta (commander-in-chief) of Kumāra Gupta.[3] The Dhanaidaha copper plate refers to the gift of a piece of land by an Āyuktaka to a Sāmavedī Brāhmaṇa,[4] and two land-grants from Damodarpur record the sale of government land to Brāhmaṇa families for the performance of *agnihotra* and daily *pañca-mahāyajña*.[5] The Kalaikuri copper plate records the gift of land by certain traders, writers and record-keepers to three Brāhmaṇa scholars to enable them to perform their daily sacrifices, the *pañcamahāyajñas*.[6] On a group of his lion-slayer coin types, Kumāra Gupta has compared himself with Narasiṃha, an incarnation of Viṣṇu (*sākṣādiva Narasiṃho Siṃha-mahendro-jayatyaniśam*).[7] On the other hand, however, non-Brāhmaṇical activities are shown by an epigraph at Udayagiri, which records the setting up of an image of the Jina Pārśva in "the augmenting reign of the family of the best of kings belonging to the Gupta lineage" (*Guptānvayānāṃ nṛpa-sattamānāṃ rājye*).[8] Similarly, a Jaina lady, Sandhyā, installed a Jaina shrine at Mathurā in 432 A.D.[9] The Mānkuwar inscription records the dedication, in order to ward off all evils, of an image of the Buddha, by Bhikṣu Buddhamitra, in 448 A.D.[10] Another Sāñchī inscription informs us that an upāsikā, Harisvāminī, wife of the Upāsaka Sanasiddha, gave twelve dīnāras as a permanent endowment (*Akṣayanīvī*) to the Āryasaṅgha of the great vihāra of Kākanādabota (Sāñchī), for the daily feeding of

1. D. C. Sircar, *op. cit.*, p. 405, verse 23.
2. *Ibid.*, pp. 299-307.
3. *Ibid.*, pp. 289-90.
4. *Ibid.*, pp. 287-89.
5. *Ibid.*, pp. 290-94.
6. *Ibid.*, pp. 352-55.
7. John Allan, *op. cit.*, p. 77, Pl. XIV. 1-4.
8. J. F. Fleet, *op. cit.*, pp. 258-59.
9. *Epigraphia Indica*, XI, p. 210.
10. D. C. Sircar, *op. cit.*, pp. 294-95.

one Bhikṣu, new to the Saṅgha, out of the interest of investment.[1]

Skanda Gupta (455-467 A.D.), though his name is an allusion to Skanda, another name of Kārttikeya, was also personally devoted to Viṣṇu, whose mage he installed at Bhītarī, allotting to it a village "in order to increase the religious merit of his father."[2] The Junāgadh rock inscription[3] likewise is a Vaiṣṇava record, commemorating the erection of a temple of Cakrabhṛt. His coins bear the Garuḍa standard and have the figure of Lakṣmī like those of his predecessors; he takes the epithet of *Parama-bhāgavata* on his silver coins.[4] It is also worthy of note that Skanda Gupta compares himself with Kṛṣṇa in the Bhītarī pillar inscription,[5] and with Rāma in terms of strength and valor, and Yudhiṣṭhira in truthfulness, in the Supiā inscription.[6] But, true to his name, he alludes in the Bihār stone pillar inscription to the worship of Skanda or Kārttikeya and the Divine Mothers.[7] An inscription found at Indore[8] commemorates a perpetual endowment by a Brāhmaṇa, Devaviṣṇu, who boasts of always reciting the hymns of the *Agnihotra* sacrifice. The endowment is made with the guild of oilmen to maintain daily, out of its interest, a lamp for the shrine of the Sun. But, according to the Kahaum inscriptions,[9] a certain Madra set up five images of the Jain Tīrthaṅkaras—Ādinātha, Śāntinātha, Neminātha, Pārśva and Mahāvīra. What is interesting is that he describes himself as "full of affection for Brāhmaṇas and ascetics" (*dvija-guru-yatiṣu prāyaśaḥ prītimān yaḥ*). This inscription compares Skanda Gupta with Śakra.[10] A Mandasor inscription of 467 A.D. records the construction of a stūpa and a vihāra for the Lokottaravādin sect

1. J. F. Fleet, *op. cit.*, pp. 260 ff.
2. D. C. Sircar, *op. cit.*, pp. 321-24.
3. *Ibid.*, pp. 307-16.
4. John Allan, *op. cit.*, pp. 119-29, Pl. XX.3-29; XXI. 1-12.
5. D. C. Sircar, *op. cit.*, p. 323, line 13 of the epigraph.
6. *Ibid.*, pp. 317-18.
7. *Ibid.*, pp. 325-28. Sircar assigns this inscription to Puru Gupta and Fleet to Skanda Gupta.
8. *Ibid.*, pp. 318-20.
9. *Ibid.*, pp. 316-17.
10. *Ibid.*, p. 316. See line 3 (*rājye śakropamasya kṣitipa-śata-pateh Skandaguptasya śānte varṣe...*).

of the Hīnayāna school by Devabhaṭa the commander of the forces of a feudatory king Prabhākara.[1]

Puru Gupta (468-? A.D.), who probably issued the Prakāśāditya coins, was also a Vaiṣṇava, for he used the Garuḍa standard and Lakṣmī; but he was an ephemeral king, ruling perhaps for a few months either before or after Skanda Gupta.[2]

Kumāra Gupta II (474-76 A.D.), whose coins show Garuḍa and Lakṣmī again,[3] adopts in his Bhītarī seal the title of *Paramabhāgavata.*[4] It was in this reign also that Abhayamitra set up an image of the lord Śāstā (Buddha).[5]

Budha Gupta (477-500 A.D.) also was a devotee of Viṣṇu, as shown by the use of coins of the Garuḍa standard and Lakṣmī[6] and by the title *Paramabhāgavata* in the Nālandā seal. Among the inscriptions of his period, the copper plate grants from Damodarpur indicate in one case that government land was granted to a Brāhmaṇa who had applied for it to facilitate performance of the *Agnihotra* sacrifice; it refers to the purpose of the grant as *pañcamahāyajña-pravartana.* In another of the Damodarpur plates, a piece of land was granted to encourage the settlement of good Brāhmaṇas for the welfare of the parents of one Nābhaka.[7] The third plate is in connection with a piece of land for the purpose of building two Śiva 'nāma-liṅga' temples, one each of Kokāmukhsvāmin and of Śveta-Varāhasvāmin by Ṛbhupāla, a city merchant.[8] A Nandpur copper plate inscription[9] records that a Viṣayapati applied to the Āyuktakas for a piece of land belonging to the Agrahāra of Nanda-vīthī, to donate it to a Brāhmaṇa so that he could perform his *pañcamahāyajñas* well. A pillar inscription (no. 19) of Mātriviṣṇu and Dhānyaviṣṇu[10]

1. *Ibid.*, pp. 406-09.
2. John Allan, *op. cit.*, pp. 134-36, Pl. XXI. 23-26 (Archer type), XXII. 1-6 (Horseman type with Prakāśāditya title). Some of these Archer types of Puru Gupta's coins are now attributed to Budha Gupta, cf. *infra*, fn. 6.
3. John Allan, *op. cit.*, p. 140, Pl. XXII. 13-14.
4. D. C. Sircar, *op. cit.*, p. 329.
5. *Ibid.*, pp. 328-29.
6. *Journal of the Numismatic Society of India*, XII, pp. 112-15, Pl. X. 1-2.
7. D. C. Sircar, *op. cit.*, pp. 332-34.
8. *Ibid.*, pp. 336-39.
9. *Ibid.*, pp. 382-84.
10. *Ibid.*, pp. 334-36.

begins with an invocation of Caturbhuja (or Viṣṇu), whose banner is Garuḍa, and the inscription seems to be connected with a double temple called the 'Lakṣmī temple'. But Budha Gupta also continued on his silver coins the use of the peacock *vāhana* of Kārttikeya, started by Kumāra Gupta I and followed by Skanda Gupta.[1] On the other hand, the Pahārpur copper plate inscription refers to the purchase of some land to be donated by a Brāhmaṇa Nāthaśarmā, and his wife to a Jaina vihāra, of the *Pañcastūpa-nikāya* founded by Nirgrantha Śramaṇācārya Guhanandī of Vārānasī.[2] Through the profits from the land were to be purchased scents, incense, flowers and lamps for the worship of the Arhats. The epigraph affirms the popularity of Jainism in Puṇḍravardhana. One short dedicatory inscription[3] on a Buddha image at Sārnāth also informs us that a Śākyabhikṣu Abhayamitra installed the image during the reign of Budha Gupta in order to earn religious merit for his parents, predecessors, guru, and humanity at large (*lokasya*). In the travel accounts of the Chinese pilgrim Hsüan-tsang, and in his biography, we find the name of Budha Gupta as one of the patrons of Nālandā Vihāra.[4]

Narasiṃha Gupta (500-? A.D.) used the epithet *Paramabhāgavata* in his Nālandā seal inscription,[5] and his coins bear the Garuḍa standard and the figure of Lakṣmī.[6] His name is an allusion to the Narasiṃha incarnation of Viṣṇu. But if he is the same as Bālāditya mentioned by Hsüan-tsang, then he was a patron of the Buddhist university at Nāḷandā.[7] A late epigraph from Nālandā also mentions the construction of "a great and extraordinary temple at Nālandā by *a* Bālāditya."[8] According to Hsüan-tsang and his biographer Hui li, Tathāgataṛāja, one of the last Gupta kings, was a patron of the Nālandā Vihāra.[9]

1. John Allan, *op. cit.*, p. 153, Pl. XXIV. 13-15.
2. D. C. Sircar, *op. cit.*, pp. 359-63.
3. *Ibid.*, p. 331.
4. Thomas Watters, *On Yuan Chwang's Travels in India.* 2 Vols., (London : Royal Asiatic Society, 1904-05), II, p. 164.
5. *Memoirs of the Archaeological Survey of India,* No. 66 (Calcutta, Government of India Press, 1942), p. 65.
6. John Allan, *op. cit.*, p. 137, Pl. XXII. 7-9.
7. Thomas Watters, *op. cit.*, II, p. 164.
8. *Epigraphia Indica*, XX., pp. 37-46.
9. Thomas Watters, *op. cit.*, II, p. 164.

The discovery of a seal at Nālandā of yet another among the last kings of the dynasty, Viṣṇu Gupta, whose name is an allusion to Viṣṇu, and who called himself *Paramabhāgavata* and whose gold coins bear the usual Garuḍa and Lakṣmī, indicates the continued Gupta extension of patronage to the Buddhists at Nālandā.[1]

Vainya Gupta (*c.* 507 A.D.) provides another representative example of Gupta religious behavior. His coins depict Lakṣmī on the reverse and he adopts the epithet of *Paramabhāgavata* on his seals, but the latter bear the figure of a bull.[2] The Gunaighar copper plate inscription describes him as a devotee of Mahādeva (*Bhagavan-Mahādeva-pādānudhyātā*), but the content of the epigraph records his approval of the gift to Śāntideva, a Mahāyāna Ācārya, of five plots of land to the Saṅgha at the request of Rudradāsa, one of his governors.[3]

Whether or not it was due to the influence of the Imperial Guptas, it is significant to note that almost all the important royal dynasties as well as most of the local chiefs and feudatories in India—North and South, East and West—belonging to the Gupta age were generally swayed by Vaiṣṇavism. There are, of course, some who, again like a few Gupta kings themselves, showed preference for another type of Brāhmaṇical system. But very few Gupta monarchs indicated their personal allegiance to Buddhism or Jainism, although the two latter religious groups remained in flourishing condition in every respect. The survey given below compares favorably with that of the Guptas in its pattern of religious behavior.

The Vākāṭakas of the Deccan (250-550 A.D.) were followers of Śaivism and performed several Vedic sacrifices, but one of them, Rudrasena II, accepted Vaiṣṇavism after his marriage to Prabhāvatī Guptā, a daughter of Candra Gupta II, and described himself as "one who earned the mass of prosperity through the grace of Bhagavat Cakra-pāṇi or Viṣṇu" (*Bhagavataścakrapāṇeḥ prasādopārjita Śri samudayasya*).[4] But it was in the Vākāṭaka period

1. D. C. Sircar, *op. cit.*, p. 340; *Epigraphia Indica*, XXVI, p. 235; John Allan, *op. cit.*, pp. 145-46, Pl. XXIII. 9-13.

2. John Allan, *op. cit.*, p. 144, Pl. XXII. 6-8. These coins are now assigned to Vainya Gupta; cf. *Indian Historical Quarterly* (1933), p. 784.

3. D. C. Sircar, *op. cit.*, pp. 340-45.

4. *Ibid.*, pp. 442-49, see lines 13-14 on p. 444.

possibly when Nāgārjuna developed the new Mādhyamika school of Buddhist philosophy at Nāgārjunikoṇḍa. It was in this period and in their realm also that most of the Buddhist caves at Ajantā with their beautiful sculptures and paintings were probably made. Some of the ministers of the Vākāṭaka kings were donors of caves, as is evident from their inscriptions. A record in the Chāndā district shows how a local king named Sūryaghoṣa erected a temple of the Buddha commemorating the memory of his son.[1]

The early Pallavas of the South, in the fourth century A.D., like the Guptas, while they performed Vedic sacrifices, subscribed to Vaiṣṇavism, although in the seals of their copper plate grants we find the figure of a bull and their banner *Khaṭvāṅgadhvaja* carried the representation of a club with a skull at the top. To give some examples of Pallava religious affiliation, Śiva Skandavarman performed the Vedic sacrifices, Agniṣṭoma, Vājapeya and Aśvamedha, and called himself a *dhamma-mahārājādhirāja.* Viṣṇugopa, his son Siṃhavarman, Kumāraviṣṇu II and others called themselves *Paramabhāgavata* and *bhagavat-pādānudhyātā.* Viṣṇugopa dedicated two hundred *nivartanas* of land to Lord Nārāyaṇa installed in the temple of Kuli-Mahattaraka.[2]

The Kadamba kings are described as in the Sirsi grant[3] of Ravivarman (500-38 A.D.), who made a gift of land to the temple of Mahādeva and whose successor, Harivarman, called himself *Paramamāheśvara.* Earlier in the dynasty, Kākusthavarman (425-50 A.D.) and Śāntivarman (455-70 A.D.), who were also devotees of Śiva, favored Jainism too. So also Kṛṣṇavarman II (550-65 A.D.), who called himself *Dharma-Mahārāja* and adored Viṣṇu and Hari,[4] prayed to Mahādeva for success in war. A Kadamba king, Viṣṇuvarman, adored Viṣṇu and called himself *Paramabrahmaṇya.*[5] Some of the Kadambas were devotees of Kārttikeya and the Mātṛkās. They are also known to have made adorations to the Buddha and the Tīrtha-

1. *Journal of the Royal Asiatic Society of Great Britain and Ireland* (1905), p. 617.
2. "Gunapadeya Copper Plate Inscription of the Time of Skandavarman", in D. C. Sircar, *op. cit.*, pp. 467-69.
3. V. S. Sukthankar, "Two Kadamba Grants from Sirsi", *Epigraphia Indica*, XVI, pp. 264-72.
4. "The Bennur Copper Plate Grant", *Epigraphia Carnatica*, pp. 594 ff.
5. "Hebbata Grant", *Mysore Archaeological Survey, Annual Report*, 1925, p. 98.

ṅkaras as well as to have made land grants in favor of Buddhist and Jain temples and in favor of Jain ascetics and the Buddhist Saṅgha.[1] One of the Kadamba kings named Mṛgeśavarman made a gift of a village which was divided into three parts: the first was given to the holy Arhat and the great Jinendra of Pūrvamahācchālā, the second to the Śvetapaṭa saṅgha, and the third to the "eminent ascetics called Nirgranthas."[2]

The Sālaṅkāyanas (fourth and fifth centuries A.D.) in Andhradeśa were mainly Śaivas, but some of them, like Nandivarman II, called themselves *Paramabhāgavata*, normally denoting Vaiṣṇava faith; the Peddavegi plates of this king record the grant of thirty two *nivartanas* of land to make a 'devahala' for the god Viṣṇugṛhasvāmin.[3] One of them, Devavarman, a Māheśvara, also performed an Aśvamedha.[4] The Ānanda kings (*c.* 400 A.D.), also of this area, were mostly devotees of Śiva,[5] but one of them, Dāmodaravarman, was a Buddhist, as he is called *Bhagavataḥ samyaksambuddhasya pādānudhyātā,* although the figure of a seated bull appears on the seal of his Mattepad plates and he believed in the efficacy of the ceremony of Hiraṇyagarbha.[6]

The Bhoja kings of the western coast (fifth and sixth centuries A.D.) registered grants to Brāhmaṇas in their charters, but one of them, Aśaṅkita (end of the fifth or beginning of the sixth century A.D.) praises Lord Buddha in the Hiregutti plates[7] and records the gift of a village for the use of the Ārya-saṅgha. Some believe that Bodhidharma, founder of the Zen School of Buddhism, was probably connected with these Bhojas.[8] The Pardi plates found

1. J. F. Fleet, "Sanskrit and Old Canarese Inscriptions", *Indian Antiquary*, VI, pp. 22-31; VII, pp. 33-38, 209-20; *Epigraphia Indica*, XXXIII, pp. 87 ff.
2. J. F. Fleet, *Indian Antiquary*, VII, pp. 33-38, esp. pp. 37-38 for the text.
3. In all the three inscriptions of Nandivarman II the king is called *Paramabhāgavata* (D. C. Sircar, *The Successors of the Sātavāhanas in Lower Deccan*, Calcutta, 1939, p. 84). See "Peddavegi Grant of Nandivarman II", *Journal of the Andhra Historical Research Society*, I, pp. 92 ff.
4. D. C. Sircar, *The Successors of the Sātavāhanas*, p. 86.
5. *Ibid.*, pp. 50-62.
6. *Epigraphia Indica*, XVII, pp. 327 ff.
7. P. B. Desai, "Hiregutti Plates of Bhoja Asankita", *Epigraphia Indica*, XXVIII, pp. 70-75.
8. *Prabuddha Karṇāṭaka*, 1933, No. 55, p. 39; E. J. Thomas, *History of Buddhist Thought*, p. 254; but see P. B. Desai, *op. cit.*, p. 74.

in Surat district state that Dahrasena (456 A.D.), who was "a worker at the feet of Bhagavat" (*Bhagavat-pādakarmakaro*) and who called himself, like Vyāghrasena, a *Paramavaiṣṇava*, also performed an Aśvamedha sacrifice.[1]

The Early Cālukyas, starting their career in the Deccan in the sixth century A.D., are described in some of their early records "as meditating on, or favored by, the feet of the holy Svāmin or of Svāmi-Mahāsena (Kārttikeya). But their boar crest, as well as the invocation of the *Varāha avatāra* at the beginning of most of their records, shows that the family-god of the Early Cālukyas was Viṣṇu (cf. also the use of the epithet Paramabhāgavata in the family), although they are known to have patronized the Jains and the Śaivas, and some of the later kings appear to have actually adopted their faiths. The title Śrī-Pṛthivīvallabha—'the enjoyer of wealth and land' or 'the husband of the goddesses Lakṣmī and Earth'—assumed by the kings of this family, suggests that they claimed to have been incarnations of Viṣṇu."[2] Pulakeśin I performed the Aśvamedha and other Śrauta sacrifices like Agniṣṭoma, Vājapeya, etc. Kīrttivarman celebrated the Bahusuvarṇa and Agniṣṭoma sacrifices and his brother, Maṅgaleśa, who had the title Paramabhāgavata and who was entrusted by his brother with the construction of the Mahā-Viṣṇu-gṛha at Bādāmī, also made benefactions to Mukuṭeśvara, a form of Śiva.[3]

In Kaliṅga, in southeast India, the Māṭhara kings of the fifth century A.D., Ānanda-Śakri-Varman and Prabhañjanavarman, were devotees of Nārāyaṇa (Viṣṇu), but Anantavarman, of the sixth century A.D., was a *Paramamāheśvara*, a devotee of Śiva.[4] Later, still another king, Hastivarman, is noted as a Paramamāheśvara, and at the same time as granting an *agrahāra* to the god Nārāyaṇa.[5] Similarly in the far northeast, in Assam, the Umachal Rock inscription[6] of the time of Mahārājādhirāja

1. *Epigraphia Indica*, X, No. 13, pp. 51 ff.
2. D. C. Sircar, "The Chālukyas", in R. C. Majumdar (ed.), *The Classical Age* (Bombay : Bharatiya Vidya Bhavan, 1962), p. 228.
3. *Ibid.*, pp. 231-34.
4. "Ningondi Grant", in J. F. Fleet, *op. cit.*, No. 17, pp. 74-76; "Sungavarapukota Plates", *Epigraphia Indica*, XXIII, p. 60.
5. "Narasingapalli Plates", *Epigraphia India*, XXIII, pp. 65-66.
6. *Epigraphia Indica*, XXXI, p. 69.

Surendravarman (*c*. 470-95 A.D.) records the construction of a cave temple for Balabhadra-svāmin (Balarāma). Another king, Bhūtivarman (533 A.D.), was a devout follower of Viṣṇu, but he also performed an Aśvamedha sacrifice (*Śrī-paramadaivata-paramabhāgavata-mahārājā-śvamedhayājināṃ-Śrī-Bhūtivarmaṇaḥ-pādānāṃ*).[1] The examples may be multiplied and spread over the length and breadth of India.

IV. CONCLUSIONS

The survey given in the preceding section is not exhaustive, but it begins to indicate the religious pluralism practiced in the Gupta period. It also confirms the general agreement about the cultural impact of the Guptas on contemporary India. Almost all the Gupta kings and most of the contemporary kings and chiefs of India personally belonged to one or the other of Brāhmaṇical religions or sects; a large number of them, in fact, were declared adherents of Vaiṣṇavism of the Bhāgavata school. Their allegiance was made public through the use of symbols and epithets on coins and in epigraphs. It is also true, however, that these kings were liberal in their outlook, and not only tolerated faiths other than their own but patronized them, whether they belonged to the Brāhmaṇical fold or to the non-Brāhmaṇical. They did not persecute heterodoxy. On the contrary, the two major heterodoxies, Buddhism and Jainism, hardly having royal patrons of their own, continued to flourish, and in fact participated freely in creatively contributing to the excellence that was the Gupta age.

Was this religious pluralism, the liberalism and catholicity of the kings of the Gupta age, a result of a consciously-followed religious policy? Or, were these kings just trying to behave as ideal kings in the Indian political tradition? Were they merely a part of the system, or were they innovating? What was meant by toleration? Was it a matter of policy or a matter of the religion itself? Why and how did they succeed in doing what they did generation after generation?

Religious policy, for our purposes, cannot be treated as a

1. "Badaganga Rock Inscription of Bhutivarman", *Epigraphia Indica*, XXVII, pp. 18-23.

straightforward story of relationship between the two institutions, State and Church, as in the West. In ancient India religion was more personal than institutionalized. Unlike in Christianity, there was in Brāhmaṇism no church, no central organization, and none of the paraphernalia of ecclesiastical power hierarchy. The question of institutional confrontation as in the West did not arise. The Brāhmaṇa in India was not only a temple priest or a royal chaplain. He also could be a king, an army general, a minister of war and peace, a poet-laureate, a land-owning farmer, and even a merchant. Brāhmaṇas were just a social group. They did not constitute a priestly order *per se*. They were more of an elite class, a controlling one for a long time until challenged by other social groups within the varṇa system. The dichotomy between *Brāhmaṇa* and *Kṣatra* power, spiritual and temporal authority, was more a compromise than a confrontation meant to resolve the social struggle between the two upper classes of the Indian society as a whole, and of Brāhmaṇical society in particular, for primacy and authority. The Buddhists, or the Jains for that matter, had no structured social order of their own. This was one of the many reasons why the Buddhists lost their identity in India. They had, of course, an organized Saṅgha, a religious order, unlike anything in the Brāhmaṇical system. But, again, there was no centralized controlling authority in the Saṅgha either. Each monastery acted as an autonomous corporation on the pattern of the tribal republics. No wonder, then, if the Brāhmaṇical political theorists were more concerned with the stability of social order than in devising counter ecclesiastical organizations. The Buddhists, too, if and when they expounded a political theory, struck at the social bases of authority and did not generally make issues out of religious or moral aspects of legitimation of authority in the institution of kingship. The Buddhists were more interested in downgrading the ranking and role of the Brāhmaṇas as a controlling social group than in creating a rival social organization. The counter group of the Brāhmaṇa was the Śramaṇa, for parity purposes, but whereas the former was ubiquitous in society, the latter's operation was restricted. So, even when a king as a matter of policy showed parity in his behavior toward the Śramaṇas, the Brāhmaṇas did not suffer. A Śramaṇa could not become a chaplain, and the Buddhist theory of State, while it did provide a new idea, did not provide any ritual or warrant for legitimation of a king's power and authority. There was, therefore, no conflict between the Brāhmaṇas and the Śramaṇas in so far as the outward symbols of legitimation of the authority of the king were concerned. The king was thus safe and could easily afford to be liberal to all religions, because they did not offer any challenge to him. The presence or absence of a challenge depended on the rise and decline of the controlling power of the Brāhmaṇa as a social group.

Toleration is a government policy of permitting forms of religious belief and worship not officially established or recognized. In India, however, it is difficult to maintain that there was an 'official' religion. Toleration in this context means a state's recognition and protection of the right of private judgement in matters of faith and worship, and a lack of persecution or obstruction of the beliefs and practices of sects or religions other than the king's own. Often, the king of ancient India does not get credit for his act of toleration by modern historians because it is wrongly assumed that toleration is an essential part of his religious practice or of *rājadharma*.

If all actions of the king were in conformity with the *rājadharma*, he was a good king, a maker of the age; if his actions did not conform to the ideals, he was not a good king. Since there were good kings and bad kings in history, we must give credit to the good ones for having done good things, and consequently *for their acts of toleration*. It is not correct, therefore, to say that the ancient Indian state was *religiously* tolerant and, therefore, patronized all sects impartially, and minimize the importance of the individual king's role. It would be wrong to assert that one of the chief functions of state was the active *promotion* and *patronage* of religion. This would be a hasty generalization and it should not be confused with the idea of *recognition* and *protection*. The country would have been strewn with temples and monasteries if all the kings were actively to promote and patronize religions. This is not to say that some of them did not patronize or promote religion or religions. In fact, this is to affirm that only some of them actively patronized and *promoted* not only their own religion or religions but also *protected* those of others *as a matter of policy* and not merely as a matter of religious duty.

Rājadharma was not a religion but a corpus of royal duties, a code of conduct, a *sva-dharma* on par with such codes or *dharmas* as those for the merchant, the priest, the doctor, the carpenter. It was a social or professional *dharma*, a secular matter rather than a religious one. Politics were separate from theology, and the concept of *Dharma* transcended religion. Belief in supernatural rituals and recognition of the work of the royal chaplain did not make Kauṭilya hesitate to recommend the exploitation of religion for political purposes. The main function of the state was not promotion of religion; instead, it was the maintenance of social order. The Brāhmaṇa became alarmed when there was *varṇa-saṅkara,* but not when the number of deities multiplied and new cults were born. The confusion in modern writing has taken place because social order has been mixed up with religion. The king's duty was to see that social equilibrium was maintained. As long as that was maintained, he did not worry about the proliferation or even the rise and fall of religions or sects.

Aśoka became a little doctrinaire about the principle of toleration. He made it a part of his *Dhamma* ideal. He knew that it was not part of the sectarian *dharmas* and that is why within his own personal *dharma* he was an advocate of discipline, whereas in his public role, where inter-*dharma* relations mattered, he emphasized the practice of toleration. Perhaps, as some would say, he failed in his mission. His policy was not continued by his successors. While he did not disturb the class division of the society, he did equate the Brāhmaṇas with the Śramaṇas and did not hesitate in indicating his prejudice against ranking, and did not support discrimination in matters of imparting justice and largesse. A counter-movement took place and a coup was led by a Brāhmaṇa *army general, not a head priest* of a religious organization, and *not even by the Purohita*, the royal chaplain. While proper ranking in the social system was re-established with the help of force and social equilibrium was restored, the religion promoted by Aśoka did not decline. The Vedic sacrifices returned more as symbols of the reassertion of authority by kings and as an instrument of legitimation of power for them than as a religious tool for people at large. The entry of a fresh group of external elements, due to foreign incursions and the resultant interaction of ideas, diversity in beliefs and practices, and overall political decentralization for almost five hundred years after Aśoka, prepared the ground for a new religious policy and the great toleration in the Gupta age.

2

HISTORICAL AND POLITICAL ALLEGORY IN GUPTA ART

FREDERICK M. ASHER

WHAT truly motivates a patron is, of course, best known to him and is seldom recorded for the historian. The ultimate goal may be the *karma* attached to the act, but on occasion the motivation may be more clearly self-serving. In any event, the expectation of rewards does not explain why the patron selects an image of one particular deity rather than of another, a temple of one god rather than another. To an extent, the devotional preferences and the advice of a learned brāhmaṇa must be the primary explanation, but one can also ask why a particular form of a particular deity was selected. In the case of certain monuments, we can postulate that the image or temple was intended to convey an allegory or to serve as a metaphor. While some precedents in the early art of India exist for the use of allegorical imagery, nowhere before the Gupta age was its use in Indian art so magnificently realized.

It was not long before the Gupta age that anthropomorphic images of the major deities were introduced[1] and that worshippers were called upon to recognize the metaphoric relationship between a stone statue and God Himself. The image was a device to facilitate devotion to God, but the devotion would not have been possible without an understanding of the perceived correspondence

1. A very few images of major deities date as early as the second century B.C., for example, a Sūrya, a Balarāma, and some Śiva *Liṅgas*, but it was not until the Kuṣāṇa age, particularly at Mathurā, that anthropomorphic images of major deities are known in abundance.

between God and statue. Thus, in a sense, the image is a metaphor for the deity it represents. Just as the Gupta poets developed metaphors with multiple meanings, so did Gupta stone carvers develop multiple meanings to the metaphors in their lithic art. And it was particularly in the realm of historical and political allegory that Gupta artists and their approximate contemporaries in other parts of India excelled. By 'allegory' here is simply meant a story which serves as an analogy to a real-life person or event, usually making that person or event more vivid, poignant, or dramatic.

Such allegory in stone was hardly an invention of the artists in the Gupta age. The Aśokan columns, among the first historical stone works in India, carry a cosmological symbolism[1] whose meaning and power were intended to be transferred to the emperor whose edicts adorn the shaft. But during the ensuing centuries, until the establishment of the Gupta authority in North India, there is no known monument of comparable nature. Perhaps that is because most of the monuments remaining from the first two centuries B.C. are Buddhist, while the contemporary rulers were Hindu. And, during the years of Kuṣāṇa authority, it seems unlikely that the rulers, regardless of their personal religious faith, would have generated the subtle sensitivity to form and idea to convey the multiple meanings which allegory requires.

Traditional Indian notions of kingship acknowledge the monarch's divine rank,[2] a view which was given special prominence during the Kuṣāṇa age when statues of the rulers were established in a shrine called a *devakula*, quite literally meaning the family of god. King Kaniṣka was called *devaputra*, for instance, literally son of the gods, in an inscription on his statue.[3] Without entering into a discussion of the possible explanations for these statues and the epithet applied to Kaniṣka, it is difficult to doubt that the king's divinity was intended. This notion must have been

1. Jean Przyluski, "Le symbolisme du pilier de Sarnath," *Études d'Orientalisme à la Mémoire de Raymonde Linossier*, II (Paris, 1932), pp. 481-98; and John C. Irwin, " 'Aśokan' Pillars : A Reassessment of the Evidence; Part IV : Symbolism," *The Burlington Magazine*, Vol. CXVIII (November, 1976).

2. Jan Gonda, *Ancient Indian Kingship from the Religious Point of View* (Leiden, 1966), pp. 24-33.

3. John M. Rosenfield, *Dynastic Art of the Kushans* (Berkeley, 1967), pp. 149-51, 202-06.

especially important for these alien rulers who did not have the authority of *kṣatriya* birth to justify their monarchy. There is no evidence, however, to show that the Guptas shared this view of kingship. In fact, their titles, while imperious, are strictly secular; the stress is, instead, upon devotion to Viṣṇu in their inscriptions. But it would be unlikely for at least the memory of the Kuṣāṇa conception of kingship to vanish altogether during the subsequent age. Hence this memory of kings who styled themselves as sons of gods, together with the more ancient and subtle rich blending of sacred symbolism during the imperial age of the Mauryas, was combined in the Gupta age to new effect.[1]

One such monument, much of whose symbolism has been recognized by previous writers,[2] is the great early Gupta relief of Varāha at Udayagiri (Plates 1-2). According to an inscription on an adjacent wall, the great Vaiṣṇava shrine of which this is part was dedicated in 402 A.D. during the reign of Candra Gupta II by one of his loyal feudatory kings.[3] Ostensibly, it is a magnificent image of the boar incarnation of Viṣṇu dedicated for pious purposes. But when we pose the question, why Varāha, why this incarnation of Viṣṇu so many times larger than the more customary anthropomorphic images of Viṣṇu on the facade of the rock-cut sanctuary to the right, the answer suggests something about the motivation of the patron. It is here that the image seems to represent a lithic allegory.

The great relief is a literal illustration of Purāṇic accounts of Varāha's lifting of the earth from beneath the cosmic waters, righting it to its proper position.[4] At the same time, when viewed in historical context, the image seems to serve as a remarkable allegory for the unification of the empire under Candra Gupta II.

1. For the revival of old ideas in Gupta times, see Joanna Williams, "A Recut Aśokan Capital and the Gupta Attitude Towards the Past," *Artibus Asiae*, XXV (1973), pp. 225-40.

2. V. S. Agrawala, *Matsya Purāṇa—A Study* (Varanasi, 1963), pp. 333-35; and S. V. Sohoni, "Varāha Avatāra Panel at Udayagiri, Vidiśā," *Journal of the Bihar Research Society*, LVII (1971), pp. 49-56.

3. J. F. Fleet, *Corpus Inscriptionum Indicarum*, Vol. III : *Inscriptions of the Early Gupta Kings and their Successors* (reprinted., Varanasi, 1963), pp. 21-25.

4. Wendy D. O'Flaherty, *Hindu Myths* (Harmondsworth, 1975), pp. 184-97.

Before the foundation of the empire, Northern India was in an essentially fractured condition, bordering on political chaos, which, to the inventive minds of the Gupta age, would have seemed akin to the dismal state at the end of an age of the world. Although the Gupta Empire had been expanded almost to its full extent during the reign of Candra Gupta's predecessor, Samudra Gupta, large parts of Western India (including Mālwā, the very area in which Udayagiri is located) remained under the authority of the Western Kṣatrapas until Candra Gupta brought them within Gupta rule. He thereby united virtually all Northern India under a single central authority, in a sense saving the world from chaos by unifying it just as Varāha did by uplifting it from submersion. If, as seems likely, the Udayagiri relief was inspired by Candra Gupta's conquests and also serves as an allegory for his victory, then it provides cosmic perspective to the historical event. Other details of the relief lend credence to the presumption. For example, the figures lined up along the back wall of the relief must represent, on a literal level, the sages who had gone between his bristles praising him.[1] But their ascetic garb at first glance appears to resemble the so-called northern dress that first served as the costume of the Kuṣāṇa rulers and was retained in the Gupta age for royal portraiture on coins; and their hands are held in the position customarily applied to these royal figures : left at the hip and right raised to shoulder level. Thus it seems likely that, on a secondary level, these figures are intended to recall royalty. Could they then represent the local kings like the patron of the relief who paid homage to the paramount Gupta sovereign, much as the sages acknowledged Varāha's supremacy ?

Further portraying the allegorical character of this relief is a pair of figures on one of the two short projecting walls (Plate 2). As indicated by their *vāhanas*, these two females are personifications of the Gaṅgā and Yamunā. These are the rivers which flow through the Gupta heartland; more significantly, they have their confluence at Prayāga (modern Allāhābād), which has recently been identified as the capital of the Gupta Empire.[2] On one

1. J. N. Banerjea, *Development of Hindu Iconography* (Calcutta, 1956), p. 414.

2. Basudeva Upadhyay, "Prayāga—The Capital of the Guptas," *Journal*

level, therefore, the ocean toward which these united rivers flow represents *Ekavarṇa,* of course, the primeval ocean from which Varāha rescued the earth. But, as the Sanskrit word for ocean is *samudra,* the ocean here may also recall Candra Gupta's father and predecessor, Samudra Gupta, literally meaning he who is protected by the ocean, the monarch who essentially established the Gupta Empire through his famous exploits. As if merging streams into a single mighty river, or great rivers into an enormous ocean, Samudra Gupta drew together under a unified central authority the disparate states of India.

It is thus altogether fitting that the Boar incarnation of Viṣṇu should have been adopted as a royal emblem by some dynasties. The Cālukyas, for example, not only used it on their seals but also frequently commenced their inscriptions with invocations to Varāha.[1] Elsewhere, too, images of Varāha have served as a metaphor for the monarch, but nowhere is the allegory stated in such magnificant visual terms as at Udayagiri.

At Eraṇ, about forty-five miles northeast of Udayagiri, an enormous but less impressive image of Varāha was erected (Plate 3) during the reign of Toramāṇa, a Hūṇa contemporary of the Guptas ruling in the late fifth century, who boldly applied to himself the full imperial titles used by the Gupta emperors.[2] On the very body of the beast is an inscription which commences :

> "Victorious is the god Viṣṇu, who has the form of a Boar, and who, in the act of lifting up the earth (out of the waters), caused the mountains to tremble with the blow of his hard snout; (and further) who is the pillar of the great house which is the three worlds."[3]

From here, the inscription goes on to glorify the reigning monarch, Toramāṇa, and his progenitors. The inscription hardly makes the analogy between the monarch and the god Varāha more explicit than the one at Udayagiri, but how can one fail to draw the connection when a statement about the boar's valorous deeds

of the Bihar Research Society, LVII (1971), pp. 11-20; and S. R. Goyal, *A History of the Imperial Guptas* (Allahabad, 1967), pp. 41-52.

1. Gulam Yazdani, ed., *Early History of the Deccan,* Vol. I (London, 1960), p. 206; and J. F. Fleet, *Dynasties of the Kanarese Districts* (Bombay, 1896), pp. 337-38.
2. Fleet, pp. 158-61.
3. *Ibid.,* p. 160.

is followed immediately by a description of the strength of Toramāṇa and his allegedly mighty family—no doubt one whose importance needed to be established by such means as they were contemporaries of the vastly more heralded Guptas and whose alien heritage cast doubt on their right to sovereignty. Thus, the image serves as a visual metaphor and Varāha's act as an allegory for Toramāṇa's usurpation of authority in Eraṇ.

The case for the allegorical role of images of Varāha is strengthened by the fact that enormous images of this deity are almost always associated with royal endowments. A third—and for this discussion final—case in point is the image at Aphsaḍ, about fifty miles east of Gayā (Plate 4). At that place, a long inscription was found belonging to Ādityasena, who ruled about 650-75 A.D. and was the best known king of the Later Guptas of Magadha, a dynasty which significantly adopted the name of the imperial Guptas but bore no known relationship to them. It commemorates the foundation of a Viṣṇu temple, perhaps containing the image of Varāha as the cult object, and also the establishment of a sanctuary of some sort, and the excavation of a temple tank.[1] Even if the inscription does not commemorate the dedication of the image of Varāha, then at least the sculpture was made about the time of Ādityasena since it and virtually every other sculpture at the site may be ascribed on the basis of stylistic evidence to his time. Except for the final lines of a very long inscription, which at last refer to the dedication, it is a wordy panegyric extolling the valor of the king more than his virtue and piety. Since the inscription, whose ostensible purpose is to record the dedication of a temple, is essentially the king's bold boast, it seems likely that he would employ a religious image to enhance the appearance of his secular deeds by implying an analogy between himself and Varāha, the divine rescuer of the earth. When one poses the question, why did Ādityasena commission an image of Varāha rather than some other form of Viṣṇu, the answer appears to be that he was in part motivated by special considerations. Either he felt a personal affinity with Varāha, the divine rescuer of the earth, or more boldly he wished to convey to his subjects his

1. *Ibid.*, pp. 200-08. Wladimir Zwolf, Department of Oriental Antiquities, British Museum, recently found the inscription, long presumed to have been lost, in the Museum's storage.

analogous relationship with the divine boar. In either case, an allegory is implied.

Images of another incarnation of Viṣṇu, that is, Trivikrama, who traversed the universe in three strides and who subdued the demon king Bali,[1] sometimes carried allegorical meaning. Here again the allegory is implied by the story of Trivikrama, the image serving as a visual symbol of the story. One such statue of Trivikrama was originally installed at Lajampat in Kāthmandu (Plate 5). According to an inscription on the statue's base, it was dedicated in 467 A.D. during the reign of King Mānadeva, thus a contemporary of the Guptas.[2] We know relatively little about the reign of this monarch, although from a second inscription, on a pillar of the Changunārāyaṇa Temple, we learn that he did defeat several neighboring kings to the east and the west—one of whom he conquered especially because of that king's misdeeds.[3] Thus it would not be surprising if Mānadeva had erected the statue of Trivikrama, shown as usual taking the three vast strides, soon after these missions of conquest. This would have cemented the correlation between Viṣṇu's divine acquisition of land and the resulting expulsion of evil personified by Bali and Mānadeva's temporal conquests. While the purpose of the Lajampat image may not have explicitly been to elevate the king's stature in the eyes of his subjects, it could have had that effect and its allegorical significance would not have gone unnoticed.

A third sort of image, the personification of Viṣṇu's wheel, was also intended to convey a political as well as the more apparent religious meaning. During the Gupta period at both the sites of Pawāyā and Eraṇ wheels were erected with a male figure sculptured against each side. The one at Eraṇ (Plate 6) still remains at the summit of a pillar; the one from Pawāyā (Plate 7), now in the Gwālior Museum, originally stood in such a location. Following the example established in Gupta times, similar wheels

1. O'Flaherty, *op. cit.*, pp. 175-79.

2. Raniero Gnoli, *Nepalese Inscriptions in Gupta Characters*, Part I (Rome, 1956), p. 6, and P. Pal, *Vaiṣṇava Iconology in Nepal* (Calcutta, 1970), pp. 38-41. A second image of Trivikrama with an identical inscription today stands at the confluence of the Tilgaṅgā and Bāgmatī rivers near Mṛgasthalī, Kāthmandu.

3. D. R. Regmi, *Ancient Nepal* (Calcutta, 1960), pp. 104-06. Note line seventeen of the inscription.

were erected at Sālār in Murshidābād District, West Bengal, and at Enda in West Dinājpur District, West Bengal, both products of the sixth century (Plates 8-9). Recently, a pair of such wheels with male figures sculptured against each side were discovered at Marūī, a few miles east of Nawādā in Gayā District, Bihār, products of the seventh century. Until the recent identification of the Pawāyā, Eraṇ, and Sālār images as personifications of Viṣṇu's wheel,[1] their meaning was lost, but, even so, their significance seems to extend beyond the customary personification of the god's weapon.

The significance of the wheel is manifold. The most apparent meaning implied by these images is its being the emblem of Viṣṇu, his fiery weapon, the agent of his might. At the same time, in a text of the Gupta period, it is said to represent the rotation of the world, the Wheel of the Law, the Wheel of Time, and the circular path of the planets.[2] Here the reference goes beyond the wheel of Viṣṇu in particular to more general concepts underlying the notion of the wheel in ancient Indian thought. In this context, we must recall the notions attached to the Cakravartin, the age-old ideal king, whose very name means wheel-turner[3] and who, in concept, followed the path of an ever-turning wheel, extending his righteous rule to the four quarters. In a well-known relief of the second century B.C. from Jaggayyapeta, a wheel surmounting a tall shaft serves as the Cakravartin's most prominent emblem.[4]

Thus, on one level the wheel was simply one of Viṣṇu's attributes, but it was also a symbol of ideal leadership and was such a basic part of Indian thought that a great wheel elevated high on a pillar unfailingly evoked in at least learned minds a vision of the universal righteous king, the Cakravartin. Here is precisely where the allegory begins its subtle work. The inscription on the pillar upon which the Eraṇ wheel stands—and presumably

1. Wayne Begley, *Viṣṇu's Flaming Wheel* (New York, 1973), pp. 45-47.

2. *Viṣṇudharmottara Purāṇa*, Ad. 60.5-6. Priyabala Shah, ed., *Viṣṇudharmottara-Purāṇa, Third Khaṇḍa*, Gaekwad Oriental Series, Vol. 130, p. 183; also Vol. 137, p. 141.

3. H. Jacobi, "Chakravartin," *Encyclopedia of Religion and Ethics*, Vol. III, pp. 336-37. Also Gonda, pp. 123-28.

4. Benjamin Rowland, *The Art and Architecture of India* (Baltimore, 1953), plate 16A.

the inscription of the other pillars as well—refers to the dedication of a Viṣṇu temple, and so the wheel serves as an appropriate emblem to stand before the temple.[1] But the inscription on the pillar proclaiming this royal endowment contains few pious phrases. It commences with the words, *jayati vibhuś-caturbhujas*, that is, "Victory to the four-armed (Viṣṇu)". From there it extols the virtues of the reigning *Mahārāja* "whose fame extends to the borders of the four oceans; who is possessed of unimpaired honor and wealth; and who has been victorious in battle against many enemies."[2] This is just the beginning; it is not until the final lines that the long inscription returns to the ostensible purpose for raising the pillar, namely, to commemorate the establishment of a temple. Could anyone seeing the wheel and reading or hearing the inscription fail to recall that the wheel is the emblem of the universal monarch, the Cakravartin ? By implication, of course, it is the dedicator of the temple, the reigning monarch who is to be seen as the righteous universal monarch.

The notion is not new in the Gupta period, for at least one of Aśoka's pillars, the most famous of all, the one at Sārnāth, was originally surmounted by a wheel supported on the backs of four addorsed lions.[3] Though at Sārnāth the context was most definitely Buddhist, it would not be surprising if that pillar served as inspiration for the Brāhmaṇical adaptation and enhancement of the theme, for, as Joanna Williams has pointed out, the Gupta age was remarkable for its interest in things past, for its historical sensitivity.[4]

In South India, as much as in the Gupta realm of North India, one encounters poignant historical and political allegory within religious art. This first appears in the early Pallava period and seems to coincide with a change in attitude toward king and temple. For example, one writer notes that the Tamil words

1. Fleet, pp. 88-90.

2. *Ibid.*

3. The wheel has not been found, but there is a large hole at the back of the lion protomes to accommodate the shaft connecting it to the capital. D. R. Sanhi, *Catalogue of the Museum of Archaeology at Sarnath* (Calcutta, 1914), pp. 2-31.

4. Williams, *op. cit.*, pp. 225-40.

which come to mean god and temple in the Pallava period had in earlier literature referred to king and palace. Thus he suggests

> "that concepts central to South Indian values (i.e., 'king' the order of the cosmos and 'palace' his home) have been usurped and transferred to new more universal objects; the transcendental king is God and the public palace is the temple."[1]

Perhaps he does not mean that the king *is* god, for the identity never seems to go beyond analogy. But the analogy is made clearly and poignantly, and it may have been stimulated by a practice well established in the Gupta North. It seems to have been adopted with such unaccustomed vigor in South India in order to legitimize the monarch's role, which, like that of the invading Hūṇas, was not sanctified by caste. Thus, in social terms, it was established by proclamation and practice; in artistic terms, it was established by analogy, that is, by allegory.

At Kāñchīpuram, the great Vaiṣṇava Temple, the Vaikuṇṭha Perumāl, dating to the eighth century, is enclosed within a huge cloister whose back wall is adorned with reliefs depicting the battles of King Nandivarman Pallava.[2] Hence in the course of circumambulation the worshipper is confronted with the exploits of the monarch, while in a comparable position on several of the temples reliefs illustrating the epics appear.[3] Thus one cannot avoid the unstated analogy between the epic heroes and the reigning Pallava king. While it may initially appear as unmitigated boasting to place one's own image where an image of God properly belongs, it was hardly uncommon or heretical, for comparable examples are ample. Quite clearly, the practice proves that the kings' names and deeds appropriately adorn this part of the temple.

This can be seen, for example, at the famed Kailāśanātha Temple, also in Kāñchīpuram but erected a few years earlier

1. Richard Kennedy, "Status and Control of Temples in Tamil Nadu," *Indian Economic and Social History Review*, XI, 2-3 (June-September, 1974), p. 263.

2. C. Minakshi, *The Historical Sculptures of the Vaikuṇṭhaperumāl Temple, Kāñchī*, Memoirs of the Archaeological Survey of India, No. 63 (Delhi, 1941).

3. For example, reliefs illustrating epic scenes were placed on the *jagati* of the Gupta Temple at Deogarh and so would have been seen by the devotee in the course of his preliminary circumambulation, that is, at ground level.

during the reign of Rājasiṃha Pallava. This temple is known today, and was called in its dedicatory inscription, the Rājasiṃh-eśvara Temple.[1] The word *Rājasiṃheśvara* may be understood in two ways, both of which were probably intended. It may be taken as the temple of the lord of King Rājasiṃha, that is, a temple of Śiva, the lord worshipped by Rājasiṃha. This meaning is made clear by the inscriptions, by the imagery of the walls, and by the *liṅga* enshrined in the *garbhagṛha*. It also may be construed as the temple of the lord who *is* Rājasiṃha; that is, the king who is identified with the lord.[2] Beyond Sanskrit grammar, it is clear that both meanings should be understood. There are fifty-five niches on the inside of the wall enclosing the main temple; on the wall of each niche is a brief inscription. The first of these commences with the name of Rājasiṃha himself, followed by phrases which describe him : "He whose desires are boundless; the conqueror in battle; the lovely." The remaining fifty-four commence with different epithets of the monarch, and include comparable praising phrases.[3] The positions of these inscriptions are virtually identical with those of the reliefs depicting the exploits of Nandivarman on the Vaikuṇṭha Perumāl Temple.

In addition to these fifty-five brief inscriptions, the dedicatory inscription on the plinth of the temple itself implicitly associates the monarch Rājasiṃha with the god to whom the temple is dedicated. After tracing Pallava genealogy from its mythic origins, the inscription continues with an explicit simile :

> "Just as Guha [i.e., Śiva's son Kārttikeya] was born of the Supreme Lord, Śiva, the destroyer of the warlike Pura, thus from the supreme Lord Ugradaṇḍa Pallava, the destroyer of the city of Ranarasika, there was born a very pious prince, Rājasiṃha, the chief of the Pallavas."[4]

Here in this line, which provides the analogy, there is a play on words. The words describing the emperor Rājasiṃha,

1. E. Hultzsch, ed., *South-Indian Inscriptions*, Vol. I (Madras, 1890), pp. 12-14.

2. In both senses, the word *Rājasiṃheśvara* would be varieties of *bahu-vrīhi* compounds as classified by the Sanskrit grammarians.

3. Hultzsch, pp. 14-21.

4. *Ibid.*, pp. 13-14.

subrahmaṇya kumāra (or "very pious prince"), are common epithets of Kārttikeya, with whom the composer of the inscription is equating Rājasiṃha. Hence an analogy in one part of the sentence becomes a virtual identity in another. The inscription continues to describe King Rājasiṃha :

> "Like Kāma, he charmed refined women in secret; like Indra, he constantly protected those who followed the three Vedas; like Viṣṇu, he tore the hearts of the enemies of Sages, the twice-born, and the gods; and like Kubera, he gratified good people with abundant wealth."[1]

In short, the analogy with the gods becomes explicit.

What precisely this means is difficult to decide. While the temple may have served as an institution to legitimize the king's authority in South India, it is clear that it enhanced his stature in a manner similar to the monuments in North India during the Gupta age. It is also clear that, in spite of early textual references, the king was never deified, in any commonly accepted notion of that term. The king's depiction in the South Indian temple, however, like other aspects of South Indian culture, may have served as the model for the practice in several Southeast Asian cultures of identifying the monarch with God.[2] It seems likely that the Indian sensibility would have been repelled by a literal identification of the king with the Divine and would have preferred a more subtle analogy.

A concluding monument of a somewhat different sort, a couple of generations earlier than Rājasiṃha's reign or soon after the Guptas lost their authority in North India, serves as a poignant allegory for a benevolent act of the emperor. The proof for this is less well-documented than for some of the other monuments, since no inscriptional evidence remains to verify the meaning of the allegory. This monument is the great rock-cut relief at Māmallapuram (Plate 10). Long known as the Descent of the Ganges because of the figures clustered around the cleft at the center of the relief, T. N. Ramachandran has adduced plausible evidence to indicate that it illustrates the *Kirātārjunīyam*, namely,

1. *Ibid.*, p. 14.

2. Sachchidanand Sahai, *Les institutions politiques et l'organization administrative du Cambodge ancien* (*VI-XIIIe siècles*) (Paris, 1970), pp. 16-18, 34-46.

the meeting of Arjuna with Śiva in the guise of a rustic hunter.[1] Hence his study attempts to confirm another common name for the relief, Arjuna's Penance, for it was this great warrior's penance which induced Śiva to appear to him in disguised form and finally to bestow upon him the ultimate weapon. Ramachandran's evidence for this identification is weighty, but he fails to explain the absence of any scene illustrating the most important episode of the story, that is, the simultaneous shooting of the boar by Arjuna and the rustic hunter (the *kirāta*) and their ensuing fight. Given the great expanse of rock with which the artist had to work, how strange it seems that he omitted the pivotal episode of the story in favor of emphasis on the asceticism of a sage. Thus it appears more likely that the relief illustrates a different story of asceticism, that of King Bhagīratha, the righteous ruler whose personal asceticism brought water to his people by the descent of the Ganges.[2] The original identification of the relief, therefore, seems correct.

For the full impact of this great relief and its allegorical character, it must be viewed together with the adjacent relief of Kṛṣṇa supporting Mount Govardhana to protect the people of Brindāvan from a deluge. On one level it is simply a story about one of Kṛṣṇa's exploits, but on another level it is like the adjacent Bhagīratha relief and pertains to the control of water. One sees both the gift of water by Bhagīratha's penance and the control of its excess by the raising of Mount Govardhana. What sort of allegory is this ? To celebrate the ending of a drought or of a flood ? At any rate, would it be likely for a monarch to take credit for a turn of nature he had in no way brought about? However, evidence of an ancient canal system at Māmallapuram exists and has been described in the following words :

> One other feature is observable at Māmallapuram, now almost obliterated, but which when in full use gave the town, and particularly its religious architecture, some of its character. This was a well-designed and extensive water system, drawn

1. T. N. Ramachandran, "The Kiratarjuniyam or 'Arjuna's Penance' in Indian Art," *Journal of the Indian Society of Oriental Art*, XVIII (1950-51), pp. 10-12.

2. Heinrich Zimmer, *Myths and Symbols in Indian Art and Civilization* (Washington, 1946), pp. 112-15.

> from the Palar River, and distributed by means of canals and tanks to all parts of the port. There are indistinct but nonetheless definite traces of this installation, so that in its palmy days such a constant supply of running water must have made it a very pleasing seaside resort.[1]

Clearly, there must have been practical purposes to the canal system beyond that of creating a pleasant seaside resort.

One can easily imagine an inscription to have existed which extolled the glory of the reigning monarch under whom the system was constructed (probably Narasiṃhavarman Māmalla), who, like the virtuous penitent Bhagīratha, brought water to his people and who, like Kṛṣṇa, controlled its excesses. But the fact is that such an inscription might even be unnecessary; the monument itself makes the allegory sufficiently clear.

It is true that much of the evidence presented is circumstantial at best, for there is little proof that an image of a deity or a relief of a sacred exploit was ever intended as more than just that. Perhaps on the conscious level of the maker and patron nothing more was intended, though on another level it seems likely that an historical allegory was intended, particularly in the case of many royal dedications. If one fails to penetrate sculptural and monumental metaphors when they are there, then we miss much of the rich meaning to a work of art. Unlike similes, the analogy of a metaphor is not made explicit, but once understood its meaning is conveyed with enormous power.

1. Percy Brown, *Indian Architecture: Buddhist and Hindu Periods* (Bombay, 1965), p. 78.

Plate 1. Varāha at Udayagiri, 401/02 A.D.

Plate 2. Left wall of Udayagiri Varāha relief.

Plate 3. Varāha at Eraṇ, c. 510 A.D.

Plate 4. Varāha at Aphsad, c. 675 A.D. Photo copyright : Archaeological Survey of India.

Plate 5. Trivikrama from Lajampat, Kathmandu, 476 A.D. Bir Library, Kathmandu.

Plate 6. Wheel Personification atop pillar at Eraṇ, 484/85 A.D. Photo copyright : American Institute of Indian Studies, Center for Art and Archaeology, Varanasi.

Plate 7. Wheel Personification from Pawāyā, early fifth century. Gwalior Museum.

Plate 8. Wheel Personification from Sālār, sixth century. Museum of the Baṅgīya Sāhitya Pariṣad, Calcutta.

Plate 9. Wheel Personification from Eṇḍa, eighth century. Photo copyright : Archaeological Survey of India

Plate 10. Descent of the Ganges. Relief, Māmallapuram

3

MAHĀNAVAMĪ : MEDIEVAL AND MODERN KINGLY RITUAL IN SOUTH INDIA

BURTON STEIN

INTRODUCTION

FEW epochs in human history are as remarkable as that of the Gupta age in India; few so deserve the label 'Golden' or 'Classical' age as this period of about four centuries. All of the criteria for determining such cultural apogees are fulfilled by the Gupta age. It was a time of successful monarchy exemplified especially in the conquering, righteous (i.e., possessing *Dharma*) reign of Candra Gupta II, the legendary Vikramāditya; there was vigorous and original literary production including the final development of the *Mahābhārata* and the *Rāmāyaṇa* epics, several of the major *Purāṇas*, several of the major *Dharma-śāstras* (but more important, the broad dissemination and knowledge of these and earlier Sacred Law texts), the dramatic works of Kālidāsa and the prose works of Daṇḍin, Bāṇabhaṭṭa, and others; there were also the religious and philosophical developments of *bhakti* hymns and completion of the six systematic philosophies (*darśana*); there was splendid visual art created in stone at Sārnāth and in painting at Ajantā; finally, there were the impressive scientific and technological accomplishments of Āryabhaṭa, Brahmagupta, and others in mathematics and astronomy as well as the metallurgical wonder of the Meharaulī iron pillar. Such attributes have provided an irrestible framing for modern historical reconstruction, both in tracing antecedent developments of the splendid and mature human achievements of the Gupta period as well as the fading of these achievements after the age of their flowering. We remain somewhat uncertain about how these accomplishments were viewed by contemporary Indians, though the persistence of an era named after the Guptas (Gupta-Valabhī era beginning in 320 A.D.) suggests some agreement from those of the great age and immediately following.

One problem with 'golden ages' is that they must be followed by leaden ones. To historians, post-Gupta kings were not as towering in their prowess or their righteous mien; literature turned to vulgar imitation or stultifying codification; ecumenical religion passed into petty sectarianism; promising science yielded to superstition and technology to closed ethnic monopolies. Add to these degradations the external predations of the Hūṇas and, later, the Turkic Muslims, and the conversion of the 'golden age' to the 'dark age' is completed. In Indian as well as in European historiography, the 'dark age' which succeeded the 'golden age' conventionally constitutes the middle period of history.

The presumed bleakness and disparagement of post-classical, or medieval, history ought not to obscure the manner in which classical forms, or a classical pattern, persisted in Indian history as it did in the history of other civilizations. Successive generations of scholars of European history have discovered ever-earlier 'renaissances' to brighten what was supposed to be a 'dark age' and to show the path to a new and glorious modernity. In Indian history, too, the classical pattern of the Gupta period provided conceptions of appropriateness and excellence which never ceased to be informing for Indians, even those quite distant from the Gupta *madhyadēśa* of the Gangetic plain. While this was most evident in the widespread, post-Gupta knowledge about and value of certain of the great literary works of the Gupta age, e.g., epics, courtly poetry (*kāvya*), sacred religious texts (*Purāṇa*), and, most especially, *Dharmaśāstras*, it is also evident in the development of conceptions of kingship until well into the later medieval period, and even near contemporary times.

FROM SACRED KINGS TO SACRED KINGSHIP

As with other sacrificial rituals (*yajña*) of pre-Gupta and Gupta India, royal sacrifices had as their purpose the transformation of their sponsor (*yajamāna*). In particular, royal sacrifices (e.g., the horse sacrifice or *aśvamedha*, the royal consecration or *rājasūya*, and the "drink of strength" sacrifice or *vājapeya*) were regenerative rituals meant to replenish the sacred power of kings in order that the latter might acquit their responsibilities

(*Rājadharma*) of protection and nourishment of people and realm. This was conceived as an extension of divine power to a human whose attributes were sacrificially altered by coming to be composed of the divine substance of several gods.[1] The coins of Samudra Gupta and Kumāra Gupta I depict the sacrificial horse being washed and cooled by a queen[2]; commemorative coins of Candra Gupta II also depict this royal sacrifice.[3] A reference to this rite is also found in Gupta inscriptions such as the Bhitari pillar inscription (Ghāzīpur district, Uttar Pradesh) of Skanda Gupta.[4] The classic age of royal sacrifice is supposed by most historians to have come to an end after the Gupta age; rarely after that time are there Vedic ritual events mentioned in inscriptions and other medieval records.

The texts which most authoritatively speak of the classical pattern of India and of kings as the preservers of that pattern are the *Dharmaśāstras*. Several of the most important of these were produced during the Gupta age. The Nārada *smṛti* is dated around 500 A.D. according to Bühler, and those of Bṛhaspati and Kātyāyana appeared about a century later.[5] This places what P. V. Kane, the historian of Dharmaśāstra, called the "triumvirate in the realm of Hindu Law and procedure" squarely in the Gupta period.[6] It is ironic that the Gupta age should have produced the last surge of royal sacrificial ritual and also legal texts which repudiated such ritual.

Dharmaśāstra (law of righteousness) texts of the Indian medieval age characteristically denigrated the divine qualities of kings.

1. J. Gonda, *Ancient Indian Kingship from the Religious Point of View* (Leiden: Brill, 1966); *The Laws of Manu*, trans. G. Bühler (Originally published as Vol. 25, *Sacred Books of the East*, ed. F. Max Müller, 1886. Reprinted, New York : Dover, 1969), p. 100 and *passim*. Also, E. Washburn Hopkins, "The Divinity of Kings," *Journal American Oriental Society*, Vol. 51 (1931), pp. 309-16; P. V. Kane, *History of Dharmaśāstra*, 2nd ed. (Poona: Bhandarkar Oriental Research Institute, 1973), Vol. 3, pp. 23 ff.

2. Parameśvari Lal Gupta, *The Imperial Guptas.* Vol. I. *Sources, Historiography and Political History* (Varanasi : Visvavidyalaya Prakashan, 1974), pp. 73 and 79.

3. *Ibid.*, pp. 303-04.

4. *Ibid.*, p. 40.

5. *The Laws of Manu*, pp. cvii and cx.

6. Kane, *op. cit.*, Vol. 1, p. 213. Kane generally dates these writers earlier by a century or so; see pp. 184, 205, 210, and 218.

Sacred Law writers continued to depict kings as protectors, to be sure. The protection of his subjects (*prajānāṃ paripālanam*) and the guarantee of their security (*abhayadāna*) express the royal function.[1] But protection was realizable only as the king was a victorious warrior, the possessor of efficacious force (*kṣatra*). To medieval law writers, the social origin or the birth qualities of kings was of minor concern. It mattered little that a king might not be the son of kings and of an established ruling lineage—something which agitated the ur-text of Dharmaśāstras, that of Manu. What did matter was that the would-be king acted like a king, that he possessed force sufficient to protect, and that this force was purified by proper anointment (*abhiṣeka*). As expressed in medieval Dharma texts, *Rājadharma*, the proper execution of kingship consisted of the protection and the regulation of the several kinds of self-governing groupings in the realm.

The king was to assure that each of three elemental units of polity—blood-linked groups (*kulam*), vocation or interest groups (*śreṇi*), and territorial groups (*gaṇa* or *puga*)—managed their own affairs properly.[2] Kingly duty, according to medieval Dharmaśāstras, consisted of royal custodianship over the Dharma of others, stated conventionally as the three polity units mentioned above; kingly intervention was latent in all social relations in a realm, but became manifest infrequently, only when regulation by other appropriate agencies in society failed. Then, royal intervention in the form of a royal command (*Rājaśāsana*) was ad hoc and administrative, not legislative in a categorical sense.[3]

In all of these, there would appear to have occurred a profound desacralization of kings by the medieval period of Indian history. By the close of Gupta times, kings were divested of the sacred stuff which they were deemed to possess, partly ascriptively, by birth as kṣatriyas, and partly by the contingent outcome of their periodic ritual regeneration; there was even a prohibition of those great royal sacrifices whose object was to infuse kings with

1. Robert Lingat, *Les Sources du Droit dans le Système Traditionel de l'Inde* (Paris : Mouston, 1967) and an English translation by J. D. M. Derrett under the title, *The Classical Law of India* (Berkeley : University of California Press, 1973).

2. *Ibid.*, pp. 272-73.

3. *Ibid.*, pp. 282-83 and 249 ff.

divine power. Many Dharma texts forbade *aśvamedha* and *rājasūya* sacrifices. It is possible, as P. V. Kane has suggested, that such prohibitions were urged on the grounds that time and wealth were prodigiously squandered in ancient, Vedic sacrifices.[1] What divine qualities were lost to individual kings, however, appear to have been gained by the institution of kingship.

Kingship became sacred in itself according to Sacred Law texts of the Gupta period and after. Thus, on the matter of the divinity of kings, Lingat writes :

> "The dominant idea of dharmasastra writers appears certainly to be that it is not the king who has a divine nature, but the royal function."[2]

The contrast here is clear. Sacred or divine kings were conceived in early Sacred Law texts (*smṛti*) and religious texts (*purāṇa*) as composed of godly attributes. Manu states :

> "The Creator created the king with the essential parts taken from Indra, the Wind god, Yama [the god of death], the Sun, Agni, Varuṇa, the Moon and Kubera the lord of wealth and therefore surpasses all beings by his majesty...it is a great deity that stands (before people) in human form as a king.[3]"

Similar statements occur in the *Matsyapurāṇa* and *Agnipurāṇa*.[4] Nārada, in his Dharmaśāstra of the Gupta period, appears to be saying the same thing; but there is a difference, and it is this difference which provides the basis for sacred kingship rather than for sacred kings. Nārada states that even kings of poor qualities deserve honor because they perform functions of five deities (Agni, Indra, Soma, Yama, and Kubera).[5] Elsewhere, Nārada also states that the king is actually Indra manifested on earth, the purāṇa conception of divine manifestation (*avatāra*) being brought to the service of kingship.

The emphasis upon royal function and the idea of earthly manifestation provide important bases for sacred kingship to which Lingat has drawn attention. Kingship is the royal function exercised by powerful, yet flawed men : men who err, who sin,

1. Kane, *op. cit.*, p. 232.
2. Lingat, *op. cit.*, p. 232.
3. Cited by Kane, *op. cit.*, v. 1, p. 23.
4. *Loc. cit.*
5. *Loc. cit.*

and who are subject to *Karma*. This powerful agent, though finite and flawed, is nevertheless active as a protector. The powerful deity to whom the king is analogized by most medieval writers or with whom he is identified by earlier writers is infinite and perfect, but gods require the intervention of men to be active. Together, the powerful human and god comprise perfect sovereignty.[1] Medieval Vaiṣṇava theology seizes this relationship in the concept of *arcāvatāra*, the manifestation of a universal deity (Viṣṇu) in a particular place and time, made efficacious by the activities of powerful men, priests and kings.[2] In medieval Hinduism and medieval kingship, gods and men complemented each other to create a sacred condition. In contrast to the pre-Gupta age, ritual did not dissolve the differences between men and gods—such that men became gods; it was rather that together, with appropriate ritual intervention, gods and men established and maintained the sacred condition of which kingship was an important manifestation.

Most writers on early Indian kings and kingship have failed to appreciate this transition from sacred kings to sacred kingship. To illustrate, it is instructive to contrast two important, recent, and quite different analyses with Lingat's Dharmaśāstra conception referred to above. All three view Indian kings and kingship in universal terms : their notions apply to all of India and for all of pre-modern time; all three locate royal institutions in their most broad social and cultural contexts. The two writings other than Lingat's are essays by Louis Dumont, 'The Conception of Kingship in Ancient India', and J. D. M. Derrett, 'Rājadharma'.[3]

The arguments of Dumont and Derrett preclude the possibility of either sacred kings or sacred kingship in any but trivial ways. Dumont's complex argument may be stated in the following propositional form. At some early point in the ancient Indian past,

1. *Loc. cit.*

2. This understanding and use of *arcāvatāra* derives from a recent discussion of the concept by Dr. Friedhelm Hardy, though he is in no sense responsible for how it is being applied here. See footnote 1, page 89 for bibliographical detail.

3. Respectively : Dumont, *Contributions to Indian Sociology*, no. 6, December, 1962 and reprinted in L. Dumont, *Religion, Politics and History in India : Collected Papers in Indian Sociology* (Paris : Mouston, 1970); Derrett, *Journal of Asian Studies*, v. 35, no. 4 August, 1976), pp. 597-609.

religious and political functions elsewhere (e.g., Egypt, Sumeria, China) combined in the ruler were "dissociated"; religious functions became the prerogatives of brāhmaṇa priests, and with this separation there was a division of religious from political domains capable of being stated as the division of *Dharma* (values and norms) from *Artha* (interests or advantage). The royal function thus "secularized," *Artha* was subordinated to *Dharma*; the king was subordinated to the priest in recognition of the superiority of *Dharma* over *Artha*. However, it was also recognized that this separation was not complete in the sense that a residue of a magico-religious sort (contrasted with moral, transcendent, or spiritual authority) clung to kings. An important consequence of the separation of spiritual and secular authority was that the priest was dependent upon the king (i.e., non-competitive with respect to power) in the secular domain. Politics was, thenceforward, understood as consisting of *Daṇḍa* (legitimate force) and *Artha* (interest) and, because it lacked the benefit of clergy, politics was set in opposition to righteousness, or *Dharma*. Finally, the secularization of kings and kingship led to a corollary theory among Buddhists, a "contract" theory of kingship. This development, Dumont argues, sprang from the Buddhist "renouncers" of Brāhmaṇical values and the "individualism" of the Buddhist adept. These ideas form an obvious and important element in Dumont's larger argument in *Homo Hierarchicus*.[1]

Derrett's formulation was framed against that of Dumont. The former's view has the effect of not only denying to kings and kingship a fully sacred quality (permitting kings a low-level magical or superstitious component much like Dumont), but goes further to virtually deny spiritual or sacred elements to either kings or brāhmaṇas. Dumont, Derrett contends, is led into error by ".... those rogue texts, the *Brāhmaṇas*...".[2] Derrett's alternative view is based upon what he calls the "classical pattern, reflected in the *dharmasastra*...".[3] Rejected is Dumont's historicistic and unprovable assumption that Indian kings (like those of the ancient Near East, Greece and Rome) once possessed significant

1. Louis Dumont, *Homo Hierarchicus* (London : Weidenfeld and Nicolson, 1970).
2. Derrett, *op. cit.*, p. 601.
3. *Ibid.*, p. 603.

religious functions. On the contrary, Derrett claims, *Daṇḍa* was always secular, not spiritual, just as *Artha* and *Vārtā* (economics) were. Such terms could acquire magical or superstitious meanings in the hands of writers like Kauṭilya whose *Arthaśāstra* recommends the deployment of magic and superstition to fortify kingly power. Indeed, for Derrett, "spiritual" authority is not an issue at all. The subordinate position of kings to brāhmaṇas in the *Varṇa* order and the support by kings of priests through fees and endowments are seen as means for non-priestly groups of all kinds, including kings, to have access to the most prized magical lore of brāhmaṇas, the Veda. "The whole basis of the brāhmin's prestige lay in his possession of the Veda."[1] With the Veda, amoral deities could be manipulated by the magico-ritual techniques of priests. To avoid the brāhmaṇas' curses and to gain brāhmaṇas' control over unseen, but manipulable divine forces, brāhmaṇas were conceded first rank and rewarded. But, this concession of rank involved "a very qualified subordination, for very limited purposes."[2] Kings also recognized that brāhmaṇas could and should advise them about *Dharma* ("the science of righteousness"), but kings were not constrained to accept such advice. *Dharma* was indeed seen as superior to *Artha*, but since kings and priests were equally subject to and custodians of *Dharma*, the special knowledge of brāhmaṇas did not confer upon them spiritual superiority. For Derrett, Rājadharma ("the way a king should comport himself in order to be righteous")[3] was bereft of any spiritual character; it had to do with utterly pragmatic consideration of ruling without disorder, of not altering a harmonious order of self-governing groups. In his view, the ancient Indian political system, because it lacked any spiritual or sacred qualities (notwithstanding the misconstrued and tendentious utterances of Indian commentators, as Derrett hears them), was constantly plagued by instability. This is a rather unexpected position from one who is rightly deemed one of the best living *Dharmaśāstra* scholars, but it is a position which is congenial to one large viewpoint on ancient Indian monarchy shared by Buddhist writers on what Dumont has

1. *Loc. cit.*
2. *Ibid.*, p. 607.
3. *Ibid.*, p. 606.

called "conventional" (contrasted to magico-religious) kingship, by materialist writers, and by those who take the *Arthaśāstra* as authoritative.[1]

If the transformation of sacred kings to sacred kingship has been neglected by scholars such as Dumont and Derrett, it is also obvious that another major element of Indian kingship has been even more neglected. That is, little attention has been given to changes in the crucial role of public ritual in sustaining the monarchical institution. It is, of course, true that over much of early Indian history kings were perceived as secular, or "conventional," by Buddhists, Jainas, and many Hindus (those who followed Kauṭilya's *Arthaśāstra*), but the dominant conception of Hindu kingship continued to give fundamental significance to public ritual, as in the ancient horse sacrifice.

As a result of the ancient royal horse sacrifice—"the king of sacrifices"—the ruler, his power, and his realm were sanctified in an extended and powerful public ritual. The age of the horse sacrifice passed with the Guptas. Denigration of this and other kingly sacrifices in post-Gupta *Dharmaśāstra*—indeed, their prohibition according to Kane—diminished the divinity or sacred qualities of kings by denying them the public staging or displaying of these kingly attributes. What, then, took the place of these earlier forms of public ritual in the altered conception of sacred kingship of the post-Gupta period ?

THE RITUAL BASIS FOR SACRED KINGSHIP IN SOUTH INDIA

In South India, "conventional" kingship—the king as a secularized political manager, the "Great Elect" (*Mahāsammata*), chosen and hence under "contract" to his subjects—is to be found. But, little research has been done on these kings.[2] Jaina kings of Karṇāṭaka from the fifth to the twelfth centuries, and a few Jaina kings in Tamil country, are spoken of in inscriptions and other literary works as towering moral figures. They and some of the notables upon whom their rule depended were chosen and ruled in recognition of being exemplars of perfected

1. Dumont, "Kingship in Ancient India," pp. 61 ff.

2. Burton Stein, "All the Kings' Mana : Perspectives on Medieval South Indian Kingship," in John F. Richards (ed.), *Kingship and Authority in South Asia* (Madison : University of Wisconsin, South Asia Studies Publication Series, No. 3, 1978), 115-68.

kingly attributes : courage, wisdom, knowledge, and compassion. Ritual played no important part in their attainment of kingly office nor in its execution. That depended alone on their inherent, perfected qualities.[1]

As to "magico-religious" kingship, South Indian historians have noted that sacrifice (*yajña*) yielded to prestation (*dāna*) as the characteristic form of kingly ritual, and the occasional references to sacrifices in medieval times are taken as anachronistic or, possibly, expressionistic archaisms. This change from sacrifice to prestation may be dated with certainty during the time of the Pallava kingdom.

Pallavas began their career in Gupta times, sharing much of the luster of that period; the dynasty endured until the tenth century. The Pallava kingdom commands attention in being a good example of the change from classical Indian kingship to medieval kingship. The long and well-documented reign of Nandivarman II, Pallavamalla (736-96 A.D.) most perfectly illustrates this fundamental change in, among other things, the stress upon kingly prestation.[2] Moreover, Pallava transformations in royal style correspond with altered conceptions of kingship elsewhere in medieval India. Kingship had changed in such ways as to make ancient forms of kingly ritual a less vital and vitalizing activity.

Most early South Indian monarchs were Hindus and were involved in sacrificial as well as prestation activities that justified and characterized their kingships. Early Pallava kings (known from a few Prākrit and Sanskrit inscriptions) expressed kingly appropriateness by claims to kingly predecessors, or genealogy, and by royal sacrifices which they or their ancestors carried out. Later Pallavas, especially Nandivarman II, Pallavamalla, and his successors, changed this idiom of kingly rule from genealogy and

1. Toshikazu Arai of the University of Hawaii has prepared an illuminating comparison of Jaina and Hindu conceptions of kingship based upon Jaina and Hindu *prabandhas* of about the 13th century, in Richards, *op. cit.* (footnote 25). See "Jaina Kingship as Viewed in the *Prabandhacintāmaṇi*," pp. 74-115.

2. T. V. Mahalingam, *Kancipuram in Early South Indian History* (Delhi : 1969); Nicholas B. Dirks, "Political Authority and Structural Change in Early South Indian History," *Indian Economic and Social History Review*, Vol. 13; Stein, *op. cit.*

sacrifice to prestation primarily, and gifting events were attended by elaborate, if localized, public rituals.[1] The establishment of the special settlement for brāhmaṇas, *brahmadēya* ("gift to brāhmaṇas"), was the usual context for such early Pallava public rituals. Temple construction was another public and ceremonial expression of sacred kingship of the later Pallavas and their successors, the Cōḻas. The apogee of this was the creation of the monumental Rājarājēśvara shrine by Rājarājacōḻa (985-1014 A.D.) in his capital of Tāñjapuri (Tāñjavūr).[2] Temple construction by kings and by chiefs continued to be the major way in which sacred rule was expressed at least until the fifteenth century. Even the greatest temples, however, remained essentially locality institutions, and the public rituals involved in their construction, consecration, and maintenance were of limited scope. In the fifteenth century, a new form of kingly public ritual came into existence that provided a vastly more encompassing form of public ritual, one that transcended locality and involved all in the realm.

Against this development of kingly, public ritual in medieval South India, the Dharmaśāstra conception of sacred kingship, based upon narrow and limited judicial functions of kings and kingly immunity from sin while executing royal functions, seems thin. Even when in some Dharma texts the basis of sacred kingship is extended by analogy, the foundation for sacred kingship (as opposed to sacred kings) remains weak. Thus, a king is at times likened to one who has undertaken a great vow (*mahāvratin*) in pursuit of the fulfilment of which he can be excused many transgressions.

This idea of kingship as a sacred condition may be augmented, made more persuasive, by consideration of forms of public ritual, especially those in later medieval South India. One such public ritual was the *Mahānavamī* ("great nine-day") festival. The *Mahānavamī* is first reported in the greatest South Indian kingdom of medieval times, the Vijayanagara kingdom. This annual ceremony was celebrated by Vijayanagara kings during the lunar

1. Especially, Dirks, *op. cit.*

2. B. Suresh Pillai, "Raajaaraajeesvaram at Tancaavuur," *Proceedings of the First International Conference-Seminar of Tamil Studies* (Kuala Lumpur : International Association of Tamil Research, 1966).

month of *āśvina* (Tamil month : *puraṭṭāci*) corresponding to mid-September to mid-October. The festival consisted of nine days of celebration followed by a tenth, final day, *daśamī*, according to its earliest commentators in the fifteenth and sixteenth centuries. The latter were foreign sojourners in Vijayanagara, the capital city of the kingdom. Thereafter, the festival became known in many parts of South India. As *Daśarā*, the festival was celebrated with the greatest éclat by the Mysore royal family from 1610 A.D., when the Rājā Wodeyar established an independent successor kingdom of Vijayanagara in Karṇāṭaka.[1] The festival is also known as *Navarātri* ("nine nights") in the Vijayanagara successor, *nāyaka*, kingdoms of the seventeenth century. In imitation of these several kingdoms, the festival conducted was eventually adopted by many minor kingly houses (e.g., the Rājās of Ramnad). As *Navarātri*, the celebration also became one of the most popular domestic rituals in South India.

The earliest eye-witness report of the *Mahānavamī* festival at Vijayanagara is provided by an Italian, Nicolo Conti, who visited the kingdom and city in 1420 A.D. A Persian ambassador to Malābār trading kingdoms, Abdur Razzak, was summoned to Vijayanagara in 1442 A.D.; he too left a brief account of the festival. The most elaborate descriptions come from two Portuguese travellers, Domingos Paes and Ferñao Nuniz in the sixteenth century.[2] From these several reports, the principal elements of the festival can be reconstructed. These elements are found to recur in descriptions of the great *Daśarā* festivals of the Wodeyar kings of Mysore and in the equally detailed descriptions of *Navarātri* celebrated by the Rājās of Ramnad in the far southern part of the Indian peninsula. In all cases, the focus of the ceremonies is upon the reigning king and the revitalization of his kingship and his realm.

1. C. Hayavadana Rao, *History of Mysore, 1399-1799 A.D.* (Bangalore : Government Press, 1943), Vol. 2, p. 68; and *Historical Sketches of the South of India in an Attempt to Trace the History of Mysore...to 1799...by Lieutenant Colonel Mark Wilks, Political Resident at the Court of Mysore*, ed. Murray Hammick (Mysore : Government Press, 1930), Vol. 1, pp. 61-63.

2. Robert Sewell, *A Forgotten Empire; Vijayanagar* (London : George Allen and Unwin, 1924); Paes' chronicle, pp. 253-64; Nuniz' chronicle, pp. 357-60. The accounts of Conti and Razzak are found in R. H. Major, *India in the Fifteenth Century : A Collection of Narrative Voyages to India* (London : Hakluyt Society, No. 22, 1857).

From the Paes account of the *Mahānavamī* at Vijayanagara, the following features may be outlined. Throughout the nine days, festivities were centered in the walled palace grounds, or "citadel" area of Vijayanagara. Here, before the palace and on two large, permanent structures the ritual was enacted. One of these structures is called "The House of Victory" by Paes, or "Throne Platform" by Longhurst, the archaeologist of Vijayanagara, or the *Mahānavamī Dibba* by modern residents of Hampi, as the place is now called.[1] The other structure is called "The King's Audience Hall." The ruins of both are massive granite slab platforms showing structural signs of having borne large wooden superstructures as described in the medieval chronicles. These structures were constructed by the Vijayanagara king Kṛṣṇa Deva Rāya around 1513 A.D. following his victory over the Gajāpati king of Orissā.

From these edifices, the king observed the many processions, displays, and games, and here he accepted the homage and the gifts of throngs of notables as he sat upon his bejewelled throne. The king sometime shared this throne, or sat at its foot while it was occupied by a richly decorated processional image of a deity; at other times the king was alone. The deity is not identified. Within the "House of Victory" was a special, enclosed, and, also, richly decorated chamber in which the deity was installed when it was not on display before the participants in the festival. At several points in the proceedings, the king, sometimes with brāhmaṇas and sometimes alone, retired to this enclosed chamber of the deity for worship. Both the Audience Hall and the Throne Platform still bear bas-relief sculptures along their granite sides depicting many of the events described by the foreign commentators.

In front of the two structures which were the stage for the activities of the festival, a number of temporary pavillions were constructed and contributed to the aura of opulence of the festival as a whole. These were elaborately decorated among other ways with the heraldic devices (*birudas*) of the grandee occupants whom the pavillions housed during the festival. Nuniz reported that there were nine major pavillions (he called

1. A. H. Longhurst, *Hampi Ruins Described and Illustrated* (Madras : Government Press, 1917), pp. 57-70.

them "castles") for the most illustrious of the notables and that each military commander also had to erect one in the broad space before the palace.[1] Razzak, in recognition of his ambassadorial status, was ensconced in one of these.[2]

Access to the guarded, central arena of festival activity was gained by passage through several tall gateways connecting the walled enclosures of the palace precincts. Paes' description of these portals suggests passage through a series of temple gateways (*gopurams*) as the medieval pilgrim proceeded toward the sanctum of the great temples of South India.[3] Once gained, the spacious open area before the palace—dominated by the Audience Hall and the House of Victory—was ringed about with the pavillions referred to and with shaded seating from which the notables (soldiers, sectarian leaders, and others) viewed the extravaganza immediately before the House of Victory on whose higher levels the king sat.

What was viewed was a combination of great *darbār* with its offerings of homage and wealth to the king and the return gifts from the king—honors, exchanges; the sacrificial reconsecration of the king's arms, his soldiers, horses and elephants—in which hundreds or thousands of animals were slaughtered; *darśana* (viewing) and *pūjā* (worship) of the king's tutelary deity as well as his closest agnatic and affinal kinsmen; and a variety of athletic contests, dancing, and singing processions focussed upon the adorned women of the king and temple dancers from throughout the realm. There were also firework displays. The center of these diverse and magnificent entertainments was always the king as glorious and conquering warrior, as possessor of vast riches lavishly displayed by him and his women (queens and their maids of honor) and distributed to his followers, as fructifier and agent of prosperity of the world.

The ritual sources of the *Mahānavamī* festival appear quite varied. Purāṇas speak of two nine-day festivals (*Mahānavamīs*) which mark the turning of the three seasons of the sub-continent : in March-April, after the harvest of the *sambā* or *rabi* crop and

1. Sewell, *op. cit.*

2. Major, *op. cit.*, "Narrative of the Voyage of Abd-er Razzak, Ambassador from Shah Rukh, A. H. 845, A.D. 1442," p. 36.

3. Sewell, *op. cit.*, pp. 253-54.

the onset of the hot season, and in September-October, after the harvest of the *kar* or *kharif* crop and the onset of the cold season. The first of these nine-day festivals is associated with the god Rāma and the second with the goddess Devī, or Durgā. Elements of both of these festivals, as described in purāṇic works, can be seen to exist in the *Mahānavamī* festival of medieval Vijayanagara; the Rāma motif may have been as important as the Devī motif though it is the latter (i.e., September-October) nine days that are celebrated at Vijayanagara.

There are other sources of this grand festival at Vijayanagara. In many ways, the festival has the appearance of being a combination of the ancient *aśvamedha*, the greatest of all ancient royal sacrifices with its celebration and consecration of kingly military prowess as symbolized by the horse of the king. Another source would appear to have been the description of Rāma's return to Ayodhyā after the conquest of Laṅkā as retold in the final book (canto 130) of Vālmīki's *Rāmāyaṇa.*

Comparing the *Mahānavamī* of Vijayanagara with the antique horse sacrifice may seem superficial or strained, for the Vijayanagara period knows no such royal sacrifices, and only one is even alluded to in the previous South Indian imperium of the Cōḻa state. Certain common features of the ancient horse sacrifice and the medieval *Mahānavamī* may indeed be superficial. Thus, both are ten-day rituals, and at least one of the most famous horse sacrifices was celebrated on a *Mahānavamī* (the March-April one) by Yudhiṣṭhira, hero of the *Mahābhārata.*[1] More persuasively, however, the anointing of royal arms by priests,[2] the central role played by royal women, and animal sacrifices are prominent features of the ancient horse sacrifice and the Vijayanagara festival; these elements figure prominently in the two most detailed descriptions of it. Paes, for example, wrote of the king's women :

> "They come in regular order one before the other, in all perhaps sixty women fair and strong, from sixteen to twenty

1. *The Mahabharata of Krishna-Dwaipayana Vyasa.* Translated by P. C. Roy (Calcutta : Oriental Publishing Company, n.d.), Vol. 12, "Aswamedha Parva," Section 84, p. 161 and *passim.*

2. Priests offer prayers to and anoint the king's horses and elephants according to Nuniz, Sewell, *op. cit.*, p. 358.

> years of age. Who is he that could tell of the costliness and value of what each of these women carried on her person? So great is the weight of the bracelets and jewels carried by them that many of them cannot support them, and women accompany them assisting them by supporting their arms. In this manner and in this array they proceed three times around the [king's] horses, and at the end retire into the palace."[1]

Compare this with the *aśvamedha* rite in *Śatapatha Brāhmaṇa*:

> "It is the wives that anoint (the horse), for they—to wit (many) wives—are a form of prosperity... the wives walk around (the horse)...thrice they walk around."[2]

An even more striking parallel feature of the *Mahānavamī* and Vedic horse sacrifice is the symbolic significance of the king's horse in the consecration of his kingship. Paes describes a troop of richly caparisoned horses brought before the king at one point in the *Mahānavamī*. Leading this troop was one horse bearing "two state umbrellas of the king and grander decorations than the others." Of this horse, Paes writes:

> "You must know that this horse that is conducted with all this state is a horse that the king keeps, on which they are sworn and received as kings, and on it must be sworn all, all those that shall come after them; and in case such a horse dies they put another in its place."[3]

This suggested comparison of some elements of the Vijayanagara *Mahānavamī* festival and the archaic horse sacrifice is more than anachronistic; it may also be flawed in being a violation of Vedic prohibitions. The bright half of the lunar month of Āśvina, when the *Mahānavamī* festival occurs, is said to be inauspicious for brāhmaṇical learning and thus by extension, perhaps, for brāhmaṇical rituals as well. In the Dharmaśāstra of Aparāka, these activities are enjoined as *anadhyāya* ("intermission from study").[4] Brāhmaṇas do figure in the *Mahānavamī* festival as

1. *Ibid.*, p. 263.

2. J. Eggeling (trans.), *The Śatapatha-Brāhmaṇa According to the Text of the Madhyandina School* in *Sacred Books of the East* (Oxford : Clarendon Press, 1900), Vol. 44, part 5, p. 313. On the anointment of the sacrificial horse, see pp. 278-79.

3. Sewell, *op. cit.*, p. 262.

4. Kane, *History of Dharmaśāstra*, Vol. 2, part 1, p. 395.

ritual performers along with the king in relation to the king's tutelary; they are also recipients of royal gifts. But, brāhmaṇas do not dominate the ritual arena, which is very much the king's, and in one description of the festival brāhmaṇas appear to have been publicly reviled.[1]

The association of Rāma with the *Mahānavamī* festival at Vijayanagara is somewhat more direct. The same mood of celebration by a people of their king found in the final verses of the Vālmīki *Rāmāyaṇa* suffuses the vivid descriptions of the festival of Vijayanagara. And, there is the further shared conception of kingly deliverance from threatening evil. Saletore captures this quality in his statement about the festival.

> "Religious in atmosphere, it is essentially political in its significance. For it commemorates the anniversary of Rāma's marching against Rāvaṇa and in its twofold aspect of the worship of Durgā and of the *āyudhas* or arms, culminating in the Vijaya-daśami [victorious tenth day], was particularly suited to Vijayanagara time when fatal issues loomed ominously in the political horizon."[2]

The god Rāma appears important in yet another way. One of the major temples of the capital city during the Tuluva dynasty of Vijayanagara, especially in the time of Kṛṣṇa Deva Rāya was that dedicated to Rāmacandra, the hero of the *Rāmāyaṇa* and the seventh *avatāra* of Viṣṇu. A separate shrine within that temple was dedicated to the consort of Rāma. This shrine was also called the "Hāzra Rāma" temple, and it was the only shrine within the palace precincts and thus proximate to the activities of the festival. The unidentified image in the sixteenth century reports of the *Mahānavamī* festival may have been the consort goddess of Rāma if the proximity of the Rāma temple is an indication of its importance and if the judgement of the archaeologist Longhurst is correct that the Rāma shrine was the private place of worship of the Tuluva kings of Vijayanagara.[3]

All historians of Vijayanagara have mentioned the *Mahānavamī* festival, often quoting long excerpts from the accounts of Paes

1. Major, *op. cit.*, p. 28; and Sewell, *op. cit.*, p. 83.
2. B. Saletore, *Social and Political Life in the Vijayanagara Empire* (Madras : B. G. Paul & Co., 1934), Vol. 2, p. 372.
3. Longhurst, *op. cit.*, p. 71.

and Nuniz. However, the festival has not received analysis as a single, unified ritual event. Culled from the detailed reports have been odd facts (e.g., the "rents" of his military subordinates (*nāyakas*) are paid to the king at this time in recognition of the idea that the latter "owns" all of the land) and descriptions of the king and his high officials and his queens. It is appropriate to view this festival, like others, as a unified system of action and meaning.

The continuity of major elements of the *Mahānavamī* over several centuries is impressive. An elaborately detailed description of the *Navarātri* festival celebrated at Ramnad by the Rāja Bhāskara Setupati in September, 1892 preserves the order of elements of the sixteenth century Vijayanagara festival in such punctiliousness as to permit use of that later description to fill out certain of the details not found in the Vijayanagara festival four centuries before.[1]

One such additional detail added by the Ramnad report pertains to the anointing (*abhiṣeka*) of the king. This anointing ceremony officially inaugurated the festival in Ramnad and emphasized the linkage of the Rājā's lineage with the great Rāma, prince of Ayodhyā and destroyer of Rāvaṇa in Laṅkā. The *abhiṣeka* ritual (*abhiṣekamahōtsavam*) involves a black granite stone seat (*pittam*) on which the Rāja Bhāskara and, it is claimed, all of the predecessors of his royal line were anointed. This rock is understood as having been used by the first Setupati king whom Prince Rāma appointed as protector of the causeway connecting the southeastern tip of India with Laṅkā. The causeway from Rāmeśvaram (now a great temple center) to Laṅkā is said to have been constructed by the Prince Rāma, and the title, *Setupati*, is derived from this primordial event (*setu* means causeway, *pati* means lord or protector). Seated on this rock, the Ramnad Rājā was anointed with water drawn from

1. Carol A. Breckenridge kindly brought this description to my attention and elsewhere. She has provided a rich analysis of this Navarātri festival. See her essay "From Protector to Litigant : Changing Relations Between Temples and the Rājā of Ramnad," to be published in a forthcoming number of *The Indian Economic and Social History Review* as part of a symposium on South Indian temples edited by B. Stein. The description was originally published in *The Madras Times*, October, 1892

sacred springs in many parts of South India, with water from the sacred Ganges, and with water used to bathe deities of his realm (hence sacred as *tīrtha*). The purification of the Rājā is also a form of reverence as is evident from the next element of the Ramnad *Navarātri* celebration—worship of the Ramnad Rājā family tutelary, Śrī Rājarājeśvarī.

This goddess is represented by a golden image in the iconic form of Durgā as Mahiṣāsura Mardinī (the destroyer of the buffalo demon). Her pedestal (*pittam*), like the granite installation seat of the Rājā, is accorded high significance. It is believed that the great Śaiva teacher Śaṅkarācārya first installed this *pittam* in Karṇāṭaka, and it became the sacred possession of the Hoysaḷa ("Ballala") kings in that South Indian territory. According to legends of the Ramnad *Navarātri*, this sacred pedestal was seized from the Hoysaḷas by a Pāṇḍya king with the aid of the Ramnad Rājā of the time, and the *pittam* was granted by the Pāṇḍya as a reward. Henceforth, the *pittam* served as the base for the Ramnad family tutelary, as a momento of conquest by and service to a great South Indian king. The goddess herself signifies the same thing.

Śrī Rājarājeśvarī, the Ramnad tutelary goddess, was the consort deity of the Cōḻa guardian deity installed at the great Śrī Rājarājeśvara temple of Tāñjavūr, the Cōḻa capital. Thus, the tutelary goddess of the Ramnad Rājā, which occupied the same central ritual function as the tutelary of Vijayanagara kings in the *Mahānavamī*, is seen to signify the connection of the Ramnad Rājās with two of the greatest kingdoms in medieval South India : the Cōḻas, from whence came the goddess, and the Pāṇḍyas, from whence came her pedestal. Here is what might be called the other side of the incorporative meaning of the *Mahānavamī* and *Navarātri* festivals, for here a minor kingly house—the Ramnad Rājās—is seen to have been incorporated by greater kingships of the past in a system of transitive meanings of royal incorporation.

Two aspects of the *Mahānavamī* festival of sixteenth century Vijayanagara and the *Navarātri* festival of nineteenth century Ramnad immediately seize attention. These are their overwhelmingly royal character and their symbolically incorporative character. Both aspects confirm conceptions of ritual kingship assumed in my conception of the segmentary state in medieval

South India[1] and in the ideas proposed some forty years ago by A. M. Hocart and since then largely ignored by Indologists[2].

Hocart's view of the king as ritual performer and as the primary agency for the prosperity and welfare of the realm, and his attention to the integrative function of temple and city are well realized in the Vijayanagara *Mahānavamī* and Ramnad *Navarātri* festivals. Kingly ritual power is expressed in numerous ways : in the manifestation of wealth displayed and elaborately redistributed at many points of the nine-day festivals; in the various consecratory actions involving the king's weapons as the means of his royal fame and protection; and also in the king's frequent and often solitary worship (and ultimately his identity with) the deity who presides with him over the festival and in whose name and for whose propitiation the festival occurs. Worship forms of the Devī (Durgā) are clear in these festivals, and they deserve notice. According to the *Devī Bhāgavatam Purāṇa*, females in procession before the goddess form an essential element of the *Navarātri* or *Mahānavamī* festival.[3] Since it is also true that the Mahānavamī is considered to be a time of danger (from disease among other things), the protective powers of the Devī and that of the king are enhanced.

Incorporative elements to which Hocart drew attention in his work included the subordination of all gods and all chiefs to the king. This incorporation is signified by various means in the Mahānavamī festival. The palace site of the festival is reached through two large gates over which towers were constructed.[4] These massive gateways were apparently destroyed by the Muslim invaders of the city during the sixteenth century; gates

1. B. Stein, "The Segmentary State in South Indian History," pp. 3-51, in Richard G. Fox (ed.), *Realm and Region in Traditional India* (Durham : Duke University Program in Comparative Studies on Southern Asia, Monograph No. 14, 1977).

2. A. M. Hocart, *Kings and Councillors* (Chicago : University of Chicago Press, 1971; originally published in Cairo, 1936). He is not mentioned by Gonda, *op. cit.*, but is by Dumont in *Homo Hierarchicus*.

3. See B. Ramakrishna Rao, "The Dasara Celebrations in Mysore," *Quarterly Journal of the Mythic Society*, Vol. 11 (July 1921), pp. 302-03; and *The Srimad Devi Bhagavatam* in *The Sacred Books of the Hindus*, trans. by Swami Vijnanananda (H. P. Chatterji) (Allahabad : Pananai Office, n.d.), "On Navaratra," part 1, ch. 26, pp. 225-29.

4. Sewell, *op. cit.*, 253-54.

in other parts of the Hampi ruins, at some distance from the palace precincts of Kṛṣṇa Deva Rāya's time, confirm Paes' description of these structures, which resemble the temple gateways of southern India.[1] King and god are at least homologized, if they are not equated. The pavillions erected in the spacious, interior courtyard fronting the Throne Platform to house the notables of the realm are called "castles" by the Portuguese witness; these were the dwellings of great men placed within the precincts of the palace and thus under the protection of the king.

Gods of the king's realm are also incorporated in this city. Installed at Vijayanagara were permanent resident deities such as the Gajāpati Kṛṣṇa of Udayagiri (Nellore district, Āndhra Pradesh) and Viṭṭhala (Viṭhobā) from distant Mahārāshtra.[2] It also appears that deities from elsewhere in the realm were brought to the capital during the festival and presented to the king for his adoration and for exchanges of honors.[3] And, servants of gods throughout the king's realm came to do obeisance to the king. These included priests, but most conspicuously it was the temple women (whom the Portuguese called "courtesans") of shrines everywhere. These temple dancers and musicians performed before the king just as they did before the god to whom they were dedicated.[4]

Following Hocart's perceptive discussion, it is possible to point to the crucial place of the city—to Vijayanagara, "city of victory"—in the total moral order over which the Vijayanagara kings exercised sway. The city, Hocart wrote, "never stands for anything specific; it is never less than the whole world. . . ."[5] And dersistently linked to the city and its establishment is the goddess

1. Several are shown in Longhurst, *op. cit.*, pp. 47-49.

2. Kṛṣṇa Deva Rāya built a temple for Viṭṭhala which is considered one of the most beautiful in South India. However, this god was worshipped in Vijayanagara before that time : K. A. Nilakanta Sastri and N. Venkataramanayya, *Further Sources of Vijayanagara History* (Madras : University of Madras, 1946), Vol. 3, p. 47 and note.

3. Sewell, *op. cit.*, p. 264.

4. *Ibid.*, p. 253, and N. Venkataramanayya, *Studies in the Third Dynasty of Vijayanagara* (Madras : University of Madras, 1935), pp. 404-05. There is another parallel with the horse sacrifice: over the ten days of the consecration of the horse, different gods are presented : *Śatapatha Brāhmaṇa*, part 5, pp. xxxi and 361-70.

5. Hocart, *op. cit.*, p. 250.

Durgā. As Bhuvaneśvarī, "mistress of the world,"[1] the goddess was by tradition propitiated by Vidyāraṇya, or Mādhavācārya, who is supposed to have been the preceptor of the fraternal founders of the city in 1336 A.D. This connection of the city of the Rāyas and the great goddess was first presented by William Taylor in his 1835 translation of several Tamil chronicles of later medieval times,[2] and though the idea continues to be accepted by most Vijayanagara historians, none have exploited fully the symbolic power of the relationships of goddess worship, the Rāyas, and the city. While scholars have failed in this, the successor states of Vijayanagara in South India—including such great states as the Wodeyar kingdom of Mysore and the Nāyaka kingdom of Madurai as well as minor kingdoms such as the Setupatis of Ramnad—did not. They maintained this royal festival in their capitals in full richness.[3]

CONCLUSION

The *Mahānavamī* or *Navarātri* festivals of medieval and modern South India re-establish royal public ritual on a grand scale. These public rituals constitute the most striking manifestation of the quality of sacred kingship implied within the formal code of the Dharmaśāstras, though, in being lavish displays of kingly wealth, these festivals may be said to violate some of the spirit of the medieval Dharma texts. Inspirations for the royal public rituals of the medieval period were varied. Elements of ancient *yajña* (e.g., the *aśvamedha*),), purāṇic ritual (Devī or Durgā festivals), and epic descriptions (e.g., the *Rāmāyaṇa*) are surely there. But what is perhaps most cogently the informing model for these ritual events is the South Indian Hindu temple. In its physical setting, the palace precincts became a temple. This is prefigured in the very names for both palace and temple : in most Dravidian languages these are the same : *kōyil*. The walled enclosures of both palace and temple are the world and the center of both. It is the ruler of that world—king or god—who is the object of that

1. Monier-Williams, *Sanskrit Dictionary*, p. 760.
2. *Oriental Historical Manuscripts, in the Tamil Language : Translated with Annotations*, by William Taylor. 2 Vols. (Madras : C. J. Taylor, 1835), Vol. 2, pp. 102-03.
3. Noted by Taylor among others, *op. cit.*, p. 103.

worship and attendant ritual interactions consisting of resources and honors.

The full implication of this comparison cannot be appreciated without recognizing that the medieval and modern South Indian temple expresses most perfectly the South Indian conceptions of sovereignty and community.[1] Sovereignty is conceived as shared between powerful humans (Rājās) and powerful divinities (Devas); the sovereignty of neither is complete; the sovereignty of both, together, is perfect. Those who fall under the sovereignty of both kings (and kingly personages like chiefs and headmen) and gods comprise a community of reverence or worship. This is a conception of community which occurs at every level of South Indian society from the village to the whole kingdom. Thus, what constitutes any South Indian village is that collectivity of persons who worship the village tutelary (*grāmadevatā*) and who submit to the moral leadership of a village chief. Within villages, families as well as segments of lineages and clans similarly define themselves (and are defined by others thereby) as co-sharers in the protection and sovereignty of gods (of family, lineage, clan) and powerful personages (fathers, lineage and clan leaders).[2] Beyond the medieval village of South India, locality (*nāḍu*) was established by worship of a locality god (*nāḍudevatā*) and chief; the realm itself was defined by the worship of the king and his tutelary as in the *Mahānavamī* or *Navarātri*. Worship is constitutive of (it establishes or creates) community; the sovereignty of great humans (fathers, clan heads, kings) and gods is realized in worship events, or ritual performances, of a public kind in which all of any corporate whole (family to kingdom) express membership and in which all witness as well as compete for the

1. The preceding formulation is based upon a recently completed manuscript to be published by *The Indian Economic and Social History Review*. This symposium of several essays under the editorship of B. Stein includes work by Arjun Appadurai, Carol A. Breckenridge, Dennis Hudson, Friedhelm Hardy, and B. Stein. The introduction of the essays, exploring the relationship of sovereignty and community, was prepared with major contributions from Appadurai and Breckenridge. The work of these two scholars informs this formulation in a very direct way.

2. Here, see the rich ethnography of Dr. Brenda Beck on these relations in modern Coimbatore (Kongu)) : *Peasant Society in Koṅku* (Vancouver : University of British Columbia, 1972).

honors which alone can be distributed by powerful personages and divinities. The divinity of kingship found by Lingat in the Dharmaśāstras was, and could only be, fully realized in the public rituals of great kings like those of Vijayanagara and lesser ones like those of Ramnad.

PART II

RELIGIOUS PLURALISM

4

THE MANDASOR INSCRIPTION OF THE SILK-WEAVERS

A. L. BASHAM

IF we were to be asked what was the finest and most typical relic of the Gupta age, we might be hard put to it to make a choice—the incredibly beautiful Sārnāth Buddhas, the great Boar Incarnation of Viṣṇu at Udayagiri, the wonderful Iron Pillar of Mehraulī, the glorious Ajantā murals, the poems and plays of Kālidāsa—all these and others quickly come to mind. But perhaps the finest relic of the Gupta age is none of these things—it is a simple block of stone found built into the wall of a flight of steps leading down to a river at Mandasor, Madhya Pradesh, on which is inscribed, in small characters of the beautiful Gupta script, most of them still legible after fifteen hundred years, the story of how a certain temple came to be built. The temple of which the block was once a part has long since vanished, its stones removed, as was the custom in ancient and medieval India, to build other structures.

One of the first things we notice as we read the inscription is that it is in verse. It forms a short *kāvya* or 'courtly' poem in Sanskrit, and at the end we read the name of the author, a local hack-poet, a brāhmaṇa who composed poetry to order for those who paid him in this small town, quite far from the main centres of literary culture. He was not a great poet—he used all the stock epithets and similes of the poetry of his time and he plagiarized some of his best stanzas from Kālidāsa's *Meghadūta* ('The Cloud-Messenger') with only slight alterations. But when the chief of a guild of respectable craftsmen approached him one day and commissioned him to write a dedicatory poem for the new temple Vatsabhaṭṭi gave of his best. Kālidāsa may have felt that some of his writings would be preserved and recited many years after his death, but this provincial brāhmaṇa, unknown outside his home-town, can hardly have thought that his poem was to become, after centuries of oblivion, one of the major sources for the social history of the period, and one of the main pieces of evidence for its high culture and urbanity.

Below we give our own translation of the poem generally known as 'the Mandasor Inscription of the Silk-weavers', with a running commentary. Our translation is rather free, for a close translation of Sanskrit poetry is impossible without sacrificing every bit of the poetic feeling of the original. The poem starts with three rather elaborate verses in praise of Sūrya, the sun-god, for whose worship the temple was built.

(May this poem be) successful.

1. Worshipped by the hosts of gods that they may live, by *siddhas* for their success,
by yogīs, only intent on meditation, their senses under control, seeking salvation,
and by sages with devotion, their only wealth their intense austerities, able to curse and bless,
cause of the sinking and rising of the world—may the Maker of Light protect you.

2. Even the divine sages (*brahmarṣi*), wise in the knowledge of the truth, do not know him fully, however hard they try;
him who with his rays far reaching feeds the whole three worlds,
praised as he rises by *gandharvas*, gods, *siddhas*, *kinnaras* and men together,
bestowing their desires upon his worshippers—hail to that Savitṛ.

(In the above verse, *gandharvas* and *kinnaras* are species of demi-gods, whose special function is to provide the heavens with song and music. *Siddhas* are another class of demigod. Savitṛ, in the *Vedas* a god distinct from Sūrya, is here identified with him.)

3. Shining forth day by-day, the net of his beams
pouring from the wide and lofty summit of the mountain of dawn
his beams as ruddy as the flushed cheek of a tipsy woman,
May Vivasvān, adorned with a garland of rays, protect you.

(The third quarter of this stanza is a commonplace simile in Sanskrit poetry of this type, and gives good evidence of the moral attitude of the times, very different from that of modern India, which turned against alcohol with the rise of popular *bhakti*. Vivasvān, the 'Shiner-forth', is a common epithet of the Sun-god.)

Now Vatsabhaṭṭi introduces us to the guild of weavers of the land of Lāṭa, from which they came to Daśapura (the modern Maṇdasor). Lāṭa is the area later known as Khāndesh, between the Narmadā and Tāptī rivers.

4. Men famed throughout the world for their craft came from the region of Lāṭa,
where the hills are covered with forests
lovely with lofty trees bowing low with the burden of blossoms,
and with fine temples, halls and monasteries.

5. Drawn by the virtues of the kings of this country,
caring nothing for the real and manifold hardships of the journey,
filled with respect, first with their minds and then bodily,
they came to Daśapura, bringing their children and kinsfolk.

(The trees bowed low with blossoms are a poetic commonplace in Sanskrit, and were part of the raw material of every hack-poet like Vatsabhaṭṭi. One wonders, however, why the group, later in the poem identified as silk-weavers, decided to leave their old home. We know very little about the history of Lāṭa at the time and there is no evidence that its rulers were oppressive, though it was outside the Gupta Empire. This region, however, largely depended for its prosperity on the sea-trade with the West, and the weavers must have exported much of their output. We surmise that with the continued barbarian attacks on the Roman Empire the export trade declined, and so the weavers decided to seek their fortunes in the Gupta Empire, then at the height of its power and prosperity. Similar migrations of large groups of people are frequently attested in later Indian history.)

In the next four stanzas Vatsabhaṭṭi praises the glories of the countryside of the small tributary kingdom of which Daśapura was the capital. Though the reader who knows little of Sanskrit poetics will find these verses delightful (which in fact they are), in their evocation of the colours and scents of Indian nature, all the phrases are the common stock of the poets of the times, and might have been applied to any region of India.

6. In course of time the city became the crest-jewel of the land,
the land adorned with a thousand hills whose rocks are damp
with the drops that fall from the cheeks of rutting elephants,
the land whose lovely ornaments are trees bowed low with flowers;

(The *dāna*, a pungent sweaty liquid produced from the heads of male elephants during their mating season, is another commonplace of Indian poetics.)

7. Where lakes are alive with wild-fowl,
their waters glittering by the banks, all bright
with many petals fallen from the flowering trees on the shore,
adorned with full-blown lotuses;

8. where on the pools the wild geese seem shut in golden cages,
formed by scattered yellow pollen from lotuses swayed by tremulous ripples,
pools radiant with many water lilies
which bend with the weight of their stamens;

9. where the trees are bowed with the burden of blossom,
and hum with bold tribes of bees made drunk with their nectar,
and where the women of the town, forever singing,
make beautiful the groves;

(*Purāṅganā*, 'woman of the town', as in eighteenth century English, implies a courtesan. The beauty and accomplishments of the local courtesans, like the piety and learning of the local brāhmaṇas, were legitimate grounds for civic pride.)

Now Vatsabhaṭṭi turns to the city of Daśapura, which he praises in terms largely plagiarized from the description of Ujjayinī in Kālidāsa's *Meghadūta*. Being a brāhmaṇa himself he places much emphasis on the virtues of the local clerics :

10. where the tall houses seem
like pale peaks of cloud bright with flashes of lightning,
so very high, so very white,
with fluttering banners and women.

(The whitewashed walls of the houses are compared to the white clouds, the banners and the brightly dressed and bejewelled women to the lightning.)

11. Other houses, high as the peak of Kailāsa,
    radiant with tall turrets and pavilions,
    are loud with the sound of music, their frescoed walls
    lovely amid the groves of swaying banana trees.

(Kailāsa is the mountain of the Himālayas believed to be the abode of Śiva and the lesser gods associated with him.)

12. The houses, wearing roof-pavilions like garlands,
    rise as though they have torn through the earth,
    like a chain of heavenly palaces
    bright as the rays of the full moon.

(*Vimānas*, in modern Indian languages meaning 'airplanes', were the mobile pavilions of the gods, which conveyed them from place to place. *Dharāṃ vidāryyaiva samutthitāni*, the second line, seems to imply that the buildings of the city form an organic whole with the earth on which they are built, like trees or out-cropping rocks. This is a noteworthy feature of much Indian architecture from the humble peasant's hut to such ornate temples as those at Khajurāho.)

13. The city shines, embraced by the dancing ripples of two fair rivers.
    like the body of Smara by large breasted Prīti and Rati.
14. With brāhmaṇas adorned with truthfulness, forbearance, restraint, peace,
    firmness in keeping vows, purity, resolution, learning,
    good conduct, modesty, strength of purpose, and intellect,
    paragons of wisdom and penance, never losing their nerve the city is resplendent, like the sky with a host of shining planets.

(Smara is a pseudonym of Kāmadeva, and Prīti (affection) and Rati (sexual pleasure) are his two wives.)

Now the poet turns to the history of the weavers. It seems that even in their new home there was not enough trade in silk cloth to keep them all employed, but they showed enterprise in finding other professional openings.

15. So, all together, through constant association
    their friendship expanding from day to day,
    honoured by the kings like their own sons,
    they [the weavers] dwelt happily, rejoicing in the city.
16. Some became pastmasters in archery, pleasant to the ear (from the twang of the bowstring);

others became knowers [i.e., tellers] of varied tales,
about hundreds of good deeds;
while others, unassumingly virtuous, fully devoted to
discoursing on righteousness [*dharma*],
were skilled in speaking that which is useful,
pleasantly, not harshly.

17. Some remained excellent in their (ancestral) craft, and others,
knowers of the self (*ātmā*), mastered astrology;
others, even today, reckless in battle,
strive to wreak harm upon their foes.

(The professions taken up by the members of the guild form a strange list. The archers referred to in stanza 16 are unlikely to be professional soldiers, who are clearly mentioned in stanza 17; probably this refers to teachers of archery, which was a popular sport as well as one of the most important skills in warfare and hunting. We have a mention of professional story-tellers, a traditional calling in most ancient societies. The class of those 'devoted to discoursing on *dharma*' may refer to professional arbitrators in domestic law, a calling ideally exercised by brāhmaṇas. The phrase 'knowers of the self' referred to in stanza 17, as an epithet of those who became astrologers, is strange; one would expect *ātmā* to be taken in a mystical sense, roughly equivalent to 'soul' in Western theology, but the words may only mean 'self-conscious', 'self-aware'.)

Next Vatsabhaṭṭi praises the virtues, social and otherwise, of the guildsmen. This poem is a conventional eulogy and its stanzas need not be taken literally, but at least it shows the ideal of middle class life in the time of the Guptas.

18. Wise, having charming wives, of famed and widespread family,
adorned with conduct worthy of their stock,
true to their vows, ready to help their friends,
others are firm and trustworthy in their friendships.

19. The guild (*śreṇi*) is even more glorious from other such men,
their attachment to the senses conquered, their conduct righteous,
gentle, with virtue predominant, like gods on an earthly journey,

noble and free from passion, the crest-jewels of their families. (Here Vatsabhaṭṭi emerges in his true colors, as a second-rate poet. In stanza 18 his use of the word *apare* ('others') is dictated solely by the requirements of the metre, and its implication that many of the guildsmen are not 'firm and trustworthy in their friendships' is certainly not what he intends. He seems to divide his clients into two classes : some, referred to in stanza 19, are more religiously inclined than the others, but all of them are praiseworthy. The phrase 'with virtue predominant' (*adhika-sattva*) probably refers to the first of the three *guṇas* in Sāṅkhya philosophy.)

In the next stanza Vatsabhaṭṭi gracefully pays tribute to the traditional profession of his clients with an evocation of the *abhisārikā*, the girl who goes out secretly at night to meet her lover, a stock character of classical Sanskrit poetry.)

20. Though she be endowed with youth and beauty, though she be adorned
with golden necklaces and garlands of flowers,
a woman will not go to meet her lover in secret
until she has put on two silken garments.

Now the poet begins to attend to the real business of his poem. The silk-weavers, though many of them had given up their traditional profession, still retained their corporate identity. They met together and decided to make an endowment.

21. And these men, who have adorned their whole earth in robes of silk,
pleasant to the touch, lovely to the eye, with varied stripes of different colors,
22. remembered that the world was very fickle, unstable,
blown by the wind like the flower in the ear of a fairy,
as was all that is human, and all wealth, however large,
and so they made an auspicious and firm resolve.

But Vatsabhaṭṭi cannot get down to the real business of his poem without some verses in praise of the local ruler. First of all, he briefly mentions the Emperor Kumāra Gupta. According to the traditional metaphor, the Earth, personified as a woman, is the wife of the Emperor.

23. When Kumāra Gupta was ruler of the earth,
whose undulous girdle is made of the four oceans,
whose large breasts are Sumeru and Kailāsa,

whose laughter is the full blown flowers wafted from the woods' edges.

(Sumeru or Meru is a mythical mountain, the centre and axis of the earth. Kailāsa is referred to in our note to verse 11.)

Kumāra Gupta is a remote monarch, and evidently has little direct impact on the citizens of Daśapura. The poet descants rather on the virtues of the local line of kings, subordinate to the Guptas. The benevolent Viśvavarman is dead, and his son Bandhuvarman, whose martial virtues are more strongly praised, now rules. From the evidence of another inscription we know that Viśvavarman, son of Naravarman, was ruling in Daśapura in 417 A.D., nineteen years before the erection of the temple of the sun. We need not assume that these minor kings were the paragons of benevolence and prowess they are said to be. Panegyrics of this kind are commonplaces in the inscriptions of the period. The importance of these flattering epithets is that they established norms of government which the kings were expected to try to live up to. They show us the ideal king, from the point of view of the subject.

24. There was (ruling in Daśapura) the governor, king Viśvavarman,
His mind was as keen as Śukra's or Bṛhaspati's;
most eminent of kings throughout the world,
his deeds in battle equalled Arjuna's.

(Śukra and Bṛhaspati are legendary sages, the reputed authors of standard textbooks on law and statecraft. Nearly all readers will recognize Arjuna as the second of the five Pāṇḍava brothers, the heroes of the *Mahābhārata*.)

25. Full of compassion for the poor, fulfilling his word to the wretched and distressed, very merciful, lord of the lordless,
a wishing-tree to those who loved him, a giver of protect ion to those in fear, he was the friend of all the land.

('Lord of the lordless—*anātha-nātha*—refers mainly to the king's care for widows and orphans. 'Wishing-trees'—*kalpadruma*—in happier ages of the world, before the cosmic rot set in, fulfilled all the wishes of those who stood under their branches.)

26. His son, endowed with firmness and good judgement,
dear to his kinsmen, as if his subjects' kinsman,
removing the sorrows of his kinsmen, King Bandhuvarman,

was supremely skilful in destroying the ranks of his proud enemies.

(Here Vatsabhaṭṭi parades his command over words and his verbal ingenuity, which was an essential tool of the ancient Indian poet's trade. *Bandhu-varman* literally means 'one whose defence is his kinsmen'. In the second and third quarters of the verse he plays with the word *bandhu* to his heart's content, and then, in the last quarter, changes to a harsher key, with a series of guttural consonant clusters :

Tasyātmajaḥ sthairyya-nayopapanno,
bandhu-priyo bandhur iva prajānām,
bandhv-artti-harttā nṛpa-Bandhuvarmmā,
dviṅ-dṛpta-pakṣa-kṣapaṇ-aika-dakṣaḥ.)

27. Handsome and young, expert in battle, endowed with modesty,
who, though a king, was never carried away by infatuation, surprise, or similar (undesirable emotions),
the embodiment of erotic sentiment, though unadorned, he shines
in beauty, like a second god of love.

28. Remembering him, even today, the large-eyed enemy beauties,
broken by the fierce affliction of widowhood,
shiver in fear, and their firm breasts
are weary and pained (from their constant trembling).

('Erotic sentiment'—*śṛṅgāra*—is one of the nine *rasas* or 'flavours' according to which literary and artistic emotions are classified. A king's physical beauty and sexual prowess were virtues almost as highly prized by his loyal subjects as his benevolence and bravery—an attitude arising from the belief in the intimate bond linking the king and his kingdom, to which he was mystically married.)

Now at last the poet comes to the point of his poem :

29. When Bandhuvarman, the noble, the bull among kings,
the strong shouldered, was well protecting this flourishing Daśapura,
the silk-weavers, who had formed a guild, skilled in their craft,
with hoarded wealth had this incomparably noble temple
made for the god with burning rays.

30. Its broad-based pointed tower is like a mountain,
    white as the mass of the pure rays of the risen moon,
    it shines, lovely to the eye, like a glorious crest-jewel
    set in (the turban of) the City of the West.

('The City of the West' is Daśapura or Mandasor itself. The size of the original temple is not known and it may have been comparatively modest, despite the hyperbole of this description; but in any case it gives evidence of the prosperity of the times that a guild of craftsmen in a comparatively small city could find the money to erect a stone temple of any kind. We cannot tell whether the silk-weavers had any other motive than the desire for religious merit and fame in their generosity to their adopted home. Possibly they were hoping that the king might bestow valuable privileges on them, for instance remission of taxes, if they disgorged their accumulated savings for a work of public utility—and such, from the point of view of the times, it was, for the whole city would share in the religious merit accruing from the building of the new temple, and thus be protected from hunger, disease and oppression.)

Vatsabhaṭṭi now gives us the date of the dedication of the new temple in a very roundabout manner, introducing a thumbnail description of the cold season (*hemanta*) from mid-November to mid-January. All the phrases here are conventional, including the eroticism of stanza 33. The theme is developed at greater length in the well-known poem 'The Garland of the Seasons' (*Ṛtusaṃhāra*) attributed to Kālidāsa.

31. At the time when women are united with their lords,
    pleasant from the slight warmth
    of the (once-) fiery rays of the sun, when the fish lie low in the water,
    when no one watches the rays of the moon or the terraces of palaces, or uses sandal paste
    or fans or garlands, when the cold destroys the lotus,

(A fragrant paste made of ground sandalwood was applied to the skin in the hot season and had a cooling effect; garlands of light colored flowers were used for the same purpose.)

32. in the season lovely with the humming of bees, drunk
    with the nectar of full-blown flowers
    of *rodhra* and *priyaṅgu*, and of jasmine,
    when the solitary branches of *nagana* trees dance with the force

of a cold wind, harsh with drops of dew;
33. when the fall of the dew is scorned by young men in the grip of passion,
closely embracing the full and swelling thighs and breasts of women they love;
34. when four hundreds of years had passed, and ninety-three more
from the establishment of the clan of the Mālavas,
when (men) look forward to the thunder of the clouds;
35. in the bright half of the month Sahasya, on the auspicious thirteenth day,
with a ceremony of benediction this temple was established.

(The calendrical information contained in the last two stanzas is too complex to explain fully here. The kingdom of Daśapura, though now subordinate to the Guptas, had not adopted the Gupta Era based on 320 A.D., but still used the Mālava Era, later known as Vikrama, based on an epoch of 58 B.C.; 493 expired years in this era are equivalent to 436 A.D. At this time the Roman Empire, under the ineffectual Valentinian III, was staggering from the attacks of Vandals and Huns, and St. Augustine was six years dead. To establish the exact day of the temple's dedication involves the use of complicated tables and is hardly worth doing at such a distance in time, but it represents a date not far off Christmas.)

This is not the end of the inscription, which commemorates not only the building of the temple, but also events which took place 37 years later. Vatsabhaṭṭi does not mention the name of the king ruling at that time, and it seems that unpleasant things had happened at Daśapura, which he preferred not to describe :

36. Then, under other kings, when much time had passed,
part of this temple fell into disrepair, so now
37. this house of the sun has been again repaired, for the increase
of their fame, and made altogether most noble, by the noble guild.
38. It is very high and white, as though touching the sky with its lovely pinnacles,
a resting place for the first clear rays of the rising moon and sun.

(It is strange that a temple built of solid blocks of masonary without arches or domes should have needed extensive repair after such a brief period, and we suspect that the troubled times around 454 A.D., when the Hūṇas made their first great attack on India, may have had something to do with the damage. Other inscriptions show that in 467 A.D., a king called Prabhākara was ruling in Mandasor and was still vaguely tributary to the Gupta emperor. In 490 A.D., there ruled another king, Ādityavardhana who, in his fragmentary inscription, admits no overlord of any kind. His successor Yaśodharman, in 532 A.D., claims to have defeated the fierce Hūṇa conqueror Mihirakula, and to be lord of lands which the Guptas never ruled. It is not clear whether there was any relationship between these kings and those of the line of Bandhuvarman, though some specialists believe that there was. In any case, the local poet Vatsabhaṭṭi prefers not to mention the new rulers by name. Despite many changes, a new generation of guildsmen carries on the tradition of the earlier one. They are still evidently fairly wealthy, and still maintain their group solidarity.)

Vatsabhaṭṭi gives the date of the restoration of the temple in a florid manner similar to the date of its consecration. He describes the season of Śiśira, when the temperature begins to rise and many flowers appear. The date corresponds to early February 473 A.D., three years before the Herulian Odoacer deposed Romulus Caesar and put an end to the Roman Empire in the West.

39. When five hundred years, and twenty more, and nine
 had passed, on the second (day) of the bright half of the month Tapasya;
40. When he whose body was destroyed by Hara has (an) increased (supply of) arrows,
 thanks to the fresh bursting forth of flowers of pendulous *atimukta* vines and of wild jasmines;
41. when every separate branch of the *nagana* bush resounds with the clans of bees, gay with drinking honey,
 in the season when the *rodhra* tree is lovely with luxuriant blossom;
42. as the clear heaven (is adorned) by the moon, as the breast of Viṣṇu by the *kaustubha* jewel,
 this wholly noble city is adorned by the best of temples.

('Hara', in stanze 40 is an epithet of the god Śiva, who, when the love-god Kāmadeva tried to wound him with his arrows, burnt him to ashes. Like the classical Eros-Cupid, Kāmadeva is an archer, but his arrows are made of flowers.)

Finally, the local poet puts his name to his handiwork, with legitimate pride. The fact that he composed his poem, 'painstakingly' (*prayatnena*) is evident from many phrases which are not quite as felicitous as they might be, but we must remember that he made no claims to greatness. He is not heard of elsewhere. Probably he turned out verses at so much a stanza on demand, and the fact that he did as well as this at the behest of a body of respectable craftsmen speaks volumes for the culture of the period.

43. As long as the Lord bears a mass of tawny matted hair
from which the pure new moon arises.
as long as Viṣṇu wears on his shoulders a wreath of full-blown lotuses,
so long may this noble temple endure. May it last forever.

44. The temple of the sun has been built with devotion (*bhakti*)
on the orders of the guild,
and the above has been painstakingly composed by Vatsabhaṭṭi.

(The 'Lord' referred to in the 43rd stanza is the god Śiva, the archetypal ascetic, who, like many human ascetics, never cuts, washes or combs his hair. It is, therefore, tangled and matted, piled in a bun on top of his head, and it is reddish in colour, partly from ingrained dust and dirt, and partly from its being bleached by constant exposure to the sun.)

And then, in prose, comes the final benediction :

May this poem be for the welfare (*svasti*) of the maker, the writer, the reader and the hearer. May there be success (*siddhi*).

Over fifteen hundred years later we still seem to share in the blessing as we read Vatsabhaṭṭi's poem. It reflects not only religious faith, but also love of the good things of this world, and behind its superficial sophistication, its complex rhythms and its occasional infelicities, we can see the best qualities of the period—loyalty, fellowship, local patriotism and honest pride in what one has achieved. No period in the history of India has a greater monument than this.

5

THE IMAGE OF THE HERETIC IN THE GUPTA *PURĀṆAS*

WENDY DONIGER O'FLAHERTY

THE Gupta Age may or may not have been the Golden Age for some—for Kālidāsa, for a lot of architects, for the privileged in that elitist society—but it may well have been the Kali Age for those outside the inner sanctum. The evidence of the *Purāṇas* and *Dharmaśāstras* may indicate that the attitude to heretics and atheists became embittered in this period, losing ground that had been gained during the more loosely structured Śaka-Kuṣāṇa era and that was to be gained once again, after the Gupta period, under the influence of Tantrism.

Heresy and diversity had flourished under the Kuṣāṇas, whose eclectic patronage stimulated the luxuriant growth of sectarian Hinduism and the emergence of highly original forms of Buddhism. Heresy and diversity continued to flourish (in an almost grotesquely syncretistic form) under the patronage of Harṣa, as is witnessed both by Bāṇa's biography of Harṣa and by Harṣa's own weird play, the *Nāgānanda*. Under these conditions, Hinduism truly borrowed from Buddhism (the influence of which over even such an orthodox document as the *Bhagavad Gītā* has long been noted). Under the Guptas, however, the need to maintain superficial political unity drove the rulers to play an uneasy game of impartial patronage; under very similar conditions many centuries earlier, Aśoka had promulgated his mealy-mouthed *dhamma* in an ultimately vain attempt to indoctrinate his subjects into an early form of reductionist comparative religion.

The Guptas patronized the Buddhists, but the Purāṇic texts composed by Brāhmaṇas in this period excoriated the Buddhists.

The most important of the anti-Buddhist myths of this period, namely, of Viṣṇu's incarnation as the Buddha, depicts the Buddhists being dishonestly used by God, much as the actual Buddhists were used by the Gupta kings for all their patronage. The enemies in these myths are the "heretics", often disguised as "foreigners" (*Mlecchas*); in this way, a myth of political extermination was crudely superimposed upon a myth of theological conflict. It is difficult indeed to tell where politics ends and religion begins in these myths, or even to tell precisely what axes are being ground in a given context. Further complications arise when one realizes that Buddhists and Jains, so often lumped together by the Hindu polemicist, each tended to regard the other as heretics, even as each of two castes may regard the other as lower and polluting; many of the myths of heresy may be expressing intercaste tensions as well as political tensions on a higher scale.

The precise dates of the relevant texts are extremely difficult to fix, but the relative chronology is reasonably clear. The rapprochement with Buddhism and other heterodoxies that enriched Hinduism during the period of the Upaniṣads and the redaction of the *Mahābhārata* is conspicuously absent from the early Purāṇas and reappears again in the works of Jayadeva and his contemporaries. A significant example of this is the myth of the Buddha incarnation of Viṣṇu, which first appears in the *Viṣṇu Purāṇa* between 400 and 500 A.D.[1] In the Purāṇic texts, the Buddha was depicted as deluded and destructive, for these texts of the Gupta period were weapons in a battle between the instigators of the Hindu revival and the still thriving establishments of Jainism and Buddhism. It has been said that the *Purāṇas* "bear the scars of the battle to this day, in the form of numerous sharp and contemptuous denunciations of the

1. Adalbert J. Gail, "Buddha als Avatar Viṣṇu's im Spiegel der Purāṇas," in *ZDMG* 1969, supplementa 1, vorträge teil 3, pp. 917-23; Radhakrishna Choudhary, "Heretical Sects in the Purāṇas," *Annals of the Bhandarkar Oriental Research Institute*, 37 (1957), p. 239; Rajendra Chandra Hazra, *Studies in the Purāṇic Records on Hindu Rites and Customs*, (Dacca, 1948), pp. 41-42 and 103; see Wendy Doniger O'Flaherty, *The Origins of Evil in Hindu Mythology* (University of California, Berkeley, 1976), pp. 188-211.

Mohaśāstras ('scriptures of delusion') and their non-Vedic adherents."[1]

Later, when Buddhism was waning in India, the Hindus could afford to be generous, and the Buddha is depicted in a more favorable light.[2]

In order to understand the development of the Hindu attitude to heretics, it is necessary to understand precisely who these heretics were—and the texts are exasperating in their imprecision on this point. Our own use of the word "heresy" is equally imprecise, though in a different way; this further obstructs our attempts to come to terms with the Indian issue. The *Shorter Oxford English Dictionary* defines heresy (from the Greek αἵρεομαι "to choose") as "theological opinion or doctrine held in opposition to the 'catholic' or orthodox doctrine of the Christian Church. Hence, opinion or doctrine in philosophy, politics, science, art, etc. in variance with what is orthodox." The Greek term, αἵρεσις, was actually applied, by a Greek of the third century A.D., to one form of Indian religion. As the men he described were ascetics living without women or children, it is conceivable that they might have been considered heretics by their countrymen, but as they were Brāhmaṇas it is more likely that they were heretics from the standpoint of the Christian author.[3] Already the dangers of cross-cultural terminologies become apparent. The primary difficulty which arises when the Greek-derived term is applied to Indian religion is that the element of choice, which characterizes not only heresy but sin in Western theology, is

1. Ronald Huntington, *A Study of Purāṇic Myth from the Viewpoint of Depth Psychology* (Unpublished Ph.D. Dissertation, University of Southern California, 1960), p. 33.

2. Cf. *Bhāgavata Purāṇa*, with the commentary of Śrīdhara (Bombay-1832), 6.8.19; *Gītagovinda* of Jayadeva (Hyderabad, 1969), 1.1.9; *Devībhāgavata Purāṇa* (Benares, 1960), 10.5.13; cf. O'Flaherty (1976), pp. 204-06.

3. Jean Filliozat, *Les relations extérieures de l'Inde* (Pondichéry: Institut Français d'Indologie, Publication 2, 1956), pp. 34-60. In 234 A.D., St. Hippolyte wrote a *Refutation of All Heresies* (Κατὰ πασων αιρεσεων ελεγχος). Portions I.24.1-3 and I.24.7 of this work refer to certain Brāhmins who said that they had rejected wrong doctrine (κενοδοξία), a term which the author applies elsewhere to certain heretic sects who were influenced by Indian doctrines. Thus the Greek term "heresy" was applied to one Indian religion which claimed to have rejected "wrong-doctrine", a term which was applied to another Indian religion.

totally inapplicable to the Hindu concept of heresy. The Hindu heretic does not choose his false doctrine; it is thrust upon him by his own ignorance, or by a curse. A heretic is often called *vedabāhya*, "outside the Vedas", a condition which results from the action of the orthodox; he is excommunicated, quite literally, the victim rather than the conscious agent of heresy. (It is interesting to note that the association of the concept of choice with heresy is preserved in the middle Persian *varan*, which is related to the Sanskrit root √*vṛ*, "to choose". *Varan* is defined as heresy or concupiscence.)

Hinduism and Buddhism differ from Christianity in that they regard heresy as a failure of understanding rather than as a deliberate choice of evil; ignorance rather than sin is the cause of all evil, "an act of intellectual misapprehension and not...an act of volition and rebellion."[1] In this, the Hindu concept of sin is less akin to the Hebrew terms which denote a conscious moral disobedience to God and alienation of oneself from him, than to the Greek concept of sin as αμαρτία—a mistake, a "going-off-the-track", which is literally approximated by the Sanskrit concept of the "wrong path" (*vimārga, pāṣaṇḍamārga*) or "error" (literally, "wandering"—*bhrānti*). Thus the element of choice implicit in the term "heretic" in Western theology but absent from the Sanskrit term for heretic (*pāṣaṇḍa*) similarly distinguishes "sin" from the more passive Sanskrit equivalents (*pāpa, adharma, moha, tamas*, etc.).

The element of choice is re-introduced into this debate in the post-Gupta period, the *bhakti* period. For in the *bhakti* cults, the individual is given a choice of action, though the choice is not entirely free—for his choice is conditioned by past *karma*, and god must choose the worshipper as well as be chosen. But viewed in terms of action, the individual consciously changes his life. This attitude toward choice in *bhakti* theology is in notable contrast with the characteristic attitude of the orthodox mythology typical of the Gupta *Purāṇas*. There, just as the individual is helpless to resist a possibly undesirable inherited social role (*svadharma*), so too his salvation is sometimes thrust upon him equally without his conscious agency or choice. Thus Guṇanidhi commits all manner of sins, including robbing a temple, and is

1. Edward Conze, *A Short History of Buddhism* (Bombay, 1960), p. 6.

saved from the tortures of hell because he had made a new wick for the temple lamp so that he could see better to steal the offerings. In this view, salvation appears to be as accidental as heresy—though it should be noted that this view was vehemently challenged by later *bhakti* texts.[1]

In spite of these differences of connotation, the English term "heretic" corresponds most closely in negative tone as well as in denotation to the Sanskrit *pāṣaṇḍa* (later, sometimes *pāṣaṇḍin* or *pākhaṇḍa*). The shift in the connotation of this term throughout its period of application supports the hypothesis of a gradual increase in intolerance. Its earliest occurrence, in the edicts of Aśoka (third century B.C.), is not necessarily pejorative; it merely denotes a sect or religious doctrine of any kind.[2] Yet, even here, the context indicates that non-orthodox sects in particular may be denoted and certainly in all later texts, from the *Mahābhārata* on, non-orthodox sects are pejoratively designated by the term *pāṣaṇḍa*. The etymology of the term is obscure. Mayrhofer suggests that it may be derived from *pāriṣada*, designating one around whom a group of disciples sat in a gathering.[3] If this is valid (though there are arguments against it, such as the subsequent appearance of the nasal[4]), the term might indicate a contrast with the *upaniṣadṣ*, for which a similar verbal base has been suggested—the *pāriṣada/pāṣaṇḍa* being the teacher around whom non-Brāhmaṇa students sat, the Upaniṣadic teacher the one beside whom Brāhmaṇa students sat, or at least students who remained within the orthodox Hindu fold.

From a very early period, the question of heresy turned upon the acceptance of the Vedas.[5] To a Westerner, this might

1. *Śiva Purāṇa* (Benares, 1964), 2.1.17-48—2.1.18.38; *Śivapurāṇamāhātmya* 1.1.2.15-40. See O'Flaherty (1976), pp. 233 and 237.

2. Seventh pillar edict; cf. Dines Chandra Sircar, *Select Inscriptions*, 2nd edition (Calcutta, 1965), p. 63, line 15. The wording of the inscription is, "I have arranged that some [Dhamma Mahāmātas] will be occupied with the affairs of the [Buddhist] Sangha···some with the Brahmins and Ājīvikas ···some with the Nirgranthas [Jains]···with other religious sects [*pāsandesu*]."

3. Manfred Mayrhofer, *Concise Etymological Sanskrit Dictionary* (Heidelberg, 1963), p. 65.

4. I am indebted to Professor Thomas Burrow of Oxford University for pointing out this etymological problem.

5. See Wendy Doniger O'Flaherty, "The Origin of Heresy in Hindu Mythology," *History of Religions*, 10, 4 (May, 1971), pp. 271-333; and Louis Renou, *The Destiny of the Vedas in India* (New Delhi), 1965.

appear to be a matter of dogma; to a Hindu, however, it is a matter of ritual. The ritualistic approach to the Vedas as a touchstone of orthodoxy/heresy is clearly apparent from the writings of Kumārila Bhaṭṭa, in the immediate post-Gupta period; his attitude epitomizes that of the Gupta *dharmaśāstrins*:

> "Like milk that has been kept in the skin of a dog, the few statements appearing in these [heretical] texts which agree with the Vedas, such as the doctrine of non-injury, etc., are not to be believed until they are found in the *dharmaśāstras*; and when the meaning is clear from the *śāstras*, the heretical texts have no use."[1]

Kumārila back-handedly acknowledges the earlier, pre-Gupta contribution which heretics made to a more receptive Hinduism when he refers grudgingly to "the doctrine of non-injury, etc."; but now the taint of heresy corrupts even the true doctrine, just as a dog pollutes an orthodox Hindu (or a cow) by his touch—indeed, sometimes by his mere shadow. And Kumārila rejects these "true" bits of heretic doctrine on the same principle as that embraced by the Muslims who burnt the library at Alexandria, arguing that those texts which disagreed with the Qur'ān were heretical, while those that agreed with it were redundant.

A similar hardening of dogmatic lines may be seen in the development of the term *nāstika.* This term is traditionally (and probably correctly) derived from the phrase "*nāsti*"; a *nāstika* is thus one who says "It/he is not", while an *āstika* says "It/he is."[2] Parmenides, perhaps under Indian influence, makes a similar distinction between two ways of inquiry : ". . . the first, that says that (it) is and that it cannot be that (it) is not", and the second that says the opposite.[13] A *nāstika* is, literally, a "nay-sayer", but that to which he says "Nay" was regarded

1. *Tantravārttika* of Kumārila Bhaṭṭa, commentary on Śabarasvāmin's *Jaiminīya Mīmāṃsā Sūtra* commentary (Benares Sanskrit Series, Benares, 1903), p. 127, commentary on Śabarasvāmin's verse 1.3.7.

2. V. S. Apte, *Practical Sanskrit-English Dictionary*, 3 Vol. (Poona, 1957), under *nāstika*.

3. Parmenides, fragment 2, cited in Edward Hussy, *The Pre-Socratics* (London, 1972), p. 81. Some striking parallels between the thought of Parmenides and the Mādhyamikas have been discussed at length by V. N. Toporov, "Маπхbямики и зπеатbı: нескоπbко πараππеπеи" in Инπийская куπbтура и Вуππизм, москва, 1972, pp. 51-68.

quite differently in pre-Gupta and Gupta times. The subject of the copula is omitted in both the Sanskrit and the Greek, which has left the more precise meaning of the term open to dispute. "It/he" may refer to a god, as in a phrase in the *Ṛg Veda* : "They say of him [Indra], 'He is not'."[1] In a passage in the *Kaṭha Upaniṣad*, however, the unexpressed subject could refer to the *brahman/ātman* : "How can [it] be comprehended except by one saying, '[It] is' ?"[2] The primary meaning of *nāstika* is generally defined by the Indian commentators as "atheist"—i.e., one who denies the existence of the gods; a secondary qualification more Upaniṣadic than Vedic is also often included : a *nāstika* believes that there is no other world nor any lord (*nāsti paraloka īśvaro veti matir yasya*).[3] Finally, this definition is almost always linked with a third criterion which brings the *nāstika* much closer to the heretic : the *nāstika* denies the validity of the Vedas. Thus Manu refers to *nāstikas* and revilers of the Vedas together,[4] and Hemacandra defines an *āstika* as one who says "The lord exists," one who accepts the authority of the Vedas.[5] Surendranath Dasgupta suggests that the term *āstikyam* originally referred to belief in the existence of another world but then came to denote "faith in the ultimate truth being attainable only through the Vedas."[6] Thus a *nāstika* is equated with a *pāṣaṇḍa*;[7] a *nāstika* is "an atheist, unbeliever, one who denies the authority of the Vedas and a future life or the existence of a supreme ruler or creator of the universe," and *nāstikyam* is thus "atheism, infidelity, heresy."[8] The St. Petersburg dictionary defines *nāstika* as an "unbeliever" (a definition which, like the Sanskrit word, leaves unspecified

1. *Ṛg Veda* 2.12.5. *utém āhur naíṣó astīty enam.*
2. *Kaṭha Upaniṣad* 6.12-13.
3. *Śabdakalpadruma* of Raja Sir Radhakant Dev Bahadur, (Calcutta, 1886).
4. *Mānavadharmaśāstra*, with the commentary of Medhātithi, *Bibliotheca Indica* (Calcutta, 1932), 2.11 and 4.163; see also Medhātithi on 4.163.
5. Hemacandra, cited in *Śabdakalpadruma.*
6. Surendranath Dasgupta, *History of Indian Philosophy*, 5 Vols. (MLBD Rept. Delhi, 1975), III, p. 62; cf. also III, 512-550, "The Lokāyata, Nāstika, and Cārvāka." He cites *Ahirbudhnyasaṃhitā*, xxxi,18-23 for the "later" view.
7. *Śabdakalpadruma*, under *nāstika.*
8. V. S. Apte, under *nāstika.*

the actual doctrine which is not believed), but an *āstika* is said to be one who believes in the truth of the tradition ("*überlieferung*", —i.e., the Vedas).[1]

By these criteria, then, it is difficult, if not impossible, to distinguish the heretic from the atheist. Louis Renou remarks upon the early connection between "the question of the *astitva* of the gods— and, therefore, indirectly that of the Veda";[2] clearly, if one does not believe in the gods, one does not believe in a canon purported to have been inspired by them. Moreover, the contrast between the *nāstika* and the *āstika* was soon refined into a distinction between specific doctrines far more complex than simple atheism versus simple faith. Thus the *āstika* religion is said to consist of the six *darśanas*, the orthodox philosophies:[3] these are usually listed as the Sāṅkhya, Yoga (of Patañjali), Pūrva Mīmāṃsā (of Jaimini), Vedānta, Nyāya, and Vaiśeṣika. There is less agreement upon the constituents of the *nāstika* school; traditionally, the *nāstikas* are Buddhists, Jains, and Cārvākas, who deny both the Vedas and the *ātman* of the *Upaniṣads*; according to Hemacandra, however, the *nāstika* religion consists of the Bārhaspatyas, Cārvākas and Laukāyatikas,[4] who are usually regarded as a single school, that of the Materialists. Other authorities observe yet finer distinctions : *nāstikas* are of six kinds : Cārvākas, Digambaras (i.e., Jains), Mādhyamikas, Yogācāras, Sautrāntikas, and Vaibhāṣikas (four great Buddhist schools).[5] In spite of these differences, it is apparent that the broad distinction between *āstikas* and *nāstikas* corresponds in application, if not always in theory, to that which came to distinguish orthodox Hindu from heretic (*pāṣaṇḍa*) in the Gupta period.

According to Jan Heesterman, the *nāstika* or atheist was originally an integral part of the agonistic structure of the Vedic sacrifice. The term denoted one who confronted the *āstika* as well as one who followed any of a variety of different teachings

1. *Sanskrit Wörterbuch* (ed. Otto Böhtlingk and Rudolph Roth), I, 742, and IV, 127.
2. Louis Renou (1965), p. 60.
3. *Ibid*., p. 2.
4. *Abhidhānacintāmaṇi* of Hemacandra (Bombay, 1896), 3, 862-863.
5. *Śabdakalpadruma*.

of materialism.[1] The doubts expressed in the *Ṛg Veda*[2] are merely part of the verbal contest with the official "reviler",[3] who does not reject sacrifice as a matter of abstract doctrine but merely rejects his opponent's sacrifice. Later, however, by the Gupta age, these complementary ritual roles gave way to mutually exclusive doctrines, one of which denied the abstract institution of sacrifice.[4] Once again, as precise terms denoting opposition within the structure give way to imprecise pejoratives directed toward outsiders, we see the handiwork of the Brāhmaṇas closing ranks in the Gupta age.

A final variation of the use of the term "heretic" arose from the development of more vehement conflict between Vaiṣṇava and Śaiva sectarians. One myth of this type shows with great clarity the imposition of specifically anti-Śaiva sentiments upon a typical myth of indeterminate heresy. In the first of the two versions of this myth, no Śaiva is involved :

> "There was a Dravidian king named Citra, who was lustful and greedy and quick-tempered. He reviled Viṣṇu and hated the Vaiṣṇavas, and he would go about saying, 'Who has ever seen this Viṣṇu ?' He oppressed the Vaiṣṇavas, refused to perform any Vedic ritual, and sided with the heretics. When he died, he went to hell and was tortured. Then he was reborn as a demon [*piśāca*], until a sage enlightened him and he found salvation."[5]

This Vaiṣṇava text calls the king a heretic both for denying Viṣṇu and for failing to perform Vedic sacrifices. Another version of the same text, however, introduces a Śaiva heretic as the instrument of the king's corruption :

> "There was a Dravidian king named Citrasena, who was famous for performing Vedic rituals. One day he met some non-Vedic [*vedabāhya*] heretic Śaivas who had matted hair and who smeared ashes on their bodies [i.e., Pāśupatas or Kāpālikas]. These

1. J. C. Heesterman, "On the Origin of the Nāstika," *Beiträge zur Geistesgeschichte Indiens, Festschrift für Erich Frauwallner, Wiener Zeitschrift zur Kunde des Sud- und Ostasiens*, 12-13 (1968-69), p. 171.
2. *Ṛg Veda* 5.30.1, 6.18.36.27.3, 8.64.7, 8.100.3, 10.22.1.
3. Heesterman, pp. 180-181.
4. *Ibid.*, p. 184.
5. *Padma Purāṇa*, Ānandāśrama Sanskrit Series 131 (Poona, 1894), 6.250.1-23.

Śaivas denounced the Vedas and the caste system and caused Citrasena to abandon Viṣṇu and to join their sect. At their instigation, Citrasena prohibited the worship of Viṣṇu in his kingdom and threw the images of Viṣṇu into the sea."[1] Although nothing is said here of the king's fate, the cause of his anti-Vaiṣṇava behavior is described at great length. His heresy becomes specific and more intense : he not only fails to perform rituals, but forbids them and speaks against the Vedas and the caste.

In these various ways, by the Gupta age heresy was in the eye of the beholder. To the Hindus as a whole, Buddhists and Jains (and Cārvākas or Materialists, with whom the former two are often confused) are heretics. To many Vaiṣṇavas, Śaivas are heretics, and to many Śaivas, Vaiṣṇavas are heretics. To many North Indians, South Indians were regarded as heretics.[2] And just to round things out, the Jains regarded the Hindus as heretics.[3] In short : "I am a true believer; you are a heretic." Hindus came to use the term "heretic" as a useful swear word to indicate anyone who disagreed with them, much as the late Senator Joseph McCarthy used the term "Communist".

Sir Richard Burton satirized this attitude in his "translation" of the story of the king and the vampire. When asked to define the term "atheist", the vampire replies :

> "Of a truth, it is most difficult to explain. The sages assign to it three or four several meanings : first, one who denies that the gods exist; secondly, one who owns that the gods exist but denies that they busy themselves with human affairs; and thirdly, one who believes in the gods and in their providence, but also believes that they are easily to be set aside...

1. *Māgha-māhātmya* of the Uttara Khaṇḍa of the *Padma Purāṇa*, in a Bengālī manuscript, Dacca University Mss. no. 931, fols. 44 ff., chapter 10 ff., cited by Rajendra Chandra Hazra, *Studies in the Upapurāṇas : II : Śākta and Non-sectarian Upapurāṇas*, Calcutta Sanskrit College Research Series 22 (Calcutta, 1963), p. 362.

2. I am indebted to Dr. John Marr of the School of Oriental and African Studies for this insight.

3. *Nandisūtra*, p. 391, cited in A.S. Altekar, *State and Government in Ancient India*, 3rd edition (MLBD Rept. Delhi, 1958), p. 15. For a useful discussion of the uneasy rapprochement between a Jain *tīrthaṅkara* and the motif of the Viṣṇu *avatāra*, see Padmanabh S. Jaini, "Jina Ṛṣabha as an *avatār* of Viṣṇu," in *Bulletin of the School of Oriental and African Studies*, Vol. XL, Part 2, 1977, pp. 321-37.

> Thus the Vishnu Swamis of the world have invested the subject with some confusion. The simple, that is to say, the mass of mortality, have confounded that confusion by reproachfully applying the word atheist to those whose opinions differ materially from their own."[1]

Sir Richard's account may have been influenced by his reading of Plato, who distinguishes three impious views held by the corrupt (σιεφδαμἔυοιζ): that the gods do not exist; that they exist but do not care for men; that they are easily bribed (παραγομἔυουζ) by offerings and prayers.[2]

As the net of heresy was cast more and more vehemently, to catch an ever-growing school of dissenters, the myth of the Buddha avatāra of Viṣṇu (a Gupta myth) became so well established that it served as the model for pseudo-historical writings. The *Skanda Purāṇa* relates that, at the beginning of the Kali Age, and under the influence of monks known as *kṣapaṇas* (i.e., Jains), the people of King Āma's kingdom renounced their Vaiṣṇava faith and became followers of the Buddhist *dharma*. The king's daughter was influenced by the Jīvika (*sic*; Ājīvika?) named Indrasūri, and the people followed the Jain teaching and disregarded the Brāhmaṇas. King Āma was surrounded by heretics and refused to shelter Brāhmaṇas who were deprived of their villages, for he considered them guilty of injury (*hiṃsā*) in their animal sacrifices.[3] The outline of this story, and many of its details, follows that of the classical myth of the corruption of the demons by Viṣṇu in the form of the Buddha,[4] but this myth has been superimposed upon a historical personage: for according to Rājaśekhara's *Prabandhakośa*, a Jain monk converted King Āma, son of Yaśovarman of Kanauj (728-753 A.D.), to Jainism.[5] History is now viewed through the screen of the dogmatic myth of the heretic. Similar stories of kings corrupted by Jains appear in other Indian texts.[6] The

1. Sir Richard Burton, *Vikram and the Vampire, or Tales of Hindu Devilry* (London, 1893; reprint ed. New York, 1969), pp. 162-63.
2. Plato, *Laws*, 10.885.
3. *Dharmāraṇyakhaṇḍa* of the *Brahmakhaṇḍa* of the *Skanda Purāṇa*, chapters 31-38, cited by Dines Chandra Sircar, *Studies in the Society and Administration of Ancient and Medieval India* (Calcutta, 1967), p. 149.
4. See O'Flaherty (1976), pp. 174-87.
5. *Prabandhakośa* of Krṣṇamiśra (Bombay, 1898), pp. 27-45, 9.36-52.
6. C. H. Tawney (trans)., *The Ocean of Story* [*Kathāsaritsāgara*], 10 Vols. (MLBD Rept. Delhi, 1967), II, 204, citing W. B. Barker, *Vaitala-pachisi*, pp. 184-91.

Bṛhannāradīya Purāṇa offers an instance of the myth of the more general heresy :

"The virtuous Bhadraśīla was in his former life a king named Dharmakīrti. He was very evil and careless, and by contact with heretics he became a heretic and lost his former merit."[1]

Heresy in a previous life is used here to explain the nature of a possibly historical figure.

It is significant that the myth of King Āma, a historical king, is set at the beginning of the Kali Age, the age in which true history begins.[2] The corrupting and heretical nature of the Kali Age is expressed in anthropomorphic terms in the *Mahābhārata* tale of Nala, in which Kali is personified :

"The virtuous king Nala married Damayantī, who chose him, a mortal, from among the gods. Kali had wanted to marry Damayantī himself, and he determined to break Nala and take Damayantī from him. For twelve years, Kali waited in Nala's presence, and finally he found an opportunity : Nala urinated at twilight and did not wash his feet. Then Kali entered Nala and caused him to commit a series of evil actions, culminating in Nala's desertion of Damayantī. Though Nala was drawn back to Damayantī again and again by his love, he was dragged away by Kali within him, and thus deluded he abandoned her. When Damayantī learned that he was gone, she said, 'Whatever evil one has done this to Nala, who has no evil thoughts—let him live in misery.' After many years, Nala mastered the science of numbers and dice, and Kali came out of his body and resumed his own form. Nala wished to curse Kali, but Kali said, 'Because of Damayantī's curse, I was tortured and lived very unhappily within you. But now I will make you famous.' Then Nala refrained from cursing Kali, and Kali, who was still afraid, hid so that no one but Nala could see him. When Kali was destroyed, Nala was free of fever, and later when he was reunited with Damayantī he said to her, 'It was because of

1. *Bṛhannāradīya Purāṇa* (Calcutta : Asiatic Society of Bengal, 1891), 21.51 ff.

2. David Pocock, "The Anthropology of Time-Reckoning," in *Contributions to Indian Sociology*, no. 7 (1964), pp. 18-29; reprinted in John Middleton (ed.), *Myth and Cosmos* (New York, 1967), pp. 303-14. See also O'Flaherty (1976), pp. 35-45.

Kali that I left you, not because of my own will. But my determination and asceticism conquered him, and the evil [*pāpa*] left me.' "[1]

Kali is the incarnation of the spirit of gambling (which is the undoing of so many *Mahābhārata* heroes), particularly of the loser, for the *kali* throw is "snake-eyes", the lowest throw of the dice; thus it is by mastering numbers and dice that Nala overcomes Kali, though he himself attributes it smugly to his own determination and asceticism. But Kali is also clearly considered to be the incarnation of the heretic, who stands ready to invade the soul of the good man in a careless moment. Kali's struggle with Nala is depicted as a psychological, moral dilemma : Nala is torn between his higher ideals and an ungovernable tendency to sin, which is personified (in dualistic fashion) as Kali within him. Subtle overtones are lent to the story by Kali's passion for Damayantī, which places him in the camp of those many gods and demons who attempt to corrupt a good man for love of his wife[2] (though Kali can hardly be said to pursue this original objective when, having entered Nala's body, he causes Nala [i.e., himself] to leave Damayantī). Another ironic and perceptive moral insight is the statement that Kali suffers in making Nala suffer.

Other texts, in the post-Gupta age, elaborate upon the myth with less subtlety than that of the Epic. The *Kathāsaritsāgara* describes Nala's moral degradation at greater length, making him a drunkard and an adulterer as well as a gambler.[3] The *Naiṣadhacarita*, probably under Purāṇic influence, attributes to Kali specific heresies as well as the general force of evil :

> "On the way to the wedding of Nala and Damayantī, the gods encountered the army of Kali. His generals were Desire, Anger, Greed, Delusion, and others. A Cārvāka in the ranks mocked the gods, citing various Buddhist doctrines. Indra became angry and called Kali's troops atheists; Yama called them materialists [Lokāyatas], while Varuṇa called them heretics and atheists. Kali stood there surrounded by evils.

1. *Mahābhārata*, ed. V. S. Sukthankar et al. (Poona, 1933-1960), 3.55-74.
2. Wendy Doniger O'Flaherty, *Asceticism and Eroticism in the Mythology of Śiva* (Oxford, 1973), pp. 184-86.
3. *Kathāsaritsāgara* of Somadeva (Bombay, 1930), 56.

When Kali determined to take Damayantī from Naia, he was at first unable to enter the city, because of Nala's virtues. He looked in vain for heretics, Jains, or Buddhists in the city. At last he found an opportunity, and he entered Nala. . ."[1] The *Mahābhārata* tale of a hero's moral dilemma is thus embroidered with traditional Purāṇic descriptions of the heresies of the Kali Age.

For men of the Kali Age, ostracized from Vedic rituals, the post-Gupta texts recommend the use of Tantric texts : people fallen from Vedic rites and afraid of Vedic penances should resort to the Tantras;[2] the Pāñcarātras, Vaikhānasas, and Bhāgavatas use Tantric texts written for people who have fallen from the Vedas.[3] The *Kūrma Purāṇa* tells of a King Sattvata, a Vaiṣṇava, who was prompted by Nārada to teach a doctrine suitable for bastard sons of married women and widows, for their welfare—this is the *sātvata* text of the Pāñcarātras.[4] In this way, the heretics who had been simply excluded during the Gupta age were received back into the fold in the post-Gupta, Tantric age by the same class of Brāhmaṇa Paurāṇikas who had originally written them off.

This general process, from tolerance to intolerance and back again to a kind of modified tolerance, may be seen in the development of the Purāṇic and *dharmaśāstra* attitudes to heretics. From the Aśokan use of the term *pāṣaṇḍa* to designate any sect, the situation changed so that by the time of the *Mahābhārata* the term had acquired definitely pejorative overtones.[5] The increasing bias against heretics is evident from many of the definitions of heresy and from such statements as Manu's "Let not the householder. . .honor heretics"[6] and Yājñavalkya's "One should

1. *Naiṣadhacarita* of Śrīharṣa, ed. Jīvānanda Vidyāsāgara (Calcutta, 1875-76), 17.13-37;—.88-201.

2. *Sāmba Purāṇa*, quoted in the *Vīramitrodaya* of Mitramiśra, 1.24, cited by Chintaharan Chakravarti, *The Tantras : Studies in their Religion and Literature* (Calcutta, 1962), p. 32. See also O'Flaherty (1976), pp. 310-20.

3. *Sāmba Purāṇa*, cited by Ananta-bhaṭṭa in his *Vidhānapārijāta*, II, 519, cited in Hazra (1958), p. 93.

4. *Kūrma Purāṇa*, ed. A. S. Gupta (Benares : All-India Kashiraj Trust, 1967), 1.23.31-34.

5. Edward Washburn Hopkins, *The Great Epic of India* (New Haven, 1920), p. 89.

6. *Mānavadharmaśāstra* 4.30.

avoid...heretics."[1] Yājñavalkya and Nārada disqualify heretics and atheists as witnesses.[2] This attitude grew more and more strict as Brāhmaṇism developed : the *Saura Purāṇa* says that Cārvākas, Buddhists, Jains, Yavanas [Greeks], Kāpālikas and Kaulas should not be allowed to enter a kingdom,[3] and the late text of the *Śukranītisāra* exhorts the king to punish atheists and those who have fallen from caste.[4] By the tenth century A.D., heresy was so widespread and so abhorred that Śiva himself was said to have become incarnate as the philosopher Śaṅkara in order to explain the Vedas, destroy the temples and books of the Jains, and massacre all who opposed him, particularly the Jains.[5]

The *Prabodhacandrodaya*, a remarkable allegorical play written during the following century, described the battle between good and evil, orthodoxy and heresy : "The *pāṣaṇḍa* books were uprooted by the sea of orthodox teachings [*sadāgama*]; the *pāṣaṇḍas*, Saugatas [Buddhists], Digambaras [Jains], Kāpālikas, etc., concealed themselves among the most abject men in the countries of Pāñcāla, Mālava, etc."[6] Yet the very vehemence of these orthodox texts hints at the strength of the threat, the degree to which heresy had penetrated Hinduism by this time. Much of the assimilation took place in the earlier, more tolerant period, and more continued to take place on a popular level—as expressed in the mythology of the *Purāṇas*—in spite of the exhortations of the orthodox Brāhmaṇas. Thus the heretical creeds were first tolerated, then assimilated or absorbed, and then—with the fanaticism which often characterizes the newly converted—excoriated by orthodox Hindus.

A similar process of historical development may be seen in the changing attitude to demons in the mythological texts. At first, the demons were barely differentiated from the gods, but they

1. *Yājñavalkya Smṛti*, Ānandāśrama Sanskrit Series 46 (Poona, 1903-04), 1.130.

2. *Ibid.*, 2.70; *Nārada Smṛti* (Calcutta, 1885), 4.180.

3. *Saura Purāṇa* (Calcutta, 1910), 38.54.

4. *Śukranītisāra* (Calcutta 1882), 4.1.97-98.

5. *Śaṅkaraprādurbhāva*, cited by Francis Wilford, "On Egypt and other countries ... from the ancient books of the Hindus," *Asiatic Researches*, III (Calcutta, 1792), p. 411. See also O'Flaherty (1976), pp. 207-11.

6. *Prabodhacandrodaya* of Kṛṣṇamiśra (Bombay, 1898), Act V, prose between verses 10 and 11.

later came to be regarded as morally neutral enemies (in the period of the *Brāhmaṇas*) and finally (by the period of the *Purāṇas*) to be described as hideous and immoral.[1] The apparently tolerant attitude of the middle period, based upon the orthodox concept of *svadharma* (that gods and demons are like two separate castes, each with his own job to do) is not found, as one might expect, in the majority of Purāṇic texts, where the *svadharma* doctrine is so strongly prevalent. In fact, the amoral view of the demons is characteristic of the earliest mythological texts (the *Brāhmaṇas*) and of the latest texts, in which the doctrine of caste duty is superseded by the idea of individual *bhakti*.[2] But the large body of Purāṇic material composed between these two periods regards the demons as "evil" in spite of the fact that these texts emphasize the necessity of following one's pre-ordained path in life. For these orthodox scriptures often display the same intolerance toward the demons as they do toward human heretics : to be other is to be bad. The *bhakti* texts, though more lenient with regard to the activities of the heterodox, display a more dogmatic attitude toward the doctrines of heretics,[3] whom they regard as *bhāvis* (worldly people), the polar opposite of *bhaktas*. But since, as we have seen, heresy in India is often defined in terms of an error of judgement rather than a wilful sacrilege, devotional sects seldom displayed the vehement disapproval of heretics that the caste-oriented texts manifest.

The general process is clear; it remains to see whether we can pinpoint the period of intolerance in the Gupta era. The texts make this a difficult prospect. We have reasonably clear guidelines at either end of the spectrum: tolerance in the period of the *Upaniṣads* and the Aśokan reign, intolerance by the time of the *Viṣṇu Purāṇa* in the Gupta age, and in subsequent *Purāṇas* until the flowering of the *bhakti* movement. In between lie many dark centuries.

Two Purāṇic myths of the Kali Age heresies include strong Gupta evidence, not beyond any question of post-Gupta tampering but at least as indicative of Gupta authorship as a trout is of water in the milk :

1. O'Flaherty (1976), pp. 64-65.
2. *Ibid.*, pp. 127-131.
3. J. F. Staal, "Über die Idee der Toleranz im Hinduismus," *Kairos, Zeitschrift für Religionswissenschaft und Theologie*, I (1959), pp. 215-18.

"When Time had reached its turning point, and the end of the Yuga had come, a chastiser of the wicked [*asādhu*] creatures arose out of destruction. He was born in the gotra of Candramas, the dynasty of the moon, and he was called Pramiti. In a former age, in the era of Manu Svāyambhuva, he was born of a portion (of Viṣṇu). For twenty years he wandered on the earth, commanding an army with many horses, chariots, and elephants, surrounded by Brāhmaṇas wielding weapons, by the hundreds and thousands. He destroyed the barbarians by the thousands and killed all the kings who were born of Śūdras, and cut down all the heretics. Those who were not excessively righteous—he killed them all, and those born of mixed classes (*varṇas*), and their dependents. Turning the wheel of conquest, the powerful one made an end of the barbarians.... At the age of 32 he set out, and for twenty years he killed all creatures by the hundreds and thousands, until this cruel act reduced the earth to nothing but seeds because of a causeless anger from one against another. He caused the lowly and the unrighteous to be generally exterminated. He and his followers established themselves between the Gaṅgā and the Yamunā, together with his ministers and his army, after destroying all the barbarian princes. When the period of the turning point set in at the end of the Yuga, there were very few subjects left over, here and there..."[1]

Another text of this myth differs on a few minor details and adds a significant list of political territories :

"When Time had reached its turning point, and the end of the Yuga had come, a chastiser of the unrighteous [*adharmin*] arose in the family of the Bhṛgus.... He was called Pramati.. For full thirty years he wandered on the earth.... Those who were unrighteous—he killed them all : those in the north, and in the central country, and the mountain people, the inhabitants of the east and the west, those in the area of the highlands of the Vindhyas, and those in the Deccan, and the Dravidians and Siṃhalas, the Gāndhārans and Pāradas, the Pahlavas and Yavanas and Śakas, Tuṣāras, Barbaras, Śvetas, Halikas, Daradas, Khasas, Lampakas, Andhras, and the races

1. *Liṅga Purāṇa* (Calcutta, 1812), 40.50-63a.

of the Colas. Turning the wheel of conquest, the powerful one put an end to the Śūdras, putting all creatures to flight. . ."[1] The basis of this myth is the old theme, the story of the dynasties of the Kali Age, which lists the standard set of Barbarians in various permutations. The list was compiled in the early part of the Gupta era (during the reign of Candra Gupta I but before that of Samudra Gupta); it occurs in the *Matsya Purāṇa, Vāyu Purāṇa, Brahmāṇḍa Purāṇa* (all stemming from the *Bhaviṣya Purāṇa*) and then in the *Viṣṇu Purāṇa* and the *Bhāgavata Purāṇa*.[2] These are the basic scriptures of Gupta paranoia and xenophobia : the barbarian kings kill women and children, indulge in the evil behavior of the age, and kill off one another; all are devoid of *dharma*, or pleasure, or wealth, and they mix indiscriminately with the Āryans.[3] None of these accounts mention Pramati/Pramiti. Pargiter suggests that the standard lists were composed in the early part of the fourth century A.D. : "The first portion of the description appears to depict the unsettled condition of the country in the early part of the fourth century," though it builds upon "gloomy Brāhmaṇic forecasts, which were no doubt based on actual calamities, but which have no historical value."[4] So we have the general "gloomy" myth of the Kali Age first embroidered with more specific descriptions in the beginning of the fourth century; shortly thereafter, early Purāṇas like the *Viṣṇu Purāṇa* insert passages describing the incarnation of Viṣṇu as Kalki to exterminate the barbarians.[5] The next step transfers the role of Kalki to an actual king, Pramati—still said to be born of a portion of Viṣṇu, as Kalki is—who first achieves a general conquest and then, in the *Matsya Purāṇa*, overcomes a specific list of political units in the sub-continent.

Who is this king ? Vasudeva S. Agrawala makes a strong case for the identification of Pramati with Candra Gupta Vikramāditya

1. *Matsya Purāṇa*, Ānandāśrama Sanskrit Series, 54 (Poona, 1907), 144.50-65.

2. F. E. Pargiter, *The Purāṇa Text of the Dynasties of the Kali Age* (Oxford, 1913), p. xiii.

3. *Ibid.*, p. 56. *Matsya Purāṇa* 273.25-34; *Vāyu Purāṇa* 99.388-412; *Brahmāṇḍa Purāṇa* 3.74.200-224; *Viṣṇu Purāṇa* 4.24.18-29; *Bhāgavata Purāṇa* 12.1-2.

4. Pargiter, p. 55.

5. See O'Flaherty (1976), pp. 200-05.

(380-412 A.D.) :[1] the reign of thirty two years, the twenty-year military campaign, the lands of his conquest, the extermination of Śūdra kings (a possible reference to the uprooted Śakas), his birth as the son of Candramas (this being a name of Samudra Gupta)[2]—all of these could indicate Vikramāditya. Agrawala also suggests that the "Brāhmaṇas wielding arms" may be the Licchavi contingent in the Gupta army. In any case, this development gives us a firm basis in time : right in the middle of the Gupta era.

A more explicit reference to Vikramāditya occurs in the *Bhaviṣya Purāṇa*, in a passage which was almost certainly composed long after the Gupta period (for parts of the work demonstrate familiarity with British rule in Calcutta[3]) but which nevertheless extends the pseudo-historical tradition that links Vikramāditya with the extermination of heretics at the end of the Kali Age. For even if we cannot prove that all of the texts in this genre were actually composed in the Gupta age (as we can in fact prove for the earliest layer), we can at least demonstrate the persistence of the Paurāṇikas' hope that the Gupta kings would exterminate heretics :

> "When King Kṣemaka had performed a great sacrifice and destroyed all the barbarians, Kali incarnate begged Viṣṇu to produce more barbarians as is appropriate to the Kali Age, and Viṣṇu created Adam and Eve and their descendants.[4] These barbarians did not penetrate into Brahmāvarta, which was protected by the Goddess Sarasvatī, but they conquered many areas of India [these are enumerated at great length], and they were lamentably unable to pronounce Sanskrit words. As the generations passed, at the time of the Mauryas and Nandas, Kali reminded Viṣṇu of his duty, and so Viṣṇu was born as Gautama, son of Kāśyapa, and he preached the Buddhist dharma. All men became Buddhists, and still the generations passed—Candragupta, Bindusāra, and Aśoka.

1. Vasudeva S. Agrawala, *Matsya Purāṇa, A Study* (Benares : All-India Kashiraj Trust, 1963), pp. 228-31.
2. R. K. Mookerji, *The Gupta Empire*, 4th ed. (MLBD Rept. 1967), p. 17.
3. R. C. Hazra, *Studies in the Purāṇic Records on Hindu Rites and Customs* (MLBD Rept. 1976), p. 169.
4. *Bhaviṣya Purāṇa* (Bombay, 1959), 3.1.4.1-60; 3.1.5.1-41. See O'Flaherty (1976), p. 44.

> Then a Brāhmaṇa performed a Vedic ceremony, and by the power of the Vedic mantras four Kṣatriyas were born: Pramara, Capahāni, Śukla, and Parihāraka. They put Aśoka in their power and murdered all the Buddhists. Pramara had many descendants, and finally, when the full and terrifying Kali Age had arrived, Vikramāditya was born in order to destroy the Śakas and to promote Āryan dharma. At the age of 20 he went to the forest and practised asceticism for twelve years, and then, at the age of 32, he established his throne, by the grace of Śiva"[1].

This text does not give the details of his conquest, but launches instead into its own version of the tale of Vikramāditya and the vampire. The conquest of the heretics has already been accomplished thrice: first, the barbarians (who murdered Kṣemaka's father) are wiped out by Kṣemaka; then, the heretics (Jews and Christians ?) created by Viṣṇu and descended from Adam are fended off by the Goddess; and, finally, the Buddhists (also created by Viṣṇu are exterminated by Pramara (in place of the usual Vaiṣṇava avatāra, Kalki). All that remains now for Pramara's descendant, Vikramāditya, to do is to destroy the Śakas—the one thing that we are fairly certain that he did actually do.

But the destruction of the Śakas is hardly equivalent to the "extermination of heretics". David Lorenzen raises this point in his discussion of imperialist attitudes in ancient Indian historiography, directing his remarks primarily against the British, though they are an equally apt description of Purāṇic historiography: "Chandragupta II (*c*. 375-415 A.D.) of the 'imperial' Guptas...was sometimes praised for his defeat of the 'foreign' Śakas in terms which are the mirror image of British encomiums of the conquests of Clive... How the Śakas, who had been in India since the beginning of the second century A.D. and were thoroughly Indianized, can have been considered foreigners is understandable only in the light of British imperialism and/or communalism."[2] It is, I think, also fully understandable in the light of Purāṇic dogmatism and jingoism.

1. *Bhaviṣya Purāṇa* 3.1.6.1-49; 3.1.7.1-26.
2. David Lorenzen, "Imperialism and the Historiography of Ancient India," unpublished paper; p. 16 and fn. 26.

For the myth of Candra Gupta Vikramāditya is embroidered with the full pomp of the ancient images of righteous conquest, political *pradakṣiṇā*, the old myth of the *dhammavijaya*, consciously evocative of the most charismatic of all ancient Indian polemicists, Aśoka himself. Perhaps by over-reacting too long after the actual event—the Śaka invasion centuries before the Guptas climbed onto the throne—in a kind of historiographic *esprit de l'escalier*, the authors of the Gupta *Purāṇas* cast the Śakas as the heavies in the drama of the simultaneous political and religious catharsis of the land of the Aryans.

In discussing the myths of the heresies of the Kali Age and the Buddha avatāra, H. H. Wilson remarked,

> "The complaints of the prevalence of heterodox doctrines... indicate a period of change in the condition of the Hindu religion, which it would be important to verify. If reference is made to Buddhism, to which in some respects the allusions especially apply, it would probably denote a period not long subsequent to the Christian era; but it is more likely to be of a later date, or in the eighth or ninth centuries, when Śaṅkara is said to have reformed a variety of corrupt practices, and given rise to others."[1]

The first period, "not long subsequent to the Christian era," would be the immediate pre-Gupta period, the period of invasions, when a "period of change in the condition of the Hindu religion" most certainly took place, but probably without any organized counter-action by the Brāhmaṇas. The second period, in the "eighth or ninth centuries", is indeed a period of reaction against heterodoxy, of which Śaṅkara is a good example,[2] but one wonders if it is beginning of that period or the aftermath of it. My guess is the latter; and this places the heresies of the Kali Age right in the Gupta era, whose much-vaunted Gold may have been little more than a desperate attempt to plate a fast-tarnishing Establishment made of baser stuff.

1. Horace Hayman Wilson, *The Vishnu Purana* (London, 1840), 3rd ed. (Calcutta, 1961), pp. 489-90.

2. *Śaṅkaradigvijaya* of Mādhava (Poona, 1915); and *Śaṅkaravijaya* of Ānandagiri, ed. J. Tarkapañcānana, *Bibliotheca Indica* (Calcutta, 1868).

6

BUDDHISM IN THE GUPTA AGE

BALKRISHNA GOVIND GOKHALE

AT the dawn of the Gupta age (*c.* 320 A.D.) Buddhism was already over eight hundred years through its history in India. The unity of its doctrine and monastic community had been sundered four centuries before Samudra Gupta (*c.* 350-76 A.D.). Its two broad divisions, Hīnayāna (more properly Theravāda) and the Mahāyāna encompassed as many as eighteen different sects which, though they followed fairly uniform rules of monastic life and conduct, differed widely about what they understood to be "Buddhism". The Gupta age saw a resurgent Brāhmaṇism with the court circles reviving the ancient Vedic sacrificial ritual and the masses increasingly attracted by the new Purāṇic Hinduism. Buddhism still maintained some of its old philosophic vigor, but as a "religion" it was obviously on the defensive, increasingly overshadowed by the emerging Tantric cults.

The purpose of this essay is two-fold. It will discuss the state of Buddhism in the various monastic centers and it will examine the social and economic background against which Buddhism lived and progressed from one phase to another. As will be shown later, Buddhism during this age seems to have been well past its original social purpose. The burgeoning "feudal" economy and polity had already permeated Buddhist organization at various levels. What we can observe in it is a number of monastic centers with little or no "organic" relationship to the lay population surrounding them. The old centers had already decayed and the new were riven by sectarian differences in their intellectual pursuits. Tantrism had begun to cast its lengthening shadow, comprising sublime mysticism on the one hand with gross magical ritual on the other.

Two points should be clarified before we begin the subject proper. The first concerns the chronological limits of the age. J. F. Fleet's hypothesis that the Gupta Era originated in 320 A.D. is still the most accepted one, though opinions differ about the event which it was supposed to commemorate.[1] The last great ruler of the dynasty was Skanda Gupta (455-467 ? A.D.) and by 550 A.D., the Gupta Empire had vanished from the historical scene. The period dealt with here, therefore, is roughly that of two centuries (350-550 A.D.). The second point is related to the sources of our information on the subject. First, there are some fifteen inscriptions of a specifically Buddhist content. These are largely votive, commemorating pious gifts to various Buddhist establishments. Of much more substantial interest is the Chinese pilgrim's (Fa-Hien, or Fa-Hsien) account of his travels in the country at the time of Candra Gupta II (376-414 A.D.), as it gives us some invaluable insights into the state of Buddhism at that time. This account may be judiciously supplemented with that of Yuan Chwang (Hiuen-Tsiang, or Hsüan-Tsang, 629-645 A.D.) which, though considerably later, does help us fill in gaps in Fa-Hsien's narrative. We also have a number of Mahāyāna Buddhist works which are ascribed to this general age. Among them the important ones are the *Prajñāpāramitā* group of texts, the *Laṅkāvatāra*, the *Saddharmapuṇḍarīka*, the *Ratnagotravibhaṅga* and the *Śikṣāsamuccaya* of Śāntideva. The Pāli commentaries of Dhammapāla and Buddhaghosa may also be drawn upon to illustrate the state of Theravāda Buddhism especially in Kāñchīpuram in South India. Finally, there are the murals of Ajantā (near Aurangābād in Mahārāshtra) which, though outside the administrative domains of the Imperial Guptas, offer a vivid commentary on Buddhist thought and life-style during the Gupta age.

1. J. F. Fleet, *Corpus Inscriptionum Indicarum*, Vol. III, *Inscriptions of the Early Gupta Kings and Their Successors* (Varanasi, 1963), p. 130, hereinafter abbreviated as *CII*, III; for other views on the event, see R. C. Majumdar *et al.*, *The History and Culture of the Indian People—The Classical Age* (Bombay, 1962), p. 16, abbreviated as *CA*; R. C. Majumdar and A. S. Altekar, *The Vākāṭaka-Gupta Age* (Delhi, 1960), pp. 131-32; R. K. Mookerji, *The Gupta Empire* (Bombay, 1959), pp. 15-16; S. Chattopadhyaya, *Early History of North India* (Delhi, 1970), pp. 176-77; H. C. Raychaudhuri, *Political History of Ancient India* (Calcutta, 1953), p. 520; B. G. Gokhale, *Samudra Gupta, Life and Times* (Bombay, 1962), pp. 32-33.

II

The history of Buddhism before the rise of the Imperial Guptas may be traced here merely as a background to the subject of this paper. The first great event was the Rājagaha Council held immediately after the passing away of the Buddha (*c.* 486 B.C.). The *Cullavagga* account of this Council may be generally accepted as historical. The same work further states that about one hundred years after the passing away of the Buddha the Second or Vesālī Council was held at which the great schism in Buddhism occurred. The Ceylonese chronicles, *Dīpavaṃsa* and the *Mahāvaṃsa* (fourth-fifth centuries A.D.), give us the names of the various sects that arose as a consequence of differences in the interpretation of Vinaya rules and doctrinal points and the number of such sects given is eighteen. The problem of the chronology of the evolution of these sects is much too involved to be dealt with here, nor is it very relevant for our purpose.[1] These chronicles also speak of a Third or Pāṭaliputra Council held during the reign of the great Aśoka (*c.* 272-232 B.C.), which seems to have been a purely Theravāda council. A Fourth Council was held in Kashmīr during the time of the Kuṣāṇa Kaniṣka (end of the first century A.D.) dominated by the Sarvāstivādins.

The first great schism seems to have occurred around the middle of the fourth century B.C. and by the time of Aśoka at least five schools were in existence.[2] Inscriptions of the period between the first century B.C. and the beginning of the Gupta age indicate the existence of centers of the Sarvāstivādins, the Kāśyapīyas, the Dharmottarīyas, the Bhadrayānikas and the Mahāsāṅghikas in various areas of the country. The Sarvāstivādins were strong in Mathurā, from where they spread into Kashmīr and Gandhāra, with some support in Śrāvastī and

1. See J. Kashyap (ed.), *Cullavagga* (Nalanda, 1956), pp. 406ff.; *Dīpavaṃsa,* verses 16-50; *Mahāvaṃsa,* verses 3-10; D. Chattopadhyaya (ed.), *Tāranātha's History of Buddhism in India* (Simla, 1970), pp. 367ff.; J. Legge (trans.), *Fa-Hien, A Record of Buddhistic Kingdoms* (New York, 1965), pp. 75ff.; T. Watters, *On Yuan Chwang's Travels in India* (Delhi, 1961), II, pp. 73ff.; N. Dutt, *Buddhist Sects in India* (Delhi, 1976), pp. 12ff.; for the latest view on the subject, see A. K. Warder, *Indian Buddhism* (Delhi, 1970), pp. 286ff.

2. For the chronology of various schisms, see A. K. Warder, *op. cit.*, pp. 214ff., 272ff.

Vārāṇasī. The Mahāsāṅghikas were also present in Mathurā and spread northward up to Kābul, westward to Mahārāshtra and were particularly strong in the Nāgārjunakoṇḍa-Amarāvatī region in Āndhra Pradesh as well as in Magadha. The Kāśyapīyas were to be found in eastern Uttar Pradesh and northwestern India and the Sāmmitīyas were strong in Magadha and parts of Bengal.[1] Fa-Hsien found in a Mahāyāna monastery a *vinaya* of the Mahāsāṅghikas; he also found a text of the rules of the Sarvāstivāda, the *Saṃyuktābhidharmahṛdaya śāstra* and one chapter of the *Parinirvāṇa-vaipulya sūtra.*[2] Fa-Hsien's statements, which will be examined in detail later, indicate that many of the sects still continued to live during the Gupta age.

The Buddhist inscriptions of the Imperial Gupta age are thirteen in number and belong to the fifth and sixth centuries A.D. Of these three are from Sāñchī, six from Uttar Pradesh, three from Bodhgayā in Bihār, and one of unknown provenance from the Calcutta Museum. Two inscriptions from Sāñchī are concerned with the monetary and land endowments and one is too fragmentary to convey any definite meaning; the six Uttar Pradesh inscriptions commemorate the dedication of images, as also the Calcutta Museum inscription. One Bodhgayā inscription deals with the setting up of an image, while two deal with benefactions at the shrine by a Ceylonese king. Admittedly, the evidence from inscriptions is much too scanty to enable us to come to any significant conclusions. Of the 81 inscriptions edited by Fleet as belonging to the Guptas and their successors only thirteen (or 16%) are Buddhistic in content while the rest are Brāhmaṇical in nature. Two of the Sāñchī epigraphs concern grants of land and money for feeding monks and lighting lamps in the shrine. One is of the year 412-413 A.D. and the other 450-451 A.D., showing the continued attention received by the establishment of Sāñchī over half a century of the Gupta age. In fact, the history of the Buddhist settlement at Sāñchī goes back to pre-Mauryan times and Aśoka served as a viceroy at nearby Vidiśā before his accession to the throne. There he

1. *Ibid.*, p. 341; B. G. Gokhale, *Buddhism in Maharashtra : A History* (Bombay, 1976), pp. 84ff.; S. Konow, *Corpus Inscriptionum Indicarum*, II/i, *Kharoshthi Inscriptions* (Varanasi, 1969), pp. 40, 45-46, 95, 136, 154, 175.

2. Legge, *op. cit.*, pp. 87-90.

married Devi and of this union were born Mahendra and Saṅghamitrā who later became missionaries to Ceylon. The railings and gateways of the great stūpa were completed during the time of the Śuṅgas (*c*.156-75 B.C.) and inscriptions of the Sātavāhana and Śaka times indicate that the establishment continued to attract pious attention through the centuries and up to the twelfth century A.D.[1] The Gupta grants refer to the great saṅgha at Sāñchī and the *ratnagṛha* (jewel-house) containing images of the Buddha. The third Sāñchī inscription is fragmentary and refers to a Rudra, son of Gośūrasiṃhabāla. He is called a *vihārasvāmin* and there are references to a *viharasvāminī* (Fleet No. 63) and a *mahāvihārasvāmin* (Fleet No. 69) at Kāsiā (Gorakhpur district) and Mathurā. The precise meaning of these terms will be discussed later.

The two most important places of Buddhist devotion were Bodhgayā (Bihār) and Sārnāth (Uttar Pradesh) where the Buddha was enlightened and preached his first sermon. The archaeological history of Bodhgayā between the period of the Buddha and Aśoka is uncertain. Aśoka is stated to have visited the spot, where the Buddha was enlightened and relics of the Śuṅga and post-Śuṅga age are numerous. Fa-Hsien, who visited the spot, says that in the city of Gayā "all was emptiness and desolation". To the south was the place where the Buddha practised austerities for six years and "all around was forest". But he says that at the place of austerities and all other places "men subsequently reared topes and set up images, which all exist at the present day." He goes on to state,

> "At the place where Buddha attained to perfect Wisdom, there are three monasteries, in all of which there are monks residing. The families of their people around supply the societies of these monks with an abundant sufficiency of what they require, so that there is no lack or stint. The disciplinary rules are strictly observed by them. The laws regulating their demeanour in sitting, rising, and entering when the others are assembled, are those which have been practised by all the saints since Buddha was in the world down to the present day."[2]

1. For the history of the monuments at Sāñchī, see J. Marshall, *A Guide to Sanchi* (Delhi, 1955), pp. 7ff.
2. Legge, *op. cit.*, pp. 87-90.

Yuan Chwang, who visited the same spot some two centuries later, describes the Bodhi tree as

> "being surrounded by a brick wall (*a wall of piled bricks*) of considerable height, steep and strong. It is long from east to west, and short from north to south. It is about 500 paces round. Rare trees with their renowned flowers connect their shade and cast their shadows; the delicate *sha* herb and different shrubs carpet the soil. The principal gate adjoins a great flowery bank. The western side is blocked up and difficult to access (*steep and strong*). The northern gate opens into the great *saṅghārāma*. Within the surrounding wall the sacred traces touch one another in all directions. Here there are *stūpas*, in other places *vihāras*."

He also speaks of the *Vajrāsana* or diamond seat and the Bodhi tree as "40 or 50 feet in height". To the east of the tree was a *vihāra*

> "about 160 or 170 feet high. Its lower foundation wall is 20 or more paces in its face. The building (*pile*) is of blue tiles (*bricks*) covered with *chunam* (burnt stone, lime); all the niches in the different storeys hold golden figures. The four sides of the building are covered with wonderful ornamental work; in one place figures of stringed pearls (*garlands*), in another figures of heavenly Rishis. The whole is surrounded by a gilded copper Amalaka fruit."

He then goes on to speak of a storied pavilion with projecting eaves, gilded pillars, beams, doors and windows, "sombre chambers and mysterious halls" and images of the Bodhisattvas Avalokiteśvara and Mañjuśrī. The place was filled with numerous stūpas marking various events associated with the first few weeks after the Enlightenment.[1]

Yuan Chwang also describes the great Mahābodhi Saṅghārāma built by a

> "former king of Ceylon. Its buildings formed six courts, with terraces and halls of three storeys, enclosed by walls between 30 and 40 feet high; the sculptures and paintings were perfect. The image of Buddha was made of gold and silver, and ornamented by precious stones of various colours.

1. S. Beal (trans.), *Chinese Accounts of India* (Calcutta, 1958), III, pp. 344-51; Watters, *op. cit.*, II, pp. 116ff.

There were elegant topes lofty and spacious containing bone and flesh relics of Buddha. On the last day of every year when the relics were brought out to be shewn a light shone and flowers fell in showers. In this establishment there were nearly 1000 ecclesiastics all Mahayanists of the Sthavira school, and all perfect in Vinaya observances."

He goes on to state that "in the old days there was a king of Ceylon" whose brother, a monk, experienced great difficulties during his visits to the places of pilgrimage, whereupon the king requested the king of India for permission to build a vihāra at Bodhgayā.[1] The Allahābād Pillar inscription of Samudra Gupta (*c.* 350-376 A.D.) refers to the Gupta emperor's receiving embassies from Siṃhala (Ceylon) among others and Yuan Chwang's account obviously refers to the Ceylonese king Meghavarṇa (*c.* 352-379 A.D.) building a monastery at Bodhgayā consequent upon Samudra Gupta's permission to do so.[2] The two inscriptions from Bodhgayā (Fleet, Nos. 71, 72) refer to the erection of a Buddhist monastery by a Mahānāma; the first is dated 588-589 A.D. and the second refers to the setting up of a statue by the Śākya Bhikṣu the Sthavira Mahānāma, a resident of Āmradvīpa. The third Bodhgayā inscription (Fleet, No. 76) is assigned to the sixth century on palaeographic grounds and mentions "the appropriate religious gift of the two Śākya Bhikṣus Dharmagupta and Daṃṣṭrasena" for "the acquisition of supreme knowledge by all sentient beings, after (*their*) parents and (*their*) *Ācārya* and *Upādhyāya*."[3]

Of the Gupta inscriptions from Uttar Pradesh there are three from obscure places (Mānkuwar, Deoriyā and Kāsiā—Fleet, Nos. 11, 68, 69). Mānkuwar is a small village on the bank of river Jamunā in the Karchhanā *tehsil* of the Allahābād district. The inscription is on a pedestal of a seated Buddha image originally discovered in a brick mound northeast of Mānkuwar. It has the date 129 years (=488-489 A.D.) and states that the image was installed by a Bhikṣu Buddhamitra "with the object of averting all unhappiness". Deoriyā is also a small village in the same *tehsil* and district. The inscription on the pedestal of a standing Buddha image is undated but is assigned, on palaeo-

1. Watters, *op. cit.*, II, p. 136; Beal, *op. cit.*, III, pp. 358-59.
2. *CII*, III, p. 14; *CA*, p. 11.
3. *CII*, III, pp. 274-79, 282.

graphic grounds, to the fifth century. It commemorates the gift of the "Śākya Bhikshu Bodhivarman" and the merit is assigned to the donor's parents and all sentient beings. Kāsiā is a village in the Gorakhpur district and is identified with Kuśinārā, the place where the Buddha passed away. It was located on a trade route from Sāvatthi to Rājagaha and was one of the important places of pilgrimage for Buddhists. Fa-Hsien very briefly notices it as "in the city the inhabitants are few and far between, comprising only the families belonging to the (different) societies of monks." Yuan Chwang found the road leading to it "a narrow and dangerous path, with wild oxen and wild elephants, and robbers and hunters always in wait to kill travellers" and "the city walls were in ruins, and the towns and villages were deserted." He refers to a stūpa built by Aśoka and several other stūpas. But the place was in ruins and desolate. Probably it maintained a monastery or two, particularly for visiting monks. The inscription is on the pedestal of a colossal Buddha figure in the *parinirvāṇa* pose and is stated to be the gift of a *Mahāvihāra-svāmin* Haribala, the image being fashioned by Dine . . . masvara.[1] Like the foregoing, this epigraph is also assigned to the fifth century.

The two inscriptions (Fleet, Nos. 63, 70) from Mathurā are dated in the Gupta years 135 and 230 (=454-455 A.D. and 549-550 A.D.), being separated from each other by an interval of over a century. The first is from a broken standing statue, probably a standing Buddha, and mentions it as the gift of the *vihārasvāminī* Devatā who assigns the merit of her act to her parents and all sentient beings, adding that everything is impermanent including *Nirvāṇa*, and stresses the happiness of making gifts. The second inscription is also from the pedestal of a standing Buddha image and mentions the gift as being assigned to all sentient beings. Mathurā was famous as a center of great religious significance for the Buddhists, Jains and Hindus. Its antiquities have a continuous history from about the first century B.C. onward and during the time of the Kuṣāṇas and Śakas the city enjoyed great prominence as an administrative center as well. Fa-Hsien

1. *CII*, III, pp. 45-47, 271-73; Legge, *op. cit.*, pp. 71-72; Watters, *op. cit.*, II, pp. 25ff.; B. N. Chaudhury, *Buddhist Centres in Ancient India* (Calcutta, 1969), pp. 50-54.

noticed some twenty monasteries with about three thousand monks and obviously "the Law of the Buddha was still more flourishing". Buddhism, according to the Chinese pilgrim, enjoyed royal patronage in those parts. He says,

> "Everywhere, from the Sandy Desert, in all the countries of India, the kings had been firm believers in that Law. When they make their offerings to a community of monks, they take off their royal caps, and along with their relatives and ministers, supply them with food with their own hands. That done, (the king) has a carpet spread for himself on the ground, and sits down on it in front of the chairman;—they dare not presume to sit on couches in front of the community."

Yuan Chwang found in Mathurā two hundred monasteries with two thousand or so monks. The monks were adherents of the Mahāyāna as well as Hīnayāna. He also mentions stūpas built by Aśoka and stūpas dedicated to the Buddha's foremost disciples as well as to Mañjuśrī and other Bodhisattvas. There were also numerous nuns. As mentioned earlier, Mathurā was a stronghold of the Sarvāstivādins and after them the Mahāsāṅghikas.[1]

Only one inscription (Fleet, No. 75) of the Gupta age comes from Sārnāth. It is from a sandstone bas-relief showing three scenes from the Buddha's life and is assigned, on palaeographic grounds, to the fifth century. It mentions that the image "has been caused to be made by the Bhikṣu Harigupta" assigning the merit to his preceptor and parents. Fa-Hsien visited the vihāra at the Deer Park where the Buddha first preached and mentioned two monasteries with monks living in them. The Dhamek stūpa is still a prominent landmark and an inscription on the pedestal of a Buddha image mentions the gift of Kumāra Gupta. Yuan Chwang found some fifteen hundred monks of the Sāmmitīya school at Sārnāth and noticed several stūpas around the site.[2]

Finally, the Calcutta Museum inscription on the pedestal of a sandstone standing image of the Buddha of unknown provenance

1. *CII*, III, pp. 262-64, 273-74; Legge, *op. cit.*, p. 42; Watters, *op. cit.*, I, pp. 301ff.

2. *CII*, III, p. 281; Legge, *op. cit.*, p. 94; B. N. Chaudhury, *op. cit.*, pp. 68-69.

records the gift of the Śākya Bhikṣu Dharmadāsa, with the merit assigned to his parents and all sentient beings.[1]

Pāṭaliputra, the old imperial capital of the Mauryas, still preserved some vestiges of its glory. Fa-Hsien reports having seen "the Royal palace and halls in the midst of the city, which exist now as of old"...adorned with walls and gates and elegant carving and sculptures. By the side of a stūpa attributed to Aśoka, Fa-Hsien saw a

> "Mahayana monastery, very grand and beautiful; there is also a Hinayana one; the two together containing six hundred or seven hundred monks. The rules of demeanour and the scholastic arrangements in them are worthy of observation." "Shamans of the highest virtue from all quarters, and students, inquirers wishing to find out the truth and the grounds of it, all resort to these monasteries. There also resides in this monastery a Brahman teacher, whose name also is Manjusri, whom the Shamans of greatest virtue in the kingdom, and the Mahayana Bhikshus honour and look up to."

Fa-Hsien then goes on to describe the custom of annual procession of images on the eighth day of the second month. The images were carried on a four-wheeled, five-storied high cart, decked with white and silk-like cloth and painted in various colors. Images of various gods made of gold, silver and lapis lazuli and Buddha figures in a niche on every side with attendant Bodhisattvas were placed on the cart accompanied by numerous other carts. Monks and laymen from all over thronged the procession at the invitation of the Brāhmaṇas, and provisions were distributed to the needy. In a Mahāyāna monastery Fa-Hsien found a copy of the Mahāsāṅghika *Vinaya*, Sarvāstivāda literature, the *Saṃyuktābhidharmahṛdayaśāstra*, the *Parinirvāṇavaipulya-sūtra* and the *Mahāsāṅghika Abhidharma*. Fa-Hsien lived in Pāṭaliputra for three years learning Sanskrit and copying the literature he found. He also found in Pāṭaliputra public hospitals set up by the heads of Vaiśya families, a tradition that went back to the days of Aśoka.[2] Yuan Chwang also gives a long account of Pāṭaliputra. He states that the city was deserted, though its foundation walls still survived. He narrates the legends of Aśoka and describes

1. *CII*, III, p. 280.
2. Legge, *op. cit.*, pp. 77-79, 98-99.

the city's various monuments. He states that there were some fifty monasteries around the ancient city with about ten thousand monks. Most of them belonged to the Mahāyāna persuasion.[1] Obviously between the time of Fa-Hsien and Yuan Chwang, Pāṭaliputra had rapidly deteriorated, though the number of monks mentioned by the latter is unusually large and may be taken to be a round number and an exaggeration. It is difficult to accept the figures given by the Chinese travellers as accurate. In the state of primitive technology of those days one monk must have needed the surplus of at least three workers to maintain himself in a monastery and this would give us a population of some thirty thousand in and around Pāṭaliputra, which, given its state of decay and dilapidation, is hard to believe.

Nālandā was one of the greatest centers of Buddhistic learning in ancient India. Situated on the outskirts of Rājagaha the Buddha visited it often. Its subsequent history up to the Gupta age is unclear. Fa-Hsien mentions a village of Nāla which is identified with Nālandā. Yuan Chwang has a long description of the seat of learning which earned very high praise from him. He gives us the names of its various patrons. Kumāra Gupta I (415-455 ? A.D.) seems to have built the first great monastery there and to this were added others by Tathāgata Gupta and Bālāditya so that by the time the Chinese pilgrim arrived Nālandā was a large complex of six great monasteries surrounded by a wall with openings through impressive gates. Its library occupied three buildings and there was also an observatory. Yuan Chwang says,

> "The priests to the number of several thousands, are men of the highest ability and talent. Their distinction is very great at the present time, and there are many hundreds whose fame has rapidly spread through distant regions. Their conduct is pure and unblamable. They follow in sincerity the precepts of the moral law. The rules of this convent are severe, and all the priests are bound to observe them. The countries of India respect them and follow them. The day is not sufficient for asking and answering profound questions. From morning till night they engage in discussion; the old and the young mutually help one another."

The rules of admission were very rigorous and the institution

1. Beal, *op. cit.*, III, pp. 320ff.; Watters, *op. cit.*, II, pp. 86ff.

boasted of many renowned teachers such as Dharmapāla, Candrapāla, Guṇamati and Sthiramati, authors of several works on Buddhistic subjects. An elaborate ritual of worship was followed and the place was supported by the revenues of one hundred villages granted it by Harṣa (606-647 A.D.).[1]

Outside the confines of the Gupta empire there were numerous Buddhist centers of monastic life and culture stretching through parts of Central Asia, Afghanistan, Kashmīr, the Panjāb, Saurāṣṭra, Mahārāshtra and in the states of Āndhra Pradesh and Tamil Nādu. Yuan Chwang mentions as many as five thousand monasteries with a total of 212,130 monks.[2] The numbers of monasteries and monks given by Fa-Hsien and Yuan Chwang cannot be taken literally, as they are obviously round numbers based very often on hearsay evidence. But even if we subtract these by 50% the number is still large, namely, 2500 monasteries and over 100,000 monks. The old centers had decayed. Kapilavastu was a "desert" with a small congregation of monks and ten families. Kuśinārā was "in ruins" with very few inhabitants; so was Vesālī, and Pāṭaliputra was little better. Rājagaha suffered a similar fate; Gayā was desolate.[3] Fa-Hsien mentions a somewhat different list of the holy places of Buddhism such as Bodhgayā and Sārnāth, both common to the old list mentioned in the *Mahāparinibbāna Sutta*, but Kapilavastu and Kuśinārā being desolate very few visitors ventured to visit them.[4] Valabhī in Saurāṣṭra grew into a prominent university in the time of the later Imperial Guptas and owed its rise to the patronage of the Maitraka kings, the first monastery there being built by Dudda, the sister of the Valabhī king, Dhruvasena I (525-545 ? A.D.). Yuan Chwang mentions that the kingdom had "some hundred samgharamas, with about 6000 priests. Most of them study the Little Vehicle, according to the Sammitiya school."[5]

1. Legge, *op. cit.*, p. 81; Beal, *op. cit.*, III, pp. 384ff.; also see R. K. Mookerji, *Ancient Indian Education, Brahmanical and Buddhist* (Delhi, 1960), pp. 558ff.; H. D. Sankalia, *The University of Nalanda* (Delhi, 1972), Chapter IX.
2. See Mookerji, *op. cit.*, pp. 523-25.
3. Beal, *op. cit.*, II, pp. 322ff.
4. Beal, *op. cit.*, I, p. 30.
5. *CA*, p. 62; Mookerji, *op. cit.*, pp. 585-86; Beal, *op. cit.*, IV, pp. 457-58.

The state of Buddhism in Mahārāshtra during the Gupta age is reflected by the Buddhist monuments at Kaṇherī, Kārle, Piṭalkhorā and Ajantā. These owed nothing to Gupta patronage. There is a "hiatus" in our knowledge of the history of Buddhism in the region between *c.* 250 A.D. and the fifth century A.D. when the old centers at Kārle, Nāsik, Kaṇhērī, Karhād, Kudā and Piṭalkhorā are astir with a new life under the Mahāyāna impetus which came from the south and the east, Āndhra and Orissā. Ellora and Ajantā lay within the territories of the Vākāṭakas of the Vatsagulma branch and Cave 16 at Ajantā refers to King Hariṣeṇa (475-500 A.D.) and his minister Hastibhoja. Cave 17 was endowed by a Vākāṭaka feudatory and the magnificent Cave 26 mentions a minister of the King Aśmaka. The thirty caves at Ajantā, with the exceptions of 9, 12, 13 and 30, were excavated during the period from the fifth to the first half of the seventh century A.D. The complex has some 18 vihāras and the Mahāyāna establishment enjoyed support from royalty and state officials.[1] Further south, the old establishments at Nāgārjunakoṇḍa and Amarāvatī had already long passed their prime, though the faith lingered on at Jaggayapetā and in Kerala and the names of Buddhaghoṣa, Buddhadatta and Dhammapāla, celebrated Pāli commentators, illumine the history of Buddhistic learning in South India from the fifth to the seventh century.[2] Yuan Chwang noticed "some hundred of *Samgharamas* and 10,000 priests" in Kāñchīpuram and the Draviḍa country.[3] Fa-Hsien states that there were twenty two monasteries in Tāmralipti where he stayed two years "writing out his *Sutras*, and drawing pictures of images." Unfortunately, he has little more to add. Yuan Chwang found there "about ten samgharamas, with about 1000 priests" whereas there were fifty Deva temples. Tāmralipti-Tāmluk lay on the Hooghly in West Bengal. In neighbouring Kaliṅga, or Orissā, Yuan Chwang found ten monasteries with five hundred priests of the Mahāyāna persuasion, but there were one hundred Deva temples with "very many unbelievers of different sorts."[4]

1. For details, see B. G. Gokhale, *op. cit.*, pp. 90ff.
2. *CA*, pp. 400-05.
3. Beal, *op. cit.*, IV, pp. 429-30.
4. Legge, *op. cit.*, p. 100; Beal, *op. cit.*, IV, pp. 407-08, 413-14.

III

This survey of the state of Buddhism during the Gupta age reveals the existence of a large number of monasteries with thousands of monks. As mentioned above, the statements of the Chinese pilgrims cannot be taken at face value and should be regarded as exaggerations. What seems clear is that, though the old centers of Buddhism were in obvious decay and desolate, numerous new centers were flourishing, with impressive monasteries enjoying royal support. Of the life of the monks Fa-Hsien has this to say :

> "The regular business of the monks is to perform acts of meritorious virtue and to recite their Sutras and sit wrapt in meditation. When stranger monks arrive (at any monastery), the old residents meet and receive them, carry for them their clothes and alms-bowl, give them water to wash their feet, oil with which to anoint them, and the liquid food permitted out of the regular hours. When (the stranger) has enjoyed a very brief rest, they further ask the number of years that he has been a monk, after which he receives a sleeping apartment with its appurtenances, according to his regular order, and everything is done for him which the rules prescribe."

He further states that there was a practice of erecting stūpas to Śāriputra, Maudgalyāyana, and Ānanda as also shrines in honor of the *Abhidharma*, the *Vinaya*, and the *Sūtras*. After the rain-retreat laymen sent the monks offerings as a way of earning merit. The monks assembled in a great assembly and preached the Law. Through the night, lamps were kept burning in the shrines and musicians were employed to perform.[1] A reference has already been made above to Fa-Hsien's obtaining texts of the monastic codes and other literature of the various sect, from which it may be concluded that many monasteries had their own libraries. Nālandā, as has been stated, had the largest library of all monasteries in India. The cult of the Former Buddhas was very popular and Fa-Hsien refers to Dīpaṅkara, Kāśyapa and Krakusandha to whom stūpas were raised. Indeed, stūpa-worship was the commonest form of ritual, though images of the Buddha and various Bodhisattvas such as Avalokiteśvara and Mañjuśrī were common, and Fa-Hsien describes the custom of the procession

1. Legge, *op. cit.*, pp. 44-45.

of images mounted on carriages. Belief in the miracles performed by the Buddha was common and stūpas were also raised over spots where events of a mythological nature occurred, some of which related to stories in the *Jātakas* and the *Avadānas*.[1] Thus, Buddhism had evolved into a highly ritualistic faith with its own shrines, mythology and miracles. Yuan Chwang refers to the unceasing discussions going on among the monks on the abstruse and finer points of the doctrine. The Chinese pilgrims mention the existence of eighteen different sects among the Buddhists though they mention only a few by name. Among them are the Mahāsāṅghikas, the Sthaviras, the Sāmmitīyas, and the Sarvāstivādins. The partisans of Mahāyāna and Hīnayāna were "content to dwell apart." The sects had their own Vinaya which differed in minor details with more or less exact attention to matters of practice, though most agreed in essentials.[2] Yuan Chwang mentions that some monks of superior rank had lay servants attached to them, while others rode on elephants and had retinues.[3]

Here we may refer to the office of the *vihārasvāmin* noticed above. The inscriptions mention *vihārasvāmin*, *anekavihārasvāmin* and *vihārasvāminī*. The first term has been rendered as "master of a *vihāra*" and is explained as a "technical religious title of office, applied to certain functionaries who came next in rank below the *anekavihārasvāmin*." However, the term *vihārasvāminī* is rendered as "mistress (lady-superintendent) of a *vihāra*" and explained as seeming "not to be technical religious title denoting office by females, but to mean simply 'the wife of a *vihārasvāmin*'." If the *vihārasvāmin* was an ecclesiastical officer heading a vihāra or monastery, he must be presumed to be a monk and the *vihārasvāminī* cannot be described as wife of a *vihārasvāmin* since neither of our Chinese pilgrims notes the violation of the vow of celibacy by any of the monks in India. In this connection reference has been made to similar titles such as *mahāsāmiya* and *pamukha* which are taken to mean similar offices elsewhere.[4]

1. Beal, *op. cit.*, I, pp. 15-17, 20, 29, 33, 35, 37, 42.
2. Beal, *op. cit.*, I, p. 44; II, pp. 137-38.
3. Watters, *op. cit.*, I, p. 162.
4. *CII*, III, p. 263; see A. M. Sastri, *An Outline of Early Buddhism* Varanasi, 1965), pp. 131-32; also see *Epigraphia Indica*, II, p. 328, and J. Burgess, *Archaeological Survey of Western India* (Varanasi, 1964), IV, p. 105.

That the person described as *vihārasvāmin* had control of the vihāra or monastery is beyond doubt as the second part, *svāmin*, indicates. The question is whether he was a monk or a layman. Hitherto, it has been taken for granted that he was a monk, though *vihārasvāminī*, which should mean a woman in control of monastery, is rendered as the wife of a *vihārasvāmin*. A careful reading of the terms *mahāsāmiya* and *pamukha* does not show that the persons associated with them were monks, but rather that they were lay officials, probably governmental officials. An inscription of the time of the Hūṇa Toramāṇa refers to a Jayavṛddhi as an *anekavihārasvāmin*, "master of several vihāras", and is nowhere indicated as a monk. Our evidence, therefore, does not support the inference that a *vihārasvāmin* was a monk. He was in all probability a layman, sometimes a local official responsible for the maintenance of a monastery or group of monasteries.

In this connection, we should bear in mind two aspects of the Gupta polity of the times. One is the office of the *vinayasthitisthāpaka* who was an official in charge of religious and moral affairs, somewhat similar to the *dharmamahāmātra* of Aśoka.[1] Either the *vihārasvāmin* was a *vinayasthitisthāpaka* specifically charged with Buddhist affairs or an officer assigned specifically to Buddhist monasteries, working under the Religious and Morality office of the state. As such, he was a layman and cannot be regarded as a holder of a "religious" office or someone who occupied a place of importance and power in the Buddhist monastic hierarchy. His general duties could have been the building, endowment and upkeep of the monasteries that enjoyed royal grants. In some cases he could have been wealthy himself, favorably disposed to Buddhism in his personal faith, considering it an act of merit to build or endow a monastery at his own expense.

Secondly, there is the fact of land-grants to Buddhist monasteries. The practice of making land-grants and/or endowment of amounts of money, the interest from which could be used for defraying costs of monastic supplies, arose much before the Gupta age. In Mahārāshtra, for instance, during the period of the Sātavāhanas a number of such land-grants were made to Buddhist monastic settlements. Such grants are specified by clauses

1. For the Gupta religious officer, see Majumdar and Altekar, *op. cit.*, p. 279.

granting immunity from taxation and it is assumed that the revenues of these lands were to be used for the upkeep of the monks and monasteries to whom these grants were made. In some cases, the entire villages were assigned; in others, specific lots of farmland or land used for growing fruit trees were given. In such cases where entire villages were involved, the state suspended many of its administrative and fiscal functions from the assigned lands and we may assume that individual farmers became tenants of the monastic establishment. This was but a part of the evolution of ancient Indian feudal polity.[1]

For the Gupta age, we have the Sāñchī inscription of the time of Candra Gupta II of the year 93 (412-413 A.D.) recording the grant of a village or an allotment of land in Īśvaravāsaka, purchased with an endowment for the purpose of support of monks living in the great *Vihāra* of *Kākanādaboṭa* or Sāñchī.[2] The grant is from Āmrakārddava, son of Udāna, an officer of Candra Gupta II. Yuan Chwang states that Nālandā enjoyed the revenues of one hundred villages, which were increased to two hundred by the time of I-Tsing (671-695 A.D.). I-Tsing describes the system of farming of such Saṅgha lands :

> "When a cornfield is cultivated by the Sangha (the Brotherhood or community), a share in the product is to be given to the monastic servants or some other families by whom the actual tilling has been done. Every product should be divided into six parts, and one-sixth should be levied by the Sangha; the Sangha has to provide the bulls as well as the ground for cultivation, while the Sangha is responsible for nothing else."[3]

I-Tsing prefaces his observation by saying that this was "according to the teaching of the Vinaya", which should suggest that the practice was not by any means recent but old enough to be included in some versions of the Buddhist *Vinaya.* Probably such a practice became prevalent by the beginning of the sixth century if not earlier. Such land-grants reflect the increasing "feudalization" of the state and society during the Gupta age. The Buddhist monastery became a part of this emerging feudal struc-

1. For details for this period, see B. G. Gokhale, *op. cit.*, pp. 122-25.
2. *CII*, III, pp. 31-34.
3. J. Takakusu (trans.), *A Record of the Buddhist Religion as Practised in India and the Malay Archipelago by I-Tsing* (Delhi, 1966), pp. 61, 65.

ture indicating the long distance that Buddhism had travelled from its original manifestation as the product of an urban and mercantilist revolution in Indian history.[1]

Though Buddhism still enjoyed some support from the common people, increasingly the monasteries had come to depend upon the generosity of kings, their courtiers, and feudal barons.[2] The Guptas generally favored Brāhmaṇism and its two leading cults, Vaiṣṇavism and Śaivism, as is indicated by their performance of Vedic sacrifices and by Vaiṣṇavite and Śaivite emblems on their coins. A recent work has argued that "in the later phase of the history of their dynasty they came under the spell of an ascetic philosophy" and that Kumāra Gupta I was attracted to Buddhism toward the end of his career and that Narasiṃha Gupta I was a devout Buddhist.[3] We have already referred to Gupta contributions to the founding of the great center of Buddhistic learning at Nālandā. The Guptas were tolerant in their religious policies and were liberal in their religious benefactions, though none of the Gupta rulers could be compared to Aśoka, Kaniṣka or Harṣa in their patronage to Buddhism. It is probable that a few of their feudatories such as Āmrakārddava of the Sāñchī inscription were especially well-disposed toward Buddhism.

The Buddhist monastic institutions also received support from Brāhmaṇas. Fa-Hsien states that at the time of the image-procession in Pāṭaliputra the Brāhmaṇas came and invited the "Buddhas to enter the city" and heads of Vaiśya families also helped a great deal in charitable works. Along with the Vaiśyas, the Brāhmaṇas distributed to the monks articles needed by them in their monastic life.[4] It is doubtful if the Buddhist laymen and laywomen formed a distinct society of their own. Probably no such distinction existed except that the laymen offered their gifts to the monasteries and at the *stūpas*, but this was also done by

1. A. K. Warder has an interesting observation concerning the relationship between Mahāyāna Buddhism and feudalism in his paper in R. S. Sharma (ed.), *Indian Society: Historical Probings in Memory of D. D. Kosambi* (New Delhi, 1974), pp. 156-74.

2. For feudalism during the Gupta age, see R. S. Sharma, *Indian Feudalism* (Calcutta, 1965), pp. 46ff.

3. S. R. Goyal, *The History of the Imperial Guptas* (Allahabad, 1967), pp. 292ff.

4. Legge, *op. cit.*, pp. 47, 49.

the Brāhmaṇas and other groups. The only distinguishing marks pertained to the monastic life of the Buddhists, for their monasteries were meant exclusively for their use and within their walls the monks studied, preserved and discussed their specific doctrines. At the travellers' hospices different arrangements were made for the Buddhist monks, as their rules of food and monastic conduct in general markedly differed from those of others. Buddhism had failed in creating its own distinctive society and was, at this time, more or less confined to the monasteries. Many of the older monasteries were in ruins and at many places the number of monks was small. Other and newer centers had risen, such as Nālandā, but these were monastic colleges dependent on royal benefactions, surrounded by ritual and pomp. The general picture is that of decline, with very little of the old social vigor left in Buddhism. Yuan Chwang frequently refers to the large numbers of Deva-temples, and their votaries who numbered in the thousands, clearly indicating that Brāhmaṇism was on the ascendant and Buddhism was on its way to disappearance.

Of the intellectual life of the Buddhist community, Fa-Hsien states that the study of the *Abhidharma*, *Vinaya* and the *Sūtras* and the practice of meditational exercises were carried on assiduously in the monasteries. In the Mahāyāna residences the Prajñāpāramitā texts were studied with great diligence.[1] Yuan Chwang states :

> "The different schools are constantly at variance, and their contending utterances rise like angry waves of the sea. The different sects have their separate masters, and in various directions aim at one end.
>
> There are Eighteen schools, each claiming pre-eminence. The partisans of the Great and Little Vehicle are content to dwell apart. There are some who give themselves up to quiet contemplation, and devote themselves, whether walking or standing still or sitting down, to the acquirement of wisdom and insight; others, on the contrary, differ from these in raising noisy contentions about their faith. According to their fraternity, they are governed by distinctive rules and regulations". . . .[2]

1. *Ibid.*, pp. 44-46.
2. Beal, *op. cit.*, II, p. 137.

Of the literature of the period the *Prajñāpāramitā* texts were the most important. The early texts probably originated in South India and the name of Nāgārjuna is associated with the consolidation of the tradition. According to Conze, it was during the Gupta age that "the re-statement of the doctrine in short Sutras and in *versified Summaries*" occurred (*c.* 300-500 A.D.). Among these are the *Heart Sūtra* and the *Diamond Sūtra*, the former described as "one of the sublimest spiritual documents of mankind" offering a re-statement of the idea of Emptiness (*Śūnyatā*). The *Diamond Sūtra* "appeals directly to a spiritual intuition which has left the conventions of logic behind."[1] The subject-matter of these texts has reference to the Absolute and the relation between the conditioned and the unconditioned. They instruct us to proceed from appearance to reality, to go beyond life which is like a dream, a bubble, even beyond concepts such as the Buddha or Nirvāṇa and realize the "sameness" between here and the concept of the "hereafter". The Absolute is unconditioned, immutable, impenetrable, unidentifiable, and spiritual advancement must begin with an awareness of the essential "unreality" of all concepts. When duality is transcended "suchness" is realized. These texts build upon the fundamentals of the Śūnyavāda, the doctrine of "emptiness" propagated by Nāgārjuna. They do not completely reject the way of "works" (merit-making) and practice of the basic Buddhistic virtues, but emphasize that these only prepare the ground for the journey into the Absolute which must involve, initially at least, an intense intellectual effort, only so that intellect itself may be shown as inadequate in the realization of the Absolute.[2]

Another important text related to this general period of Buddhistic thought is the *Saddharmapuṇḍarīka*. The work has had a long history, in the course of which it underwent numerous textual modifications, and is devoted to the glorification of the Buddha as the incomparable Lord of healing, a savior ever present

1. E. Conze, *Selected Sayings from the Perfection of Wisdom* (London, 1968), pp. 11-14.

2. See *Ibid.*, pp. 16-24; also E. Conze, *The Prajñāpāramitā Literature* ('S-Gravenhage, 1960), pp. 18-20; E. J. Thomas, *The History of Buddhist Thought* (London, 1971), pp. 214ff., 285-87; A. B. Keith, *Buddhist Philosophy in India and Ceylon* (Varanasi, 1963), pp. 216ff.

to succour suffering humanity and ever responding to faith. The work was first translated into Chinese in 223 A.D. and in different recensions later. It is the principal text of devotional Buddhism with all its elaborate rituals, acts of faith, miracles and savior cult. More than the *Prajñāpāramitā*, the *Saddharmapuṇḍarīka* reflects the popular Buddhist temper of the Gupta age and inspired numerous and great works of art.[1]

The *Laṅkāvatāra Sūtra* is another outstanding work which may be generally related to the ethos of Buddhism of the Gupta age. It was translated into Chinese in 443 A.D. and hence must have been in existence at least by the middle of the fourth century. It espouses the Vijñānavāda school of Buddhist philosophy which, while denying the reality of the external world, accepts that the phenomena of consciousness have a subjective reality. Its main thrust is directed toward the "realization that things are nothing but mental creations; that external things can be said to exist or not exist only in the sense of a mirage, being produced from mental impressions from of old, and through the true apprehension of things in their ultimate nature." This apprehension is the essence of the "Buddha-nature," the leap into "suchness" (*tathatā*) transcending reason and discrimination. The path leading to it is that of meditation which later became embellished with the contemplation of "constructs" (*dhāriṇīs*) and chants (*mantras*) finally culminating in Vajrayāna ("Thunderbolt vehicle"), Mantrayāna, and Tantrayāna from the seventh century onward.[2]

Dominating the background of this development in Buddhism were the two concepts of the transcendental Buddha who had long gone beyond the historical Buddha. In his aspect of the *dharmakāya* (Truth-body) he was eternal, ineffable, fully capable of saving human beings who approached him with hearts filled with faith and absolute surrender (*bhakti*). But even more important than this Buddha was the Bodhisattva (one who had in him the essence of perfect wisdom). He symbolized in his person and career the two supreme virtues of transcendental wisdom (*prajñā*)

1. M. Winternitz, *A History of Indian Literature* (New York, 1971), II, pp. 303-05; H. Kern (trans.), *Saddharmapuṇḍarīka or The Lotus of the Good Law* (New York, 1963), pp. xxxiii ff.

2. Winternitz, *op. cit.*, II, pp. 332ff.; A. B. Keith, *op. cit.*, pp. 249ff.; D. T. Suzuki, *Studies in the Laṅkāvatāra Sūtra* (London, 1968), pp. 96-100.

and unbounded compassion (*karuṇā*). He defers his own *nirvāṇa* so that he may operate in the world to save all those who come unto him with their hearts filled with faith (*śraddhā*) and supplication, the eternal companion of the lonely traveller, ready to wipe the tears of the afflicted, the agonized and the forlorn.

The origins of the Bodhisattva cult have been long debated and various sources are cited for them. One view is that it was a Buddhist response to the growth of the *bhakti* cult centered around Kṛṣṇa and Śiva worship. Archaeological evidence for the Viṣṇu-Kṛṣṇa cult dates back to the second century B.C. and it is possible that the *bhakti* tradition goes back to a much earlier time than that. Among the Buddhists the early development of the *stūpa* as a place of worship indicates the influence of elements of the bhakti-cult. The *Bhagavad Gītā*, assigned in its present form to a period between the second century B.C. and the second century A.D., is the first formalized and institutionalized statement of the role of the bhakti-cult in the newly emerging Hinduism. It is also argued, on the other hand, that the Hindu bhakti-cult was, in itself, a Brāhmaṇical response to developments in Buddhism. But perhaps both Buddhism and Hinduism in their bhakti traditions centered on the Bodhisattva and Kṛṣṇa-Viṣṇu savior concepts were, in fact, classical expressions of what was originally a folk cult. That folk cult was based on Yakṣa worship. Yakṣa worship among the merchant and artisan groups has an antiquity much greater than both Buddhism and the new Hinduism. The Yakṣa and his female counterpart, the Yakṣi, reflected a complex of ideas and expectations related to travel, wealth, crafts and arts of music and dance, erotica, *maṅgala* (auspiciousness), and fertility. Among a host of Yakṣas mentioned by name in Buddhist and Brāhmaṇical literature two are prominent, namely, Maṇibhadra and Pūrṇabhadra, whose icons were worshipped in shrines. These were deities of merchants, travellers, craftsmen, artists and, in general, the plain common folk. They were too ubiquitous and powerful to be ignored by both Buddhism and Hinduism. The most vital part of the Yakṣa cult was the role of bhakti (devotion, supplication, succour) which was assimilated by the two classical traditions of ancient India. Some aspects of the cult, such as assistance to travellers and merchants' patronage of the arts and crafts, are common to some of the Yakṣas as well as the Bodhisattvas Padmapāṇi and Vajrapāṇi. The iconography of these Bodhisattvas reveals close relationships with Yakṣa iconography. It is more than probable that the new Buddhism drew upon folk cults to a much greater degree than has been suspected and the twin aspects of bhakti and succour may have been concepts assimilated from the folk cults.

This new Buddhism had gone far past the spirit of the old, for the Buddha "now appeared as a god of the first order, invested with all the qualities that the most extravagant mythopoetic imagination could suggest." The new mythology conjured countless heavens presided over by Buddhas and Bodhisattvas, among whom was Avalokiteśvara, "the self-appointed votary seeking eagerly to procure happiness for his fellow-creatures at any cost, even if he must surrender his own right to spiritual advancement as the price." The ability of one person to transfer his own merit to others now looms large as a dominant belief, evidence of which appears in the votive inscriptions cited above in this chapter. Images of the two Bodhisattvas, Padmapāṇi and Vajrapāṇi were worshipped all over northern India and in Mahārāshtra during the Gupta age. Also worshipped was Mañjuśrī, who conferred on his devotees qualities of intelligence, wisdom, memory and eloquence, and his cult became popular from the fourth century A.D. onward.[1]

These developments paralleled similar movements in Hinduism expressed in the philosophy of the paths (*mārgas*) of ritual action (*karma*), selfless devotion (*bhakti*), and wisdom (*jñāna*). The ethical earnestness of the old school was still there, but now it was heavily overlaid with elaborate ritual, image-worship and meditative and mystical practices and cults. The two outstanding texts of the Bodhisattva cult were Śāntideva's *Bodhicaryāvatāra* and the *Śikṣāsamuccaya*, the first being called "the finest poem in Buddhism" and the latter a compendium of lore bearing on the training of the Bodhisattva and the Buddha.[2]

1. For a history of the Bodhisattva, see Har Dayal, *The Bodhisattva Doctrine in Buddhist Sanskrit Literature* (Delhi, 1976) pp. 13ff.; for the two Bodhisattvas, see B. Bhattacharyya, *The Indian Buddhist Iconography* (Calcutta, 1958), pp. 101-03, 124 ff.; L.D. Barnett, *The Path of Light* (London, 1959), pp. 22-30; for the Yakṣa cult, see B. G. Gokhale, *Indica*, XIII/1 & 2 (1976), pp. 52-58.

2. Thomas, *op. cit.*, p. 196; Winternitz, *op. cit.*, II, pp. 366-75.

Mention must also be made here of the intellectuals assigned to this period. Among them were Dignāga (Diṅnāga), the celebrated Buddhist logician, and Dharmapāla who belonged to Vasubandhu's school; Sthiramati, the author of the *Ratnakūṭa*; and Buddhapālita and Bhāvaviveka, assigned to the beginning of the fifth century. Tradition associates the name Vasubandhu, "one of the most prominent figures in the history of Buddhist literature," with either Candra Gupta II or Kumāra Gupta or both.[1]

Among the schools prominently mentioned by the Chinese travellers were the Mahāsāṅghikas, the Sarvāstivādins and the Sāmmitīyas. The Mahāsāṅghikas are regarded as the precursors of the Mahāyānists and date back to the time of the Second or Vesālī Council. The Mahāsāṅghikas were strong in Pāṭaliputra, in Mathurā, Western India, and Āndhra. They developed their own views of the nature of Buddhahood and especially the Bodhisattva doctrine. The Sarvāstivādins are so-called because of the attribution to them of the claim *sarvam asti* (Everything exists) which really pertained to the ontological reality of certain elements. The Sāmmitīyas were strong in Valabhī in Saurāṣṭra and also at Nālandā. The old Theravādins were largely confined to the Tamil Nādu area and Śrī Laṅkā

The Buddhist educational system and art vividly reflect the intellectual temper and the emotional ethos of Buddhism in the Gupta age. Yuan Chwang's account of the university of Nālandā contains some very perceptive observations on the educational methods in use. They consisted of expository lectures, discussions, learning by rote, debates and expositions of the doctrines. Some of the keenest Buddhist minds lived at the center and the students were put through a complex curriculum comprising grammar, Sanskrit language, philosophy, logic, and astronomy as well as non-Buddhistic thought. Its library contained hundreds of texts laboriously copied and handed down from generation to generation, and Nālandā served as the pre-eminent intellectual center of the Buddhist world not only in India but also in all Asia. While its later development betrays preoccupation with magic and mysticism, the earlier decades undoubtedly reflected all that was best in the Buddhist intellectual tradition. The Buddhist feeling is exquisitely brought out in Buddhist works

1. Winternitz, *op. cit.*, II, pp. 356-67; Warder, *op. cit.*, pp. 357ff.

of art of which the Sārnāth Buddha figure and the murals of Ajantā are the outstanding examples. The Sārnāth Buddha figure is at once the flower of a mature sculptural tradition, displaying utter sophistication in the handling of intractable material and infusing it with a spiritual greatness so characteristic of this great age. The Ajantā murals delight in the portrayal of the many facts of life encompassing in their broad sweep the world of kings and princesses as well as common people, the animal and vegetable realms, and the realms of gods, Nāgas, Yakṣas, and Bodhisattvas. The over life-size figure of Avalokiteśvara Bodhisattva epitomizes the noble ideal of the Being of infinite wisdom and compassion transmuting with tender gaze earthiness into spiritual sublimity. Long past is the phase of tentative probings and experimental heaviness of the Kuṣāṇa and Mathurā schools, for the Gupta artist is now completely a master of his material and technique, revealing through the half-closed gaze of the Buddhas and Bodhisattvas the variety of the macrocosm merging into the subliminal unity of the world within. Buddhism had created a great culture, a noble and integral part of an age of classicism.

PART III

LITERARY AND ARTISTIC EXPRESSION

7

MICROCOSMS OF A COMPLEX WORLD: CLASSICAL DRAMA IN THE GUPTA AGE

BARBARA STOLER MILLER

VARIOUS chapters in this volume emphasize the heterogeneous nature of Indian society and cultural life during the period that is usually described in terms of its social harmony and artistic classicism.[1] Even at the height of Gupta power (*c.* 390-470 A.D.),

1. For an encyclopedic account of Western literary notions of what is classical, see "Classicism" in the *Princeton Encyclopedia of Poetry and Poetics*, edited by Preminger, Warnke, and Hardison (Princeton University Press, 1965), pp. 136 ff. The closest Indian equivalent for "classical" is *saṃskṛta*, referring to the language and cultural values associated with it. This point raises an immediate paradox with reference to classical Indian drama, since it was composed in mixed Sanskrit and Prākrits, non-classical languages. Sanskrit was the hieratic language of the brāhmaṇa priests from ancient times —an Indo-European language brought to India by the tribes of nomads who filtered into the Panjāb at the end of the 2nd millenium B.C. By the time it entered court circles it had long-since undergone codification by the grammarian Pāṇini (in the *c.* 4th century B.C.) and subsequent grammatical refinement. It had become highly artificial—regularized and grammatically dense. Highly inflected forms were embedded in complex constructions and elaborate metrical patterns governed by accentless quantitative prosody.

Good introductions to the norms of Indian poetry and drama are found in chapters two and three of *The Literature of India : An Introduction*, edited by E. C. Dimock, Jr., et al. (Chicago, 1974); in *Sanskrit Court Poetry*, translated by D. H. H. Ingalls (Cambridge, Mass., 1965); in *Two Plays of Ancient India*, translated by J. A. B. van Buitenen (New York, 1968). A knowledge of basic forms, theories, and examples is presupposed by my discussion; a survey of the subject is provided in A. B. Keith's *The Sanskrit Drama*. Sylvain Lévi's *Le Théatre Indien* (Paris, 1890) should also be consulted; the latest edition is prefaced by an excellent essay by Louis Renou, published in English as "Research on the Indian Theatre since 1890," *Sanskrita Ranga*

the conservative ideals of the Sanskrit renaissance only partially represented the cultural values of the society. It seems significant that the five major Sanskrit plays whose composition and original performance are traditionally placed in the Gupta period are complex, multi-layered works that display and explore conflicting social values.[1] The three dramatic romances attributed to Kāli-

(Madras, 1966). A. Rangacharya's *Drama in Sanskrit Literature* (Bombay, 1967) offers some provocative ideas.

In this attempt to formulate relevant questions about the nature of classical Indian drama, I have searched the literature of Western and Indian esthetic theory, as well as analyses of the relation between drama and ritual. I have found a few primary texts and studies particularly suggestive, beginning with Bharata's *Nāṭyaśāstra*, edited and translated by M. Ghosh (Calcutta, 1956-67); Dhanañjaya's *Daśarūpaka*, edited and translated by G. C. O. Haas (Delhi preprint, 1962); and Aristotle's *Poetics*, translated in *Aristotle On Poetry and Style* by G. M. A. Grube (New York, 1958). I have found it useful to re-read the comedies of Aristophanes and Shakespeare, especially Shakespeare's *As You Like It*, *Twelfth Night*, *Midsummer Night's Dream*, *All's Well That End's Well*, and *Love's Labour's Lost*. I have culled interpretations and perspectives from Sigmund Freud's *Civilization and Its Discontents*; Northrop Frye's *Anatomy of Criticism*; Herbert Gans's *Popular Culture and High Culture : An Analysis and Evaluation of Taste* (1975); Theodore Gaster's *Thespis*; Norvin Hein's *Miracle Plays of Mathurā* (1972); Johan Huizinga's *Homo Ludens : A Study of the Play Element in Culture*; Suzanne Langer's *Feeling and Form*; Gilbert Murray's *The Classical Tradition in Poetry*; Victor Turner's *The Ritual Process*; and Jesse Weston's *From Ritual to Romance*.

1. Readers are referred to Edwin Gerow's translation of the *Mālavikāgnimitra*, *Journal of South Asian Literature*, VII (1971), pp. 67-127; David Gitomer's translation of the *Vikramorvaśīya* (unpublished Columbia University M. A. Thesis, 1976); and Arthur Ryder's translation of the *Śākuntala*, as this play is often referred to. Translations of the *Śākuntala* used here are my own, based on the Bengālī-Kashmīrī recension, most recently edited by S. K. Belvalkar (New Delhi, 1965). There are plans to publish the Gerow, Gitomer, and Miller translations with critical essays in a volume on Kālidāsa's plays. For other translations and studies, as well as texts, see S. P. Narang, *Kālidāsa Bibliography* (New Dehli, 1976). *Mṛcchakaṭika* and *Mudrārākṣasa* are best read in the translations of J. A. B. van Buitenen in *Two Plays*.

The history of classical Indian drama certainly antedates the Gupta period. There exist fragments of plays attributed to the Buddhist poet Aśvaghoṣa [see Keith, *Sanskrit Drama*, pp. 80-90; C. R. Devadhar, *Plays Ascribed to Bhāsa* (Poona, 1962)] and at least some of the plays attributed to Bhāsa must have been known to Kālidāsa, since Bhāsa is acknowledged in the prologue of the *Mālavikāgnimitra*. But it is in these five plays that the dramatic form became a sophisticated vehicle. Exact dating of the dramatists or the plays is impossible. No mention of any of them is known before

dāsa (*Mālavikāgnimitra, Vikramorvaśīya, Abhijñānaśākuntala*), the satiric comedy attributed to Śūdraka (*Mṛcchakaṭika*), and the political drama attributed to Viśākhadatta (*Mudrārākṣasa*) are all sophisticated theatrical pieces whose esthetic impact depends on the radical interplay of levels of language, culture, emotional tone, and artistic taste.[1] The formal and thematic complexity of the plays is theoretically underscored by the earliest extant work on dramaturgy, the *Nāṭyaśāstra* attributed to Bharata, which was probably compiled in the Gupta period.[2]

The theatre of any society is a cultural institution that depends on patronage; the dramatist composes for an audience whom he imagines gathered into a tangible group. All literature is social, using as its medium language, which is a social creation, and basing its conventions on norms which arise in society, but drama is more directly social than other forms of literature by virtue of its performance before live audiences. The Indian term *dṛśya-kāvya* may be rendered "public poetry" to contrast drama with lyric and epic forms whose structure takes little direct notice of

Kālidāsa is named in an inscription at Aihole, dated 634 A.D., which simply proclaims him a great poet. Legends are convincing in associating him with Vikramāditya, an epithet of Candra Gupta II, and the title *Vikramorvaśīya* may be a direct reference to the Gupta patron. See R. D. Karmarkar, *Kālidāsa* (Dharwar, 1960); K. Krishnamoorthy *Kālidāsa* (Delhi, 1972); D. H. H. Ingalls, "Kālidāsa and the Attitudes of the Golden Age," *Journal American Oriental Society*, 96, no. 1 (1976), pp. 15-26. Historical data related to the other two dramatists is even scantier; see van Buitenen, *Two Plays.*

1. Recognition of the elaborate categories of language operating in the plays raised my interest in defining the "classical" form of Indian drama (*nāṭya*, also called *dṛśya-kāvya* or "public poetry" in relation to the academic Sanskrit lyric and epic poetry, *khaṇḍa-kāvya* and *mahā-kāvya*). My work on Jayadeva's 12th century Sanskrit dramatic lyric poem *Gitagovinda*, published as *Love Song of the Dark Lord* (New York, 1977) provides the perspective. That poem resists classification in any genre of classical literature and has been considered by some critics to be a "translation" from one of the non-classical languages. My work on it has suggested that the relations between genres, levels of literature, and levels of classical language in India are extremely complex.

2. References to the *Nāṭyaśāstra* are cited from the text and translation of M. Ghosh (Calcutta, 1956); these are easily located in the four-volume edition of R. Kavi with the commentary of Abhinavagupta (Baroda, 1926). On the dating of the extant text, see S. K. De, "The Problem of Bharata and Ādi-Bharata," in *Some Problems of Sanskrit Poetics* (Calcutta, 1959), pp. 156-76; cf. Ghosh, text introduction pp. lxxix-lxxxii.

the audience.[1] In our attempt to cultivate a sympathy for the values of the Gupta age, analyses of the conventions of the theatre as they are presented in the plays of Kālidāsa, Śūdraka, and Viśākhadatta, and in the dramaturgy of Bharata may provide valuable insights.

Indian dramatic theory recognizes the emotional and ethical instruction afforded by the spectacle of drama, which is said to mimic the conduct of people more closely than other forms of poetry. In Bharata's mythic account, drama is a kind of holy presentation that the gods originated to offer ethical instruction through diversion when people were no longer listening to the Vedic scriptures.[2] The first production of a play legendarily

1. See Wellek and Warren, "Literature and Society", in *Theory of Literature* (New York, 1942), ch. 9.

2. *Nāṭyaśāstra* I.1-129; IV. 269. Aritstotle also stressed emotional satisfaction through action. Both Greek and Indian plays present spectacles which are antidotes to disorder within the microcosm of the theatre, but the modes of ordering experience are vastly different. Classical Indian plays characteristically re-establish harmony between conflicting elements by exploring the latent essence within things; this produces the *rasa* of a dramatic experience. Greek tragedies present heroic struggles against gods and established order; the experience effects a purgation, or *catharsis*, of emotions of fear and pity.

To understand why the German poet Goethe was more sympathetic to the rhythm of Kālidāsa's drama *Śākuntala* than the modern-day Indian holy man could be is to begin to appreciate the purpose of classical Indian drama. Delight, even delight in the beauties of the natural world, is dangerous for an ascetic; it threatens to undermine his narrow vision of reality.

Willst du die Blüte des fruhen, die Früchte des späteren Jahres,
Willst du, was reizt und entzückt, willst du, was sättigt und nährt,
Willst du den Himmel, die Erde, mit einem Namen begreifen,
Nenn' ich Śakuntalā dich, und so ist alles gesagt.

If you want blossoms of young and fruits of later years,
If you want what charms and enchants, fulfills and nourishes,
If you want heaven and earth contained in one name—
I say Śakuntalā and everything is spoken.

J. W. von Goethe, first printed
in *Deutsche Monatsscrift* in 1791.

I have never read the Shakuntala of Kalidasa, and I never shall. I do not learn the language of the gods to amuse myself with love stories and literary trifles.

Vinoba Bhave, speaking in Banaras,
quoted by Lanza de Vasto in
Gandhi to Vinoba : The New Pilgrimage (1956)

took place at the popular rainy-season festival of Indra known as the "Banner Festival". Indian dramas are still generally presented as sources of diversion at seasonal festivals, marriages, and other auspicious occasions. Bharata stresses the profit a king will gain if he allows his subjects to enjoy dramatic performances without payment.[1] The ideal of education through dramatic spectacle is codified in Bharata's definition of drama (*nāṭya*). The god Brahmā speaks to the gathered demons who threaten the performance[2] :

> "In drama there is no exclusive representation of you demons or of the gods. Drama is a representation of the emotional states of the three-fold universe. It includes concerns of duty (*dharma*), play (*krīḍā*), material gain (*artha*), peace (*śama*), mirth (*hāsya*), war (*yuddha*), passionate love (*kāma*), and death (*vadha*). It teaches duty to those who violate duty, passionate love to those who are addicted to love; it reprimands those who behave rudely, promotes restraint in those who are disciplined; gives courage to cowards, energy to heroes; it enlightens fools and gives learning to learned men."

Throughout its history, Sanskrit literature concentrates on establishing correspondences between the world of men and the world of the gods, between the microcosm and the macrocosm; the idea was that if one discovers the correspondence in any aspect he gains magical power of the whole. This fascination with finding hidden correspondences lies at the basis of the proliferation of literary forms and figures of speech that are elaborated in Sanskrit. The earliest recorded Indo-Aryan literature, the *Ṛg Veda*, expresses the notion that language does not serve the function of separating things; instead, it is a unifying force. In the Vedic hymns, which are songs to propitiate the gods, composed to accompany offerings poured on the sacrificial fire, the Word, personified as the goddess Vāc, is seen as being representative of the power of men to communicate with the divine.[3] The hymns were composed by a hereditary priesthood who were called "inspired," "quivering," "seers,"—poets (*kavi*), who

1. *Nāṭyaśāstra* XXXVI.80.
2. *Nāṭyaśāstra* I. 106-109.
3. See W. Norman Brown, "The Creative Role of the Goddess Vāc in the *Ṛgveda*," *Journal of South Asian Literature*, VII, nos. 3-4 (1971), pp. 19-28.

composed poetry (*kāvya*), within an oral tradition that placed great emphasis on the effectiveness of both sound and sense.

There is ample evidence in works of literature and inscriptions that the courts of Gupta India delighted in eloquent speech.[1] Poems of counsel and love and religious celebration, composed in stylized forms of lyric, epic, and drama, were recited before the king and his courtiers. Poets were valued for their skill in conjuring up universal correspondences which echoed ancient mysteries; the beauty of poetry (or any art) was valued for its power to remind the audience of ancient truths by creating an appropriate mood. A poet's skill was recognized to be related to his inspired insight. Like the ancient priest-singers to whom all poets traced their lineage, their central work was to create verbal bridges to the divine as a means of glorifying and strengthening the kings they served.

Despite the absence of historical evidence to confirm the traditional Gupta associations of specific authors like Kālidāsa, Śūdraka, and Viśākhadatta, attempts to establish their relative dates in terms of the style and content of their works are significant.[2] In his cogent article on Kālidāsa, Daniel H. H. Ingalls argues that Kālidāsa's literary ideals of conservatism and harmony, as well as his practical innovation, appear to reflect closely the ideals of the Gupta Age. Ingalls stresses that Kālidāsa's works complement other evidence of efforts carried out during the reigns of Samudra Gupta and his son Candra Gupta II (375-415 A.D.) to revive the customs of the Vedic and Hindu past, including ancient rites and the sacred Sanskrit language. It is noteworthy that Kālidāsa's poems, like the Gupta inscriptions, are all in elegant, stylized Sanskrit. The poems are characterized by descriptive richness, slow narrative movement, and minimal dialogue. Descriptions are constructed by elaborate use of diverse imagery and subtle metaphors. Kālidāsa, alluding to his own craft, describes the creation of Pārvatī in a stanza in his great epic poem the *Kumārasambhava*, "Birth of the Prince," which is a celebration of the creative love of the god Śiva for the daughter of the Himālayas, Pārvatī : "It was as though the creator, wishing to see all loveliness concentrated in one spot, had composed her form

1. See Ingalls, "Kālidāsa", in R. C. Majumdar, et al., *The History and Culture of the Indian People*, Vol. III (Bombay, 1954), ch. XV.

2. See note 1 on Page 156 above.

with effort, by gathering together all the things that serve as standards of comparison (for the beauty of women) and distributing them in appropriate places (in her body) [I.49]."[1]

The digressive elegance and standardized courtly language of Kālidāsa's poems were for an audience of highly educated men who could be responsive to the poet's esthetic presentation of his harmonious vision of reality. An audience that had to be cultivated in the linguistic subtleties of a refined, sacred, classical language like Sanskrit was certainly limited.[2] The high tone of the poetry is unrelieved by excursions into humor or lower registers of language and thought.

Kālidāsa's plays belong to a less academic tradition of Sanskrit composition, which includes the works of the playwrights Bhāsa, Śūdraka, Viśākhadatta, Bhavabhūti, and Harṣa, as well as anonymous works like the early monologue plays (*bhāṇa*). Kālidāsa is, however, the only classical author known to have composed both poems and plays. Sanskrit verses in the plays share the linguistic and esthetic norms of poetry, but these verses are only one component of the complex structure of a classical Sanskrit drama. In plays the Sanskrit language is mixed with various stylized forms of vernacular languages, called Prākrits. Sanskrit is the language of only one set of characters in the plays, the king and certain other characters of high status; the brāhmaṇa buffoon (*vidūṣaka*), the women of the court and city and hermitage, as well as various minor characters, speak Prākrits. This linguistic diversity is conventionalized in the plays and codified in the *Nāṭyaśāstra* (XVIII.1-61).[3] It seems reasonable to assume that the Prākrits used by the classical dramatists must have been drawn from current mediums of the day, stylized for purposes of characterization, musical sound, and emotive contrast.[4]

1. Cited by Indira Shetterly in "Recurrence and Structure in Sanskrit Literary Epic : A Study of Bhāravi's *Kirātārjunīya*" (Unpublished Ph.D. Dissertation, Harvard University, 1976), p. 392.

2. The special relation between connoisseur and poet is central to the doctrine of later rasa theorists like Bhoja, Ānandavardhana, and Abhinavagupta; see V. Raghavan, *Bhoja's Śṛṅgāra Prakāśa* (Madras, 1963), pp. 466ff.; Masson and Patwardhan, *Śāntarasa and Abhinavagupta's Philosophy of Aesthetics* (Poona, 1969).

3. See L. Nitti-Dolci, *Les Grammairiens Prākrits* (Paris, 1938), ch. 2; S. M. Katre, *Prakrit Languages and their Contribution to Indian Culture* (Poona, 1964), pp. 25-27, 60.

4. The Prākrits spoken by the *vidūṣaka* and the women in the plays

The characters in the plays are also diverse, drawn not only from divine and exalted human stations, but from every corner of society. One does not find policemen, fishermen, dancing masters, buffoons, boorish royalty, masseurs-turned-monks, and the like in classical Sanskrit poems. The poems focus on gods and kings who obey the brāhmaṇical law-books by modelling their behavior on the protective and punitive roles of various Vedic gods. The plays show "humanized" kings who enjoy varied society, indulge in all diversions, and have brāhmaṇa buffoons for advisors. The buffoon, called *vidūṣaka* in Sanskrit literature, in a verbal parody of his role as "wise man," is an important aid in the king's adventure. He accompanies the king everywhere and frequently commits the critical errors that propel the plot to its conclusion. He is usually in close contact with his counterparts in the realm of pleasure, the Prākrit-speaking females, and acts as a go-between with the audience too, thus sustaining relations at various levels in the theatre. He ironically answers the king's Sanskrit with Prākrit and is obsessed with satisfying his hunger. His gluttony and absurdity confound the brāhmaṇical pretence of wisdom and help to undermine the authority of brāhmaṇical law.[1] The range of social types represented in the plays is often used only for comic effect, but it adds to one's sense that plays were created for an audience that must have included people of varied taste and learning. This is confirmed by Kālidāsa when he says, "the play, though men have many different tastes, is the one delight of all" (*Mālavikāgnimitra*, I.4). The *Nāṭyaśāstra* contains references to the medley of spectators who assemble to enjoy a dramatic performance.[2] The

create verbal environments of comedy and love. Phonetic ambiguities of the Prākrits are conducive to comic play, and misunderstanding the high frequency of vowels allows a softer language of love than Sanskrit (like French and Italian versus Latin).

1. On the types of character and distribution of roles in classical drama, see *Nāṭyaśāstra*, XXXIV-XXXV. For a discussion of the values of kingship in the Gupta period, see Charles Drekmeier, *Kingship and Community* (Stanford, 1962); cf. *The Laws of Manu*, VII; IX.248-313; translated by Georg Buhler in *Sacred Books of the East*, Vol. 25 (MLBD, 1970). The *vidūṣaka* is mentioned in the *Kāma Sūtra*, IV, as one of the persons who provides diversion for a man-about-town (*nāgarika*); see Rangacharya, *Drama in Sanskrit*, ch.10.

2. Though limited in size (about 400 as compared with the 15,000 spectators a Greek amphitheatre could accommodate), the diversity of the audience

theatrical occasion for renewing contacts with perennial conflicts of human emotion was clearly shared by the king, or rich merchant, with an audience who made demands on the playwright's ability to divert them.

Kālidāsa, like Śūdraka and Viśākhadatta, opens each of his plays with a benediction, followed by direct reference to himself and his audience. Kālidāsa's poems, by contrast, all open with a verse which designates the subject and context of the poem, on which subsequent verses elaborate. The poems contain metaphorical references to the poet's creativity, but there is no direct reference to the poet or his audience. The prologue in a classical Sanskrit play serves to underline the importance of the audience in the world of theater while it highlights the actors' passage into the on-going universe of the dramatic action. This mode of dramatic beginning prepares the audience for the multilevelled theatrical spectacle.

Comparison of the opening verses and selected stanzas from two of Kālidāsa's poems with the prologues and selected scenes from his plays suggests a great deal about the purpose, setting, performance, and structure of Sanskrit drama. The basic function of the prologue is the same in the plays of Śūdraka, Viśākhadatta, and later playwrights.[1]

At the opening of the *Kumārasambhava* Kālidāsa sets the scene by presenting a series of metaphors designed to infuse aspects of the mountainous world with nature's sensuous, erotic divinity.[2]

> "Far in the north divinity animates a majestic mountain range
> called Himālaya—a place of perpetual snow
> sinking deep into seas on its eastern and western wings
> and standing over earth like a towering barrier. [1]

in an Indian theatre is clearly reflected in Bharata's theory of theatrical success, *Nāṭyaśāstra* XXVII.1-17.

1. The prologues of the *Mṛcchakaṭika* and *Mudrārākṣasa* are well-translated in van Buitenen's *Two-Plays*; readers are referred there.

2. Few translations do justice to the poetry of Kālidāsa, but I can recommend the stray translation by D. H. H. Ingalls in his article on Kālidāsa and his book *Sanskrit Court Poetry* for a wonderful taste of Kālidāsa's style. The translations here are my own, based on the critical edition of Suryakanta (New Delhi, 1962).

Himālayan mountain high peaks hold a wealth of minerals
whose red glow diffuses through clefts in the clouds
to produce an aura of untimely twilight—
making heavenly nymphs hasten to put on their evening jewels. [4]

Filling the hollow spaces of bamboo reeds
with winds rising from the mouths of caves,
Himālaya strives to sustain the droning tonic note
that celestial musicians need for their singing. [8]

Himālayan herbs shine at night
deep inside cave shelters
where wild forest men lie with their rustic women—
herbs like lamps burning without oil to excite sensual love. [10]

Bearing sprays from Gaṅgā river waterfalls,
making cedar trees quake,
parting the peacocks' plume feathers,
Himālayan wind is worshipped by tribal hunters stalking deer." [15]

In every section of the poem the sacred landscape of India is intertwined with the power and beauty of Śiva and Pārvatī enacting sacred rites. Ingalls points out that the correspondences intended are made explicit by Kālidāsa in a stanza in the first section [I.28], where aspects of Hindu religion are merged in the beauty of Pārvatī through a chain of similes (*mālopamā*) :

"As the altar lamp by means of its flame, as the night by means of the Ganges that flows through it, as the Milky Way, as speech by means of the Sanskrit language, so was the mountain purified by the goddess and thereby rendered beautiful."[1]

In Kālidāsa's lyric monologue the *Meghadūta*, "Cloud Messenger,"[2] a demi-god (*yakṣa*) who is exiled from his Himālayan home by his master Kubera for negligence of duty asks a thundercloud moving northward at the start of the rainy season to convey a message to his estranged wife. Kālidāsa begins :

1. Ingalls, "Kālidāsa," p. 20.
2. See Leonard Nathan, *The Transport of Love : The Meghadūta of Kālidāsa* (Berkeley, 1976); the translations here are my own, based on the critical edition of S. K. De (New Delhi, 1957).

"A yakṣa careless in his office
had lost his honored rank.
His master cursed him to endure
a year in exile from his love.
He lived on Rāma's mountain
in the hermit groves—
trees cast soft shadows,
waters were pure from Sītā's bathing."

From this opening, an immediate correspondence is made between the demi-god's separation from his wife and Rāma's separation from Sītā; as in the *Kumārasambhava* Kālidāsa sets the subtle movements of erotic emotion in a timeless sacred landscape, full of ancient mythological reverberations and natural beauty. In the first part of the poem, the demi-god gives striking, erotically-charged descriptions of the cities and countryside on the northward route of the dark cloud. In the second part he evokes his own divine city on Mount Kailāsa and his sorrowing wife—he paints her charms in glowing colors, imagining her tossing on her couch, sleepless and wan through the watches of the night. Kālidāsa's profound intimacy with nature allows his imagination to interpenetrate with the landscape; his vision is expressed in simple and complex metaphors that relate the natural world in its seasonal transformations to the pain and joy of love. The desire of parted love is constantly straining for fulfilment in the cloud's sensual contacts with creatures of the forest and the court:

"Spying the first weak shoots
of golden green, valley flowers,
and plantains' tender buds
along the river banks,
scenting the rich fragrance
of forest earth,
deer will trace the path
of raindrops that you loose." [21]

Then:

"Yakṣas in the company of beautiful women
ascend to their palace balconies,

crystal-paved and studded
with reflections of flower-like stars.
They ascend to enjoy aphrodisiac wine
pressed from a wish-granting creeper
while drums gently beat
with the deep sounds of muffled thunder." [66]

The culminating possibility of resolution is expressed in the message verse which concretely equates the demi-god's wife with aspects of nature, but reminds her of her unique place in his heart :

"In twining creepers I see your body,
in eyes of startled does your glance,
in the moon, the glow and shadow of your cheek,
in the peacocks' crested plumes your hair,
in the flowing waters' quick ripples
the capricious frown on your brow—
but never in a single place, alas,
can I find an image in your likeness." [101]

In Kālidāsa's dramas, each prologue is a play-within-a-play that initiates a conventional pattern of structural oppositions; these have parallels in the prologues of Śūdraka and Viśākhadatta. They include contrasts between verse and prose, Sanskrit and Prākrit, authority (in the person of the director[1]) and common sense (in the person of the assistant or actress[2]), as well as solemnity and wit.[3] Each of the three Kālidāsa prologues is quoted, without the benediction to Śiva with which it begins.

MĀLAVIKĀGNIMITRA

Director [Looking in the direction of the wings—dressing room] : Māriṣa, come here !

1. The characteristics of the director (*sūtradhāra*) are given in the *Nāṭyaśāstra*, XXXV.65-74, 98.

2. The assistant director (*pāripārśvika*) is mentioned in *Nāṭyaśāstra* XXXV.74-75; the qualities of an actress (*nāṭakīyā*) are given in general terms and in terms of her role as courtesan or other heroine, XXXIV.25-70, 78-79; XXXV.81-87, 101.

3. See S. K. De, "Wit, Humour, and Satire in Sanskrit Literature," in *Aspects of Sanskrit Literature* (Calcutta, 1959), pp. 257-89.

Assistant : [Enters] Sir, I am here.

Director : The learned assembly has instructed me, on the occasion of the spring festival, to arrange for the performance of a play. It's called *Mālavikā and Agnimitra*—something put together by a certain Kālidāsa.

(So) Let the musical Prelude begin.

Assistant : What ? Not so fast ! Such an honor for the work of a contemporary poet—Kālidāsa—did you say ? Why do you ignore the compositions of Bhāsa, Saumilla and Kaviputra—established, well known ?

Director : Your remark does not survive examination. Listen :

> Not all is justified by the name of *old*;
> Nor is a new poem ne'er extolled.
> Wise men consider, and select the best of both;
> Only fools are in their thoughts to independence loath.

Assistant : Your Honor is, of course, the authority.

Director : Then hurry : for

> I can but wish to accomplish the assembly's command, already taken with bowed head; from now on I am the skillful servant of Queen Dhāriṇi.

[They leave.]

Translated by E. G.

VIKRAMORVAŚĪYA

Director : [Looking towards the backstage area] Māriṣa, come here, right away.

Assistant : [Entering] Sir, here I am.

Director : Māriṣa, the audience has frequently seen the plays of older poets. Today I will stage a really new play, called *Urvaśī Won by Valor*. Tell the cast the play is to be developed by serious efforts in the individual parts.

Assistant : As you order, sir. [Exits]

Director : As far as you good people out here now, I request

> From kindness towards servants
> Or esteem for the spirit of the house,

Listen with attentive minds
To this work of Kālidāsa.

[Offstage] : Gentlemen, help, help !

Director : [Listening] Oh ! What sound is this I hear in the sky interrupting my requests ? It is like female ospreys in distress. [Anxiously reflecting] Ah, now I know.

A maiden of the gods, born from Sage Narasakha's thigh,
Was returning after service to the Lord of Kailāsa,
On the way was taken captive by the gods' demon foes;
So this group of nymphs is crying pitifully.

[Exits]

Translated by D. G.

ABHIJÑĀNAŚĀKUNTALA

Director : [Facing the dressing room] Madam, if you have finished putting on your costume, please come here.

Actress : [Entering] Sir, I'm here. Please explain the role I am to play.

Director : Madam, our audience is well-educated. We shall present them with Kālidāsa's new drama called *The Ring of Memory and Śakuntalā*. We must be attentive to every detail of it.

Actress : You direct the performance so well, sir, that nothing can be criticized.

Director : [Smiling] Madam, I tell you the real truth :
I don't think performance technique is perfect unless the connoisseurs are satisfied.
So skillful experts train the mind without egotistical confidence.

Actress : You are right. Now direct me what to perform next.

Director : A song is the best way to engage the attention of the audience—this is the thing to do now.

Actress : What season shall I sing about ?

Director : Sing about the new summer season initiating its pleasures—right now :

Bathing in refreshing water
swept by scented forest winds,
then sleep in easy shadows,
makes each day end delightfully.

Actress : [Sings]

See how love-intoxicated women weave
wreaths from the soft tips of
pistils in śirīṣa flowers
constantly kissed by bumble bees.

Director : Madam, you sang to perfection. The mental state of this entire theatre is enchanted by your melody—the audience is like a painting. What play should we stage to content them ?

Actress : But didn't you just say that we should present a new play named *The Ring of Memory and Śakuntalā* ?

Director : Madam, I have regained consciousness. For the moment I forgot :

I was deeply captivated
by your charming melody in song—
as King Duṣyanta was captivated
by the swift deer he chased.

[While exiting]

Translated by B. S. M.

What is treated with seriousness in Kālidāsa's dramatic romances is parodied in the broadly-played prologue of Śūdraka's satiric comedy, which introduces the brāhmaṇa buffoon Maitreya babbling about his empty belly and his master's hard luck. Consonant with the tone and movement of the play, the buffoon sets the stage for the *Mṛcchakaṭika*. The prologue of Viśākhadatta's political drama, the *Mudrārākṣasa*, opens with an appropriately ambiguous dialogue between Śiva and Pārvatī, followed by the director's announcement and his dialogue with the actress, which is full of puns on the names of the Machiavellian minister Kauṭilya and his master, King Candragupta. Kauṭilya, presumed author of the *Arthaśāstra*, then appears on the stage in a state of preoccupation with the security of the kingdom he serves. The art of punning introduced here is central to the plays' plot—ambiguous words are the main device for effecting deception. Śūdraka's prologue contains a racy dialogue on festive preparation and fasting and Viśākhadatta's is filled with puns on the moon and its eclipse. The discussion between Kālidāsa's director and his assistant or the actress serves to establish the relevance of the play's action to some event with definite artistic significance and seasonal associations—a spring festival in the *Mālavikāgnimitra*, sun worship and the nymph's abduction by demons in the *Vikramorvaśīya*, sensual summer and evocative singing in the *Śākuntala*.

At the close of the prologue in the *Śākuntala* the director is so enchanted by the actress's song of summer describing love-intoxicated women weaving wreaths from the soft tips of pistils of śirīṣa flowers that he forgets his role and even forgets the name of the play, *The Ring of Memory and Śakuntalā* (*Abhijñānaśākuntala*). He says :

"I was deeply captivated
by your charming melody in song—
as King Duṣyanta was captivated
by the swift deer he chased." [I.5][1]

Then the king enters, chasing a deer, armed with bow and arrows, accompanied by his charioteer, who compares him with the god Śiva, who is Lord of the Animals (*Paśupati*). The king, intent on his prey, responds in an elaborate Sanskrit verse :

1. This is echoed in Act V.8-9 (Belvalkar V.5-6) in an exchange between the *vidūṣaka* and the king. Haṃsapadikā's singing reminds the king that he was once in love with her and its emotion calls up vague memories which produce longing in the king. In his commentary on the *Rasasūtra* of Bharata (*Abhinavabhāratī* I, pp. 279-88), Abhinavagupta cites the second verse of this little scene (*ramyāṇi vīkṣya*..., V. 9) : "Seeing moving sights, hearing soft sounds, even a man who is happy is filled with strange longing. Surely it is because he vaguely remembers, though he is not fully conscious, affections found in an earlier life that are fixed inside him through latent impressions they leave behind." (quoted in Masson and Patawardhan, *Śāntarasa*, pp. 57-58). Abhinava explains that Dushyanta's experience is an esthetic experience in which his memory is brought to life by hearing the music; the impressions bring to his esthetic attention intimations of a pleasure he formerly had—heightened now by distance and artistic evocation. The king says, "Why, on hearing the meaning of the song, am I filled with such deep sadness—I am not estranged from any one I love."

"There he is now
gracefully bending his neck back to glare
as the racing chariot runs him down,
his haunches folded into his chest
in fear of my falling arrow—
strewing the path with half-chewed bits
of grass from his limp and panting mouth.
Watch how high he leaps—bounding in air,
barely moving on earth." [I.7]

The chase continues and the movement builds in intensity until the king is about to kill the deer. At that moment he is interrupted by two hermits who identify the deer with the sage Kaṇva's hermitage, which is the home of Śakuntalā. The scene shows the king "at play", abandoning himself to the passion of the hunt, captivated by the graceful creature of nature he is committed to killing. The king's passion (*kāma*) threatens the calm of the forest and a creature of the hermitage it is his duty (*dharma*) to protect. But the hermits remind him of his duty and order is restored.[1] In his encounter with Śakuntalā, the king's passion and pursuit of his prey create a disturbance of such intensity that the lovers have to undergo a trial of painful separation before order is restored and Duṣyanta finds his son, Bharata, and his chaste wife.

Here, as in the other dramas of Kālidāsa, and in the *Mṛcchakaṭika*, the hero's adventure draws him away from strict adherence to his orthodox role as the embodiment of duty (*dharma*) through an encounter with a woman who is somehow unusual. Śakuntalā is the daughter of a nymph and a royal-sage, inappropriately living in a hermitage; Mālavikā is a princess in disguise as a serving maid; Urvaśī is a nymph kidnapped by demons and then cursed to earthly existence for falling in love with a mortal king; Vasantasenā is a courtesan who dares to fall in love with a brāhmaṇa. Through the union of the hero with a heroine who embodies the mystery of erotic passion through her affinities with

1. The scenes of the hunt and the hermitage heighten the sense of interpenetration between natural and social realms through action and dialogue as well as lyric poetry. The natural sphere is personified in Śakuntalā, the social sphere in King Duṣyanta.

nature (Śakuntalā) or her artistry in dance (Mālavikā, Urvaśī) and the arts of love (Vasantasenā), the conflict of duty and passion is exposed and resolved; their ideal balance is restored. The structural parallelism between these relationships of erotic passion in the romances and comedy and the relationship of the male rivals in Viśākhadatta's drama of political intrigue is striking. The shrewd ascetic Mauryan minister Kauṭilya, who is devoid of normal social ties and values, is paired with the passionately loyal Nanda minister Rākṣasa, whose defeat is engineered through his own loyalty in order to win him over to his rival's side. Just as the highly stylized dramas of love explore the conflicting demands of social duty and passionate love, the stylized drama of politics explores the conflicting demands of statecraft and social duty.[1]

In all the plays the relationship between the hero and the audience is made explicit since the hero himself is portrayed as a sensitive connoisseur of beauty and art. Duṣyanta appreciates painting; Agnimitra is a lover of dance, as is Purūravas and his heavenly counterpart Indra[2]; Cārudatta is a cultivated critic of music;[3] Rākṣasa continually shows his sympathy for worldly beauty. In the statements about the chaos of unrestrained passion, the classical dramatists are revealing their attitudes towards artistic creation—emotion (*bhāva*) without the tempering discipline of stylized performance (*nāṭyaśāstra*) and poetic ornamentation (*alaṅkāraśāstra*), would be, like passion or statecraft untempered by duty—transient and shallow. Intense esthetic experience (*rasa*), like deep love or political obsession, had to be disciplined.

The dramatic exposition of the conflict and complementarity of order and spontaneity is rooted in the ancient Indian concern

1. Greek tragedy, by contrast with Sanskrit drama, permits no resolution but death for its protagonist and no reconciliation between the survivor and the universe. In the Sanskrit plays, the lasting separation of Śakuntalā and Duṣyanta, the madness of Vikrama, the impending death of Cārudatta, and the suicide of Rākṣasa are all finally frustrated.

2. When the king lapses into love-madness, all nature dances for him, *Vikramorvaśiya* IV.12; cf. II.4, where the breeze makes a creeper dance. See Kapila Vatsyayan, *Classical Indian Dance in Literature and the Arts* (New Delhi, 1968), pp. 231-80.

3. *Mrcchakaṭika* III.3.-4; van Buitenen, *Two Plays*, pp. 83-84.

with reconciling life's multiple possibilities. These are codified in classical literature into a worldly triad of duty (*dharma*), material gain (*artha*), and pleasure (*kāma*), and a supermundane concern for liberation from worldly existence (*mokṣa*).[1] In the context of stylized dramatic relations, the resolution of social, psychological, and physical disharmonies was enacted, encoded in elaborate verses, dialogues, dance gestures, sounds, and signs of emotion. The concentration on subtle manifestations of changing erotic emotion, or passionate loyalty, can be appreciated today, even in translated versions, as paradigms for understanding the frustration and fulfilment of human desire and ambition in a complex world.

1. The relation between these concerns, known as the "pursuits of a person" (*puruṣārtha*), is widely debated in Indian literature of the classical period. The best debate is found in chapter II of *The Kāma Sūtra of Vātsyāyana*, translated by Sir Richard Burton (New York, 1962). The four form the organizing principle of the book *Classical India, Readings in World History*, Vol. 4, edited by W.H. McNeill and J. W. Sedlar (Oxford, 1969). See also Karl Potter, *Presuppositions of India's Philosophies* (New Jersey, 1963), pp. 5-11, for a succinct statement on these "four attitudes;" McKim Marriott, "The Feast of Love," in *Krishna : Myths, Rites, and Attitudes*, edited by Milton Singer (Honolulu, 1966), pp. 200-12; Richard Robinson, "Humanism versus Asceticism in Aśvaghoṣa and Kālidāsa," *Journal of South Asian Literature*, XII, nos. 3-4 (1977), pp. 1-10.

8

FROM CLASSICISM TO BHAKTI

A. K. RAMANUJAN AND NORMAN CUTLER

INTRODUCTION

IN this paper we attempt some notes toward a chapter of Indian poetry—the transformation of classical Tamil genres into the genres of bhakti. Early bhakti movements, whether devoted to Śiva or Viṣṇu, used whatever they found at hand, and changed whatever they used—Vedic and Upaniṣadic notions; mythologies; Buddhism; Jainism; conventions of Tamil and Sanskrit poetry; early Tamil conceptions of love, service, women, and kings; folk religion and folksong; the play of contrasts between Sanskrit and the mother-tongue.[1]

The Gupta period (fourth-sixth centuries A.D.) was not only the great classical period of Sanskrit literature, but, it also truly prepared the ground for the emergence of bhakti. For instance, the Gupta kings called themselves devotees of god (*bhāgavatas*). They took the names of the gods; put the figures of Lakṣmī, Viṣṇu's consort, and Varāha, his incarnation as a Boar, on their coins; made mythology a state concern, enlisting particularly Viṣṇu and his heroic incarnations for their politics. The Guptas sponsored Viṣṇu and believed almost that Viṣṇu sponsored the Gupta empire. Kṛṣṇa as a god with his own legends and cults emerged in the later Gupta period. Not only were the first Hindu temples built and the first Hindu icons sculpted during this period, but the official forms of Hindu mythology were set down in great syncretic texts called the *purāṇas*. By the fifth century A.D., Viṣṇu, Śiva, their families, minions, and enemies seem to have become as real as the human dynasties.

1. For an essay on this theme, see Ramanujan (1981).

In South India, the Pallavas had arrived by the sixth century A.D. Their inscriptions record the end of an era in South Indian history and the beginnings of a new one. In the culture of this time, the two "classicisms" of India, that of the Guptas and that of Tamil classical poetry, seem to have met. Of the various elements mentioned earlier, we shall study in detail only one—the *puṟam* tradition of Tamil heroic poetry—and the way its conventions were transformed by the Vaiṣṇava bhakti poets. After a few preliminary remarks on classical Tamil poetry, we shall look at one of the earliest poems on Viṣṇu in the *Paripāṭal*, a late classical anthology (fifth-sixth century A.D.); we then focus upon the poetry of the first three *āḻvārs* (*c.* sixth century A.D.) before we examine the work of Nammāḻvār (*c.* eighth-ninth century A.D.), the greatest of the Vaiṣṇava poet-saints; we close with remarks on the use of classical Tamil models in an influential theological work, the *Ācārya Hṛdayam* (*c.* thirteenth century A.D.). We have narrowed our story to early Tamil Vaiṣṇava poetry and to only one element of the classical Tamil heritage. Similar studies can be undertaken for other Tamil or Sanskritic elements and other poets (Śaiva or Vaiṣṇava) of the bhakti tradition.[1]

I. Classical Tamil Poetry[2]

A few elementary remarks (or reminders) about classical Tamil genres may be appropriate at the outset. *Caṅkam* or classical Tamil poetry is classified by theme into two kinds : poems of *akam* (the "inner part" or the Interior) and poems of *puṟam* (the "outer part" or the Exterior). *Akam* poems are love poems; *puṟam* poems are all other kinds of poems, usually about good and evil, action, community, kingdom; it is the "heroic" and "public" poetry of the ancient Tamils, celebrating the ferocity and glory of kings, lamenting the death of heroes, the poverty of poets. Elegies, panegyrics, invectives, poems on wars and tragic events are *puṟam* poems.

The *Tolkāppiyam*, the most important expository text for the understanding of early Tamil poetry, distinguishes *akam* and

1. For a more comprehensive study of Tamil bhakti poetry and its constitutory elements, see Cutler (1980).

2. For detailed studies and translations, see Ramanujan (1967).

puṟam conventions as follows : "In the five phases of *akam*, no names of persons should be mentioned. Particular names are appropriate only in *puṟam* poetry." The dramatis personae for *akam* are idealized types, such as chieftains representing clans and classes, rather than historical persons. Similarly, landscapes are more important than particular places.

The love of man and woman is taken as the ideal expression of the "inner world", and *akam* poetry is synonymous with love poetry in the Tamil tradition. Love in all its variety—love in separation and in union, before and after marriage, in chastity and in betrayal—is the theme of *akam*. "There are seven types of love, of which the first is *kaikkiḷai*, unrequited love, and the last is *peruntiṇai*, mismatched love." Neither of these extremes is the proper subject of *akam* poetry. The middle five represent well-matched love and divide its course, now smooth, now rough, into five kinds, moods, or phases : union, patient waiting, anxious waiting, separation from parents or lover, infidelity. Each mood or phase is paired with a landscape, which provides the imagery : hillside, wooded pastoral valley, seashore, wasteland, and fertile fields. The bhakti poets, however, "revived" the *kaikkiḷai* genre in poems that express the anguish of the devotee who is separated from god.

Unlike *akam* poems, *puṟam* poems may mention explicitly the names of kings and poets and places. The poem is placed in a real society and given a context of real history. The *Tolkāppiyam* also divided the subject matter of *puṟam* poetry into seven types, but in this case all seven are of equal standing. The type called *pāṭāṇ* (elegy, praise for heroes, for gifts, invective) was very popular among classical *puṟam* poets, and somewhat transformed, it was equally popular among bhakti poets. Poeticians regarded *pāṭāṇ* as the *puṟam* equivalent of *kaikkiḷai* in *akam* poetry which also is well represented in the poetry of the saints.

II. THE HYMNS TO TIRUMĀL IN *Paripāṭal*

By and large the poets of the *caṅkam* anthologies did not compose poems on religious themes. Though we find references to deities and we catch glimpses of ritual practices, rarely do these occur as the principal subject of a *caṅkam* poem.[1] However,

1. As Hart has shown, the early Tamil poems contain a wealth of

there are two notable exceptions to this generalization. The *Tirumurukāṟṟuppaṭai*, one of the ten long songs, is a poem in honor of Murukaṉ, the Tamil god who, by the time of this poem, had coalesced with the Sanskrit Skanda, the warrior-son of Śiva and Pārvatī. This poem is composed in the form of an *āṟṟuppaṭai*, a genre which accounts for three other long poems among the ten (*Ciṟupāṇāṟṟuppaṭai, Perumpāṇāṟṟuppaṭai* and *Porunārāṟṟuppaṭai*) and for a number of shorter poems included in the *puṟam* anthologies. The setting of an *āṟṟuppaṭai* is a meeting between two bards, who apparently depended on the patronage of generous kings and chieftains for their survival. In an *āṟṟuppaṭai* one bard praises the liberality of his patron to the other and urges him to seek his livelihood by visiting the court of this generous ruler. In *Tirumurukāṟṟuppaṭai* the roles of the two bards are taken by an initiate in Murukaṉ's cult and a neophyte. The god is praised as a patron-king would be in other poems of this genre, but the gift he offers his suppliants is personal salvation instead of the food and wealth kings usually gave to bards who sought their patronage. In the eleventh century A.D., *Tirumurukāṟṟup-paṭai* was incorporated into the eleventh *Tirumuṟai* ("sacred arrangement") of the Tamil Śaivite canon.

We also find some moving devotional poems in *Paripāṭal*, one of the later *caṅkam* anthologies. Originally, this anthology, which takes its name from a poetic meter, included seventy poems dedicated to the gods Tirumāl (Viṣṇu), Cevvēḷ (Murukaṉ) and the goddess, the river Vaiyai (presently known as Vaikai) and the ancient Pāṇṭiya capital Maturai which is situated on its banks, Only twenty four poems have survived however : seven to Tirumāl, eight to Cevvēḷ, and nine of the Vaiyai poems. The seven poems to Tirumāl included in *Paripāṭal* are the only explicitly Vaiṣṇavite poems in the *caṅkam* corpus. Critics have suggested that *Paripāṭal*, *Tirumurukāṟṟuppaṭai* and *Kalittokai*, an anthology of *akam* poems in the *kali* meter, belong to a later era than most of the other poems of the classical corpus. Zvelebil suggests 400-550 A.D. as a probable date for *Paripāṭal* (Zvelebil, 1974 : 50).

According to the *Tolkāppiyam*, love (*kāmam*) is the proper

information concerning ancient Tamil conceptions of the sacred (Hart, 1975; especially pp. 21-50). But they are not religious poems.

subject for poems composed in the *paripāṭal* meter, but in reality the poems of *Paripāṭal* deal with both *akam* and *puṟam* themes. The theme of love, treated in accord with the rules governing *akam* poetry, appears primarily in the Vaiyai poems. Many *puṟam* elements appear in the poems dedicated to the gods Cevvēḷ and Tirumāl, but there they have been transformed to serve poetry which is simultaneously devotional and heroic.

The panegyric genre is the most visible feature shared by the Tirumāl poems in *Paripāṭal* and *puṟam* poetry. Somewhat artificially, the *Tolkāppiyam* subdivides the *puṟam* universe into seven sub-genres called *tiṇai*, and one of these, *pāṭāṇ tiṇai*, is the genre of "praise". A large portion of the poems included in the *puṟam* anthologies are classified under the heading *pāṭāṇ*, and even *puṟam* poems classified under other *tiṇai* often include words of praise for a warrior or a king. The *puṟam* world is a world of kings, chieftains, and heroic warriors. The classical poets, therefore, praised their patrons for their valor in combat and for their virtuous rule. Most of the Tirumāl poems in *Paripāṭal* are poems of praise for the god, and they display a number of the specific thematic "situations" or *tuṟai* which are characteristic of *puṟam* poetry. Thirteen of the eighteen *tuṟai* which are treated in the *puṟam* anthology *Patiṟṟuppattu* (Kailasapathy, 1968 :195-96) are in one way or another related to the theme of praise, and many have direct counterparts in the poems to *Tirumāl*. Following is a list of the thirteen :

centuṟaippāṭāṇ pāṭṭu — poem in praise of hero's fame : in praise of might, mien, and glory.

iyaṉmoḻi vāḻttu — theme of extolling a hero by attributing to him all the noble deeds of his ancestors.

vañcittuṟaippāṭāṇ pāṭṭu — poem in praise of invading warriors : king's wrath and praise of him.

nāṭu vāḻttu — blessing the country : in praise of wealth and abundance in the land of the hero.

vākaittuṟaippāṭāṇ pāṭṭu — Praise of victorious hero : victor wears *vākai* flowers and rejoices over vanquished.

kaḷavaḻi — battle-ground : the theme of a minstrel praising the spoils of a victorious king in war.

vākai — in praise of conqueror : the bard exalts victory leading to liberality.

viṟalivāṟṟuppaṭai — directing a danseuse : directing a danseuse to a generous patron.

kāṭci vāḻttu — praise of a sight : reaction on seeing either a great hero or a hero-stone, etc.

pariciṟṟuṟaippāṭāṇ pāṭṭu — praise of hero and request for largesse.

pāṇāṟṟuppaṭai — directing a minstrel (lutanist) : usually one minstrel directing another to a generous patron.

mullai — hero's victory : praise of the hero including reference to his wife.

kāvaṇmullai — praise of rule : extolling king's rule for providing shelter and security.

We can almost say that all we need do is substitute the word "god" wherever the words "hero" or "king" occur in this list, and we end up with a list of thematic elements in the *Paripāṭal* hymns to Tirumāl. Themes such as praise of a hero's (god's) fame, praise of a victorious hero (god), and praise of a king (god) for providing shelter and security fall into this category. In other instances we find elements in the poems to Tirumāl which are analogues of *puṟam* elements. For example, *iyaṇmoḻi vāḻttu* is defined as the situation in which the hero is praised by attributing to him all the noble deeds of his ancestors. References to the heroic deeds Tirumāl-Viṣṇu performed in his various *avatāras* function in much the same way in *Paripāṭal*. The god's *avatāras*, if not an ancestral lineage in a literal sense, can be viewed as such in a metaphoric sense. Here the noble deeds of the god's "ancestors" literally *are* his own deeds : he sets his own precedents.

In his excellent study of *puṟam* poetry Kailasapathy analyzes a panegyric poem from one of the classical anthologies and identifies nine thematic units in the poem which, he tells his reader, "are traditional and typical of the entire bardic poetry" (Kailasapathy, 1968 : 208). Kailasapathy's prose translation of the poem and his nine thematic units are given below :

"Worthy scion of those kings who ruled the whole world with undisputed wheel of command ! The kingdom of your ancestors extended from the Comorin river in the south to the high mountain Himālayas in the north and from sea to sea in east and west. Their subjects wheresoever they lived—in hill, mountain, forest, or town—unanimously praised them. They eschewed evil and their sceptre was stainless; they took only what was due and were just and impartial. O warlike lord of Toṇṭi ! Your town is fenced by mountain; the white sand in its broad beaches shines like moonlight. There grow tall palms laden with bunches of coconuts. There are also extensive fields; and in the back waters flowers blossom which are like bright red flames. Even as a mighty and proud elephant contemptuous of the pit-hole whose mouth is cunningly overlaid, impetuously falls into it, and with its full-grown tusks gores the sides, fills it up with earth it has dug up, steps over and joins its loving herd, so you escaped because of your irresistible strength and now remain in your realm and among your kindred, who are extremely happy. Those defeated kings whose lands and precious jewels you captured, now feel that they could only regain them if they gained your sympathy; those who retook their lost possessions (while you were in captivity) now live in mortal fear of having provoked your fury; they feel certain of losing their forts surrounded by moats, encircling woods and thick walls atop of which fly their tall banners. Consequently, all these alien kings hasten to serve you. Such is your might and I come to praise it. O great one ! The innumerable shields of your warriors vie with the mass of rain-clouds; large swarms of bees settle on your war-elephants, mistaking them for huge hills. Your large army—the nightmare of your foes—is vast as the ocean upon which the clouds drink; the sound of your war-drums resembles the roar of thunder which makes venomous snakes tremble and hand down their hooded heads. But great above all is your unlimited munificence." (*Puṟanāṉūṟu* 17)

Thematic units

1. The extent of the king's domain.
2. Toṇṭi, and its description.
3. Some aspects of the king's benign rule
4. Reference to his illustrious ancestors.
5. The simile of an elephant escaping from a pit-trap.
6. The reactions of the king's foes.

7. Description of forts.
8. Description of the king's troops, elephants, etc.
9. His boundless munificence.

If we were to similarly analyze the hymns to Tirumāl in *Paripāṭal*, we should find that they display many of the same thematic units. In *Paripāṭal* 2 (translated by AKR), which appears as an addendum to this paper, we find at least strong hints of six of Kailasapathy's thematic units. The following description of Tirumāl's chest appears in the *Paripāṭal* poem :

"Wearing jewels
many-colored as rainbows
bent across the high heavens
on your chest, itself a jewel studded
with pearls, you always wear
the Red Goddess
as the moon
his shadow."

Immediately following this passage is another that makes "reference to the king's ancestors".

"You as the Boar
with white tusks, sharp and spotted,
washed by the rising waves, lifted
and wed the Earth-maiden
so not a spot of earth
is ever troubled by the sea."

The recital of the god's mythic history can be regarded as a transformation of the thematic unit which appears in the *puṟam* poem. Here the god's ancestor, the Boar, is his own *avatāra*.

Following this is an extraordinary depiction of Viṣṇu in battle which brings to mind Kailasapathy's thematic units, the reactions of the king's foes, and description of the king's troops, elephants, etc. (Here it is not troops, but Tirumāl's potent weapons, the conch and the discus, that are described.)

"O lord fierce in war,
the loud conch you hold
sounds like thunder

to the enemy
rising as one man,
unafraid in anger,

rising like a hurricane
to join battle;

banners break and fall,
ears go deaf,
crowns shiver on their heads,
and the earth loosens
under their feet

at the thunder of your conch.

O lord fierce in war,
the discus in your hand
cuts the sweet lives
of enemies;

heads fall and roll
wreaths and all;
their stand lost,
like the tens of thousands
of bunches
on the heads of tall black palmyra-trees
not stripped yet
of root, branch,
frond or young fruit,
falling to the earth
all at once;

not one head
standing on its body,
beheaded all at one stroke, they
gather, roll, split,
come together and roll apart,
and lie dead at last
in a mire of blood.

That discus
that kills at one stroke;
Death is its body,
its color the flame

of bright fire
when gold burns in it."

The similarity between this battle scene and another depicted in a poem from the *puṟam* anthology *Patiṟṟuppattu* is truly remarkable :

"beheaded bodies, leftovers,
dance about
before they fall
to the ground;

blood glows,
like the sky before nightfall,
in the red center
of the battlefield"

from *Patiṟṟuppattu* 35
(trans. AKR)

The *Paripāṭal* hymn to the Tirumāl (*Paripāṭal* 2) celebrates the "king's" benign rule and his boundless munificence.

"If one looks for your magnificent patience
it's there, wide as earth;

your grace,
a sky of rain-cloud
fulfilling everyone".

And in another passage,

"As soon as your heart
thought of ambrosia,
food of the gods,
the deathless ones received
a life without age,
a peace without end".

The poet's metaphorical description of Tirumāl's grace as "a sky of rain-cloud" has many parallels in *puṟam* poetry where a king's generosity is frequently compared with the rain.

"It was as if rain showered down
with thunder whose voice makes men tremble,

nourishing the forest
whose grass is burnt by the bright rays of the savage sun :
he gave rice and ghee and spicy meat."

from *Puranāṉūṟu* 160
(trans. Hart, 1979),

The association between generosity and rain is a strong one, especially in the Tamil area where, except for the three months of the unpredictable monsoon, water can be scarce. In the hymn to Tirumāl the metaphor is significant in yet another way, for Tirumāl's complexion is blue-black; he is often said to resemble a storm cloud. Sometimes he is even said to *be* the cloud that sends life-giving rain.[1] *Māl* or *māvōṉ*, literally means "the dark one." In Sanskrit he is *nīlameghaśyāma*, "dark as a black cloud."

Conspicuously absent from *Paripāṭal* 2 are references to sacred places which could be considered the counterparts of the king's domain, his capital and his forts in *puṟam* poetry. But these elements appear in other Vaiṣṇavite poems of *Paripāṭal*. The fifteenth song is a eulogy of Māliruṅkuṉṟam, "Māl's dark hill," which is located about twelve miles north of Maturai and even today is the site of a popular Viṣṇu temple known by the name

1. For instance, *Tiruppāvai*, a very popular bhakti poem by the woman poet Āṇṭāḷ, identifies Kṛṣṇa with a rain-cloud :

"Kaṇṇaṉ, Storm cloud,
Don't hide !
Black as the Era's First One,
You dive into the ocean;
You scoop up its waters
And raise peals of thunder.
Your lightning flashes
Like the cakra held by Padmanābha,
The Lord with shoulders renowned for their beauty.
And you thunder like his conch.
Send your rains right away
Like a shower of arrows from the Śāraṅga-bow,
So the world will prosper.
We too rejoice
And bathe in *mārkaḻi* month.
Accept, Consider our vow."

Tiruppāvai 4
(trans. NC)

Aḻakar Kōyil.[1] Unlike the other Tirumāl poems which are hymns of praise addressed directly to the god, in *Paripāṭal* 15 the poet extols the glories of Māliruṅkuṉṟam to a human audience.

"This is the place where the lord
who wears garments of gold
stays with his brother
    like a halo of cool sunbeams
    shimmering around a core of darkness :

Think about it, mortals,
and listen—
    fragrant blue lilies
    blossom in all its ponds,
    the branches of *aśoka* trees
    growing at their edge
    are covered with blossoms,

    the colors of green fruit
    and ripe fruit
    play against one another
    and bright clusters of buds
    on the *kino* trees
    burst into bloom :

    the beauty of this place
    is like the Black God himself.
You people
who have never gone there to worship,

gaze on that mountain and bow down :

the name Iruṅkuṉṟam
has spread far and wide,
on this great, bustling earth
it boasts fame in ages past

1. Aḻakar, the name Viṣṇu bears in this temple, means "the beautiful one". As Cuntarar, Śiva bears a name with identical meaning in the great Mīnākṣī-Cuntareśvarar temple of Maturai.

for it is the home of the dear lord
who eradicates delusions
for people who fill their eyes
with his image."

from *Paripāṭal* 15
(trans. NC)[1]

The poet praises Māliruṅkuṉṟam, the most praiseworthy of all the earth's mountains, because it is the god's abode on earth. (The poem begins with an introduction to the many great mountains on earth, and then Māl's mountain is singled out as the most dazzling of all.) The eulogy of Tirumāl's locale reminds us of the *puṟam* poet's eulogy of his patron's country and its capital city. In particulars, however, this loving picture of Māl's dark mountain is more like an *akam* landscape. The *puṟam* poet does not usually linger over descriptions of nature. For him, the fertility of the countryside is useful primarily as a reflection of a hero's glory. But careful description of natural scenes lies at the very heart of *akam* poetry. Its interior drama of anonymous characters is bodied forth in the details of the scene and is set not in particular places, but in landscapes—the mountains, the forest, the seashore, the cultivated countryside, and the desert. Here, every landscape is a mood. In *Paripāṭal* 15 the poet evokes a mountain landscape by describing mountain pools and flowering plants (in the passage cited above), waterfalls and birds (in other passages), much as an *akam* poet would. However, here natural detail is not meticulously coordinated with the human psyche as in *akam* poetry. It is probably fair to say that Māl's dark mountain stands somewhere between the specific locales of *puṟam* poetry and an *akam* landscape.

The thematic units which link the Tirumāl poems in *Paripāṭal* with other classical Tamil poems do not in themselves constitute a complete profile of these early Tamil hymns to Viṣṇu. The authors of these poems relied a great deal upon classical Tamil sources, but they also received influences from other quarters. *Paripāṭal* 2 opens with a stirring account of the earth's creation which, but for its language, could have been

1. In these translations from *Paripāṭal* I am indebted to François Gros' French renderings (Gros, 1968).

lifted straight out of a purāṇic cosmology. Later in the same poem we come upon a very striking passage which, detail for detail, identifies Tirumāl with the Vedic sacrifice. In these poems we also find descriptions of Tirumāl which are addressed to the god himself. While the *puṟam* panegyric is the Tamil prototype for this element in the *Paripāṭal* hymns, one is also reminded of Vedic hymns where descriptions *of* gods are addressed *to* the gods themselves. In *Paripāṭal* such descriptions can be divided into two kinds. The first kind is physical and iconographic, as in *Paripāṭal* 1 where the poet salutes Tirumāl :

"Lord with eyes the color of flowers
red as fire,
with body the color
of an open *pūvai* blossom,

Tiru rests upon your chest
and fulfills her desire,
your chest adorned
with a sparkling jewel,

clothed in garments of gold,
your body is like a dark mountain
surrounded by flames"

from *Paripāṭal* 1
(trans. NC)

The second kind, quasi-philosophical descriptions of the god, closely follows an Upaniṣadic pattern. Here philosophy is grounded not so much in logic as in esthetics; it is both idea and experience, a description of the lord's ubiquity as well as its celebration :

"Your heat and your radiance are found in the sun,
your coolness and your beauty in the moon,
your graciousness and your generosity are found in the clouds,
your protective nature and your patience in the earth,
your fragrance and your brightness are found in the *pūvai* blossom,
the form you manifest and your expansiveness appear in the waters,
your shape and the sound of your voice in the sky :

all these things—near, far, in-between
  and everything else,
detach themselves from you, the source of protection,
and rest in your embrace."

from *Paripāṭal* 4
(trans. NC)

Such passages show that the authors of the *Paripāṭal* poems, perhaps the earliest devotional poems in Tamil, were heirs to two classicisms. In these poems Vedic and Tamil bardic traditions meet and interweave to form a distinctly Tamil devotional poetry.

III. PUṞAM INFLUENCES IN THE POETRY OF THE "FIRST THREE ĀḺVĀRS."

The hymns to Tirumāl in *Paripāṭal* are devotional poems, but they are not sacred poems in the same sense as the poetry of the twelve Tamil Vaiṣṇavite saints, the *āḻvārs*. *Paripāṭal* certainly extends the classical literary universe into the realm of devotion—but its classical associations have always overshadowed their devotional subject in the minds of Tamil audiences. Proof of this is easy enough to find : *Paripāṭal* is counted as one of the eight anthologies of *caṅkam* poetry, and the hymns to Tirumāl were not canonized with the *āḻvārs*' poems.[1]

By most estimates the first three *āḻvārs*, Poykai, Pūtam and Pēy, who are collectively called "the first three" (*mutal mūvar*) in Tamil, lived some time during the sixth century A.D. They, therefore, lived not much later than the *Paripāṭal* poets, but their poems are very different in form and effect. Each of the early *āḻvārs* is credited with an *antāti* of one hundred verses in the *veṇpā* meter, a meter which was also used by the authors of the didactic works often grouped together as the *patiṉeṇ kīḻkaṇṇakku*, the so-called "eighteen minor works" which date from about the same time. When we turn to the poems of the first three *āḻvārs* after reading *caṅkam* poetry, we immediately sense that we are dealing with a different poetic sensibility. *Caṅkam* poetry is, by this time, a classical literature, part of a poet's learning. Only an audience well-schooled in classical

1. Even though they are not canonized, the *Paripāṭal* poems are clearly related to the later *āḻvār* poems. They share the Viṣṇu mythology, the sacred geography, the motifs, the ideas. See Damodaran, 1978 : pp. 262-67.

literary conventions could have understood these poems composed in a language far from the language of everyday speech. The bhakti poets, on the other hand, used an idiom which must have been close to the Tamil spoken during their time; they make a point of it. The work which has been accorded the highest place of honor in Tamil Vaiṣṇavite canonical literature, Nammāḻvār's *Tiruvāymoḻi*, literally means "the sacred spoken word" (*vāy*, 'mouth'+*moḻi*, 'language'). Māṇikkavācakar's *Tiruvācakam*, a Śaivite text of equal renown, bears a name derived from Sanskrit *vāc*, 'speech'. Bhakti poetry is also poetry for performance. Tamil Vaiṣṇavites and Śaivites regularly recite the hymns of the saints in their homes, and at least since the tenth century A.D. the hymns have been recited in the major temples of Tamilnadu (Nilakanta Sastri, 1955 : 637, 639).

Unlike classical poetry, the poetry of the saints is a "personal" poetry, though they too use personae or masks. In *akam* poetry the personality of the poet is almost completely effaced by internal narrators and a conventional poetic vocabulary. Only in *puṟam* poems we often understand the narrating voice to be the poet's own, but still only a few of these poets ever tell us much about themselves in their poems.[1] Even the *Paripāṭal* hymns to Tirumāl, which follow the panegyric model, tell us a great deal about the god, but not much about the poet who eulogizes him. The early *āḻvārs* were more inclined to leave traces of their personalities in their poems, even while following panegyric models. One *āḻvār* is not like another.

As Zvelebil points out (Zvelebil, 1974 : 93-94), the *pāṭāṇ* genre, or poem of praise, continued to be an influential model for the saint-poets. He condenses the parallels between the classical panegyric and the poetry of the saints in the following scheme :

1. Zvelebil cites a story from the *Tiruviḷaiyāṭal Purāṇam* (51 : pp. 30-37) (seventeenth century) which makes this point in an amusing manner.

"The forty-eight poet-academicians in Maturai composed innumerable beautiful poems which, however, were so much alike that those who wanted to comment upon them could not ascribe them to individual poets, unable to recognize any difference (*veṟupāṭu aṟiyātu*) and being much amazed (*viyantu*); not only that, the poets themselves could not recognize their own poems, and were bewildered. It was Śiva-Sundara himself who appeared in their midst in the guise of a poet, sorted out their works, and accepted the chair of the president of the Academy" (Zvelebil, 1974 : p. 43).

"The bardic poet's praise of the patron; he asks for gifts; the patron grants him gold etc.; rarely, but still, the poet scolds the patron for his wretched and miserly attitude.	The poet-saint's praise of Śiva or Viṣṇu; he asks for knowledge of himself, and of God; God grants him knowledge, grace, redemption; rarely, but still, the saint blames and reproaches God for his misfortunes."

This scheme is a useful one, for it relates two bodies of Tamil poetry, but the saints' poems do not all fit neatly into this scheme. We find in the poetry of the saints many poems that are not addressed directly to a god. Not all *puṟam* poems are addressed to a patron. Often the bhakti poet speaks about his lord to an audience who is either explicitly invoked or whose presence must be inferred. The voice of the saint is the pivot on which these poems turn, and this voice is given flesh and blood in the saint's sacred biography which is as well known as his poems : Tamil Vaiṣṇavites and Śaivites hear the life-stories of the saints in their poems.[1] In this poem by Poykai, for example, we overhear the poet talking to Viṣṇu about the best-known event in the composite biography of the first three *āḻvārs*.[2]

1. The poets of the *puṟam* poems, like Kapilar or Auvai, often have legendary biographies, like the saints, which are considered explanatory of the poems. See Kapilar's poems on his friend and patron, Pāri. There are fewer examples of this matching of poems with poet's life in the *akam* poems : see index of poets in Ramanujan (1967), especially the note on Ātimanti (p. 120).

2. In this poem Poykai speaks of an experience which ended in a revelation. The three early *āḻvārs* did not know one another until Viṣṇu simultaneously induced in each a desire to visit his shrine at Tirukkōvalūr (Kōval). On the night of his arrival, Poykai sought shelter in the small antechamber of a *ṛṣi*'s *āśrama*. Not much later Pūtam and then Pēy arrived with the same intention, and the three devotees gladly shared the small room though they had to stand to fit inside. As if to add to their discomfort, Viṣṇu enveloped Tirukkōvalūr in a blanket of storm clouds so thick the three saints couldn't even see one another, though they stood only inches apart. Huddled together, the saints began to feel more and more crowded for no apparent reason. Finally, in a flash of insight, they realized that Viṣṇu too had joined them in the tiny room, and they at once were able to see by the light of the lord's grace.

"Lord who lifted a mountain to block the driving rain,

in this beloved town of Kōval
you neither departed through the gate
nor came inside,
but chose to stay, together with your goddess,
here in this entrance hall."

Mutal Tiruvantāti 86
(trans. NC)

Poykai, Pūtam and Pēy were early voices in the evolution of a personal poetry of devotion in Tamil. If *Paripāṭal* represents an extension of classical Tamil poetry, the *antātis* of the first three *āḻvārs* represent the beginning of a new kind of Tamil poetry. Not surprisingly, the classical influences are not pervasive in the poems of the early Vaiṣṇavite saints. Nevertheless, many verses display or extend classical motifs and techniques. Pēy envisions Viṣṇu as a mighty warrior who looks after his devotees' well-being :

"The victorious lord
who wields eight invincible weapons,
the eight-armed lord
who aimed his wheel
and cut down the crocodile-monster in the pond[1]

is our refuge
down to the soles of his feet."

Mūṉṟām Tiruvantāti 99
(trans. NC)[2]

Poykai's invocation of Viṣṇu in the first line alludes to the story in which Kṛṣṇa lifted the mountain Govardhana to protect the cowherds from a downpour sent by the jealous god Indra. The mythological allusion is an ironic complement to the biographical event. In the myth Kṛṣṇa shelters the cowherds from the rain sent by Indra. In the biographical story Viṣṇu inundates Tirukkōvalūr, and his devotees are forced to run for shelter.

1. "The eight-armed lord" is a reference to Viṣṇu in his form Aṣṭabhujākāra. This poem alludes to the story of Gajendra, the elephant, who was a devotee of Viṣṇu. When Gajendra was gathering lotus blossoms to offer the god, a crocodile grabbed him by the leg and began to pull him into the pond. Gajendra called to Viṣṇu for help, and the god saved him.

2. All translations of poems by the first three *āḻvārs* and by Nammāḻvār credited to NC in the paper appear in Cutler (1980), and the *Tiruppāvai* translation found in note 4 appears in Cutler (1979). All translations of Nammāḻvār's poetry by AKR appear in Ramanujan (1981).

Whenever Viṣṇu is invoked as protector and hero we detect resonances of the bards' eulogies of their patrons. Here the heroic mode has become a signifier for devotion, as in this poem by Poykai :

"My mouth praises no one but the lord,
my hands worship no one but the lord
who bounded over the world,
my ears hear no name, my eyes see no form
but the name and form of the lord
who made a meal of the poison he sucked
from the she-devil's breast."

Mutal Tiruvantāti 11
(trans. NC)

The *caṅkam* bard commends himself to the liberality of his patron, and, similarly, Poykai implies that he gives himself over to Viṣṇu without reservation. We sense that Viṣṇu is more than capable of protecting Poykai from his enemies. After all, didn't he destroy the she-demon Pūtanāsura when he was only an infant ? For the *ālvār* devotion takes the form of incessant contemplation of Viṣṇu's heroism.

IV Puṟam Elements in Nammāḻvār's poetry

Nammāḻvār's position in Tamil Vaiṣṇavite tradition is a special one. The Śrīvaiṣṇava *ācāryas* equated his Tamil poems with the four Vedas, and the poems of the other *āḻvārs* with the "limbs" (*aṅgas*) and "subsidiary limbs" (*upāṅgas*) of the Vedas. The other *āḻvārs* are described as *aṅgas* for Nammāḻvār who is their *aṅgī* (one who possesses limbs). Tradition also accords Nammāḻvār a critical role in the story of the canonization of the *āḻvārs*' hymns.[1] The personal voice which we begin to hear in

1. When Nāthamuni, the first Śrīvaiṣṇava *ācārya* (tenth century A.D.), happened to hear a group of Vaiṣṇavite devotees singing a few verses by Nammāḻvār, he was so taken with these hymns that he resolved to learn everything the saint had composed. Unfortunately, at this time there was no one who knew more than the few verses Nāthamuni had heard, but still he remained firm in his resolve. After he recited the hymn of praise for Nammāḻvār, composed by the saint Maturakavi, twelve thousand times, Nammāḻvār came to him in a yogic vision and taught him not only his own compositions, but the hymns of all the other *āḻvārs*. Nāthamuni later

the compositions of the early saints comes to maturity in Nammāḻvār's poems.

Nammāḻvār was a prolific poet—his greatest work *Tiruvāymoḻi* alone contains over one thousand verses—and thus there is considerable scope for variety in the saint's poems. Multiple strands of influence come together in Nammāḻvār's poetry, as in the bhakti tradition as a whole. In *Tiruvāymoḻi* love poetry, mythology, philosophy and heroic poetry alternate with one another and blend together in new ways. A great deal has already been written about Nammāḻvār's use of *akam* conventions,[1] but commentators on *Tiruvāymoḻi* and Nammāḻvār's other poems have not paid nearly as much attention to the significant *puṟam* elements in the saint's poetry. The following poem about Rāma's conquest of Laṅkā is as graphic as the battle scene from *Paripāṭal* 2 and draws as freely on the imagery of battle :

"Crowding each other
face to face
as the arrows sang
and jangled

demon-carcasses fell
in hundreds

rolled over
like hills
the sea stained with blood
backed upstream into the rivers

arranged these in their canonical form and instituted their recitation in the temple of Śrīraṅkam.

By the estimates of most modern scholars, Nammāḻvār and his disciple Maturakavi were the last of the twelve *āḻvārs*, and they lived sometime during the ninth century A.D. However, Śrīvaiṣṇava tradition places Nammāḻvār fifth in the chronology of the *āḻvārs*, after Poykai, Pūtam, Pēy and Tirumaḻicai, and consequently dating of the saint's lifetime has not been unanimous.

1. Two recent works which attend to *akam* elements in Nammāḻvār's poetry are Srinivasa Raghavan (1975) and Damodaran (1978). Zvelebil (1973 and 1974) and Varadarajan (1972) take a longer view of the *akam*/bhakti connections in Tamil literary history. For a more general account of love symbolism in Indian bhakti, see Vaudeville (1962).

when our Lord and Father
ravaged the island

and left it
a heap of ash"

Tiruvāymoḻi 7.4.7
(trans. AKR)

Nammāḻvār also eulogized places sacred to Viṣṇu in a manner that calls to mind the *puṟam* poets' songs of praise for the lands ruled by their patrons. The saint composed a set of ten verses in praise of Viṣṇu's abode at Māliruñcōlai ("Māl's dark grove"), the same site near Maturai known to the *Paripāṭal* poet as Māliruṅkuṉṟam ("Māl's dark hill"). Nammāḻvār may well have composed these verses as a bhakti equivalent to the classical *āṟṟuppaṭai* or "guide to patrons".

"Casting off the strong bonds of deeds,
wandering in search of salvation,
reaching the magnificent temple
on the mountain, veiled in clouds
at Māl's dark grove,
home of the lord who lifted a great mountain,

that is real strength.

To gather strength,
turn from evil deeds
and travel to the temple
on the mountain, surrounded by clear pools
at Māl's dark grove,
the temple of the lord
who upholds virtue with his wheel,

that is real skill."

Tiruvāymoḻi 2.10.4, 2.10.5
(trans. NC)

Here Nammāḻvār encourages his audience to travel to Viṣṇu's temple at Māliruñcōlai, much as the *puṟam* poet urges other bards to travel to the court of his patron where they are sure to receive food and other gifts. But the bhakti poems differ from the classical *āṟṟuppaṭai* in at least one important way. An *āṟṟuppaṭai* documents a conversation between two bards at a specific point in time, and the noble deeds of the patron-hero are deemed historical events. Nammāḻvār's poems celebrate a god-hero who performs noble deeds in mythic time, no less real than historic time; and because they do not particularize their audience, they are immediately relevant to all audiences. The virtue of pilgrimage to Viṣṇu's sacred places is universal in its appeal.

The *puṟam* influences in Nammāḻvār's poetry are not confined solely to poems which are directly descended from *puṟam* prototypes. Images of Viṣṇu the warrior-hero appear in many and varied contexts. They often appear as telescoped references to particular incidents in the god's mythology. One favorite episode is the story of Rāma's conquest of Laṅkā. Another is Kṛṣṇa's betrothal to the cowherd maiden Piṉṉai : Kṛṣṇa won Piṉṉai for his bride by subduing seven of her father's bulls in a bull-baiting contest.[1] The following poem, which gives us a glimpse of the intimate sparring which the bhakti poet and his lord sometimes engage in, includes allusions to both these incidents :

Lord burning bright as a lamp
  who conquered seven bulls
  and turned splendid Laṅkā to ashes,

don't trust me !

When I reach your feet of gold
don't let me run off again.

Tiruvāymoḻi 2.9.10
(trans. NC)

Puṟam images also slip into poems that are directly descended from *akam* love poetry. Almost one-third of the verses in *Tiruvāymoḻi* take over the situations and characters of *akam* poetry,

1. In the classical corpus, the *Kalittokai* anthology (seventh century ? A.D.) has poems on bull-baiting contests. They describe heroic fights with bulls in an *akam* context, as a lover's ordeals before he can win his beloved's hand. Here again *akam* and *puṟam*, love and heroism, meet. These poems probably celebrate an ancient cowherding custom, and resonate in the Kṛṣṇa-Piṉṉai myths.

only here the *āḻvār* is traditionally identified with the narrative voices of the heroine, her mother and her girl friend (three of the conventional character-narrators of *akam* poetry),[1] and the hero, who does not take a speaking role in Nammāḻvār's love poems,[2] as he does in classical *akam* poetry, is identified as Viṣṇu. These two poems, the words of the heroine's mother, include the ubiquitous allusion to Rāma's conquest of Laṅkā.

"*What Her Mother Said*
Like a bar of lac
 or wax
thrust into fire
her mind is in peril
and you are heartless.

What shall I do for you,
lord who smashed Laṅkā,
 land ruled by the demon ?

Night and day her peerless eyes
swim in tears,
 lord who turned Laṅkā's fortune into smoke,
 don't scorch this simple girl
 or make her gentle glances wither."

Tiruvāymoḻi 2.4.3, 2.4.10
(trans. NC)

By virtue of the heroic deed they allude to, the epithets in these poems bring to mind *puṟam* themes, but they function within the poems very much like the suggestive insets of nature images in *akam* poetry. The *akam* poets devised subtle, implied

1. The stock characters of *akam* poetry include the hero (*talaivaṉ*), the heroine (*talaivi*), the hero's friend (*pāṅkaṉ*), the heroine's girl friend (*tōḻi*), the heroine's mother (*naṟṟāy* or *tāy*) and her foster mother (*cevili tāy*). In its colophon each *akam* poem is designated *talaivaṉ kūṟṟu* ("the words of the hero"), *talaivi kūṟṟu* ("the words of the heroine"), etc. For further discussion of the narrative structure of *akam* poems, see Ramanujan (1967).

2. There are some verses in Nammāḻvār's *Tiruviruttam* in which the hero is the speaker, but in these the hero is not explicitly identified as Viṣṇu (e.g., *Tiruviruttam* 50).

comparisons (called *uḷḷurai* : "inner statement") between events in nature and a drama of human characters, and in the saints' poems mythological allusions sometimes function in a similar manner. In these verses Nammāḻvār implies that Viṣṇu, the lover, can save the love-lorn heroine as he saved Sītā from the demon Rāvaṇa, or, by neglecting her, he can destroy her utterly as he demolished Rāvaṇa's kingdom, Laṅkā. In 2.4.10 the connection is reinforced by the images of burning which join purport and vehicle in the implied simile.

V. Akam Tradition and Bhakti Poetry

The two great classical Tamil gods, Cĕyōṉ, the Red One (Murukaṉ), and Māyōṉ, the Dark One (Viṣṇu-Kṛṣṇa) are lovers and warriors. One presided over the hills, the other over wooded pasture-land. They were the gods of both *akam* and *puṟam* milieus.[1] Bhakti poets are direct inheritors of this erotic/heroic ambience and its poetic genres.

The *akam* tradition runs deep in Tamil bhakti poetry. This is generally recognized by traditional and modern scholars, and if we have mainly attended to *puṟam* threads in the saints' poems, it is only to redress the balance. A strong *akam* strain appears in Tamil devotional poetry a little later than the *puṟam*. *Tirumurukāṟṟuppaṭai*, which may be the earliest devotional poem in Tamil, is a direct outgrowth of a *puṟam* genre. As we have seen, the poems to Tirumāl in *Paripāṭal* contain many *puṟam* elements, but *akam* and *puṟam* elements are mixed together in the *Paripāṭal* poems to Cevvēḷ (another name for Murukaṉ), who appears in this text both as a warrior god and as the lover of Vaḷḷi, the mountain maid who became his consort. Murukaṉ's love affair with Vaḷḷi evolves in much the same way as the affairs of *akam* lovers, beginning with clandestine meetings on the mountain slopes.

In these late classical poems the characters, situations and images of *akam* poetry are absorbed into Murukaṉ's mythology. In *puṟam* poetry the bhakti poets found an ideal language to express the devotional idiom of master and servant, as they found in *akam* the idiom of lover and beloved. We find touches of *akam* influence in the poems of the early *āḻvārs*, but in the works

1. For a detailed treatment of these early Tamil gods, see Zvelebil (1977).

of later Vaiṣṇavite poets such as Tirumaṅkai and Nammāḻvār we find poems dominated by an *akam* vocabulary. Nammāḻvār most clearly displays the imprint of classical Tamil love poetry in his *Tiruviruttam*, a poem of one hundred verses, and in the two hundred seventy love poems of *Tiruvāvmoḻi*, the so-called *akapporuḷ* portion of the text. These verses are precisely keyed to the conventions of *akam* poetry, and in most, Viṣṇu is cast in the role of the *akam* hero. It is almost paradoxical that Nammāḻvār, a poet who puts so much of himself into his poems, should draw so heavily upon *akam* tradition, because in classical *akam* poetry the poet is completely concealed from his audience by the veils of internal narrators and an elaborate repertoire of conventional situations and images. Śrīvaiṣṇava commentators, however, attempted to neutralize the distance separating poet from poem in this genre by identifying Nammāḻvār with the female character-narrators, especially with the heroine to whom they gave the name Parāṅkuśa Nayaki.[1] (And in so doing they violate one of the fundamental principles of *akam* poetry—that its characters are never named.) According to this influential interpretation, Nammāḻvār's love poems document the poet's own love affair with god. Thus in this poem, which describes a situation which is very familiar to the audience of *akam* poetry—the heroine is languishing in separation from the hero—we are said to hear how Nammāḻvār suffers when he is left alone without Viṣṇu's support.

"*What She Said*

Evening has come,
  but not the Dark One.

Without him here,
  what shall I say ?
  how shall I survive ?

The bulls,
  their bells jingling,

1. This name is a "feminization" of Parāṅkuśa, one of the several names by which the saint is known. Parāṅkuśa, which literally means "he whose goad is held by another" denotes the *āḻvār*'s complete dependence on Viṣṇu.

have mated with the cows
and the cows are frisky.

The flutes play cruel songs,
bees flutter in their bright
white jasmine
and the blue-black lily.

The sea leaps into the sky
and cries aloud."

Tiruvāymoḻi 9.9.10
(trans. AKR)

In bhakti a whole poetic tradition is taken over as a signifier for a new signification. Here bhakti is the new signification, and classical poetry, like Vedic and Upaniṣadic concepts, *purāṇa* mythologies, folk motifs and the many other sources from which the bhakti poets gathered their materials, is its signifier. An example will make this clear. Here is a classical Tamil poem :

"These fat *koṉṟai* trees
are gullible :

the season of rains
that he spoke of
when he went through the stones
of the desert
is not yet here

though these trees
mistaking the untimely rains
have put out
their long arrangements of flowers
on the twigs

as if for a proper monsoon."

Kōvatattaṉ
Kuṟuntokai 66
(trans. AKR)

And here is what Nammāḻvār does with it. He follows the classical score closely, yet transposes it to a new key :

"They haven't flowered yet,
the fat *kon̠rai* trees,
nor hung out their garlands
  and golden circlets
in their sensual canopy of leaves
along the branches,

dear girl,
dear as the paradise of our lord
who measured the earth
  girdled by the restless sea :

they are waiting
with buds
for the return
of your lover
  once twined in your arms."

Tiruviruttam 68
(trans. AKR)

In the earlier poem, the flowering tree, the rain, the anxious beloved, etc. were the signifiers for the erotic mood of waiting (*mullai*). In the later poem, the entire erotic tradition has become a new signifier, with bhakti as the signified. Now the classical tradition is to bhakti what the erotic motifs are to the tradition.

SIGNIFIER$_1$	SIGNIFIED$_1$
(rain, flowering tree, etc.)	(the erotic mood/ akam)

SIGNIFIER$_2$	SIGNIFIED$_2$
(the entire erotic tradition)	(bhakti)

Or, we can speak of "framing" the erotic poem in a new context of bhakti—in *Tiruviruttam* 68 above, the "framing" is achieved by the presence of a reference to Paradise and the lord who measured the earth. Past traditions and borrowings are thus re-worked into bhakti : they become materials, signifiers for a new signification : as a bicycle seat becomes a bull's head in Picasso. Often the listener/reader moves between the original material and the work before him—the double vision is part of the poetic effect.[1]

VI. The Tamil Classics and Vaiṣṇava Theology

Nammāḻvār's *akapporuḷ* poems may represent a peak in the history of classical influence in Tamil Vaiṣṇavite tradition, but they do not represent its end. Śrīvaiṣṇava commentators developed elaborate allegorical interpretations of the *āḻvārs*' love poems.[2] Aḻakiyamaṇavāḷaperumāḷnāyaṉār, the author of *Ācārya Hṛdayam*, a theological work of the late thirteenth or early fourteenth century, develops a theological interpretation for every detail in the *akapporuḷ* verses of *Tiruvāymoḻi*.[3] Even the heroine's ornaments carry an allegorical meaning in this interpretation. The commentator's mode of exegesis is a secondary signification

1. The diagram and the examples are from Ramanujan (1981).

2. Following their canonization by Nāthamuni in the tenth century A.D., the hymns of the *āḻvārs* were treated as sacred literature in Śrīvaiṣṇava tradition. Side-by-side with the Vedas and other sacred texts in Sanskrit, they were recited in temples and valued as a *pramāṇa* or basis for religious-philosophical discussion. Beginning in the late twelfth century A.D., the Śrīvaiṣṇava *ācāryas* began to write commentaries on the works of the *āḻvārs*, and of all the *aḻvār* texts *Tiruvāymoḻi* received the largest share of attention. The *ācāryas*' commentaries on the *āḻvārs*' poems are sometimes referred to as *anubhavagranthas* or "works of enjoyment" to signify that these works embody the *ācāryas*' "enjoyment", i.e., esthetic and intellectual experience of the *āḻvārs*' hymns. The *āḻvārs* in turn are revered because they dedicated themselves to "enjoyment" of the lord. The word *anubhavagrantha* is revealing, for it shows that the *ālvārs*' hymns are polysemous texts. Each commentary is the record of a meeting between the *āḻvārs*' poems and one especially well-schooled member of the *āḻvārs*' audience. Five commentaries on *Tiruvāymoḻi* have become classics in Śrīvaiṣṇava theological literature, and perhaps the most influential of these is the *Mūppattāyirappaṭi* ("the thirty-six thousand") by the thirteenth-century commentator, Vaṭakkuttiruvīti-ppiḷḷai. (The name of the text is derived from the number of *granthas* or metric units it contains.)

3. The author of *Ācārya Hṛdayam* is the son of Vaṭakkuttiruvītipiḷḷai (see note 2) and brother of Piḷḷai Lokācārya, who is looked upon as the founding father of the Teṅkalai or Southern school of Śrīvaiṣṇavism. *Ācārya Hṛdayam* ("the *ācārya*'s heart") is not a direct commentary on the verses of *Tiruvāymoḻi*. Instead, the author aims to acquaint his audience with Nammāḻvār's innermost thoughts and feelings.

system.[1] In his discussion of the heroine's physical characteristics, for example, he isolates a number of metaphors which Nammāḻvār and other poets often include in their descriptions of the *akam* heroine. From the quality which binds purport to vehicle in each of these metaphors, he develops a theological interpretation. In this way, the commentator takes over the poet's metaphorical identification of the heroine's forehead with the moon as a signifier for the purity of the soul. We may envisage the interpretive process as follows :

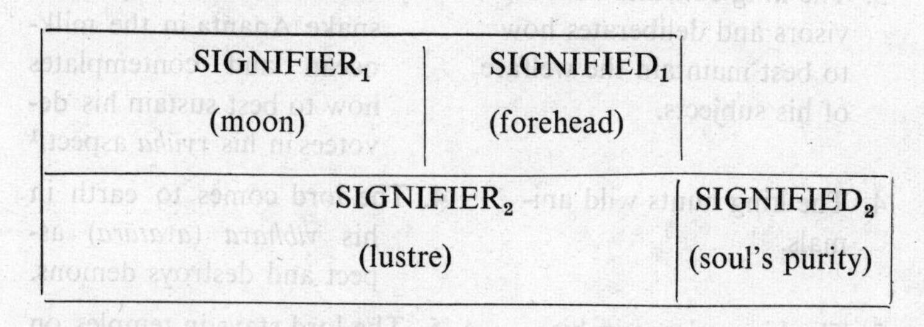

SIGNIFIER$_1$
(moon)
SIGNIFIED$_1$
(forehead)
SIGNIFIER$_2$
(lustre)
SIGNIFIED$_2$
(soul's purity)

The commentator thus uses the signs of bhakti poetry to generate theological discourse.

The *akam* dimension of Nammāḻvār's poetry receives far more attention in *Ācārya Hṛdayam* than the *puṟam*, but the latter is not overlooked altogether. The author also develops the idea that Viṣṇu presides over the universe as a king presides over his realm. He equates the traditional five functions of the king with the five aspects of Viṣṇu that are discussed in Pāñcarātra āgamic literature (Damodaran, 1976 : 96).[2] The five functions of the king are equated with the five aspects of Viṣṇu as follows :

1. For a discussion of signifier, signified, and secondary systems, see Barthes (1968).

2. The Sanskrit sectarian texts called *āgamas* are ideally supposed to cover four topics : *caryā*, *kriyā*, *yoga* and *jñāna*. In general *caryā* denotes rules pertaining to the maintenance of temples; *kriyā* pertains to the conduct of ritual and the construction of temples; the *yoga* portion deals with methods of physical and spiritual discipline; and the subject of the *jñāna* portion is religious philosophy. There are two important Vaiṣṇavite āgamic schools : the Vaikhānasa and the Pāñcarātra. The Vaikhānasa is usually considered to be the more conservative of the two, and Rāmānuja's campaign to introduce Pāñcarātra modes of worship into Vaiṣṇavite temples is usually interpreted as a drive to popularize Vaiṣṇavism. The Śrīvaiṣṇava *ācāryas* introduced many Pāñcarātra ideas into their writings.

1. The king reigns in state on his throne surrounded by the insignia of royalty.	1. The lord reigns in heaven (*paramapada*) in his *para* aspect.
2. The king circulates among his subjects incognito during the night.	2. The lord dwells within all creatures in his *antaryāmin* aspect even though they may not be aware of his presence.
3. The king consults with advisors and deliberates how to best maintain the welfare of his subjects.	3. The lord reclines upon the snake Ananta in the milk-ocean and contemplates how to best sustain his devotees in his *vyūha* aspect.[1]
4. The king hunts wild animals.	4. The lord comes to earth in his *vibhava* (*avatāra*) aspect and destroys demons.
5. The king relaxes in his pleasure garden.	5. The lord stays in temples on hills and in forested areas such as Tiruvēṅkaṭam in his *arcā* aspect.

While it is true that classical Tamil *puṟam* poetry is a poetry of kings, heroes, and warfare, Aḻakiyamaṇavāḷapperumāḷnāyaṉār's discussion of Viṣṇu's kingly attributes is guided by discussions of a king's duties found in Sanskrit *śāstras,* but blended with classical Tamil conceptions. In this respect Śrīvaiṣṇava exegetical tradition is like the poetry it purports to explain : like the *āḻvārs,* the *ācāryas* were heirs to two classicisms, Sanskrit and Tamil.

1. The four *vyūhas* or "emanations" of Viṣṇu are Vāsudeva, Saṅkarṣaṇa, Pradyumna and Aniruddha. In mythology these are the names of Kṛṣṇa, Kṛṣṇa's brother, his son, and his grandson. According to the vyūha doctrine, Vāsudeva represents the supreme reality, Saṅkarṣaṇa primeval matter or *prakṛti,* Pradyumna cosmic mind or *manas,* and Aniruddha represents cosmic self-consciousness or *ahaṅkāra.* From the latter springs Brahmā, the creator of the phenomenal world. Apparently it is because the *vyūhas* give rise to Brahmā that they are associated with the reclining Viṣṇu who "gives birth" to the creator-god through his navel.

The transposition from poetry to theology takes the same form as the earlier transposition from classicism to bhakti. It keeps the signifiers, transposes them to another level, and writes them with new signified elements. In bhakti poetry, both signifier and signified are "experiential", their relation is poetic. In the theological commentary, the signified has become abstract, and the relation between signifier and signified is allegoric. In this theological allegory, the love-lorn girl's messenger-bird is really the *guru* who mediates and relates her to god; her mother is no mother, but the soul's "conviction in the right means"; her hips and breasts are no longer erogenous and of the flesh, they are but the soul's attainment of bhakti and the lord's enjoyment of the soul.

With this commentator we are in the thirteenth century. The saints' poems are a permanent part of the Hindu religious scene. They live on, in all their full-bodied beauty and devotional power, subject of sect and temple politics, of allegory and ingenious commentary, of ritual and festival; they are also the moving resource of singers, thinkers, poets, and ordinary men. The saint as man speaking to god as beloved and protégé, offering Him his interior *akam* and exterior *puṟam*, is at the same time, in the same words, a poet in a tradition, a "man speaking to men". His past gives him a language for the present.

Hymn to Tirumāl (*Viṣṇu*)

"When the sun and the moon,
given to alterations
from the oldest times
went out,

and the fresh golden world above
and the earthen one
were ruined :

there were ages of absence
even of sky
rolling time after time;

sound was born first
in the first age of sheer sky—

womb of every growing germ
though yet without forms,

then the ancient age of winds
driving all things before them,

the age of red fire
in flames,

the age of mist and-cool rain
falling,

and when all four elements
drowned in the old flood,
the particles of earth
lay there,

recovering their own
natures, getting themselves
together;

then came the age of great earth
lying potential
in them all;

beyond the times counted
in millions, billions, trillions,
quadrillions and zillions,

came the time of the Boar
that raised the earth
from the waters
and let it flourish;

knowing that it is only one
of your Acts,

no one really can know
the true age
of your antiquity;

O First One, Lord of the Wheel,
we bow,
we sing your praise.

O you,
to those who say
you're younger, and brother
to the conch-colored One,
you appear young;

to those who say
you're older
than the one dressed
in clothes dark as all-burying darkness
with a gold palmyra for banner,
you appear older;

in the wisdom of the ancients
sifted by the high ones
with flawless intent,
you're in a state of in-between;

yet in any search
of things one can see
in this state or that,
you show only your own,
the excellence
of your most ancient state.

Wearing jewels
many-colored as rainbows
bent across the high heavens
on your chest, itself a jewel studded
with pearls, you always wear
the Red Goddess
as the moon
his shadow.

Which doesn't agree at all
with those who read the Vedas
and say,

You as the Boar,
with white tusks, sharp and spotted,
washed by the rising waves, lifted
and wed the Earth-maiden

so not a spot of earth
is ever troubled by the sea.

O lord fierce in war,
the loud conch you hold
sounds like thunder

to the enemy
rising as one man,
unafraid in anger,
rising like a hurricane
to join battle;

banners break and fall,
ears go deaf,
crowns shiver on their heads,
and the earth loosens
under their feet

at the thunder of your conch.

O lord fierce in war,
the discus in your hand
cuts the sweet lives
of enemies :

heads fall and roll
wreaths and all;
their stand lost,
like the tens of thousands
of bunches
on the heads of tall black palmyra-trees
not stripped yet
of root, branch
frond or young fruit,
falling to the earth
all at once :

not one head
standing on its body,
beheaded all at one stroke, they
gather, roll, split,
come together and roll apart,
and lie dead at last
in a mire of blood.

That discus
that kills at one stroke :
Death is its body,
its color the flame
of bright fire
when gold burns in it.

Yours is the lustre
of the great dark blue-sapphire;

your eyes, a pair
of famed lotuses;

the truth of your word
certain as the returning day.

If one looks for your magnificent patience
it's there, wide as earth;

your grace,
a sky of rain-cloud
fulfilling everyone;
so say

the sacred texts
of the learned brāhmans.

O lord with the red-beak
Garuḍa-bird
on your banner,

you're like all that
and also like all else,

you're in these,
and in all things.

As said in the Vedas :
in the sacrificer's word,

in the sacrificial pillar
built step by step,

and also in the seizing
of the sacrificial animal
strapped to that pillar,

the kindling of a raging fire
according to charted text
and famous tradition,

and in the building of that fire
to glowing light
and prosperous flame

is your form,
your food :

in such,
brāhmans see
(and even aliens agree)
your presence.

As soon as your heart
thought of ambrosia,
food of the gods,
the deathless ones received
a life without age,
a peace without end;

O lord unfathomable,
at your feet
we bow,
clean of heart,
putting our heads to the ground

over and over
we bow,
we praise,
we celebrate

and we ask O lord
with our dear ones around us
we ask :

May our knowing
know
only what is."

Kīrantaiyār
The Second Song,
Paripāṭal
trans. by A. K. Ramanujan

REFERENCES

Barthes, Roland. 1968. *Elements of Semiology* (with *Writing Degree Zero*), tr. by A. Lavers and C. Smith. Boston : Beacon Press.

Cutler, Norman. 1979. *Consider Our Vow : An English Translation of Tiruppāvai and Tiruvempāvai*. Madurai : Muthu Patippakam.

—. 1980. *The Poetry of the Tamil Saints.* Ph.D. dissertation, University of Chicago.

Damodaran, G. 1976. *Ācārya Hṛdayam : A Critical Study.* Tirupati : Tirumala Tirupati Devasthanam.

—. 1978. *The Literary Value of Tiruvāymoḻi.* Tirupati : Sri Venkatesvara University.

Gros, Francois. 1968. *Le Paripāṭal : Texte Tamoule.* Pondicherry : Institut Français d'Indology.

Hart, George L. III. 1975. *The Poems of Ancient Tamil : Their Cultural Milieu and Sanskrit Counterparts.* Berkeley : University of California Press.

—. 1979. *Poets of the Tamil Anthologies.* Princeton : Princeton University Press.

Kailasapathy, K. 1968. *Tamil Heroic Poetry*. Oxford : The Clarendon Press.

Nilakanta Sastri, K. A. 1955. *The Cōḻas*. Madras : Madras University.

Ramanujan, A. K. 1967. *The Interior Landscape : Love Poems from a Classical Tamil Anthology*. Bloomington : Indiana University Press.

—. 1981. *Hymns for the Drowning : Poems for Viṣṇu by Nammāḻvār*. Princeton : Princeton University Press.

Srinivasa Raghavan, A. 1975. *Nammāḻvār*. New Delhi : Sahitya Akademi.

Varadarajan, M. 1972. *Tamiḻ Ilakkiya Varalāṟu*. New Delhi : Sahitya Akademi.

Vaudeville, Charlotte. 1962. "Evolution of Love Symbolism in Bhāgavatism", *Journal of the American Oriental Society*, 82 : 31-40.

Zvelebil, Kamil. 1973. *The Smile of Murugan : On Tamil Literature of South India*. Leiden : E. J. Brill.

—. 1974. *Tamil Literature*. Wiesbaden : Otto Harrossowitz.

—. 1977. "The Beginnings of Bhakti in South India", *Temenos*, 13 : 223-57.

9

VĀKĀṬAKA ART AND THE GUPTA MAINSTREAM

JOANNA WILLIAMS

THE caves of Ajantā (Ajaṇṭā) have been used for a variety of purposes : as a bridge to eternity (by the donors), as dwelling halls (by monks and later inhabitants), as historical and religious documents (by modern scholars). The historian of Indian art may on the one hand seek to appreciate and understand them as fully as possible in their own terms. On the other hand, he may concern himself with their relationship to the art of contiguous times and places. It is the geographical aspect of this last question to which this paper will be addressed. Baldly put, is Ajantā part of Gupta art ? If art historical boundaries followed political ones, the answer would clearly be no. We know that this region came closest to Gupta hegemony at the beginning of the fifth century A.D., when Prabhāvatī Guptā, daughter of the emperor Candra Gupta II, married Rudrasena II of the main branch of the Vākāṭaka dynasty, ruling in the area of the modern Nāgpur. This powerful woman continued as regent for her sons, but by the second half of the fifth century A.D., when the Ajantā caves were excavated, the Gupta dynasty was a dying if not a dead letter and was unrelated to the Vākāṭakas. Moreover, the caves fell within the territories of the western or Vatsagulma branch of the Vākāṭaka family. Nonetheless, narrowly political divisions seem useful neither in general for Indian art, nor in particular for the Gupta period.[1] Such a definition would,

1. For illustrations which give a very just picture of the Gupta *oeuvre*, see J. C. Harle, *Gupta Sculpture* (Oxford, 1974). A reaction against excessive

for example, exclude most of the significant remains from Central India, executed under various successors to the Guptas, whose styles were deliberately continued. The truly imperial extent of Gupta artistic forms in geographical terms and over a period of 150 years justifies the presumptuous term in my title "Gupta mainstream". It seems to me that the question of Ajantā's relationship to this, as a shining example, as a provincial reflection, or as a distinct alternative, must be answered fundamentally in terms of artistic form and content. Yet the geography of style has a bearing on larger issues of unity and diversity in Indian culture, matters of regionalism and the reality of the so-called "Great Tradition".[1]

Such concerns immediately raise questions of chronology. I do not propose to make dating the focus of this paper, having discussed the subject *ad nauseam* elsewhere. At the same time, a discussion of relationships presupposes some sense of whether we are talking about contemporary or successive phenomena. To summarize my position, the dates proposed by Walter Spink in *Ajanta to Ellora*, 465 to 505 A.D., seem acceptable for the Ajantā caves.[2] For the Gupta works used here, the following list gives my rough chronology :

Udayagiri Cave 1 : *c.* 410-15 A.D.

Tigowā, Kaṅkālī Devī Temple : *c.* 445-70 A.D.

Nāchnā, Pārvatī Temple : *c.* 490-500 A.D.

concern with dynasties is visible not only in much recent historical writing about India but also in art historical literature (*e.g.*, Pramod Chandra, "The Study of Indian Temple Architecture," in *Studies in Indian Temple Architecture*, P. Chandra, ed., (Varanasi : 1975), pp. 35-36.)

1. For a searching consideration of the dispersal of power as the paradoxical strength of a fabric interrupted by intermittent attempts at centralism, see J. C. Heesterman, "India and the Inner Conflict of Tradition," *Daedelus*, 102:1 (1973), 97-113.

2. Walter Spink, *Ajanta to Ellora* (Ann Arbor : 1967). This range is generally accepted by the French scholars Philippe Stern and Odette Viennot, who, however, differ radically from my placement of the major Gupta monuments. Professor Spink has refined his chronology in subsequent articles, as well as shifting back the range of Ajantā's dates to *c.* 460 to 485 A.D. I am not convinced of so early a termination. For a detailed reconstruction of the history of the period, see Vasudev Vishnu Mirashi, *Inscription of the Vākāṭakas*: *Corpus Inscriptionum Indicarum*, Vol. V (Ootacamund : 1963); and S. R. Goyal, *History of the Imperial Guptas* (Allahabad : 1967).

Nāchnā, Kumra Math (=Temple on South Hill): *c.* 500-20 A.D.

Deogarh, Dasavatāra Temple : *c.* 500-30 A.D.

Bhūmarā, Śiva Temple : *c.* 520-30 A.D.

We are thus dealing with a period when actual Gupta power was shrinking and when both branches of the Vākāṭaka family were also in their final years.

AJANTĀ

It is the clearest to begin with the sculpture of Ajantā; although that is by no means the whole of the art produced in the Vākāṭaka area. Ajantā is frequently included in general discussions of Gupta art, and the case for this position should be stated first. The aesthetic of some figural scenes is clearly close to that of sculpture which we think of as Gupta. For example, the Nāga-rāja with Two Queens from Cave 19 (Plate 1) is similar to the Nara and Nārāyaṇa from Deogarh (Plate 24), not only in detail but also in the nature of its composition. Both depend upon a careful balance between figures arranged with subtle asymmetry. Each forms a clearly defined unit against the wall, enclosing a real if shallow space. For all the difference in texture of the two stone types, both balance simple volumes against areas of elaborate detail. The two, in short, seem conceived deliberately as artistic compositions, unlike the later art of medieval India in which the sculptural unit is generally subordinate to the architectural whole. This aesthetic concern is, however, lost in the latest carvings of the site, where in a frenzy of insecurity and religiosity, the patrons began to cover the walls with carvings less coherently planned.

Some specific motifs at Ajantā show the same form, spirit, and frequency with which they run throughout Gupta art. An obvious example is the foliage visible in Plate 3. Here this ebullient vegetation, based upon parts of the lotus but defying botanical classification, displays the same variety to which we are accustomed within a single Gupta monument. Thus in Plate 3 we see both a version with strong central axis and a band with alternating curves side by side, as at Sārnāth (Plate 25). The undulating central band in Plate 3 does represent a type which I have not found outside Ajantā. Flowers are particularly prominent, and the curling nodules and aquatic rhysome are subordinated to broader leaf forms which must rise above the water. Similar foliage appears in painted form on the Ajantā ceilings.[1] It is possible that for painters the flowers and variegated leaves were a more attractive aspect of such a plant than the endive-like root portions, and that this version was in turn passed back to the sculptors at a site where the two media were more intertwined than was usual in free-standing stone architecture. Other motifs such as the twisted band to the outside in Plate 3 are indistinguishable from Gupta versions, as in Plate 25.[2]

Some motifs are, however, used in a distinctly more limited way at Ajantā than in Gupta art as a whole. The outer door to Cave 23, for example, is the only case of a band of large, fan-shaped leaves commonly called "overlapping acanthus" (Plate 6, outer band). This element appears towards the very end of the fifth century at Deogarh and in the later remains of Nāchnā, probably reflecting developments in Mathurā and Sārnāth slightly previously.[3] Thus the absence of the overlapping acanthus in the rest of the final caves of Ajantā is surprising. The door to Cave 23 also exhibits in the center of the lintel the only sculptural example at the site of a *candraśālā* or arch doubled with a split version below. This form had appeared by *c.* 475 A.D. at Tigowā. While this type did not, of course, universally replace the plain arch, it is unusual not to find it in so large a body of carving as the final caves of Ajantā. In general, the doorway to Cave 23 suggests direct contact with contemporary developments in Madhya Pradesh and Gangetic India in the last

1. G. Yazdani, *Ajanta* (Oxford : 1930), II, Pl. Xb.

2. The twisted band is of Kuṣāṇ origin but disappears in the western Deccan under the Kalacuris. Another motif which appears with equal frequency at Ajantā and elsewhere in Gupta art is the meander band, found at Caves 2, 14 and 27. Cf. Odette Viennot, *Temples de l'Inde centrale et occidentale*, *Publ. École Française d'Extrême Orient*, *Memoires archéologiques*, XI. (Paris : 1976), p. 123.

3. W. Spink, "A Temple with Four Uchchakalpa (?) Doorways at Nāchnā Kutharā," *Chhavi*, ed. Anand Krishna (Banaras : 1971), 319, 322, 334 and 335. The late occurrence of this motif is one reason that I am reluctant to think of the work at Ajantā (where, to judge from the single occurrence of the acanthus, the motif could hardly have originated) as concluding by 485 A.D.

fifteen years of the fifth century.[1] The very strength of its Gupta flavor contrasts with the other caves.

The *pūrṇa ghaṭa* or overflowing vase as a capital for pillars and pilasters raises a slightly different problem. This motif had appeared quite early in the fifth century A.D. at Udayagiri Cave 1 and was common thereafter, although like all Gupta motifs it was never entirely *de rigueur* (occurring, for example, rarely at Nāchnā). At Ajantā the overflowing vase appears with slightly eccentric form on the lower door to Cave 6 and on that to Cave 15, both relatively early excavations.[2] The motif is strikingly absent in the elaborate Caves 16, 17, 1 and 2, only to reappear in the porch of 19 and to become common in the final caves. Here we have an established Gupta motif known but not catching on until the last phase of activity at the site.

Finally, the T-shaped outline for the doorway, a feature standard in Gupta architecture until the second quarter of the sixth century A.D., is haphazardly used at Ajantā.[3] While generally present, as we would expect at this point, the T-shape is absent in Caves 1, 2 and 21 and in the main porch at Ghaṭotkacha. Since these are by no means the latest excavations, the loss of the T-shape here cannot be made to coincide with what seems to be a subsequent development in Gupta art. On the contrary,

1. This wave might be associated with the emissaries of the rulers of Aśmaka, a state to the south, however, along the River Godāvarī. These are mentioned in the donative inscription of Cave 26 (J. Burgess, *Report on the Buddhist Cave Temples and their Inscriptions, A.S.W.I.*, Vol. IV, 134-35). Aśmaka machinations have been credited with the downfall of the Vākāṭakas on the basis of Daṇḍin's *Daśakumāracarita* by V. V. Mirashi ("Historical Data in Dandin's *Daśakumāracharita*," *Annals of the Bhandarkar Oriental Research Institute*, 26 [1945], 20-31) and by Walter Spink ("Ajantā's Chronology: The Crucial Cave," *Ars Orientalis*, X [1975], 175).

2. Philippe Stern, *Colonnes Indiennes d'Ajantā et d'Ellora, Publications du Musée Guimet, Recherches et Documents d'Art et d'Archéologie*, Vol. XI (Paris : 1972), figs. 56, 57. Stern places these caves in his first phase at Ajantā, but in his discussion of the overflowing vase, which he notes is less abundant than elsewhere, he leaves open the possibility that these parts are later additions to the excavations (p. 55).

3. As Walter Spink has pointed out, there is an increasingly structural logic in the relationship between jamb pilasters and lintel at Ajantā, but this seems to me an issue separate from the profile of the entire doorway (*Ajanta to Ellora*, 40).

we must envision some opposing local pattern, to which Gupta forms were added in spurts.

This brings us to elements found at Ajantā which are absent elsewhere in Gupta art, forming the strongest case for a local or Vākāṭaka idiom. The columns of a few caves and the doorway pilasters of many, such as those of Caves 20 and 2 seen in Plates 3 and 5, show a bulbous, fluted capital with several out-turned edges of a type totally unknown in Gupta monuments. Philippe Stern has suggested that this represents a version of wooden columns copied in stone.[1] The pronounced curve of the arches above the doors to Cave 6 (lower)[2] and Cave 20 (Plate 3) likewise seem to reproduce actual *toraṇas* or gates made of pliable materials, a type not reflected in structural temples of this period. In short, the acquaintance with wooden architecture, in part no doubt secular, which has long been noted in the Ajantā paintings, clearly contributes to differentiating the architectural decor from the more consistently lithic Gupta traditions.

Certain decorative motifs appear at Ajantā which are not out of keeping with the Gupta style, but which are employed in a distinctive way here. For example, a band of large petals arranged side by side is a very common feature on the doors and windows of these caves throughout the course of the excavations. It is usually the outer band of decor, as in Caves 23 and 27 (Plates 6 and 7) or the lintel of Cave 20 (Plate 3). While such petals frame *candraśālā* arches and form bands in the superstructure of Gupta temples,[3] nowhere else in the fifth or early sixth century do they occur on doorways. Likewise, the common inner band that consists of alternating lozenges and elliptical forms, probably representing jewels (Plate 3), is not part of the Gupta repertoire, although it is similar in spirit to the symmetrical foliate band on the inside of the Sārnāth door illustrated

1. P. Stern, *Colonnes indiennes*, 11. The closest Gupta form of which I know is a pair of pilasters found at Besnagar, where, however, the many small flutes are superimposed across a vase shape (*A.S.I.W.C.*, 1914, Photo 4046),

2. O. Viennot, *Les Divinités fluviales Gaṅgā et Yamunā* (Paris : 1974), Plate 5.

3. For example, at Mathurā : Vincent A. Smith, *The Jain Stupa and Other Antiquities of Mathura, A.S.I., N.I.S.*, Vol. XX (Varanasi : 1969), Plate LXXXIII. Also, Bhītargaon : J. Harle, *Gupta Sculpture*, Plates 131 and 135.

in Plate 25. Such idiosyncratic regional motifs begin to appear elsewhere towards the end of the fifth century A.D. Often they are passed on by lingering networks of communication, so that they appear in the subsequent art of other regions. For instance, the jewelled band just described may give rise to the starker lozenges of Central Indian and Pratīhāra decor in the eighth century A.D.[1]

One puzzling element is the absence at Ajantā of the differentiated river goddesses, *Gaṅgā* and *Yamunā*. While there are numerous pairs of female figures at the ends of lintels, in each case both stand upon the *makara* or crocodile of Gaṅgā. This feature is a prime reason for French scholars' assumption that those Gupta temples on which the two rivers are differentiated belong to a period following most of the work at Ajantā, a suggestion which I find improbable on other grounds. In fact, on the antechamber to the shrine of Cave 20, we see an example in which the small male attendant to the goddess stands on a tortoise (Plate 4). This might indicate a formative stage in the identification of the River Yamunā, but that figure had already been shown directly on the tortoise at Udayagiri much earlier in the fifth century.[2] Thus it is more probable that we have here a distant echo of a motif established elsewhere. Perhaps the Vākāṭaka patrons avoided the pair for political reasons, since the two rivers define the heartland of the Gupta empire and since their representation may have originated at Udayagiri with reference to the exploits of Candra Gupta II.[3] Perhaps the sacredness of Prayāga (Allahābād), where the union of the two rivers occurs, was less generally recognized in the Deccan, which had its own *tīrthas* or pilgrimage centers. The theme is remarkably rare in this area even later in the sixth and seventh centuries.[4]

1. *E.g.*, O. Viennot, *Temples*, Plates 116, 151, 214, etc.
2. This occurs in two panels at the end of the Varāha relief, which I would associate with the inscription of Cave 6.
3. The theory that the Varāha relief of Udayagiri was a political allegory and that the River Goddesses at its end represent Madhyadeśa was suggested by Vasudeva Sharan Agrawala, *Solar Symbolism of the Boar* (Varanasi : 1963), pp. 35-36.
4. The pair are differentiated four times in the Hindu caves of Ellora (nos. 14, 21, 26, 29). While Odette Viennot classifies the third doorway at Jogeśvari as belonging to the phase when the River Goddesses are 'differentiated

At any rate, we see a clear distinction between Ajantā and North India under the Guptas in the use of the River Goddess motif.

Finally, to turn to more subjective matters, it is hard to resist the impression that the figure types of the Ajantā sculptures are as a whole heavier than those of Gupta art proper. This tendency is most striking in the case of the Buddha images that loom in the shadows at the rear of the *vihāra* caves, where great bulk emerging luminously from the shadows is particularly appropriate. The Nāgarāja of Plate 1, with which I began, and the Buddha seated against the *stūpa* of Cave 26 support this generalization less well. On the whole, while it seems that the carvers at Ajantā followed the Sārnāth pattern of drapery unblemished by folds, it is hard for me to envision that any Sārnāth sculptor actually worked at Ajantā. In short, there seems to have been a local workshop which cannot be traced to any of the other great centers of Buddhist art.

To my eye, the difference between the Ajantā and that of the mainstream Gupta monuments is greater than the difference among those monuments themselves. While one can distinguish the drapery and halos of Buddha images from Sārnāth, Mathurā, and Sāñchī, let alone from the Gandhāran incursions at Devnimori (to stick to Buddhist subjects), these seem to pale before the complex distinctions which set apart Ajantā.

Should Ajantā thus be considered provincial Gupta art, perhaps precocious in its degree of regionalism, or should it be considered a separate dialect in limited ways influenced by the Gupta? The choice is hard to make on the basis of data which cannot be quantified, and the distinction may seem ultimately an arbitrary, semantic one. Part of the difficulty, however, lies also in our focus upon Ajantā alone as a sample of Vākāṭaka art.

THE CENTRAL VĀKĀṬAKA WORKS

If we look east to those parts of northern Mahārāshtra, known as Vidarbha, we find no single body of monuments from this

she does not in fact claim that this is true there, nor is that the case (*Les Divinités fluviales Gaṅgā et Yamunā*, 31). The later prominence of the theme in the Deccan may be connected with the announcement by the Cālukya ruler Vijayāditya that he had brought south the banner of Gaṅgā and Yamunā (*Epigraphia Indica*, Vol. X, 14 ff.).

period as coherent and well-preserved as the caves of Ajantā. We do, nonetheless, find a variety of isolated images which seem related to the sculpture of Ajantā. If these are unified in style, it seems reasonable to ascribe them to the rule of the main branch of the Vākāṭaka dynasty. The last ruler of this family, Pṛthvīṣeṇa II, was in rough a contemporary of Hariṣeṇa, the last of the Vatsagulma branch. The date of each of these dispersed pieces merits individual consideration, since none has been published with much discussion. For all of them it can be said at the outset that a date after the early sixth century A.D. is unlikely in terms of what we know of the later sculptural style in this area. The peculiarities of these works are not explained as an early stage of the medieval styles of central India, such as the southern branch of the Haihaya-Kalacuri.

Several possible interpretations of the bearing of these images on the Ajantā-Gupta problem present themselves. It is in the first place conceivable that the Vidarbha works represent an offshoot from the western Vākāṭaka style slightly later in time and derivative. I find this unlikely in view of the superior quality of several Vidarbha pieces, which seem to be more than sheer refinements upon the Ajantā style. In the second place, it is possible that the Vidarbha group should be seen as the filter or immediate source from which Gupta influence was transmitted to Ajantā, itself being provincial Gupta. This is improbable, for it would imply that the Vidarbha *oeuvre* is more Gupta than that of Ajantā, which does not appear to be the case. Finally, it is possible that the Vidarbha region was the source for at least some non-Gupta elements at Ajantā and that its role as an independent force in relationship to our so-called mainstream needs to be dissected. To summarize what is argued below in detail, I would consider the Vidarbha Vākāṭaka idiom to be a principal counterforce to the Gupta "mainstream", if at times related; this seems to explain some of the non-Gupta elements both in the Western Deccan and in the early medieval period of Central India itself.

In the first place, scattered fragments of architectural décor survive from Vidarbha and its periphery. The hill station Panchmarhi, on the northern edge of this area, preserves doorways such as that in Plate 8, which might pass for a simplified version of the Ajantā pattern of, for example, Cave 2 (Plate 5). Specifically, the inner band consists of lozenges alternating with elliptical forms set in foliage, and the outer band consists of petals arranged side by side, both features already discussed as peculiar to the portals of Ajantā. We have no indication of the precise political history of Panchmarhi in the fifth and sixth centuries A.D. Yet three hundred kilometers to the northwest, the inscriptions of the Ucchakalpas indicate Vākāṭaka hegemony towards the end of the fifth century.[1] Thus it is possible to suggest connections between Panchmarhi and Ajantā. The relationship to the mature phase at Ajantā would imply that the Panchmarhi door is contemporary or slightly later, although I cannot be very positive of this date.

Rajim, in the ancient province of Kosala to the east of Vidarbha, preserves a doorway that seems to precede the bulk of seventh-century monuments of this region (Plate 9). This door, set into the later Rāmacandra Temple, again shows the lozenge-ellipse and petal bands that occur at Ajantā. Moreover the third major face of the jambs bears a pilaster topped with the bulbous capital whose facets continue upward in several tiers with out-turned edges. This is precisely the form noted at Ajantā as lying outside the Gupta architectural repertoire and perhaps derived from wooden sources (Plate 3, 5). Other features of the Rāmacandra door occur at Ajantā although they are not exclusively limited to that site : the prominent, complete medallion and the meander band.[2] Moreover, the unemphatic treatment of the base of the jambs, with dwarves and lions set in niches, is similar to many of the early caves at Ajantā and runs counter to the general Gupta placement of larger male or female figures here. Some elements at Rajim are of course already indicative of a localized Kosala idiom. For example, within the niche above the standing figures low on the pilaster is a pendentive, which becomes a characteristic detail of seventh century architecture in this area. The fact that the lateral face of the jamb is carved

1. V. V. Mirashi, *Inscriptions of the Vākāṭakas*, 89-92. If the *Daśakumāracarita* describes a Vākāṭaka prince as ruling at Māhiṣmatī, this would document the dynasty's power along the Narmadā River (Walter Spink, *Ars Orientalis*, Vol. X, 149).

2. The Rāmacandra door meander band consists of overlapping acanthus, a motif not used this way at Ajantā.

is another local touch. Much later recutting of most of the figures on the outer three bands impedes any stylistic assessment of the figural treatment. But, on the whole, a date in the first quarter of the sixth century A.D. seems plausible, both on the basis of the resemblance to Ajantā and on the basis of differences from the Somavamṣi remains of the end of the sixth century A.D.[1] We know that both the main branch (under Pṛthiviṣeṇa II) and the Vatsagulma branch (under Hariṣeṇa) of the Vākāṭaka family claimed ascendancy over Kosala in the last quarter of the fifth century.[2] While the obvious conflict between these two claims as well as the absence of any Vākāṭaka inscriptions in Kosala would seem to undermine any Vākāṭaka title to the area, the Rāmacandra doorway may indicate some influence from the dominant neighbors.

The great Vaiṣṇava shrine atop the hill of Rāmtek is more clearly documented in connection with the central Vākāṭaka family. Apparently known as Rāmagiri, this religious center lay five kilometers from the first capital, Nandivardhana, and was the spot from which Vākāṭaka charters were issued in the first third of the fifth century A.D.[3] This site is still venerated, and among the many later shrines which crown the hill, Vākāṭaka remains are tantalizingly few and scattered. A small building on the spot sacred to Trivikrama may represent a vestige of some original temple (Plates 10-12).[4] The pillars are similar and might be compared to examples from Nāchnā and Deogarh in the late fifth and early sixth centuries A.D., although the resemblances are not very specific. The only peculiarity is a flat, anchor-shaped element below the lower vase (Plate 11), perhaps a simplified version of the palmette which often appears in this

1. One other early monument in Kosala, the Devarani at Tala, seems considerably closer to Gupta traditions, although it does show a band of petals side by side on its lintel. For a fuller discussion, see Donald M. Stadtner, *From Sirpur to Rajim*, unpublished Ph.D. dissertation, University of California, Berkeley, 1976.

2. V. V. Mirashi, *Inscriptions of the Vākāṭakas*, 81, 110.

3. V. V. Mirashi, *op. cit.*, 35, 37.

4. Architecturally, this is difficult to place. The base, while following fifth century molding types, is unusually high. The spaces between the columns were originally open. Perhaps we have the porch or *maṇḍapa* to a *garbhagṛha* on the east (in Plate 10).

position.[1] Much-damaged dwarves or *pramathas* form a dado below (Plate 12), alternating with panels of foliage that bear traces of the lozenge and ellipse characteristic of Ajantā. One isolated fragment shows complete foliate medallions (Plate 13), again an element rare in Gupta art but common in the Western Deccan. The Nṛsiṃha Temple at Rāmtek also preserves inset vertical panels of dwarves (Plate 14). These invite comparison with the similar jolly troupes of Bhūmarā and Nāchnā (Plate 26).[2] At both of those sites, however, the poses are more varied and one does not find the same bird-like disjunction between stiff legs and rotund body. The resemblance is unexpectedly striking between the Rāmtek dwarves and the colossal guardians of Ajantā Cave 19 in pose, body-type, and head-dress (Plate 2). One puzzling feature of all the Rāmtek remains is the lack of reference to wooden prototypes, as was hinted at Rajim and widespread at Ajantā. One might suppose that the paucity of stone architecture in the area indicates the use of wood for sacred architecture, yet this is not reflected in the stone fragments found so far. On the whole, these pieces suggest some independence from Gupta standards, although the degree is again unclear. The precise date of these fragments is likewise indeterminable. It is possible that they go back to the second quarter of the fifth century A.D., when we know that nearby Nandivardhana was the capital. Yet on the basis of stylistic correspondence with Nāchnā, and the mature phase at Ajantā, I would date the pieces just considered closer to the year 500 A.D.

Turning to figural sculpture, we confront the imposing stump of an image of Trivikrama still in worship at Rāmtek (Plate 15).[3] The free-standing form of this carving and the strongly diagonal stride set this image apart from either sketchy Mathurā precedents

1. W. Spink, "A Temple with Four Ucchakalpa (?) Doorways," *Chhavi*, fig. 329. M. S. Vats, *The Gupta Temple at Deogarh, Memoirs, Archaeological Survey of India,* 70 (Delhi : 1952), Plate XIXa.

2. The Rāmtek panels are roughly 30 cm. wide. The top figure appears to represent a lion. For Bhūmarā, see R. D. Banerji, *The Temple of Śiva at Bhumara, Memoirs, Archaeological Survey of India*, 16 (Calcutta : 1924), IX-XI. The unpublished grille from Nāchnā in Plate 26 is closer to Rāmtek (cf. the borders in Plate 12) than are the larger dwarves from Nāchnā.

3. V. V. Mirashi, *Inscriptions of the Vākāṭakas*, Plate A.

or later Deccani versions.[1] The slender figural form as well as head-dress and ornament surely lie somewhere between 425 and 550 A.D., but beyond that it is difficult to assess chronological position or regional affinities.

A second early figure has recently been discovered some five kilometers from Rāmtek on the facing hill of Manasar. This site is associated with Buddhism today, and it is the find-spot of one Vākāṭaka inscription.[2] The image in Plate 16, now kept in the National Museum, New Delhi, is clearly Śaiva and hence distinct in religious iconography from other Vākāṭaka works.[3] Comparison with an image of Kubera from the area of Udaipur in Rājasthān (Plate 27), admittedly at least a century later in date, demonstrates the extraordinary quality of the Manasar piece. While the pose is essentially the same, the Śaiva figure sits with subtle asymmetry, hips and head tilted off axis. The chubby anatomy of the Udaipur *yakṣa* is defined with geometrical regularity, whereas the curves of the Manasar work are broken, composed of small, interlocking folds of flesh. The creases in mid-arm, chest and leg have no counterpart in the Kubera. The clenched right hands of the two contrast clearly, one formed by abstracted, flower-like curves, the other bending squarely to indicate underlying knuckles. The big toe bends upward in the Manasar piece, unlike the regular feet of the Udaipur one. Similar variety and irregularity animate every detail of jewelry, drapery and head-dress. As a result, the image conveys a gripping sense of immediacy. The Manasar carving is, of course, not quite a Grant Wood portrait. The face is of a generalized types. The rendition of the flesh itself retains a sphericity in stomach and lower chest folds, exemplifying the sense of abstract expansiveness in the description of human anatomy

1. An early Gupta image from Mathurā (70.58) in the Mathurā Museum was published in *Indian Archaeology, A Review*, 1970-71, Plate LXXVIIIC. A now broken eight-armed image in the center of the Pawaya lintel represented Trivikrama (*A.S.I.A.R.*, 1924-25, Plate XLIIIc). For Bādāmī versions, see Gary Tarr, "Chronology and Development of the Chāḷukya Cave Temples," *Ars Orientalis*, VIII (1970), Figs. 25-27.

2. V. V. Mirashi, *Inscriptions of the Vākāṭakas*, 73.

3. I have not found an exact parallel for this figure in iconography and thus cannot identify the specific form of Śiva. For corpulent Śiva images, see V. S. Agarwala, "Terracotta Figurines of Ahichhatrā, District Bareilly, U. P.", *Ancient India* 4 (1947-48), Pls. LXIII-LXIV.

that runs throughout Indian art. As in those other monuments in which the Indian tradition comes closest to reproducing the visual forms of reality (for example, at Amarāvatī or in the Kuṣāṇa *yakṣīs* of Mathurā), the specific is always combined with the ideal.

The richly ornamented, corpulent dwarves at Rāmtek (Plate 14) invite comparison in terms of style. For all their difference in size and condition, there are real resemblances of general proportions and asymmetrical pose. The head-dress cascading to one side of the top right figure in Plate 14 occurs in much more complex form in the Manasar piece. Most distinctive of this figure is its subtle, irregular modelling, for example, in the multiple creases in its pudgy arms or the way the waist bulges irregularly over the central sash. Some of the same effect emerges in the lower right dwarf of Plage 14, where the flesh doubles over a similar sash or fold of the body.

The guardians of Ajantā Cave 19 are yet closer to the Manasar figure in the general quality of their carving (Plate 2). For example, the top of the chest shows the same small fold on either side below the armpit, although such modelling is not apparent in the limbs, perhaps because of the guardian's greater stature. In general the Ajantā figure shows a similar richness of detail in head-dress and ornament, while it does not follow the unique style of coiled locks from which the Manasar figure's curls descend. The pearled band or *yajñopavīta* in both twists with subtle irregularity, as do many of the swags of pearls in the Ajantā paintings. Allowing for differences of iconography and position here, I find the two carvings similar in spirit, although the Ajantā carver did not show the extraordinarily inventive handling of detail that distinguishes the Manasar artist.

I must frankly admit that the comparisons with Ajantā are not sufficient to indicate a date conclusively. If the supposition that the Cave 19 guardians derive from such a source is correct, it could be argued that the Manasar image precedes the year 475 A.D. Perhaps it corresponds to the first part of the reign of Pravarasena II (*c.* 420-50 ? A.D.), when we know of the prominence of the Manasar-Rāmtek region. Yet it is unlikely that images ceased to be produced here when the nearby Nandivardhana was no longer the capital.

By the same token, images from the region of the second capital need not be dated exclusively to the period after the shift.

V. V. Mirashi has argued that Pavnar should be equated with Pravarapura, which he suggests became Pravaraṣeṇa's capital some time after the eighteenth year of his reign, *c.* 438 A.D.[1] A number of images have been found here in the course of building an *āśrama* for the followers of Vinobā Bhāve, where most are preserved. An extremely interesting set of large reliefs are unfortunately so weathered that all surface detail has been lost (Plates 17-21). These have in the past been identified as illustration of the *Rāmāyaṇa*, but more recent Indian scholarly opinion would favor Kṛṣṇa scenes as the subject.[2] Thus the panel in Plate 17 may represent Vasudeva transporting the baby to Gokul, and that in Plate 19 shows Balarāma killing the ass-demon Dhenuka in a grove of palm trees.

These reliefs invite comparison with the somewhat smaller Kṛṣṇa and *Rāmāyaṇa* scenes that originally surrounded the plinth of the Gupta temple at Deogarh (Plates 28, 29). While no examples of precisely the same incident are preserved from the two sites, a comparison in style is proper. On the whole, the Pavnar panels are more complex in composition and contain more figures, often three-dimensionally interrelated. Nothing at Deogarh approaches the tangled battle scene of Plate 20. The complexity is in part the result of the variety and naturalness of individual poses at Pavnar. For example, Vasudeva stands rather stiffly at the moment of Devakī's handing the baby to him in the Deogarh example (Plate 28). In Plate 17, on the other hand, a previous and apparently more suspenseful moment is selected, and the actions of the surrounding figures contrast with the emphatic stride of Vasudeva. Whereas Gupta versions of the killing of Dhenuka stick to Balarāma, the ass, and a tree, the Pavnar example in Plate 19 sets off the assured action of the central figure with three spectators in consternation.[3] The rags

1. V. V. Mirashi, *Inscriptions of the Vākāṭakas*, 22ff.; "Pravarapura, Ancient Capital of the Vākāṭakas," in *Studies in Indology* (V. V. Mirashi) II, 272-84 (which also appeared in *Sarūpa-Bhāratī*, Vishveshvaranand Vedic Research Institute, Hoshiarpur, Publications Series no. 6).

2. Mirashi (*ibid.*) suggested the *Rāmāyaṇa*. The revision has been proposed by Dr. A. Jamkhedkar, State Director of Archaeology in Maharashtra. I am grateful to Dr. Devangana Desai for informing me of this.

3. One example is on a slab from Mandor, near Jodhpur (*Archaeological Survey of India, Annual Report* 1905-06, p. 138, fig. 2 top). A second version of this scene occurs on a pillar from Mathurā, now in a French private

of the kneeling onlooker here or of the seated figure in Plate 18 are convincingly foreshortened, unlike the jarring pose of Śūrpaṇakhā, whose nose is cut off in Plate 29, or of other seated figures from the Deogarh base. Finally, the Pavnar figures are taller in canon and seem slenderer as a result of their tapered waists, unlike their more columnar counterparts at Deogarh. In short, the artists of Deogarh and Pavnar differ substantially. For some panels in the Pavnar group, a later date and affinities to the south (Rāṣṭrakūṭa sculpture, for example) are tempting. Yet the analogy between the seated figures in Plate 18 and the paintings on the porch of Ajantā Cave 17 are equally great. Without surface detail, one can go no further.

A Buddha image also found at Pavnar seems more strongly allied with Gupta styles than anything we have seen so far from Vidarbha (Plate 22). Its drapery-folds recall Mathurā, yet their symmetrical form and wide spacing are not those of the great center on the Yamunā in its mature Gupta phase, which the very articulate body forms and bent knee suggest.[1] The modelling of the hand on the right is as subtle and sensitive as that of the Manasar Śiva, more so than that of any preserved Mathurā Buddha. This image suggests a localization of forms perhaps distantly and somewhat earlier derived from Mathurā.

Finally, the life-size image of Gaṅgā found at Pavnar as well serves to link all the pieces from Vidarbha (Plate 23). The inscription to the side of her right knee has been read by V. V. Mirashi as *Gaṅgā Bhagavatī* and ascribed to the Vākāṭaka period.[2] It is obviously impossible to determine whether this corresponded to a Yamunā on the opposite side of a doorway, although the general absence of the pair at Ajantā should make this unlikely.

The figure type of this Gaṅgā resembles in a general way those of the Pavnar *Rāmāyaṇa* panels, with slender proportions and tapered waist. The sensitive modelling of the stomach, with the

collection (another face of which is reproduced in Plate a of Jean Filliozat, "Representations de Vāsudeva et Saṃkarṣaṇa," *Arts Asiatiques* XXVI, 1973). These two abbreviated examples show that Deogarh provides at least some basis for comparison with Pavnar, in scale and in formal effect.

1. A Buddha image from Mathurā in Calcutta shows symmetrical folds, perhaps an early fifth century feature. Sāñcī Buddhas frequently have more closely spaced, incised, symmetrical folds.

2. V. V. Mirashi, *Inscriptions of the Vākāṭakas*, p. lxii.

waist subtly bulging on one side is reminiscent of the sense of flesh in the Manasar Śiva. The delicate treatment of drapery is also in keeping with what we have seen on the Manasar figure, although no specific element is precisely the same. At the same time, the vigorously foliate *makara* resembles many at Ajantā as well as countless Gupta examples. It is impossible to think of the Ajantā examples as small versions of this dramatic model.

For all these connections with the rest of Vākāṭaka and with Gupta art, the Pavnar Gaṅgā has a puzzling South Indian flavor. The clear elongation of the body and head is largely responsible for this effect; yet the breasts are larger than the characteristic Pallava type, nor do details support such a comparison. Likewise, one is reminded of Rāṣṭrakūṭa figures (again different in detail) or even early Cōḻa examples (yet less borne out in specifics).[1] I am left with the conclusion that the figure is part of a style entrenched in Vidarbha, not an intrusion from farther south, although it is possible that the style is a northern extension of that sinuous figure type which is most characteristic of the south from Amarāvatī on. To judge from this image in particular, the Vidarbha Vākāṭaka style was *sui generis* in figural type for the fifth century A.D. Thus, again, a precise date is impossible.

CONCLUSION

In conclusion, it seems to me that the Vidarbha pieces represent an idiom independent of the Gupta *koine* which spread from Gujarāt to Bengāl. Sensitivity of surface modelling and willowy anatomy for all but corpulent types seem to distinguish works of this area, as well as some specific decorative motifs. Both the Pavnar Gaṅgā and the Manasar Śiva evade classification as Gupta works in any significant sense. In fact, it is just conceivable that a few works from major Gupta centers show Vākāṭaka influence.[2] Thus, a Vidarbha Vākāṭaka style explains much of what is peculiar to Ajantā, which I would understand as a vigorous provincial version of that idiom. The Pavnar Gaṅgā

1. For example, compare the River Goddess Shrine of the Kailāśanātha at Ellora or the figures of the Nāgeśvara temple at Kumbhakonum.

2. I would propose, for example, the friezes of Gadhwa which show an unusually sinuous figure type : J. C. Harle, *Gupta Sculpture*, Plates 71-78. Not all of the Gupta carving at Gadhwa is of this style.

resembles figures in the painting there, but not in the sculpture as a whole. The Manasar Śaivite figure is reflected in the facade of Cave 19 at Ajantā. At least some architectural motifs link the two Vākāṭaka areas. One must admit that some direct Gupta influence as well as sheer localism were also at work at Ajantā. But, on the whole, the answer to the questions with which we began seems to be this : indeed, there was a Vākāṭaka style, and it was more independent from the Gupta than not. Gupta influence was felt in that part of Bundelkhand that had been briefly controlled by the Vākāṭakas, to judge from the Ucchakalpa inscriptions, for I understand nothing at Nāchnā as particularly derived from Vidarbha. Yet farther south in Kosala we come to an area where Gupta communication networks must have given out and where influence from the southern sphere was dominant. The styles are not rigidly limited to dynastic boundaries, but they are at least associated with the political fortunes of the two great powers.

The fact that most of the Vidarbha works are Brāhmaṇical, while Ajantā is clearly Buddhist, might be taken to have some bearing on one of the themes to which several other essays in this volume are devoted, the question of religious tolerance. Clearly, the fact that the Vākāṭaka rulers were themselves Hindu did not prevent them from having ministers such as Varāhadeva, an ardent donor of Buddhist caves. Beyond that, however, it would be misleading to use the evidence of stylistic commonalities to indicate religious toleration. The same artists seem to have been employed by patrons of different religions throughout the history of Indian art, even in situations of competition and incompatibility.

Should the fifth-century style of North and Central India be dubbed the "Vākāṭaka-Gupta", Majumdar and Altekar's term for the period as a whole ? To my mind, the two are too different and the points of contact too limited to justify uniting the dynastic terms. Nor are the two necessarily synchronous, although a discussion of chronology is probably premature. The Vākāṭaka style seems different in broad historical terms from the Gupta. On the one hand, Vākāṭaka work continues a sense of specificity in modelling which was characteristic of the second century A.D., both in Kuṣāṇa Mathurā and Amarāvatī. At the same time, the Gupta artists had shifted the balance

Plate 1. Ajantā, Cave 19, Nāgarāja with Two Queens

Plate 2. Ajantā, Cave 19, Guardian (photo courtesy J. and S. Huntington)

Plate 3. Ajantā, Cave 20, porch doorway
(photo courtesy J. and S. Huntington)

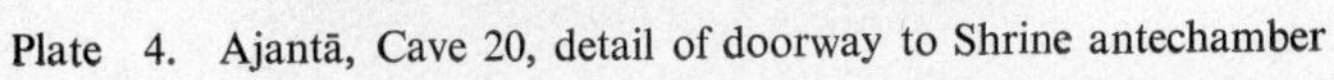

Plate 4. Ajantā, Cave 20, detail of doorway to Shrine antechamber

Plate 5. Ajantā, Cave 2, porch doorway

Plate 6. Ajantā, Cave 23, porch doorway

Plate 7. Ajantā, Cave 27, doorway to side shrine

Plate 8. Panchmarhi, cave doorway

... Temple (photo courtesy D. M. Stadtner)

Plate 10. Rāmtek, Trivikrama Shrine

Plate 11. Rāmtek, detail of Trivikrama Shrine

Plate 12. Rāmtek, detail of Trivikrama Shrine

Plate 13. Rāmtek, pilaster fragment

Plate 14. Rāmtek, doorway to Nṛsiṃha Shrine

Plate 15. Rāmtek, Trivikrama image

Plate 16. Manasar, Śiva image (photo cortesy National Museum, New Delhi)

Plate 17. Pavnar, Vasudeva transporting Kṛṣṇa

Plate 18. Pavnar, relief panel

Plate 19. Pavnar, Balarāma killing Dhenuka

Plate 20. Pavnar, relief panel

Plate 21. Pavnar, relief panel

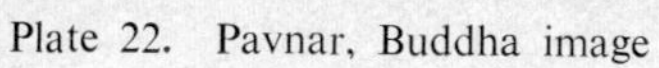

Plate 22. Pavnar, Buddha image

Plate 23. Pavnar, Gaṅgā image

Plate 24. Deogarh, Daśāvatāra Temple, Nara-Nārāyaṇa

Plate 25. Sārnāth, doorway to Main Shrine

Plate 26. Nāchnā, window grille

Plate 27. Kalyanpur, Kubera image

Plate 28. Deogarh, Daśāvatāra Temple, Devakī handing Kṛṣṇa to Vasudeva

Plate 29. Deogarh, Daśāvatāra Temple, Lakṣmaṇa and Śūrpaṇakhā

toward the ideal. The relationship between the image and the real world is distinctly different in the two. On the other hand, the Vākāṭaka style may well usher in elements of the medieval before these are apparent in the Gangetic north. Ajantā in its later years shows the gush of religiosity reflected in frenzied carving, some colossal in scale, that distinguishes later periods from the Gupta sense of aesthetic control. *Bhaktic* concerns are also evident in the very size of the Pavnar *Rāmāyaṇa* cycle, whereas such themes seem to have been treated in isolation or at least in smaller scale to the north. Similar developments took place in the second half of the sixth century with the disappearance of the Gupta style. This very time-lag is a testimony to the strength of Gupta influence within its own sphere, apparently resisting new religious currents a bit more strongly than was the case with the slightly younger Vākāṭaka artistic tradition.

To base such conclusions largely on two well-preserved Vidarbha images undoubtedly seems foolhardy. Yet in reshaping our stereotypic picture of Gupta art, I feel it is important not simply to chip away at details or to supplement the old with new pieces of information. Rather we should replace the faulty generalizations with better ones. In order to do this, hypotheses must be formulated. The existence of a Vākāṭaka style linking Ajantā with Vidarbha and largely independent from the Gupta is still only a hypothesis. If I were a scientist, I might conclude by proposing to comb Vidarbha for different kinds of images and architecture which would confirm or deny what I have argued here. It is a frequent mistake in dealing with works of art and with ancient India in general to assume that we will be more correct if we dwell on particulars and avoid interpretations. Particulars do not speak for themselves. For example, the common enumeration of Buddhist works from Sārnāth and Mathurā asserts the primacy of those centers. Moreover, most attempts at chronology involve some assumption about geographical dynamics. Thus to date the bulk of "Gupta art" after Ajantā is to assert that Ajantā was squarely within the mainstream. Finally, the high aesthetic quality of the Pavnar Gaṅgā and the Manasar Śaivite figure is surely itself an aspect of their form and one which cries out for understanding. To hypothesize a sophisticated and independent Central Vākāṭaka style is a tribute to this excellence.

10

THE GREAT CAVE AT ELEPHANTA: A STUDY OF SOURCES

WALTER M. SPINK

ELEPHANTA Island, a short distance from the city of Bombay, is a great attraction for visitors now as it must have been many centuries ago, because there we find a vast Śaivite cave temple renowned for the beauty of its huge sculptures and for its impressive interior. In this study I shall try to show that this famous temple was created in a much earlier period than is generally recognized, and that it is, in fact, strikingly connected with the artistic tradition of Gupta times.

The so-called Great Cave at Elephanta—sometimes called "Cave 1" and sometimes just "Elephanta"—is the main monument on the island, although there are a number of smaller caves there also. It appears that the latter were under way when the Great Cave was started and that they were left somewhat unfinished in most cases when that great excavation became the absorbing center of attention.[1] There are also traces of a few brick structures of uncertain function. One, recently unearthed, may have been a large dock down near the shore, although it now appears to be above sea level due to the silting in of the area. This "dock" appears to have been contemporary with the Great Cave, judging from the size and the shape of the bricks from which it was built; its presence suggests that there may have been

1. The lesser Elephanta caves bear close stylistic connections with the relatively early Śaivite caves at Jogeśvari and Mandapeśvar. Furthermore, the Great Cave, with its eastern orientation, would probably have opened where Cave 2 is now located, had not the latter already been under way.

considerable commercial and/or pilgrimage activity at that time, which we would expect if the Great Cave was by then completed. A huge stone elephant, now standing outside the museum at the Victoria Gardens in Bombay, also may belong to the same period. It once stood prominently on the island and because it was a landmark it provided the island (properly called *Ghārāpuri*) with its present popular name.

Of all Elephanta's ancient relics, there are none more intriguing than the vast numbers of apparently identical small copper coins with which the island appears to have been virtually seeded in ancient times. In my excursions around the island, I have never yet found a modern coin underfoot, but I have happened upon a number of these earlier issues.[1] Such hints of their abundance are confirmed by the fact that one can procure them in considerable numbers from the children who live there. Admittedly, no one has ever collected them with much fervor; they are generally so eroded and so encrusted with copper oxides that they have little value either for their metal or for beauty's sake. Their surface designs and legends are so hard to see that numismatists have long been baffled about their origin, particularly since no similar small coppers have been collected or identified at other sites in India.

Now, however, the mystery surrounding these little coins seems to have been solved, and the solution is a revealing one. Dr. (Mrs.) S. Gokhale of Deccan College has concluded that these coppers were issued by King Kṛṣṇarāja, the great ruler of the Early Kalacuri dynasty, who was reigning in western India in the mid-sixth century A.D.[2] Previously only his silver coins (Kṛṣṇarāja-rūpakas) have been known; they have been found at a number of sites in western and central India.[3]

Judging from the number of these coins that I alone have seen collected by the local people, it is fair to assume that thousands

1. V. M. Vani of the SW Circle, Archaeologicl Survey of India, Aurangābād, has been resposible for bringing much of this new material to attention.

2. Dr. (Mrs.) Gokhale kindly sent me a typescript of her paper entitled "Elephanta Hoard of Copper Coins of Kṛṣṇarāja" read at All India Numismatic Conference, Indore, 1975. I understand that S. R. Rao is also planning to publish some of these new finds.

3. See V. V. Mirashi, *Inscriptions of the Kalacuri-Cedi Era*, Corpus Inscriptionum Indicarum. Ootacamund, 1955. Vol. 4, Pt. 1, pp. clxxx-clxxxii.

have turned up on this small island in the last few decades. A number of these may have come from hoards buried in early times, which the action of water or of plough later dispersed, but by far the greater number appear to be scattered surface finds of coins which were misplaced or dropped long ago by their ancient owners. Since any such scattered surface finds can represent only a very small percentage of the coins in circulation at a given time, it seems that this currency must have been in remarkably intensive use on the island when Kṛṣṇarāja was ruling.

How does one explain this remarkable concetration of Kṛṣṇa-rāja's copper coins on such a very small island ? The explanation would seem to be that they were connected with the presence there of the Great Cave. It is significant that, long before this new numismatic evidence was revealed, V. V. Mirashi proposed that the Great Cave was an Early Kalacuri dedication, "excavated in the second half of the sixth century A.D. when the Kalacuri power was at its peak".[1] More recently, I suggested that it was a royal dedication of Kṛṣṇarāja himself, and assigned it to *c.* 535-50 A.D. on the basis of various historical and art historical considerations which will be mentioned below.[2] The new numismatic evidence lends strong confirmation to these views, which are quite at variance with the traditional "textbook" dating of the monument to the eighth century or (now more commonly) to the seventh century A.D. Admittedly, Kṛṣṇarāja's silver issues continued to be circulated throughout much of India long after his death—a fact which might be accounted for by the great numbers of coins which this famous king must have minted as well as the acknowledged consistency of their silver content. For this reason one cannot conclude that a site necessarily dated from his reign just because his coins are found there. However, at any very much later date his currency would not have been used so exclusively or found in such intensive concentrations as were the copper coins on Elephanta Island. Therefore, we can certainly believe that the coppers became scattered around on the island in the same general period in which they were issued.

1. *Ibid.*, p. cxlviii.

2. See W. Spink, *Ajantā to Ellora*, Ann Arbor, 1967 simultaneously published as *Mārg*, 22 (2) (March, 1967), p. 9; for a more detailed view, see forthcoming article on Jogeśvari in *Journal of the Indian Society of Oriental Art*.

Mrs. Gokhale has suggested that the coins—being of very small denominations and so far found nowhere else but on the island itself—may have been minted especially for the purpose of paying the workmen who carved the Great Cave. This may well be, since the king could obviously have done this on his own authority; if so, it would be one further reason to assume that the Great Cave was a royal benefaction. Of course, the coin finds would also reflect the great devotional activity seen at the site during its heyday, as well as the "commercial" activity which even today surrounds any flourishing temple. This activity presumably dropped off drastically after the sixth century, for finds of later coins on the island are relatively rare, although as we would expect ihey do occur, as do finds of certain earlier types also.

Having shown how numismatic evidence helps to establish the date and perhaps even the specific patronage of the Great Cave at Elephanta, we will now review other evidence bearing upon the matter. We will first give arguments to suggest that Elephanta is a *mid-sixth century* A.D. monument; secondly, we shall try to show that it is a mid-sixth century *Early Kalacuri monument*; and, thirdly, we shall try to establish it as a mid-sixth century Early Kalacuri monument *sponsored by the great King Kṛṣṇarāja.*

I. ELEPHANTA IS A MID-SIXTH CENTURY A.D. MONUMENT

In previous studies we have proposed that the Great Cave can be assigned a mid-sixth century date on the basis of a combination of artistic and epigrahic evidence. We will outline some of this evidence here.

A. *Evidence from related later cave temples at Bādāmī and Ellora.*

1. The Great Cave at Elephanta is the architectural prototype for the very similar excavation called the Dhumar Lena (Cave 29) at Ellora; the Dhumar Lena adjusts and actually improves upon Elephanta's layout, and furthermore copies its iconographic program. Other caves at Ellora such as the Rāmeśvara (Cave 21) belong to the same period as the Dhumar Lena and also reflect the influence of Elephanta in their

sculptural style and in their iconography.[1]

2. These early Hindu (Śaivite) caves at Ellora bear many close connections with the Hindu caves at Bādāmī, but most particularly with Bādāmī Caves 1 and 2, which are quite different in type from Bādāmī Cave 3.[2]

3. Bādāmī Caves 1 and 2 are related to but clearly earlier than Bādāmī Cave 3, which was completed or nearing completion in 578 A.D., as we know from a dated inscription therein.[3] Therefore, Caves 1 and 2 must date prior to 578 A.D.; they were probably undertaken at about 560 A.D., although such a date is necessarily approximate.[4]

4. Since the early Ellora caves (e.g., the Dhuṃar Lena and the Rāmeśvara) are clearly derived from the Great Cave at Elephanta and since they in turn are related to Bādāmī Caves 1 and 2, Elephanta must have been begun by the mid-sixth century.

B. *Evidence from related earlier cave temples.*

1. The latest Mahāyāna caves at Ajantā, along with Aurangābād caves 1 and 3, are the stylistic source for many features in the relief panels and decorative carvings of the Śaivite caves at Jogeśvari and Mandapeśvar, which in turn directly influence the Great Cave at Elephanta.[5]

2. Work on the above Ajantā and Aurangābād caves had completely ended by *c.*485 A.D., so that a date no later than the first half of the sixth century for Jogeśvari, Mandapeśvar, and Elephanta is eminently reasonable.[6] Some of the Ajantā and Aurangābād craftsmen undoubtedly moved to

1. See W. Spink, "Ellora's Earliest Phase", *Bulletin of the American Academy of Benares*, Vol. 1 (1967), pp. 11-22.

2. M. Neff in *Mārg*, 13 (4) (September, 1960), pp. 21-60, recognizes many of these connections; but she believes that Elephanta derives from the Dhumar Lena rather than vice versa, and thus dates it to the seventh century A.D.

3. *Indian Antiquary*, Vol. VI, p. 363; Vol. X, p. 57 ff.

4. R. D. Banerji, in *The Bas-reliefs of Bādāmī*, Memoirs of the Archaeological Survey of India, 25 (1928) dated Cave 3 (therein called Cave 4) earlier than Caves 1 and 2, as have a few later writers.

5. See W. Spink, *Ajantā to Ellora* for many comparisons.

6. For a detailed analysis, see "Bāgh : A Study", *Archives of Asian Art*, 30 (1976-1977), pp. 53-84.

the Bombay region to find work after patronage at those Buddhist sites collapsed with the fall of the Vākāṭaka dynasty. Until recently much of the work at Ajantā and Aurangābād was assigned to the seventh and even to the eighth century A.D. This seemed to support the old view that Elephanta and Jogeśvari belonged to the eighth century. However, now that Ajantā and Aurangābād Caves 1 and 3 appear to date not later than the late fifth century, Elephanta's dating to the mid-sixth century is clearly allowed—in fact, it is practically demanded as a conclusion.

II. ELEPHANTA IS A MID-SIXTH CENTURY EARLY KALACURI MONUMENT

If Elephants should be dated, on the above evidence, to the mid-sixth century or slightly earlier (say 535-50 A.D.), the question arises about its dynastic patronage, since previously it has been considered as an eighth century Rāṣṭrakūṭa monument, or a seventh century monument of either the Cālukyas or the local Maurya dynasty. The assumption that it is an Early Kalacuri (*Kaṭacuri*) benefaction solves this problem and is far more reasonable.[1]

A. Epigraphic evidence proves, and numismatic evidence appears to confirm the conclusion, that the Early Kalacuri dynasty controlled the Konkan and much of the western and northern Deccan during the last half of the Sixth century.[2] Their sovereignty over the Konkan must have started sometime prior to 533 A.D., when the former Traikūṭaka capital, Aniruddhapura, came under their control. The Matvan inscription of the year 284 (=533 A.D.) speaks of the "victorious Aniruddhapura of the Kaṭachchuris" (i.e., Kalacuris).[3] Thus Elephanta was in the Early Kalacuri domains during this period; their control could have started any time between

1. C. Sivaramamurti has proposed a fifth to sixth century A.D. Vākāṭaka date in *Indian Sculpture*, New Delhi, 1961, p. 58, while R. Parimoo, in "Elephanta in the Context of Evolution and Significance of Śaiva Sculpture", *Journal of the Oriental Institute*, Vol XXVI, No. 3 (March, 1977), pp. 282-305, also suggests that it may have been begun by the Vākāṭakas. However this would place it too early if, as we believe, Vākāṭaka rule had ended by *c.* 482 A.D.

2. V. V. Mirashi, *Inscriptions of the Kalacuri-Cedi Era*, pp. xliv-li.

3. S. Gokhale, "Matvan Plates of Vikramāṣeṇa, K 284 (=A.D. 533)" *Prof. G. H. Khare Felicitation Volume*, Poona, forthcoming.

505 and 533 A.D. In 505 A.D. the Traikūṭakas were still dominant in the region as we know from another inscription.[1]

B. Elephanta's Great Cave and the other two major early Hindu cave temples in the Bombay region, at Mandapeśvar and Jogeśvari, all appear to have been monuments of the Pāśupata sect of Śaivism, the very sect which Kṛṣṇarāja is said (in an inscription of his son and successor) to have ardently espoused.[2] Both Elephanta's Great Cave and Mandapeśvar have two extant images of Lakulīśa, an incarnation of Śiva worshipped by the Pāśupata sect, while Jogeśvari (whose doorway motifs are better preserved) has four such images, all on its main (east-west) axis. The famous Parel Śiva stele, which like Mandapeśvar and Jogeśvari probably dates to the first half of the sixth century, provides evidence of the vigorous quality of Śiva worship in the Bombay region at this time. This may support the view (discussed later) that Kṛṣṇarāja's predecessors, and Kṛṣṇarāja himself, retained strong connections with Māhiśmatī (the traditional capital of the Early Kalacuri dynasty) even after they had extended their power into the Konkan.

C. The early Hindu phase at Ellora, which is so closely connected with Elephanta on stylistic grounds, is also connected in its iconography. The Rāmeśvara has a figure of Lakulīśa at the exact center of its facade, as does Cave 19, while the Dhumar Lena has his figure at one of the entrances. All of the earliest Ellora caves are Śaivite, again supporting our assumption that they are Early Kalacuri monuments and confirming the view that the Early Kalacuris were the dominant power in Western India from about 530-600 A.D.

III. ELEPHANTA IS MID-SIXTH CENTURY EARLY KALACURI MONUMENT SPONSORED BY THE GREAT KING KṚṢṆARĀJA

A. The very grandeur of the Great Cave at Elephanta, which could only have resulted from a vast expenditure of time,

1. S. Gokhale, "Matvan Plates of the Traikūṭaka king Madhyamaṣeṇa, K 256 (=A.D. 505)", *Proceedings of the All-India Oriental Conference*, 26th Session, Ujjain, October, 1972.

2. See Ābhōṇa Plates of Śaṅkaragaṇa of the year 347, in V. V. Mirashi, *Inscriptions of the Kalacuri-Cedi Era*, p. 42.

labor, and money, suggests that it is a royal monument. If our approximate dating is correct, and if we are to seek a likely candidate for its patron, Kṛṣṇarāja is the prime contender. Neither the roughly contemporary Yaśodharman, nor Cālukyan rulers, nor any of the successors of the Guptas are known to have had influence in the Konkan at this time.

1. According to the Ābhōṇa grant of his son Śaṅkaragaṇa, the "illustrious Kṛṣṇarāja, who brightened the world with his fame...was devoted to Paśupati (Śiva) from his very birth...He acquired wealth (*only*) for the sake of religious merit, and accumulated religious merit (*only*) to secure final liberation."[1] Even allowing for conventional overstatement, the reference gives us an insight into Kṛṣṇarāja's interests and character.
2. The fact that the Great Cave at Elephanta, although later than the caves at Jogeśvari, Mandapeśvar, and the other lesser caves at Elephanta, is the only one which was finished, suggests that its patron had the necessary power and wealth to hire workmen away from the other projects and to begin even greater undertakings of his own, perhaps in the desire to announce his successes; this again suggests that Elephanta's Great Cave may be a royal monument.
3. If, as Mrs. Gokhale suggests, the abundance of copper coins on Elephanta island is due to their being specially minted to pay the workers on the Great Cave, this would clearly confirm the connection of the king with the cave. In any case, the abundance of his coins on the island certainly suggests—perhaps proves—that the cave belongs to his regnal period.

If our arguments for dating Elephanta as a mid-sixth century monument are convincing, we can better let it assume its appropriate position as the culminating example of what could (loosely) be called the "Gupta" style in western India. How much more satisfactory this is than to consider it, as has been done so often in the past, as contemporary with the eighth century Kailāsa temple (Cave 16) at Ellora, which has a completely different

1. *Ibid.*, p. 42.

esthetic. In fact, such a mid-sixth century dating has the effect of placing Elephanta very near the beginning of the sequence of major Hindu cave temples in India—well before the important Hindu excavations at Bādāmī, Aihole, and Māmallapuram, as well as before those at Ellora.

There are, of course, a series of very small Hindu excavations at Udayagiri in Central India, which mostly date from the early fifth century, but Elephanta's only large scale Hindu prototypes are to be found in the Bombay region itself, the most important examples being the nearby caves at Jogeśvari and Mandapeśvar, which appear to have been excavated in *c.* 520—*c.* 525 A.D., shortly before Kṛṣṇarāja's reign and his establishment of the Early Kalacuri house as such. Kṛṣṇarāja's line does not appear to have been called Kaṭacuri (i.e., Early Kalacuri) prior to his time, even though it is quite possible that this predecessor was his father (or father-in-law) as we will later suggest.

Jogeśvari and Mandapeśvar are ambitious works, both in terms of their size and their detailing, and were clearly the productions of artisans trained in or at least familiar with complex excavation procedures and with established modes of decorating such features as pillars and doorways. Thus, it is hardly surprising that they bear some remarkable connections with the later Mahāyāna caves at Ajantā and with the contemporary Caves 1 and 3 at Aurangābād, for these late fifth century Buddhist caves were paramount examples of the excavators' art, created by artisans among whom many of the fathers and grandfathers of the Bombay region artists must have been numbered.

Using the Śaivite cave temple at Jogeśvari as a focus, we can point out certain of these connections with Vākāṭaka prototypes, in order to support this assertion, and to show how certain adjustments are being made to conform with the new sectarian or ritual needs. Unlike the Buddhist vihāras, Jogeśvari was not a residence cave. It is essentially a shrine for a Śiva liṅgam, which appears at the very heart of the large main hall, within its four-doored garbhagṛha (Plate 5, 9). The main axis of the cave complex, following the conventions of the time, runs from east to west. Along it, in a series of separate vestibules and courts, various significant images or scenes are carved in relief, appearing in a haphazard variety of locations and shapes and sizes (Plate 6, 7, 8). The plan is far from focussed. In fact, despite the fact that four images of Lakulīśa, the form of Śiva especially honored by the Early Kalacuris, appear at various points along the east-west axis, one's attention in the cave interior tends to be drawn to the less important south side with its long colonnaded porch, from which light streams into the cave through three large doors and two large windows (Plate 9). The prototypes for this powerful but distracting architectural feature is to be found in the standard Vākāṭaka vihāra, where the only access to the cave was through the porch (Plate 13). This conventional type was retained, and indeed distractingly emphasized, in this formative Hindu cave, despite the different function of the new cave, and despite the fact that it opens onto a blind court and therefore cannot function as a major entrance[1] (Plate 10). The Vākāṭaka Buddhist caves also prove to be the source for a number of important sculptural motifs which are used in this and other Early Kalacuri cave temples. We can readily compare many of the beautifully ornate doorways at Jogeśvari with Vākāṭaka prototypes. The South Porch doorway (Plate 11), very comparable to that of Aurangābād Cave 1's (Plate 12), is but one of many examples, while a number of reliefs and guardian figures show a similar "family" connection.[2]

Jogeśvari is, all in all, a somewhat clumsy conception; its parts are strung together additively, yet it is an ambitious undertaking—its east-west axis is actually one of the longest of any cave temple in India, measuring 250 feet from where it starts to where it ends. This is remarkable when we consider that Jogeśvari is the inaugural example in a series of related Early Kalacuri excavations and that it has no really developed prototypes. It could hardly be called a successfully composed monument, but it has the vigor which one might well expect at the start of a new era of patronage as intensive as that of the Early Kalacuris. It is the first truly impressive Hindu cave temple in India.

A few years later, at Elephanta (*c.* 535-550 A.D.) we find that some remarkable transformations have taken place. The main

1. The only entrance to the court from the outside is a narrow path leading past a shrine once dedicated to Durgā (now to Hanumāna); the "path" may have originally been made to drain off water during the monsoon, when the deep-set cave always floods.

2. See W. Spink, *Ajantā to Ellora* for illustrations.

hall of the cave, instead of being dark and enclosed like a Buddhist monastic dwelling, is now defined as a vast open pillared space (Plate 16). The primacy of the east-west axis is maintained; the main (east) entrance being approached through a deep excavated court (Plate 15), while the liṅgam shrine is moved toward the west, allowing a larger space in front of the shrine for ritual use and incidentally allowing an unobstructed view from across the cave of the three great figural panels on the south wall (Plate 17). Towering guardians (Plate 20), more svelte and developed versions of the heavy colossi in Jogeśvari's east porch, are now placed on either side of the four shrine doorways, giving a new emphasis to the crucial shrine area.

Jogeśvari's unbalanced and conflicting entrances have now been replaced, at Elephanta, by three large pillared openings of equal size; furthermore, it is possible that the original plan for the cave may well have included a fourth such opening at the south, deep in the heart of the mountain. This would have necessitated the cutting of a large blind court and extremely deep light well in that area, but the fact that the Dhumar Lena *has* a blind court (Plate 26, 27) of almost exactly the depth (about 80 feet) which would have been required at Elephanta shows that such an undertaking would have been possible. In this regard, we should remember that Elephanta's East and West courts (Plate 15), although less ambitious in scale, are of this same general type, as are Jogeśvari's East and South courts (Plate 7, 10). Plans for this hypothetical South court at Elephanta may have been given up because of the difficulties anticipated in its excavation, or else because the new idea of including the colossal Mahādeva image (which along with the Ardhanārīśvara and Gaṅgādhara panels are nowhere to be found at Jogeśvari) took precedence. Possibly both of these reasons played a part.[1]

1. The ceiling of the Great Cave is the lowest (16-17 feet) at the North Entrance, where we would expect the excavation to have been begun, it being the easiest of access. The cave's height was increased as excavation continued; in front of the Mahādeva the ceiling height is nearly twenty-one feet, while the south wall reliefs are all at least six feet higher than those at the north. It seems clear that the total conception of the cave underwent significant changes shortly after the cave was started and that the cave height was adjusted in the interest of increased grandeur, and because the idea of a south portal, balancing that on the north, was given up.

At Elephanta, remarkably effective and major changes are made in the overall conception of the monument, reflecting both the brilliance of the architect and the temper of the times—times which were energetically fostering new architectural and iconographic formulations, which were to provide a secure basis for future developments.

Not only is the interior of the central hall vastly enlarged, but all of the sculptural panels, found in such scattered and often incidental locations at Jogeśvari (Plate 5), have been brought into the interior, composed much more uniformly, and placed in the well-lighted and important positions on either side of the east, west, and north entrances. (Plate 14). These paired groupings of narrative reliefs, representing Śiva meditating, dancing, battling demons, or associated with his consort Pārvatī (Plate 18), culminate with the scenes on the south wall, deep in the heart of the cave, where the giant Mahādeva image, a towering presence, looms in the shadows. (Plate 17). The whole arrangement has something of the quality of a maṇḍala or mystical devotional diagram into which the devotee can penetrate more and more deeply as the stories of the god reveal their meanings. The colossal Mahādeva, like some emergent cosmic man rising out of the heart of the mountain itself, finally gathers these different meanings into the complex single form, where the polarities of masculine and feminine, of the furious and the benign, of the destructive and the protective ultimately are merged. Finally, more abstract still, the liṅgam in the garbhagṛha or womb-house at the ritual center of the great hall, could be considered the symbolic seed out of which all these instructing meanings have come forth (Plate 20). It represents the intersection point between the world of space and time and history in which the gods and their powers are revealed, and the unmanifest realm which lies beyond, or within, this revelation.

Elephanta's eloquent impact is due not only to the impressiveness of its interior organization, but equally to the calm intensity—the serene authority—of the huge images which it contains. Filled with a florescent vigor, they are at the same time suffused with a radiant inner calm. The following description by J. Rosenfield beautifully describes the interplay of form and meaning which invests them :

"here the...image is more than a symbolic formula... (It is) also an aesthetic conception whose formal properties project an essential aspect of the faith...This imagery is suffused with a spirit of tranquillity and equipoise, avoiding extreme and violent emotion, and projects something of the flawless spiritual states of serene confidence, untouched by rage, or by egoism, by...delusion, anxiety or doubt...These images have an extraordinary quality of weightlessness and equipoise because the surface is so plain and the parts of the body are interconnected in a free-flowing, smooth manner one with the other. The face bears a benign expression, the eyes are cast downward, projecting a sense of introspection and calmness."[1]

Yet Rosenfield's description was not written to describe these images, but rather to characterize the type of Buddha image which was developed at Sārnāth during the late Gupta period ! The reason it can be applied to the Elephanta figures is that they still partake so deeply of the Gupta esthetic ideals which had developed by the late fifth century, not only in eastern India but in the Vākāṭaka domains in central and western India as well. We can see how striking the connections are when we compare typical late fifth century images from the Vākāṭaka caves (e.g., Bāgh (Plate 1) and Ajantā (Plate 2) and Sārnāth (Plate 3) productions of the same general period with the slightly later Elephanta carvings (Plate 4). It is for this reason that we can rightly consider the sculptures at Elephanta to be among the culminating examples of what we can call—in an admittedly imprecise way—the Gupta style; indeed, these figures might even be considered that style's most impressive formulation.

As we have pointed out, there seems to be an intimate link between the Vākāṭaka productions of the late fifth century and the many monuments—Jogeśvari, Mandapeśvar, Elephanta, and various Buddhist caves too—which developed in the Bombay region in the first half of the sixth century. We shall now analyze some of these stylistic and iconographic connections by comparing a few characteristic works from Ajantā on the one hand and Elephanta on the other. At both Ajantā and Elephanta this characteristically "Gupta" mingling of energy, serenity and

1. J. Rosenfield, in an unpublished paper for Association of Asian Studies Seminar, 1961.

authority is expressed in many ways. But we shall limit our present discussion to the large painted Bodhisattva panels which are common at Ajantā, and to the equally characteristic and rather comparable scenes of Śiva's manifestations which are sculptured at Elephanta.

We should mention one surprising fact at the very start : the carvings at Elephanta are even more comparable to the Ajantā *paintings* than they are to the Ajantā *sculptures*. This is not to suggest that clear relationships between the sculptures of Ajantā and Elephanta are lacking; one need only study some of the figures in Cave 26 at Ajantā or compare the heads of the large yakṣas in Cave 2 or on Cave 19's facade with certain heads at Elephanta to see definite parallels. Equally telling comparisons could be made with some of the remarkable sculptures in Aurangābād Cave 3, which is also a late fifth century cave. However, in general, the larger sculptures in these late Vākāṭaka monuments, to which we might look for relationships, have less of that fluid and rhythmic grace than the paintings, even though they belong to exactly the same phase of patronage (Plate 23). Ajantā's sculptured compositions tend to be rather stiff and formal, whereas the painted groups overflow with crowded forms and often include dramatically effective spatial devices (Plate 21).

To explain such differences we must recognize that the medium of relief sculpture confronted the Ajantā artist with particularly difficult technical problems, especially when his goal was to suggest a complex interplay of forms. It was almost certainly a medium with which the artists of the region were relatively unfamiliar at this particular time. The dearth of fifth century sculpture from the area, either in rock-cut monuments or as stray finds, suggests that there was no long-standing local tradition of stone-carving out of which the Ajantā sculptural style could easily have grown.[1] On the other hand, we have every right to assume that painting had been flourishing here as elsewhere in the fifth century, being

1. A recently found seated yakṣa from Manasar, now in the Prince of Wales Museum, Bombay, could well date from Hariṣeṇa's period (*c.* 460-*c.* 480 A.D.). Its provenance, its Śaivite iconography, and its "imperial" quality all suggest that this unique stone figure might have been a production of a royal court artist. No other free-standing stone piece datable to Hariṣeṇa's period is known.

employed for the decoration of structural temples, important residences, and other buildings. Indeed, representations of palace architecture in the Ajantā paintings show painted designs on ceilings and pillars.

By contrast, when Elephanta was created, the sculptor was able to approach the stone with considerably increased assurance, for he had a developed and sustaining tradition behind him. There is a clear sense not only of what should be but what could be achieved, and in the face of these convictions technical difficulties recede. The Elephanta reliefs rival the Ajantā paintings in their complexity, achieving an expressiveness which, however much desired, was still beyond the reach of Ajantā's sculptors.

The connections between the Ajantā and the Elephanta panels, which are seen in the plastic and expressive qualities of their figures, are evident in many other ways as well. Modes of composition are a case in point. When we compare the compositions of those paintings at Ajantā which show bodhisattvas in the midst of their retinues (Plate 21) with the various figure panels at Elephanta (Plate 18) numerous striking parallels emerge, despite the fact that the themes of the latter are Śaivite.

The ambitious spatial arrangements at Ajantā and Elephanta, where figures are placed in a convincingly "natural" setting—in a kind of landscape niche with clear suggestions of depth—represent a high point and a turning point in this mode of rendering. Such successful "three-dimensional" groupings are seldom either attempted or achieved again in relief sculpture. Analogous compositions at Ellora, even though it is geographically much closer to Ajantā than it is to Elephanta, have far fewer similaritises; and the same is true at other sites throughout India. The most complex compositions of the Cālukyas and of the Pallavas including the famous Descent of the Gaṅgā are uni-planar in comparison; their landscapes are merely a grid of motifs adhering to, or emerging from, the arbitrarily defined background of the relief. Even the famous Rāṣṭrakūṭa relief of Rāvaṇa Shaking Kailāsa in Ellora Cave 16 (Plate 31) although generally considered a paradigm of compositional complexity, is less spatially sophisticated than its Elephanta forebears. The three-dimensionality of its separate figures is indeed striking, but there is not much illusionistic overlapping; instead, the compositional treatment reflects the subject's theatrical placement in a very deeply carved niche, beneath the body of the great temple. Like Śiva himself, who effectively holds down the raving Rāvaṇa, Śiva's mountain abode rises above the demon's cave, proclaiming the triumph of divine order over the intrusions of chaos.

In order to emulate the complex compositional effects achieved in the painted panels at Ajantā, the Elephanta sculptor had to work in a relatively deep "niche-like" space. Thus he carved his emphatic figures in a very high relief; but instead of isolating them against a flat background-plane to which subsidiary figures are merely "added" he thought of his groups as complex burgeoning units. The figures at the sides and above literally enclose the great central images, being cut out of the surrounding matrix, often standing out in very bold relief (Plate 19). We automatically think of such smaller participants as background figures, and yet whole groups of them sometimes project dramatically forward. In some cases, such secondary figures are placed in such a way as to somewhat interrupt a direct view of the central objects of our attention. In other cases, we are not even aware of their presence until we move close to the panel itself, and glancing to right or left, discover them almost beside us. In one startling case, a creature hovers in the "air" directly above us[1] (Plate 19). The sense of immediacy and the visual impact thus engendered accounts for what is often called the emergent quality of these reliefs.

This sense of immediacy and "emergence" found at Elephanta was already anticipated in the thronged arrangement of the painted compositions at Ajantā. At Ajantā no less than at Elephanta, the figures are integrated physically and psychologically. They crowd each other, they overlap, and they react in concert, in accordance with their roles. The rhythms of their response accumulate around the looming figures they attend (Plate 22). A similar array of types appears at both the sites : luxuriant females, grotesque dwarfs hovering at the feet of the larger figures, and playfully pious inhabitants of the mountain and the sky. Soaring celestial couples, an increasingly frequent feature of

1. This flying figure can be seen at the very top edge of the photographs of the Umāmaheśvara panel (Plates, 18, 19); it is somewhat broken.

iconic compositions as art develops in the late fifth and early sixth centuries, crown the compositions.[1]

At Ajantā, although Indra sometimes appears among the celestial hosts, specifically identifiable Brāhmaṇical gods are generally absent; varied groupings of musicians, garland bearers, loving couples, and even animals complete these essentially non-narrative conceptions. At Elephanta, on the other hand, the members of Ajantā's retinues yield their places without difficulty to Śiva's entourage; the seats vacated by Ajantā's lovers are transformed into an airy perch for the lord Brahmā, and mountain yields to sky in order to provide room for the numerous members of the Hindu pantheon who are transported into the environs of Śiva upon their appropriate vehicles. Pertinent details of various Śaivite tales are also necessarily included. But even with such understandable iconographic changes, the total arrangement and the concomitant effects are notably similar. The Elephanta sculptor adjusts but at the same time respects the authoritative precedents established at the earlier site, which must have been characteristic of painting in that highly creative period. Under his hand the compositions of Ajantā, although transformed into stone, are still viable; essential iconographic changes are made without violating the established formal context.

At Ajantā, forms do indeed flourish far more vigorously around the central figures than at Elephanta; the Ajantā environment is a more "natural" one. The flowers, forests, cliffs, and clouds, together with the denizens of this composite world, provide a subjective and generalized setting, a descriptive overflow of an ideal world which gods inhabit—perhaps a foretaste of Paradise. No plot demands attention and usurps the stage in these bodhisattva panels. At Elephanta, on the other hand, detailed landscape elements are included only where demanded by the subject, such as in scenes where Śiva and Pārvatī sit upon Mount Kailāsa. The Elephanta artist gives less of his attention to incidentals of the environment. He concentrates instead upon presenting a clearly

1. Flying couples never appear above *sculptured* Buddha images at Ajantā until after 475 A.D., whereas they appear in *painted* compositions at least a decade earlier; artists at this time were much more at ease in handling painted compositions, and certainly would have had much experience working in this medium when decorating structural temples and palaces. Such edifices, judging from representations in Ajantā murals, were built of wood.

defined resumé of the stories he is telling. It is not that the lesser figures (musicans, animals, etc.) were inappropriate—only that they were unnecessary and, as such, were easy and perhaps tempting to omit.[1]

The suppression of Ajantā's free narrative play of forms by a new formalizing tendency is already hinted at in the somewhat more "iconic" images at Elephanta, although the basic connections in style and attitude which link the two sites still are revealed in every gesture and in every form. It is only later that an encroaching didacticism begins to triumph over the exuberance of the great compositions we have described. It is only later, as the hieratic burden of the compositions increases, as the demands of convention mount, and as the sense of creative excitement and instinctive wonder declines, that we begin to deplore the manifest transformations which are evidently under way.

If Elephanta represents a vigorous continuation and, for the medium of sculpture, a culmination of the mode of representation characteristic of Ajantā, the Dhumar Lena could be said to represent a stage in its dissolution, or (if one prefers) in its transformation to other less pictorial ends. A more rigid compositional formula is evident; there is more concern for the central images and their main attendants, with a consequent suppression of much peripheral detail. The sense of the group's being enclosed in a deep niche, in a complex spatial setting, is gone. Narration tends to be concentrated in one plane; the groupings are often self-consciously symmetrical, and the subtle rhythmic counterpoint of the Elephanta and Ajantā compositions is largely gone. The compositions, like the figures they contain, are relatively static. The characters in the Dhumar Lena reliefs are less "involved", both literally and figuratively : the complex psychological and physical interplay so characteristic of both Elephanta and Ajantā is lost.

A comparison of the scene of Śiva and Pārvatī upon Kailāsa at Elephanta (Plate 18) with the scene of Rāvaṇa Shaking Kailāsa (Plate 30) at the Dhumar Lena will point out some

1. The preceding twelve paragraphs have been excerpted, with slight changes, from a paper for the Dr. Motichandra festschrift, being published by the Prince of Wales Museum, Bombay.

of these differences. The pictorial content in the latter example is much reduced, even though the iconography of the scene necessarily demands some attention to the mountain form under which Rāvaṇa (now rather blandly) rages. The great abode has become a simple seat; no crowded cliffs reach up to a sky burdened with devotees. Indeed, its crags are reduced to a simple plaque behind the seated couple. A few flying figures are placed in the upper corners of what is now more a "panel" than a "niche", but they in no sense surge out of the turbulent celestial realms, as they do at Elephanta. They have become unnecessary. Emphasis is placed instead on the larger flanking figures who stand upon the arbitrarily defined line of the ground which separates the upper from the nether regions. The scene has become more formal, more heraldic, a mere abstract of the story.

Even though the sculpture of the Dhumar Lena—and we have discussed its noblest relief !—seems to be the work of a particularly stolid and provincial artist who is more concerned with meaning than with form, the architecture of the cave is very well thought out indeed (Plate 25). It has none of the conflicts of focus which are to be found at both Jogeśvari and Elephanta. Obviously closely based upon Elephanta (Plate 14), it nonetheless rearranges the placement of the three portals in order to achieve a perfect bilateral symmetry, which further enhances the importance of the central liṅgam shrine. The same reliefs flank the portals as in Elephanta, although their arrangement is slightly different and they are all somewhat unfinished, due to the disruption of the cave's patronage late in the sixth century. It seems evident that the Ardhanārīśvara, Gaṅgādhara, and central Mahādeva images found on Elephanta's south wall were to have been duplicated on the rear wall here; places have been prepared for them (Plates 28, 29), even though they were never carved.[1] With this new arrangement the planners would have avoided the unconventional asymmetry of Elephanta; the colossal Mahādeva would have been directly lined up on the cave's main axis, complementing the liṅgam shrine in its placement, and no longer vying with it as the visual focus of the cave. This would,

1. The rear and side walls of these shallow niches at the rear of the Dhumar Lena were neither fully smoothed nor even plastered, suggesting that work on them was never completed.

in our opinion, have been an esthetic loss, but from a ritual and iconographic point of view would have provided a better cohesiveness for the total interior arrangement.[1]

The many stylistic connections between the Vākāṭaka caves at and near Ajantā and the Great Cave of Early Kalacuri times at Elephanta can be explained in part by their proximity in time and space. A mere two hundred miles and less than six decades separate them, so it is very reasonable to think that the immediate descendants of the Ajantā craftsmen moved, sometime after the disruption of Vākāṭaka patronage, to the Bombay region where there was much new work to do, first under the Traikūṭakas and then under the victorious Early Kalacuris, as we shall explain below.

One of the earliest witnesses to this new phase of patronage, after a hiatus of over three hundred years (during which time there is no evidence that any carving had been done in the caves of the Konkan and Western Ghāts), may well be the gigantic standing Buddhas which were added to the porch ends of the Buddhist chaitya hall at Kaṇherī, just a few miles from Bombay. These huge figures (Plate 24) stand in remarkable contrast both in size and in style to the modest little Buddha images which were carved on the right stambha in the court when the chaitya hall was being excavated in the second century A.D. (Plates 32, 33). The early sculptures are themselves of peculiar interest, being the only extant Buddha images known from the earlier phase of Buddhism in western India.[2]

The Kaṇherī colossi are not inscribed, but it is tempting to relate them to the very same new phase of patronage as a small

1. In a number of later (Rāṣṭrakūṭa) caves at this and other sites, a Mahādeva image is indeed placed directly on axis behind the liṅgam, but is on the back wall of the garbhagṛha itself. An earlier (probably Early Kalacuri) example is to be found at Ankai; it may be as early as the late sixth century A.D. Such an arrangement actually provides more visual impact than the (hypothetical) Dhumar Lena one, for at the Dhumar Lena the view of the Mahādeva would have been largely blacked by the presence of the shrine.

2. For other illustrations of these important early figures, see I.D.C. Microfiche for Kaṇherī Caves, ed. W. Spink, nos. 2:34-2:49; 3:1-3:2; published in American Committee for South Asian Art Project.

brick stūpa which was constructed directly in front of the chaitya hall's court. This little relic mound (Sanskrit : *Caitya*) now much damaged, contained an inscribed copper plate (now lost) which stated that it was the gift of one Buddharuchi, a devotee from the Sindh region. He hoped to be blessed by this benefaction "for as long as the milky ocean, the waters of the whirl-pool of which are whirled by the aligators tossed about by thousands of (*its*) waves, is an ocean of milk, as long as the rugged Meru is piled with huge rocks, as long as rivers of very clear water flow with (*their*) water into the ocean...".[1] How he has fared we cannot say, but he has earned our gratitude, at least, by stating *when* the gift was made ! Records in this general period are not only scarce but they are all too often undated, so this one is a particular boon to scholars. It begins :

> "Obeisance to the Omniscient (Buddha) ! In the augmenting kingdom of the Traikūṭakas, in the year two hundred increased by forty-five, in the Great Monastery at Kṛishṇagiri (i.e., Kaṇherī), budharuchi...has erected this *Chaitya* with dressed stones..."

The year 245, which scholars all agree must be referred to the so-called Kalacuri era which began in 249 A.D., provides us with a date of 494 A.D. for the benefaction.[2] The reference to the Traikūṭakas is also very illuminating; the statement "in the augmenting kingdom of the Traikūṭakas" suggests that this old dynasty was becoming newly established in the Konkan region at this time. Two other Traikūṭaka inscriptions from this coastal region, one dated in 490 A.D.[3] and one in 505 A.D.[4], further confirm this strong re-establishment of Traikūṭaka power in the late fifth/early sixth century A.D. Prior to this, judging from the evidence of the Cave 16 inscription of Hariṣeṇa's period at Ajantā and from the evidence of a historically-based tale called the *Daśakumāracarita*, the Traikūṭakas had been feudatories of

1. Kaṇherī Plate of the Traikūṭakas, K 245 : see V. V. Mirashi, *Inscriptions of the Kalacuri-Cedi Era*, pp. 29-32.

2. The date would be 493-4 or 494-5 A.D. depending upon whether the year 245 was current or expired.

3. V. V. Mirashi, *Inscriptions of the Kalacuri-Cedi Era*, pp. 25-29 : Surat Plates of Vyāghrașeṇa, K 241. (The year 241 is equivalent to 490 A.D. or possibly 489 A.D.; see *ibid.*, p. 26, note 3).

4. Ref. p. 241, note 1.

the Vākāṭakas.[1] This political tie could help to explain the relationship between the art of the two regions, which can well be characterized by comparing the Kaṇherī colossi with quite similar ones developed during the latest phase of Vākāṭaka patronage at Ajantā.

The Traikūṭaka inscriptions of 490 A.D. and 494 A.D. are very important in helping us to determine the approximate date of the collapse of the Vākāṭaka dynasty, and the collapse of the Mahāyāna phase at Ajantā, which had been the product of their patronage. This in turn has a direct bearing upon the date of Elephanta as we explained earlier, since Elephanta cannot be very far removed from Ajantā in time. The *Daśakumāracarita* reveals that the Traikūṭakas were the feudatories of the great Vākāṭaka king Hariṣeṇa and of his weak son and successor, and that they took part in the insurrection which caused the final overthrow of the dynasty, after which they (the Traikūṭakas) and the other feudatories became independent powers once again. This had certainly happened by 490 A.D., since neither in that inscription (issued from the "victorious Aniruddhapura"—i.e., the Traikūṭaka capital) nor in the 494 A.D. Kaṇherī inscription are the Vākāṭakas referred to as the Traikūṭakas' overlords; in fact, there are no later inscriptions anywhere in India where the Vākāṭakas are ever mentioned again as a ruling power—their overthrow appears to have been not only drastic but final.

The collapse of a power as great as that of the Vākāṭakas could not help but have vast repercussions upon the cultural and political history of central and western India. The years at the end of the fifth century and at the beginning of the sixth century, when the great Gupta power to the east was breaking up and the powerful Hūṇas were making inroads from the north, were clearly ones of shifting allegiances and changing fortunes. Somehow, out of this confusion, the Early Kalacuris—the patrons of Elephanta—emerged as a major force in the first half of the sixth century. We can understand this better if we analyze the events—such as we know them—surrounding the Vākāṭaka fall. In doing so, perhaps we can even more directly connect the patronage of the Great Cave at Elephanta with that of the great Vākāṭaka sites of Ajantā, Bāgh, and Aurangābād.

1. For further discussion, see W. Spink, "Bāgh : A Study", pp. 53-59.

In the following discussion we shall often refer to evidence from Daṇḍin's *Daśakumāracarita*, the eighth ucchvāsa of which is generally considered to have an historical basis.[1] Referring to this chapter, the account by Prince Viśruta of his adventures, Mirashi has pointed out : "Daṇḍin's narrative faithfully reflects the actual political situation in the Deccan" at the time of the Vākāṭaka fall.[2] It refers to actual places, powers and events, even though "Daṇḍin has plainly changed the names of the characters who figure in the story."[3] Thus, as scholars would nearly all agree, Daṇḍin's Puṇyavarman stands for the great Vākāṭaka king Hariṣeṇa, who was ruling in *c.* 475 A.D. (in our view his regnal dates being *c.* 460-*c.* 480 A.D.); Anantavarman is Hariṣeṇa's ineffectual son and successor; Mitravarman is a second son of Hariṣeṇa "by another wife" who was acting as viceroy in Māhiṣmatī at the time of the Vākāṭaka fall; and so forth. For convenience, when referring to the characters and their activities as described by Daṇḍin, we shall avoid their pseudonyms, referring to them in terms of their relationship to Hariṣeṇa instead, apprising the reader that we are utilizing the *Daśakumāracarita* as our informational source by italicizing Hariṣeṇa's name in such contexts. In the case of Prince Viśruta and of Caṇḍavarman of Mālwā, however, we will not make any such substitution, since our identification of these characters with Mahārāja Subandhu of Māhiṣmatī and the Hūṇa ruler Toramāṇa respectively has not been previously proposed, and may not find such

1. For translations of the *Daśakumāracarita*, see M. R. Kale (trans.), *The Daśakumāracarita of Daṇḍin*, Delhi (4th ed.), 1966; A. W. Ryder (trans.), *The Ten Princes*, Chicago, 1927 (reprint 1960); V. Satakopan, V. Anantacharya, and N. Bhaktavatsalam (trans.), *Daṇḍin's Daśakumāracarita*, Madras, 1963. I have generally used Ryder's translation because of its greater accessibility, but occasionally opt for Satakopan's or Kale's more precise renderings. For discussion, see V. V. Mirashi, "Historical Evidence in Daṇḍin's Daśakumāracarita", *Annals of the Bhandarkar Oriental Research Institute*, 24 : 20 ff., in *Studies in Indology*, Vol. 1, Nagpur, 1960, pp. 164-177. See also M. Collins, *Geographical Data of the Raghuvaṁśa and Daśakumāracharita*, 1907.

2. V. V. Mirashi, *Historical Data*, p. 176. Mirashi's conclusions are somewhat different from ours, since in his view the Vākāṭaka dynasty survived until the early sixth century A.D.

3. V. V. Mirashi, *Historical Data*, p. 169.

ready acceptance. We must leave it to the reader to judge the validity of such identifications after reviewing our arguments.

Only the eight ucchvāsas forming the central section of the *Daśakumāracarita* as usually published are from Daṇḍin's own hand. The long beginning portion (Pūrvapīṭhikā) and the short end portion (Uttarapīṭhikā) probably bear some relation to the missing sections of Daṇḍin's original, but we have no way of knowing to what degree they reflect Daṇḍin's own creation and to what degree they are merely reconstructed as later authors saw fit. The Uttarapīṭhikā of our translations, for instance, makes particularly crucial and anachronistic mistakes.[1] Kale, having used one version, mentions that he knows of four other different versions of the Uttarapīṭhikā alone, and warns that "criticism on Daṇḍin's work will only be pertinent when it is made with reference to the main body of the text as it is available in its eight Uchchhvāsas".[2] This is important from our point of view, since we would agree with Mirashi that the generally-used Uttarapīṭhikā, which says that Prince Viśruta re-established the Vākāṭaka house, must be corrupt. As we explain later, it seems that Daṇḍin left the ending of the eighth ucchvāsa (Viśruta's account) ambiguous, for the very reason that the prediction of the Vākāṭaka house's restoration—which we are, in effect, asked to take on faith alone—was never in fact fulfilled. On the other hand, the author who later reconstructed the missing final portion of Daṇḍin's tale quite understandably supplied the expected and conventional ending to what to him must have seemed purely a work of fiction; in the process, by claiming that the fallen house was indeed restored, he imposed an unreal ending upon a tale which Daṇḍin had left purposely unresolved.

According to the *Daśakumāracarita*, when the Vākāṭaka dynasty collapsed due to the overthrow of *Hariṣeṇa's* weak son and successor, the young heir to the throne and his sister (*Hariṣeṇa's* grand children) fled for safety to the city of Māhiṣmatī, where their

1. The Uttarapīṭhikā has the abdicated Mānasāra of Mālwā still ruling; the Mālwā princess, who married the crown prince of Magadha, still imprisoned in the enemy camp; and the Mālwā prince who was killed at the behest of Viśruta still alive and ruling (rather impossibly) in the Bengal-Orissā area (i.e., Utpala).

2. M. R. Kale, *Daśakumāracarita*, pp. xxxvii-xxxviii.

uncle was still in power as viceroy. Anūpa, of which Māhiṣmatī on the Narmadā River was capital, appears to have been one of the few parts of the Vākāṭaka's previously extensive empire which had not fallen to the coalition of Vākāṭaka feudatories from the south and west which destroyed the empire shortly after 480 A.D.[1] However, one can well imagine that with the central Vākāṭaka power shattered, the Anūpa viceroy—now on his own —was in a very precarious political position. Not surprisingly, he fell from power very soon, as is clear from the evidence of the Barwāni plate inscription which proves that by 486 A.D. the capital city of Māhiṣmatī was in the hands of one "Mahārāja Subandhu".[2]

It is our belief that this Mahārāja Subandhu, whose rise to power in the Anūpa region appears to have been made possible by the collapse of the Vākāṭaka dynasty, can be identified with the hero-protagonist of the eighth chapter of Daṇḍin's *Daśakumāracarita*, the pseudonymous Prince Viśruta; and, if so, this greatly enlarges our perspective on events in this crucial period.

We have little absolutely sure information about Mahārāja Subandhu, although it is clear from his Barwāni and Bāgh inscriptions that he was ruling independently in Māhiṣmatī as early as the year 146 (=486 A.D.), that he not only made gifts to Brāhmaṇas but also repaired the Buddhist caves at Bāgh at some time during his reign, and that he may have had familial and/or cultural links with the great Gupta power to the east, since he used that era in dating his inscriptions, if our interpretation of the evidence is correct. Furthermore, if he is the same person as the Subandhu of the *Mṛcchakaṭika* as Buddha Prakash convincingly suggests, he was still recognized as an important ruler in this general region in the early sixth century.[3]

1. Māhiṣmatī is generally identified with modern Oṁkār Māndātā, but it seems just as likely that it could be identified with the more spacious modern Maheśvar. In any case, the two cities, both on the Narmadā River, are only about thirty miles apart.

2. V. V. Mirashi and various other scholars have assigned the Barwāni plate of the year 167 to the Kalacuri-Cedi era, equivalent to 417 A.D. See Mirashi, *Inscriptions of the Kalacuri-Cedi Era*, pp. 17-19; see also discussion of related Bāgh Cave plate of Subandhu, *ibid.*, pp. 19-21. For objections to this view and arguments for the Gupta era dating, see W. Spink, "Bāgh : A Study".

3. Buddha Prakash, *Studies in Indian History and Civilization*, Agra, 1962, pp. 399-416.

The *Daśakumāracarita* describes Prince Viśruta as a forceful prince from Magadha (i.e., the Gupta homeland) who became the ruler (as regent for the eight year old grandson of *Hariṣeṇa*) in Māhiṣmatī just after the main Vākāṭaka house had fallen—an event which must have occurred about 482 A.D. if our reconstruction of events is valid.[1] Assuming that Viśruta's rule continued for some years after this date—and he would hardly have been remembered by Daṇḍin over a century later if he had not been a force in history—his flourishing coincides precisely with that of Mahārāja Subandhu, whose Barwāni inscription places him as ruler of Māhiṣmatī in 486 A.D. Furthermore, an identification with Viśruta could explain Subandhu's otherwise surprising use of the Gupta era for dating. Viśruta not only hailed from Magadha himself, but also appointed a courtier from Kosala (the territory adjacent to Magadha, where the Gupta era was also commonly used) as his chief counsellor. Even Viśruta's typically expedient marriage to *Hariṣeṇa's* granddaughter (see below) amplified his eastern connections, for the young girl's maternal grandfather was the Kosala king.[2] Even though the vast Gupta empire was itself weakening during the late fifth century, Viśruta's ties with the Guptas and their allies must have been politically advantageous in this period of dynastic upheaval in western and central India.

According to the *Daśakumāracarita* account, the Vākāṭaka viceroy at Māhiṣmatī, who was a son of the great king *Hariṣeṇa* "by another wife" recognized that his position was threatened when his young step-nephew (*Hariṣeṇa's* grandson) was brought for protection to his court; for this nephew, born to *Hariṣeṇa's* chief queen, was actually the new heir to the Vākāṭaka throne and as such was not only his step-uncle's guest, but actually his overlord ! For this reason, the worried step-uncle "heartlessly strove to kill this lad" in order to secure his own position as the inheritor of whatever remained of the former Vākāṭaka power.[3]

1. W. Spink, "Bāgh : A Study", pp. 53-59; where, however, we suggest that the fall took place around 483 A.D. instead of *c.*482 A.D.

2. This information, from the *Daśakumāracarita*, is discussed at greater length below.

3. Quoted from A. W. Ryder, *Ten Princes*, p. 215.

However, a trusted servant managed to get the boy out of the city. This is where Viśruta first enters the narrative; he finds the boy in the Vindhya forest, hears his story from the servant, and announces his decision to become the lad's protector. As the account continues, Viśruta and the young prince, disguised as Kāpālikas (Śaivite mendicants) manage to get back into the city, where Viśruta contrives to have the jealous uncle assassinated. This accomplished, he then establishes himself in the position of regent for the little heir, thus effectively consolidating his own power as *de facto* ruler. As the *Daśakumāracarita* account ends, having "employed the priest to instruct the prince in statecraft" he himself (i.e., Viśruta) was discharging the duties of the king", vowing to re-establish the power of the Vākāṭaka house and to restore the young boy to his ancestral throne.[1] Just how much of this vow—possibly an empty one—was actually realized is not stated; but it is clear that Viśruta very cleverly improved his own position at every opportunity.

First, Viśruta managed to prevent a marriage alliance between the young princess (*Hariṣeṇa's* granddaughter) and a prince of the important neighboring state of Mālwā by conspiring to have the Mālwā prince murdered—after which he enhanced his own already powerful position by marrying the girl himself. As if this were not enough, he managed to lay the blame for the treachery upon the ruler of Aśmaka, a former Vākāṭaka feudatory who had instigated the Vākāṭaka overthrow and had emerged as the dominant force in the former Vākāṭaka domains. Thus Viśruta appears to have set these two great powers against each other and to have strengthened his own position in the process.

The countering of Aśmaka interests was apparently a keystone of Viśruta's policy, committed as he was—at least in his public statements—to avenging the defeated Vākāṭaka house and to winning back their former domains. "Then I took a vow," he declares in the *Daśakumāracarita*. "The king of Aśmaka is proud of his diplomacy. I shall overthrow him by diplomacy alone."[2] And this is, of course, exactly what he was intending by such tricks as falsely implicating Aśmaka in the murder of the

1. Quoted from V. Satakopan, *Daśakumāracarita*, p. 160.
2. Quoted, *ibid.*, p. 154.

Mālwā prince, for Mālwā was then a great power—one whose anger Viśruta might well prefer to have directed away from himself in any case, since both the adjacent Mālwā region and the now extended Aśmakan domains were too close to Māhiṣmatī for comfort.

Aśmaka, fortunately for Viśruta, appears to have been having other problems too. In the *Daśakumāracarita* when the insurrection of former Vākāṭaka feudatories against their overlord had a successful outcome, the ruler of Aśmaka "baited all of the (other former) vassals into a ruinous squabble, and himself swallowed the whole plunder";[1] that is, he himself took over effective control of the former Vākāṭaka domains. This must have occurred in *c*.482 A.D.; but within a few years, Aśmaka power was already eroding. By 490 A.D. the Traikūṭakas were re-establishing themselves in the North Konkan, which the Aśmakas may have held for a brief period as part of their "whole plunder"; in 494 A.D. we have, at Kaṇheri, a further reference to "augmenting kingdom of the Traikūṭakas" in this region; the Matvan plate of 505 A.D. equally supports the conclusion that they were firmly in power in this region from at least as early as 490 A.D. up until sometime early in the sixth century.[2]

Kuntala, also a former Vākāṭaka feudatory, may have been even more of a threat to the new Aśmaka authority. The Pāṇḍuraṅgapallī charter lauds the Rāṣṭrakūṭa king Mānāṅka as "the ruler of the glorious Kuntala country and the conqueror of Aśmaka together with Vidarbha".[3] If Sircar's view that Mānāṅka "probably flourished in the latter half of the fifth century" is correct,[4] then the Rāṣṭrakūṭa conquest could represent yet another incursion into the Aśmakan domains. According to the *Daśakumāracarita*, the Aśmakas did indeed hold their own territory "together with Vidarbha" in the period just after

1. A. W. Ryder, *Ten Princes*, p. 215. Only the ruler of Vanavāsī, probably an independent king of the Kadambas who helped the feudatories, was given "a petty fraction" by Aśmaka.

2. For inscriptions, see refs. notes 32, 30, 16.

3. V. V. Mirashi, "The Rāṣṭrakūṭas of Mānapura", *Annals* of the *Bhandarkar Oriental Research Institute*, 25, pp. 25 ff. in *Studies in Indology*, Vol. 1, Nagpur, 1960, pp. 178-188. Quote : p. 182.

4. D. C. Sircar, *Studies in the Geography of Ancient and Medieval India*. Delhi, 1960, p. 153.

the Vākāṭaka collapse, although it appears that the Early Kalacuris had taken over most of it by the mid-sixth century.[1]

In fact, it is just possible that the Rāṣṭrakūṭa incursion was commemorated in a problematic intrusive inscription on a wall at the juncture of Ajantā Cave 26 and its left wing (i.e., Cave 27).[2] This elaborate chaitya hall, the most ambitious excavation at the site, was largely completed between *c.* 475 and *c.*480 A.D., when the Aśmakas, as feudatories of the Vākāṭakas, ruled over the region.[3] Built in honour of the Aśmaka minister, standing as a symbol of their power, and quite possibly still a center of local worship in the decades just after the collapse of active patronage at the site, it would have been a tempting location for the victorious Rāṣṭrakūṭas to have placed a proclamation of their power. Although the very ruinous inscription has generally been referred by Chhabra and others to the eighth or ninth century, Chhabra has pointed out that "earlier instances of this script occur in such records as the Poona plates of the Vākāṭaka queen Prabhāvatīguptā."[4] This has led Weiner to suggest the possibility that "the inscription may in fact, on palaeographic grounds, be dated as early as the late fourth century."[5] If such a change is warranted, we would think that the inscription might well belong to a period not too long after the site's abandonment, perhaps in the opening years of the sixth century. A Rāṣṭrakūṭa king Nanarāja (probably = Nannarāja) in the opening line is referred to, but it is not clear whether he is an ancestor or a successor of Mānāṅka.[6]

Such pieces of evidence suggest that the Aśmaka control of the Vākāṭaka empire, which they had so effectively shattered,

1. The Viṣṇukuṇḍin king Mādhavavarman (ruled *c.* 468-*c.* 518 A.D., according to recent studies) married a Vākāṭaka princess, possibly a daughter of Hariṣeṇa; finds of coins near Nāgpur suggest he may have dominated part of Vidarbha in *c.* 500 A.D.

2. See translation and discussion by B.C. Chhabra in G. Yazdani, *Ajantā*, Vol. 4, pp. 121-24.

3. W. Spink, "Bāgh: A Study," p. 55.

4. B. C. Chhabra; see ref. note 53; p. 121.

5. S. Weiner, *Ajaṇṭā: Its Place in Buddhist Art*, Berkeley, 1977, pp. 24-25.

6. Two other Nannarājas are known among later kings of this lineage, but one need not identify them with this one; the name was apparently commonly used in the family, as often is the case in such dynastic lines.

was short-lived; and the lack of any records which attest to the continuation of Aśmaka power in the sixth century lends further support to this view. It seems likely that by *c.* 500 A.D., after the Aśmaka's brief moment of glory, the political situation in the former Vākāṭaka domains was very much in flux, for even if the Rāṣṭrakūṭas had extended their power northward for a time, we have no evidence that their hold was very secure or of long duration.

It is at this point that Prince Viśruta—whom we would identify with Mahārāja Subandhu of Māhiṣmatī—having consolidated his power in the Anūpa capital, may well have started his campaign to retrieve as much of the former Vākāṭaka domains as possible. It would appear from the *Daśakumāracarita* account that he had prepared himself well. He was now not only regent for the young heir to the throne (*Hariṣeṇa's* grandson) but also was the husband of the crown-princess (*Hariṣeṇa's* granddaughter); these two roles must have gone far to justify what was in effect the totality of his rule. At the same time, it appears from the account that he very successfully ingratiated himself with the queen-mother (*Hariṣeṇa's* daughter-in-law) to whom we discover he was in fact distantly related, a fact which could only further enhance his "legitimacy" as regent.

Always intent on further consolidating his position, Viśruta now decided to appoint as his chief counselor the same man who had served the former (now murdered) Vākāṭaka viceroy, reasoning that "...if he could be secured, it would be a blessing" particularly since "having his origin in Kosala, he (would be) loyal to the prince's mother" (she being the daughter of the Kosala king) and thus to her confidante and protector, Viśruta himself.[1] Again we sense the importance of such cultural affiliations with the power to the east—affiliations which, of course, Viśruta shared. Needless to say, there were also other advantages, both psychological and political, to be gained by continuing to use the former viceroy's counselor as his own counselor too. It emphasized the continuity of his own rule—which was still technically a regency—and it would have made him partisan to much inside information. The psychological advantages to be gained by associating himself with the deeds and policies of the

1. Quotes from A. W. Ryder, *Ten Princes*, p. 223.

Vākāṭakas might also explain why Subandhu (= Viśruta), probably in the 490s' A.D., repaired the Buddhist caves at Bāgh, which had been created when Hariṣeṇa controlled the region.[1]

The manner in which Viśruta examined this new counselor before appointing him is particularly interesting, and seems very significant when we "read between the lines", for it introduces shadows of doubt about Viśruta's vaunted altruism on behalf of the young prince. Viśruta devises what is, in effect, a "loyalty test"; he has a confidante, pretending concern about his (Viśruta's) actions and intentions, speak accusingly of him, in order to test the potential counselor's reaction. The potential counselor is asked (in presumed confidence) if he thinks that Viśruta really wants to restore the young prince to power or if he (Viśruta) is actually working in his own self-interest, with an ultimate goal of destroying the prince and declaring himself as ruler instead :

> "Who is this mystery man that enjoys the glory of our kingdom ?", the conniving confidante asks the potential counselor. "You know the snake has caught our young prince. Will he spew him out or swallow him ?"[2]

Fortunately for the counselor-to-be, he passes this "loyalty test" with flying colors; "Do not say so", he replies. "His ancestry appears to be pure. The power of his mind is extraordinary, his bodily strength is super-human, his generosity is unbounded..." After further enlarging upon Viśruta's virtues, he adds a prediction : "Uprooting the king of Aśmaka who is proud of his skill in state-craft and re-installing the prince on his ancestral throne—this you can take as having been realised. There need be no doubt in this matter."[3]

Viewed from a later perspective, this conversation appears very curious indeed. Could Viśruta actually be guilty of the crimes which Daṇḍin, writing over a century later, still makes reference to ? If some suspicion—or even proof—of ignobleness did not cling to Viśruta's memory, why should Daṇḍin, who normally treats his prince-protagonists as paradigms of virtue, so compulsively include these curious negative references in this one

1. W. Spink, "Bāgh : A Study", p. 58.
2. A. W. Ryder, *Ten Princes*, p. 223.
3. V. Satakopan, *Daśakumāracarita*, pp. 161-62.

instance ? Furthermore, Daṇḍin, writing in the seventh century A.D., obviously knew the outcome of the events about which he leaves us so surprisingly ill-informed. He clearly reveals what, from an orthodox point of view, represents the proper approach which a noble such as Viśruta *should* have taken in such a situation; but by failing to reveal the known facts in a simple and direct way, he leaves us wondering if it is really true that "there need be no doubt in this matter".

The situation is the more curious because Viśruta's story in the *Daśakumāracarita* is given a particular emphasis by Daṇḍin, as if it were of particular importance. It is the last and (except for one other) the longest of the tales told by the princes of their accomplishments and adventures when they all meet together some years after the events which Viśruta describes with his strangely selective retrospective vision. Furthermore, Viśruta's tale closes with a serious discussion about the realities of political power rather than with the more conventional "happy ending" of most of the other tales. It also appears to be the most specific in terms of its inclusion of detail about political and psychological motivation. All these things support the idea that it may reflect a real historical situation. Yet Viśruta's account is the only one with such an ambiguous—can we say ambivalent ?—outcome, where we are left in the dark about the future. *Did* Viśruta give up his own power by re-establishing the Vākāṭaka prince upon his throne—a restoration about which, we might add, history is notably silent ? Or did he, in his Machiavellian way, manage to become a ruler, instead of a mere regent, himself ? Needless to say, the latter option would better explain why he was so well remembered over a century later, when Daṇḍin wrote.

I submit that the strange and guilt-laden questioning of the potential counselor in the story reflects a knowledge on the part of Daṇḍin that Viśruta, "enjoying the glory of the kingdom", did indeed "spew out" or "swallow" the young heir and take over total power for himself. I would further submit that this is why the story ends in such an inconclusive way—without any evidence that the prince was actually restored to power. If Daṇḍin knew that the prince *had* been restored to power—and he obviously did know whether this occurred or not—would this not make the only reasonable and logical ending for such a heroic and high-minded tale as Viśruta's purports to be ? So

Daṇḍin's omission of the expected ending leads us to conclude what a study of history would also lead us to believe, namely, that things did *not* turn out all right for the Vākāṭakas.[1] The Rāma-like Viśruta, in reality, may have ended up as a Rāvaṇa. That is, he may have arranged the death of the boy, just as he had arranged that of the viceroy and of the Mālwā suitor.[2]

But why then should Daṇḍin decide to include this tale at all, if Viśruta, the central figure, did indeed use his prestigious situation for his own self-aggrandizement and if he ultimately failed to re-establish the fallen Vākāṭaka house; that is, if he was as ruthless and self-seeking as an unbiased reader might be led to suspect?

There seem to be two reasonable (and related) answers which we can suggest. First, judging from the apparent historicity of this chapter as a whole, it seems likely that Viśruta, like the other main characters, was indeed an historical figure; and he was probably one to reckon with—one whose deeds did indeed have a great impact upon the future, even if certain things that he did were too ignoble to include mention of in an insistently "noble" tale such as the *Daśakumāracarita.* Viśruta was someone whom Daṇḍin, writing about events related to the fall of the Vākāṭaka house, could not disregard, even if he knew about and disapproved of some aspects of his career.

This brings us to our second point, namely, that the *whole Daśakumāracarita* perhaps should be recognized as reflecting, at least in its general outlines, a real historical situation, in which the role of Viśruta was a significant component. We would suggest that the whole account refers to events which occurred within the Gupta sphere of influence in the late fifth/early sixth

1. Except for the *Daśakumāracarita,* which apparently refers to Hariṣeṇa's son and grandson, there is no reference to any successor of Hariṣeṇa in any known source. In our opinion the Vākāṭaka caves present the most striking evidence of the dynasty's collapse; see W. Spink, "Ajantā's Chronology : The Crucial Cave ", *Ars Orientalis,* 10 (1975), pp. 143-69.

2. The reader should be reminded that we only *infer* that Viśruta plotted such a regicide, although we believe that the evidence warrants such an inference. He might have equally benefitted if the boy had died a natural death, although in the latter case—unless Viśruta then seized the throne from some other more rightful heir—one would think that Daṇḍin would state the case directly.

century A.D. Daṇḍin's over-riding concern, which provides the plot of the story, is with the affairs of "Magadha", and Magadha in the period to which we wish to refer it was ruled—not without many problems—by the Gupta dynasty, which still had extensive domains and influence in central and western India too. Viśruta's accomplishments, from this perspective, are recounted in the text because he is, after all, a Magadhan prince, while Daṇḍin's interest in the events surrounding the Vākāṭaka fall must have been due to the fact that the Guptas had strong political stakes in the affairs of "Vidarbha" as well as familial connections with that extremely important fallen house.[1]

If, as is generally agreed, Viśruta's tale in the eighth ucchvāsa of the text is a reflex of late fifth century events, it certainly is reasonable to suggest that the whole of the *Daśakumāracarita* equally refers to this same general period, particularly since they are united in terms of plot.[2] Admittedly, the *Daśakumāracarita* includes many fanciful and conventionalized elements, and historical documentation from this period leaves many gaps, so it is hard to correlate the literary and the historical evidence with assurance, but the situation Daṇḍin describes, if it does indeed have a historical basis, conforms better to late fifth/early sixth century realities than to those of any other period. As he describes it, it was a time when the Magadhan power was still very strong, with many regions in north India and the upper Deccan joined to it in a feudatory relationship or by ties of friendship, marriage, and/or political expediency. The greatest problems came from Mālwā, which was in the midst of a see-sawing power struggle with Magadha throughout the tale, just as appears to have been the case in actuality.

The historicity of the whole account—as opposed to that of the eighth ucchvāsa—appears to have been discounted in the past because so many of the separate tales follow a somewhat arbitrary formula whereby the princes "each won a throne and a

1. Admittedly, much of the discussion of Magadha is in the reconstructed Pūrvapīṭhikā, but the main portion of the text confirms the fact that all of the protagonists (i.e., the ten princes) are from Magadha and are very pro-Magadha in attitude.

2. It is significant to note that Caṇḍavarman of Mālwā, who figures in Viśruta's tale, plays an important part in other earlier tales also.

beautiful lady".[1] Admittedly, most (but by no means all) of the stories do end with some variation upon this theme. However, we must remember that Daṇḍin, for all of his historical interests, was quite obviously committed to putting together an instructive tale about princely virtues, so it is hardly surprising that he chose situations where expedient marriage alliances and/or victorious military campaigns could be revealed as the expected outcome of noble birth and noble action. The fact that the situations upon which he reports are "ideal" does not mean that they were not "real"; after all, since he was writing from the perspective of the seventh century about events which had occurred over a century before, he could use a certain amount of selectivity in his choice of the events which he described. Furthermore, from this much later vantage point, using some literary license (as he obviously does), he could bring events which were not absolutely contemporaneous into a narrower time-span, and (following generally accepted conventions for the description of important historical figures) he could make all his noble heroes young and fair. The Pūrvapīṭhikā or introduction, although an unreliable later interpolation or reconstruction, probably reflects Daṇḍin's original use of such a device; in it, all of the ten princes are born at almost precisely the same time—an occurrence about which the king of Magadha "straightway experienced the extremity of joy"[2] when he thought how they would help to protect him from his enemies, which of course they later do throughout the tale, whose plot is comprised of their adventures.

The chief trouble spot for Magadha was clearly Mālwā, and the chief antagonist was the powerful regent Caṇḍavarman, who had become *de facto* ruler of the region after the old Mālwā king "being far advanced in years" had given up the throne and after the new king—who probably took his orders from Caṇḍavarman rather than *vice versa*, for he appears to be little more than a puppet ruler—had "gone to the mountain Kailāsa to practise religious austerities".[3] This Caṇḍavarman, though

1. Quoted from the jacket blurb of A. W. Ryder *Ten Princes* (Phoenix edition).

2. A. W. Ryder, *Ten Princes*, p. 19.

3. *Ibid.*, pp. 39-40; this information is from the Pūrvapīṭhikā which is a later addition; however, since the data accords with related matter in the

he wielded great power, was clearly an "outsider", both in the eyes of Daṇḍin and of the ten princes. Whereas the old Mālwā king, who had himself raided Magadha, was highly respected by his opponents, Caṇḍavarman is consistently spoken of with scorn, as doing "dreadful deeds" and as worthy of death not at all the conventional way in which Indian nobles traditionally looked upon other nobles, even when they were doing battle with each other. Caṇḍavarman, after treating the Magadhan crown prince, who had married the Mālwā princess, in an unwonted and ungentlemanly manner, was himself killed on a campaign which he had mounted "to destroy the king of the Aṅgas, who had refused his (Caṇḍavarman's) request for his daughter's hand."[1] Two of Caṇḍavarman's younger brothers were also killed, as Daṇḍin reveals with apparent approval.[2]

Perhaps Daṇḍin treated this Caṇḍavarman with scorn merely because Caṇḍavarman was such a threat to Magadha (that is, to the Guptas), whom Daṇḍin obviously lauds. But can we go farther than this, at least in our conjectures ? Is it not possible that this powerful but despised Caṇḍavarman is a reflex of the hated Hūṇa king Toramāṇa who, early in the sixth century, "conquered the major part of the Gupta empire and reduced the emperor to the status of his vassal"?[3] Admittedly, Daṇḍin does not go so far as to say that the upstart Caṇḍavarman, who pene-

main body of the text (cf. p. 61), it may fairly closely reflect Daṇḍin's original. In general, the Pūrvapīṭhikā impresses one as probably being closer to the original than the Uttarapīṭhikā; they are likely to have been written at different times by different writers. Unless otherwise stated, all of our quotations are drawn from the main body of the text; in A. W. Ryder (Phoenix edition, 1961) the main part comprises pp. 59 through 224.

1. A. W. Ryder, *Ten Princes*, p. 62.

2. *Ibid.*, p. 62, and p. 220.

3 S. R. Goyal, *A History of the Imperial Guptas*, Allahabad, 1967, p. 343. Toramāṇa and Mihirakula are generally regarded as Hūṇas, although this is sometimes disputed. For arguments pro and con, see Goyal, p. 338. Since the conventionally accepted date for the arrival of the Hūṇas in India is *c.* 500 A.D. and since it seems likely to us from our interpretation of Viśruta's tale that Caṇḍavarman (=Toramāṇa ?) was ruling in Mālwā at least ten years earlier than that, perhaps we should opt for these rulers *not* being Hūṇas. However, the arguments for the 500 A.D. terminus post quem, based on Chinese accounts, are far from convincing, and indeed are rather contradictory; see Goyal, p. 346, notes 1 and 2; also R. C. Majumdar and A. S. Altekar, *The Vākāṭaka-Gupta Age*, Delhi, 1967, pp. 193-201.

trated deep into the Magadhan domains, was actually a foreigner and (even worse !) a Hūṇa; within the context of his tale he may have preferred to pit his heroes against a more acceptable opponent.[1] In any case, the Hūṇas apparently did espouse Hinduism, probably partly in an effort to improve their public image, and in line with this same policy of legitimizing their rule they probably effected marriage alliances with conquered and/or threatened regions when they could.[2]

We know from an inscription on the boar avatāra of Viṣṇu at Eraṇ, written when "the Mahārājādhirāja, the glorious Toramāṇa, of great fame (*and*) of great lustre, (was) governing the earth[3]..." that Eastern Mālwā was ruled by this great Hūṇa conqueror sometime after 484 A.D. But even before Toramāṇa's conquest, earlier Hūṇas might have succeeded in forming a marriage alliance between their house and Mālwā, particularly in the mid-fifth century, when the region "passed through some sort of political trouble or confusion" which seems to have included internal dissensions as well as assaults from the Vākāṭakas.[4] Whether or not the Hūṇas launched several invasions into India at this time—the matter is still disputed—they were certainly a power to reckon with.

If a princess of Mālwā had indeed married a Hūṇa prince in the period just after the mid-fifth century, it would be quite possible to conceive of Toramāṇa, who appears to have been ruling in Mālwā by the late fifth century, as their son, and thus to identify him with Caṇḍavarman. This hypothesis finds support in the Pūrvapiṭhikā of the *Daśakumāracarita*, which states—without any reference to his father—that Caṇḍavarman was the son of the sister of the great Mālwā king. Could the father have been a Hūṇa ?

Again, if the *Daśakumāracarita* does indeed have an historical basis, it seems possible to determine approximately when

1. We must allow the possibility that Caṇḍavarman (=Toramāṇa ?) was an unpopular adversary on grounds other than being a Hūṇa, although we find the Hūṇa connection tempting.

2. In the *Daśakumāracarita*, Caṇḍavarman tries to marry the Aṅga princess and to marry his brother to the Vākāṭaka princess.

3. J. F. Fleet, *Inscriptions of the Early Gupta Kings and Their Successors*, Corpus Inscriptionum Indicarum, Vol. III, Calcutta, 1888, p. 160.

4. S. R. Goyal, *History of Imperial Guptas*, p. 288.

Caṇḍavarman (=Toramāṇa) began ruling in Mālwā, for Daṇḍin tells us that Caṇḍavarman sent his younger brother from Mālwā to Māhiṣmatī with the intention of marrying Hariṣeṇa's grand-daughter, who was already thirteen years old at the time of the Vākāṭaka fall (*c.* 482 A.D.).[1] Allowing a few years for certain intervening events recounted in the tale, this abortive trip—during which Viśruta had the Mālwā suitor killed and then declared that he would marry the girl himself—would seem to have been made about 490 A.D., for her younger brother (who was eight years old, or less, when she was thirteen) would still have been a young lad at that time, as he is said to have been in Viśruta's account.[2] It is quite reasonable to suppose that Toramāṇa had already declared himself Mahārājādhirāja, at least in Eastern Mālwā, at this date.

The assumption that Toramāṇa came to power in Mālwā sometime between 484 A.D. (when Budhagupta was still ruling) and 490 A.D. seems reasonable too when we realize that his reign had ended by about 511-12 A.D. At that time, according to the *Ārya Mañjuśrī Mūla Kalpa*, he fell ill in Kāśī (Benares) and after crowning his son, Mihirakula, died.[3] This account may be suspect, but it does support other evidence showing that he penetrated well into Magadha and surrounding territories. The *Daśakumāracarita's* account of his death, wherein he was stabbed by a prince of Videha during an invasion of Aṅga,[4] may be equally imaginative, but here and elsewhere it also reflects the fact that he was recognized as a great threat to the stability of the Gupta empire, which he appears to have often troubled with his campaigns.

1. Daṇḍin's "recollection" of the princess' age is so precise that it is tempting to accept it, although one should hardly place *too* much faith in it. The date of the Vākāṭaka fall cannot, in our opinion, vary from 482 A.D. by more than a year or two; for discussion, see W. Spink, "Bāgh : A Study", p. 53 ff.

2. A. W. Ryder, *Ten Princes*, pp. 199, 221-222. Since Viśruta's marriage was based upon political expediency, the age of the princess would not seem to be aproblem; she would have been 21 in *c.* 490 A.D. According to the *Daśakumāracarita*, Caṇḍavarman (=Toramāṇa ?) was ruling in Mālwā by the time of this marriage.

3. S. R. Goyal, *History of Imperial Guptas*, p. 343.

4. A. W. Ryder, *Ten Princes*, pp. 105-106.

Although the incursions of Toramāṇa into the centers of Gupta power may have been violent, they were probably of brief duration—this, in fact, is how Caṇḍavarman's raids into eastern India are described by Daṇḍin. However, Toramāṇa's hold over Eastern Mālwā appears to have been much more secure, probably because it lay closer to the Hūṇa power centers than did regions such as Aṅga, Videha, and Magadha itself.[1] It seems likely that Toramāṇa eventually ruled over both parts of Mālwā, since Gupta influence in western Mālwā must have suffered a dramatic setback (or complete disruption) as soon as the Hūṇas had come into control of the Eastern half of that region. In this regard we should note that whereas in Mandasor inscriptions of 467/8 and 473/4 A.D., the Guptas are referred to in laudatory terms, we have no references to them in the region after that.[2] Perhaps, like Dhanyaviṣṇu of the Eraṇ inscription, the local rulers of western Mālwā also shifted their allegiance to the Hūṇas when the pressure was on.[3] In any case, the *Daśakumāracarita* relates that Caṇḍavarman held Avantī (western Mālwā) and ruled from Ujjayinī at some time during his reign, although there is no proof as to just when. The fact that a King Gauri was ruling there in 491 A.D. might suggest that Caṇḍavarman (=Toramāṇa) entered western Mālwā after that date, for Gauri does not mention any overlord in his inscription.[4]

As we have seen, Viśruta foiled the projected marriage alliance between the Mālwā prince and *Hariṣeṇa's* granddaughter, instead of marrying the young Vākāṭaka princess himself. As a Magadhan prince and ally, this may have been an important political move for him to make—it is certainly remembered by Daṇḍin, who is partisan to Magadhan concerns—just as was Viśruta's assumption of the role of regent for the young heir. The Vākāṭaka collapse had certainly been a blow to Magadha, which despite earlier disputes, seems to have been connected with Vidarbha by ties not

1. S. R. Goyal, *History of Imperial Guptas*, p. 341, points out that "at least most of the upper Gaṅgā Valley (must have been) conquered by the Hūṇas before they advanced as far south as Eran" if they were to be secure in holding the latter.

2. J. Williams, "The Sculpture of Mandasor", *Archives of Asian Art*, 26, (1972-1973), pp. 50-66; see pp. 50-52.

3. S. R. Goyal, *History of Imperial Guptas*, p. 82.

4. J. Williams, "The Sculpture of Mandasor", p. 51.

only of blood and culture but also of mutual political interests during the time-period which the *Daśakumāracarita* describes. The insurrection of the Vākāṭaka feudatories, which put central and western India into a turmoil for some years, must have greatly weakened the resistance of the Vākāṭakas and their allies to the Hūṇa pressures from the north, at the very time when the Gupta resistance was also weak, and for this reason may have encouraged the Hūṇa ruler (probably Toramāṇa) to extend his conquests into regions such as Mālwā. Mālwā had, it appears, been supportive of the Vākāṭakas during the feudatories' insurrection—at least it did not join them, perhaps because its interests were then tied to those of the Guptas, who would hardly have welcomed the further chaos which any extension of that conflict would have caused.[1] But now, either because Mālwā had come under Hūṇa rule and/or because the situation had changed with the Vākāṭaka collapse, things were different. It would appear that Viśruta was working both in the Gupta interest—and in his own—when he planned the death of the Mālwā prince, and managed to lay the blame on Aśmaka at the same time, possibly succeeding in setting those important powers against each other in the process; it seems likely that he was only exacerbating what must have been a long-standing tension.[2]

In the Magadha-Mālwā conflict which underlies the plot of the *Daśakumāracarita* and was so important for political developments within the Gupta sphere of influence in the early sixth century, Viśruta seems to have occupied a key position—one fittingly recollected by Daṇḍin a century later in his tale. By

1. We know from the Eraṇ pillar inscription that Budhagupta was ruling in eastern Mālwā in 484 A.D. (Fleet, *Inscriptions of the Early Gupta Kings*, p. 88); western Mālwā may still have been under strong Gupta influence at this time (see note 81).

2. Aśmaka, as leader of the feudatory insurrection, must have been a threat to Mālwā, which may have retained some political or family alliances with the Vākāṭakas since the mid-fifth century A.D., when (Narendraṣeṇa's) commands were honored by the lords of Kosala, Mekala, and Mālava. See "Bālāghat Plates of Pṛthivīshēṇa" in V. V. Mirashi, *Inscriptions of the Vākāṭakas*, pp. 79-81. The fact that Caṇḍavarman, in Viśruta's tale, assumes that his brother can marry Hariṣeṇa's granddaughter suggests a tie between the regions, despite Viśruta's concern about this plan, which he foiled.

stabilizing the political situation in Anūpa after the Vākāṭaka fall and by starting to extend his power into other former Vākāṭaka territories, Viśruta played a significant role in resisting the Hūṇa encroachments which were such a threat to the Guptas. His domination of territories at least as far north as the Narmadā, and his mutually supportive relationship with the Guptas may explain how the latter power still managed to retain some influence over the Lāṭa region (including Valabhī), despite the Hūṇa thrust into Mālwā.[1]

But even though Viśruta was so important to the Guptas—thus receiving such prominent notice in Daṇḍin's account—it seems evident that his own interest must have been paramount in his own mind. His friendship with the Guptas was just as expedient as was the resistance to Mālwā which Daṇḍin suggests he waged with such ruthlessness and success on the diplomatic level. Meanwhile, with the Guptas and the Hūṇas in conflict to the north and east, we can imagine that his own sights were fixed to the south and west, where the old Vākāṭaka territories, perhaps still largely under tenuous Aśmakan control, were ripe for reconquest and reconsolidation, a task which his marriage to Hariṣeṇa's granddaughter could help to justify.

Thus, following the *Daśakumāracarita,* we might reconstruct the political situation and the described intentions of Prince Viśruta who, in the late fifth century to early sixth century A.D. held the reins of power in Māhiṣmatī, the capital of the Anūpa region. And thus, from other documentary sources, we might also reconstruct the political situation of Mahārāja Subandhu who, as is clear from the evidence of the Barwāni plate, was in an identical position both in time and space, having come to power in Māhiṣmatī in about 486 A.D., just after the Vākāṭaka fall.[2] In other words, Daṇḍin's Viśruta *is* Subandhu, just as Daṇḍin's Puṇyavarman is Hariṣeṇa. At least, in our view, this is a reasonable assumption.

1. S. R. Goyal, *History of the Imperial Guptas*, pp. 301-2; 357-58.
2. It appears that Anūpa, up until the Vākāṭaka fall, was securely under Vākāṭaka rule; see W. Spink, "Ajantā's Chronology : The Crucial Cave," p. 147. The recent discovery at Thalner (thirty miles from Sirpur on the Tapi) of a (still unpublished) copper plate issued in the third year of Hariṣeṇa's reign is one further indication of the size of his kingdom, even before his many conquests.

Going even beyond this, we further hypothesize that this Viśruta/Subandhu, by consolidating his power in Māhiṣmatī, laid the basis for the foundation of the great Kaṭacuri (Early Kalacuri) house, which soon occupied much of the previous Vākāṭaka domains.

Mirashi, some years ago, was also tempted to connect Subandhu with the Early Kalacuris, but could not bring them so closely together in terms of time, because he dated Subandhu's inscriptions according to the wrong era, in our opinion. "It is not known", he wrote, "whether the Early Kalacuris were descended from Mahārāja Subandhu who ruled from Māhiṣmatī in an earlier age; for there is a long period of nearly 150 years which separates them and for which no records have yet been discovered."[1]

Our own views, on the other hand, close the gap to such a degree that it is conceivable the Kṛṣṇarāja was the immediate successor of Subandhu, the transfer taking place in about 525 A.D. However, we prefer to suppose that there was an intervening ruler between them, since Kṛṣṇarāja's reign perhaps continued until *c.*575 A.D., according to generally accepted and reasonable calculations.[2] Such an intervening king, who may have been Kṛṣṇarāja's father or father-in-law, could be assigned a regnal period of *c.* 515 to *c.* 530 A.D.

We know that between 505 and 533 A.D., King Kṛṣṇarāja must have conquered or inherited the territories of the Traikūṭakas in the Konkan; this is clear from an inscription of the latter date issued from the former Traikūṭaka capital, now called "Aniruddhapura of the Kaṭacuris".[3] Thus the Early Kalacuris, who according to a long established tradition appear to have had their capital at Māhiṣmatī, dominated a large area of western India in the second quarter of the sixth century. Kṛṣṇarāja or his predecessor(s) must have extended their domains well beyond the Anūpa region into the former Vākāṭaka territories to the south and west as soon as they had strength enough to confront the rulers of those regions (the Aśmakas, Traikūṭakas, and perhaps the Rāṣṭrakūṭas). Their path of conquest would have gone through ancient Ṛṣika, which since the period of Vākāṭaka decline had been in

1. V. V. Mirashi, *Inscriptions of the Kalacuri-Cedi Era*, p. xlv.
2. *Ibid.*, p. xlvi.
3. Ref. note 15.

Aśmakan hands; beyond that lay the Western Ghāts (ancient Trikūṭa) and the coastal regions which were gained at the expense of the Traikūṭakas.[1]

The extension of the rule of Mahārāja Subandhu or his successor—the predecessors of Kṛṣṇarāja—into the Konkan in the second or third decade of the sixth century A.D. would convincingly explain the sudden surge of intense Śaivite patronage which resulted in the creation of caves as impressive as Jogeśvari and Maṇḍapeśvar and of sculpture as authoritative as the Parel stele. Such works directly anticipate the culminating example, the Great Cave at Elephanta, which dramatically proclaims the realities of Kṛṣṇarāja's political power as well as his pious concerns. Kṛṣṇarāja, as we know, was devoted to Śiva "from his very birth"; and he confirmed his devotion by representing Śiva's bull on both his silver and copper coinage.[2] We have clear evidence that his successors were ardent Śaivites too, so it seems reasonable to think of Śaivism as the family faith. This establishes yet a further connection between the Early Kalacuris and Mahārāja Subandhu, for Subandhu's capital city of Māhiṣmatī appears to have been a Śaivite stronghold, and Prince Viśruta (whom we would identify with Subandhu) was certainly a Śaivite; at one point he disguises himself as a Kāpālika; elsewhere he centers his actions in the temple of a Śaivite goddess; and ultimately he marries Hariṣeṇa's granddaughter, whose brother (the young heir) was given the title Āryāputra—the son of Śiva's consort Āryā.[3] Hariṣeṇa himself, as this and other evidence suggests, must have been a Śaivite too, even though he supported Buddhism, as did members of his court.[4] Subandhu, as the Bāgh plate proves, carried on this tradition, quite possibly for astute political reasons.[5]

We have shown that in terms of regnal period (*c.* 485 A.D. to either *c.* 515 A.D. or *c.* 525 A.D., depending upon whether there was a ruler who came between Subandhu and Kṛṣṇarāja or not),

1. Trikūṭa, mentioned in the Ajantā Cave 16 inscription, appears to have been roughly equivalent to the Nasikya of the *Daśakumāracarita*, where its ruler is mentioned as one of Hariṣeṇa's feudatories.
2. V. V. Mirashi, *Inscriptions of the Kalacuri-Cedi Era*, pp. cxlvii, clxxxi.
3. A. W. Ryder, *Ten Princes*, esp. pp. 219-222.
4. V. V. Mirashi, *Inscriptions of the Vākāṭakas*, xl-xliii.
5. For Bāgh plate, see V. V. Mirashi, *Inscriptions of the Kalacuri-Cedi Era*, pp. 19-21.

religious orientation (Śaivite, and tolerant of Buddhism), and political goals (to expand into territories previously held by the Vākāṭakas), Mahārāja Subandhu—whom we identify with Viśruta—may well have prepared the way for the foundation of the Early Kalacuri line, which shortly thereafter rose to power and successfully followed what appears to have been Subandhu's own plan of conquest.

The centrality of Subandhu's role in events of this period could well explain the surprising fact that Daṇḍin, when he composed his *Daśakumāracarita* well over a century later, seems to recall so precisely the part which Viśruta (i.e., Subandhu) played in affairs subsequent to the Vākāṭaka fall and during the period when Magadha and Mālwā (i.e., the Guptas and their antagonists, notably the Hūṇas) were in conflict.

However, a problem remains : why is Subandhu not mentioned in the Early Kalacuri inscriptions, if he was such an important predecessor and the link between Hariṣeṇa's dynasty and that of Kṛṣṇarāja ? We have no evidence that he himself was called either a Vākāṭaka or a Kalacuri king. We only know of him from records as the Mahārāja of Māhiṣmatī—as ruling from that important city where, it would seem, Vākāṭaka rule ended and Early Kalacuri rule began.

Subandhu may have been constrained not to vaunt his Vākāṭaka connections if, as we have hypothesized, he actually did "spew out or swallow" the young Vākāṭaka heir, whom in his role as regent it was his duty to protect. As the husband of the heiress-to-the-throne and *de facto* ruler of what was left of the shattered domains, even if he was implicated in such a regicide he would certainly have been able to justify reclaiming his wife's family domains; but his rule would hardly have been quite legitimate. In any case, he may have preferred to emphasize his independence, and perhaps to stress his links with the still important Guptas more than his links with the defeated Vākāṭakas.

As for Subandhu's connections with the Early Kalacuris, it seems likely that his power base in Māhiṣmatī was that upon which the Early Kalacuri rulers built. However, the first reference to the Kaṭacuris (i.e., Early Kalacuris) as such is in the Matvan grant of 533 A.D., when Kṛṣṇarāja was probably already in power. There is little reason to suppose that Subandhu could have been ruling that late. Furthermore, we have no evidence that Subandhu ever extended his own domains as far as the Konkan, although it is certainly possible that he did. In any case, later inscriptions from the time of Kṛṣṇarāja's son and grandson do not refer to Subandhu in their genealogies, but instead start off with a reference to "the illustrious Kṛṣṇarāja, who brightened the world with his fame...revived the prosperity of his family...(and) conquered the regions marching about fearlessly."[1] Even though these inscriptions do speak—perhaps conventionally—of Kṛṣṇarāja's illustrious lineage, it would appear that the Early Kalacuri house as such was not inaugurated until his (i.e., Kṛṣṇarāja's) time, and that this may have happened only after a period of decline in the family's fortunes.[2] Such a decline might quite conceivably have taken place during the reign of the hypothetical king (at present unknown) whose regnal period we would place from *c.* 515 to *c.* 530 A.D.—i.e., between Subandhu and Kṛṣṇarāja. This would have been a difficult time in any case for any ruler established at Māhiṣmatī, since it is precisely the period when Toramāṇa's notorious son and successor, Mihirakula, was wreaking havoc throughout much of the weakened Gupta domains and possibly causing great problems in Anūpa itself.[3] After Yaśodharman's dramatic defeat of Mihirakula in about 530 A.D.,[4] whereby the latter seems to have been fully humbled, it might well have been easier for Kṛṣṇarāja, coming to power at this time, to "revive the prosperity of his family" than it would have been before.

Assuming that Jogeśvari, Maṇḍapeśvar, and some of the lesser caves at Elephanta were under way in *c.* 525 A.D., under the aegis of Subandhu's successor whose domains apparently included this region, the fact that none of them were ever finished might also be a reflection of the political and/or economic troubles which beset

1. See Ābhoṇa Plates of Śaṅkaragaṇa of the year 347 (=597 A.D.); the identical epithets are repeated in Buddharāja's Vaḍner Plates of the year 360 and Sarsavṇī Plates of the year 361 (=610 A.D.); see V. V. Mirashi, *Inscriptions of the Kalacuri-Cedi Era*, pp. 38-56.

2. Note that in the later inscriptions of his son and grandson (ref. note 1) Kṛṣṇarāja not only is said to have "revived the prosperity of his family" but is the earliest king of the line to be mentioned.

3. S. R. Goyal, *History of the Imperial Guptas*, p. 344ff; J. F. Fleet, *Inscriptions of the Early Gupta Kings*, p. 142 ff.

4. S. R. Goyal, *History of the Imperial Guptas*, p. 352.

this king at this time. The fact that Kṛṣṇarāja, after consolidating his power in the Konkan, did not trouble to complete his predecessor's monuments, may only reveal that he had more interest in his own great efforts of which the Great Cave at Elephanta was the first and most startling example;[1] or it may suggest that he dissociated himself to some degree from his immediate predecessors, despite the debt that he owed to them. He may not have wished to stress the familial links which (if our suppositions are valid) he had with the ruined Vākāṭaka house, or the debt which he owed to his presumed forbears in Māhiṣmatī, including the (possibly regicidal) Mahārāja Subandhu (= Viśruta).

Of course, even if Kṛṣṇarāja was in the direct line of succession from Mahārāja Subandhu, he may not have been a blood-relation, but may have taken over some or all of Subandhu's lands and power by virtue of marrying the latter's grandaughter. Possibly Kṛṣṇarāja did not even come from Anūpa himself, but from somewhere nearer to the western coastal sites where his dynasty's first great monuments were excavated. This could account for his establishment of a dynastic line distinct in name from Subandhu's. It could also explain why the Early Kalacuri kings used the Kalacuri-Cedi era, as was common in this region, rather than the Gupta era (as Subandhu did) for dating their inscriptions.[2]

We must also admit the possibility that power and territories may have passed from Subandhu to Kṛṣṇarāja through conflict rather than through ties of blood or marriage—that Kṛṣṇarāja finished what Subandhu had started, but did so by wresting his power from Subandhu's house rather than by inheriting it. In our opinion, the laudatory treatment of Viśruta (= Subandhu) and of his ambitions in the *Daśakumāracarita* argues against the

1. Numerous examples could be cited from this general period in which kings did not complete their predecessor's monuments but started their own instead. One might ask if the Traikūṭakas had begun these monuments, but we find this doubtful. There is no evidence that the Traikūṭakas were still ruling in the Konkan at this time, while the monuments find a logical place as prototypes, both stylistically and iconographically, for later Early Kalacuri dedications.

2. The use of the Kalacuri-Cedi Era, which commenced in 249 A.D., was well established long before the rise of the Early Kalacuri dynasty. See V. V. Mirashi, *Inscriptions of the Kalacuri-Cedi Era*, pp. i-xi.

latter view; all of the nine other princes in that account have highly successful careers, so we cannot imagine that Subandhu would have been commemorated in it if his career had ended in a defeat. The apparent political stability and cultural continuity which facilitated the emergence of a monument such as the Great Cave at Elephanta early in Kṛṣṇarāja's reign also suggest that his accession was accomplished with little or no traumatic upheavals. We might also note that Kṛṣṇarāja's coins reflect some of the western issues of the Gupta emperor Skanda Gupta, which according to Mirashi "were undoubtedly in circulation in the Anūpa country, the home province of the Kalacuris, before the rise of Krishṇarāja".[1] This provides but one more suggestion of Kṛṣṇarāja's links with both Subandhu of Māhiṣmatī (the capital of Anūpa) on the one hand and with the great Gupta house on the other.

In any case, the essential point is that by reconsidering the relationships between the Vākāṭakas, Subandhu of Māhiṣmatī, and the Early Kalacuris, with the help of literary, epigraphic, and art-historical evidence, we can develop a more substantial understanding of developments in this crucial period when the Mahāyāna caves at Ajantā (perhaps the prime Buddhist undertaking in India) and the Śaivite cave at Elephanta (perhaps the prime Hindu monument in India) were both created.

If our reconstruction of events is correct, then the Mahāyāna caves at Ajantā and the early sixth century Śaivite caves in the Bombay region have a remarkable link : they are products of the same genealogical line, even though the lineage has been obscured by a shift in dynastic nomenclature with the founding of the Kaṭacuri (Early Kalacuri) house. Hariṣeṇa, the great emperor who may well have been the patron of the most splendid vihāra (Cave 1) at Ajantā and who made the site's development possible through the strength of his rule,[2] would according to

1. *Ibid.*, p. clxxxi.

2. Cave 1 has no extant inscription, perhaps because its elaborate portico has broken away. However, there are many reasons to hypothesize that Hariṣeṇa himself may have sponsored it. As in other vihāras, its jātakas and even its ceiling motifs stress kingship; of all the vihāras started in the 460's A.D. it is the most elaborately and consistently designed and decorated; unlike other caves which were started when Ṛṣika ruled the region, it shows no sign of a break in its development due to the takeover of the

our hypothesis be the great-great-grandfather of Kṛṣṇarāja, the great patron of Elephanta. The keystone of this remarkable (some might say shaky !) arch would be Mahārāja Subandhu, the heroic Gupta prince Viśruta of the *Daśakumāracarita*, who usurped what remained of the shattered Vākāṭaka power, "justified" his takeover through his marriage to the Vākāṭaka heiress-apparent, and laid the foundations of a vigorous line which was to become the Early Kalacuri dynasty. The Early Kalacuri house, with its roots in Anūpa, may have continued to rule, like Mahārāja Subandhu, from the holy city of Māhiṣmatī, despite the threat of the Hūṇa power and possibly also of their vanquisher, the great Yaśodharman, not far to the north. But the Early Kalacuri field of conquest and of expansion was into the old Vākāṭaka domains; throughout the sixth century A.D. they appear to have extended and consolidated their power in the northern Deccan. The important early Hindu caves at Ellora are witness to this spread of power and influence, and show the fervent adherence of the Early Kalacuri rulers to the Pāśupata cult of Śaivism,[1] even though (like their ancestors the Vākāṭakas) they still allowed Buddhism to flourish, as the evidence of important excavations at Aurangābād and in the Konkan proves.

In 601 A.D. the Cālukyan king Maṅgaleśa boasts, in his Mahākūṭa Pillar inscription, that "long desirous of conquering the northern regions" he has finally succeeded in depositing "the wealth of the Kalacuris in the treasury of the temple of (his) own god." Probably because of this and subsequent territorial raids, the developing Early Kalacuri caves at Ellora are left unfinished. Indeed, after a number of generations of dramatic growth, the Early Kalacuri house itself is going into a decline, and with this decline some of the last and most luminous reflections of India's earlier "Gupta" age are extinguished.

region by Aśmaka; when it was started other caves suffered setbacks, probably from consequent loss of workmen; when work on it ended (prematurely and probably with Hariṣeṇa's death) it did not, like all other caves in active use, have intrusive paintings and/or sculptures added to it.

1. See W. Spink, "Ellora's Earliest Phase", pp. 11-22.

AAAUM—Asian Art Archives, University of Michigan.
ASI—Archaeological Survey of India.

Plate 1. Bāgh Cave 2, Shrine antechamber, Bodhisattva on left wall, *c.* 476 A.D.; copyright ASI.

Plate 2. Ajantā Cave 2, Shrine, Bodhisattva at left of image, *c.* 478 A.D.; copyright ASI.

Plate 3. Sūrya, from Benares area, *c.* 500 A.D.; private collection.

Plate 4. Elephanta Cave 1, Mahādeva, central face, profile, *c.* 545 A.D.; AAAUM 105/69.

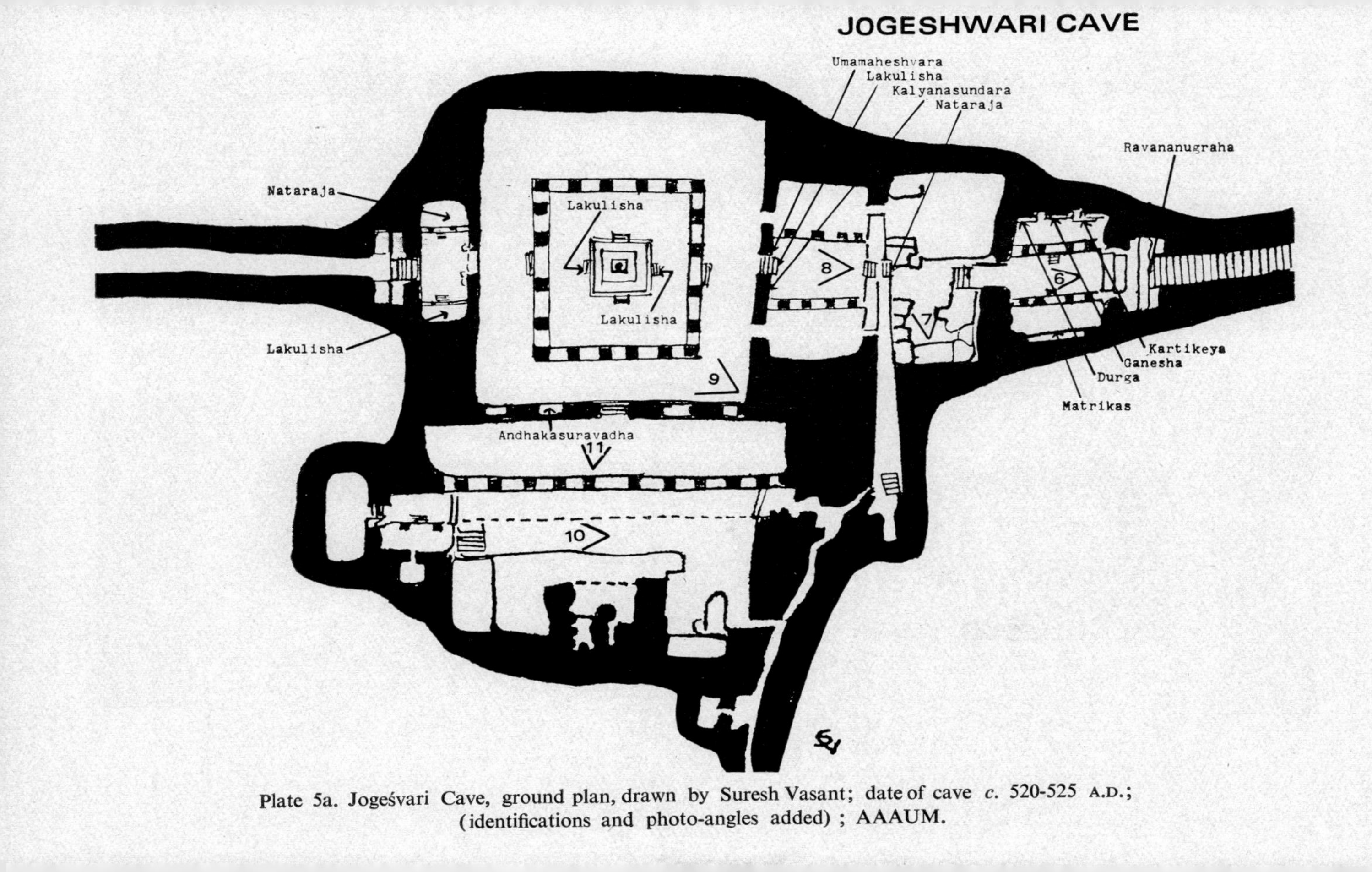

Plate 5a. Jogeśvari Cave, ground plan, drawn by Suresh Vasant; date of cave *c.* 520-525 A.D.; (identifications and photo-angles added) ; AAAUM.

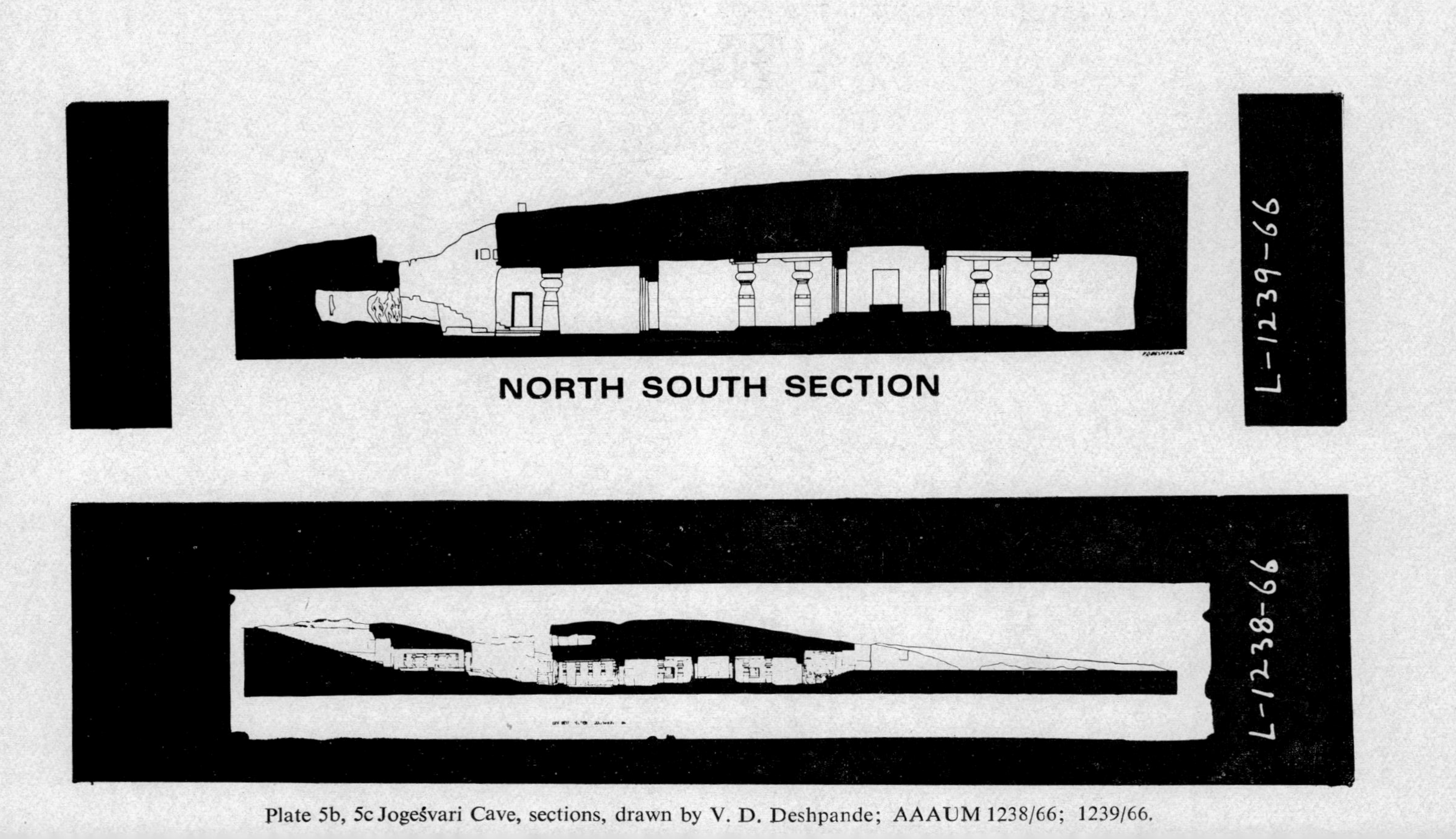

Plate 5b, 5c Jogeśvari Cave, sections, drawn by V. D. Deshpande; AAAUM 1238/66; 1239/66.

Plate 6. Jogeśvari Cave, East Entrance, doorway with Rāvaṇa shaking Kailāsa, looking through East Gallery toward deep East Court; AAAUM SF 26.

Plate 7. Jogeśvari Cave, East Court, showing doorway into East Vestibule; AAAUM 11,400.

Plate 8. Jogeśvari Cave, East Vestibule, view toward Main Hall; AAAUM 73/69.

Plate 9. Jogeśvari Cave, Main Hall, view of south wall and central shrine; AAAUM 15, 196.

Plate 10. Jogeśvari Cave, South Court and South Porch, from SE; AAAUM SG 14.

Plate 11. Jogeśvari Cave, South Porch, central doorwal (lower portion eroded away); AAAUM 11,401.

Plate 12. Aurangābād Cave 1, Main doorway (unfinished), *c.* 480 A.D.; AAAUM 15,401.

Plate 13. Aurangābād Cave 1, Facade, from right front, *c*. 480 A.D.; AAAUM 15,053.

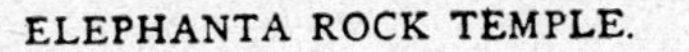

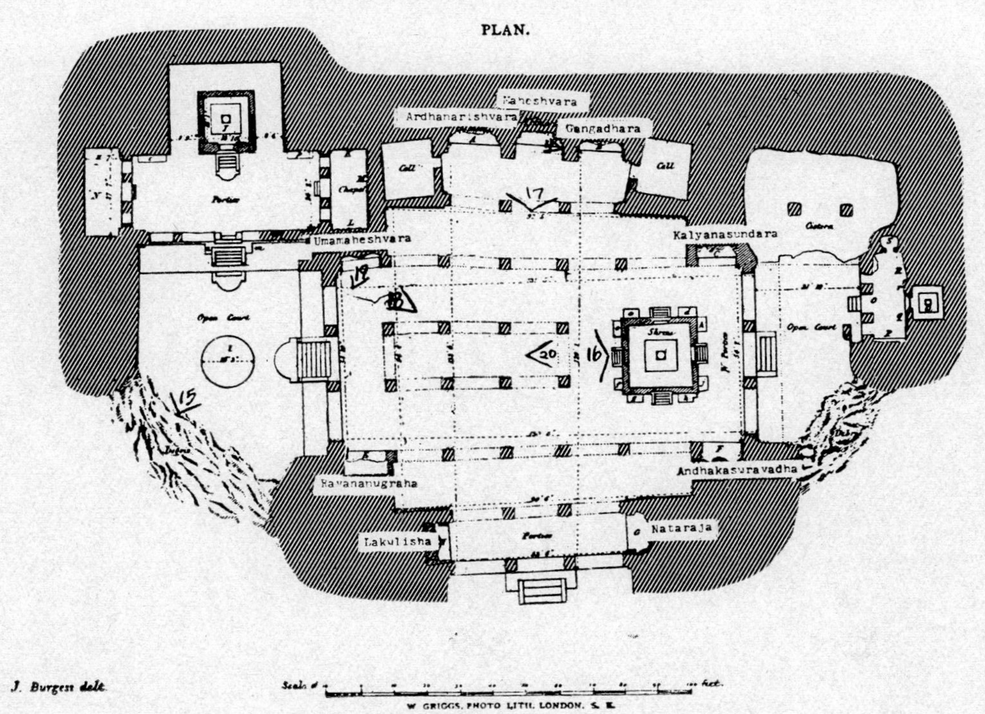

Plate 14. Elephanta Cave 1, ground plan. Based on J. Fergusson and J. Burgess, *Cave Temple of India* (London, 1880), Plate LXXXV. Date of cave *c.* 535-550 A.D. (Identifications and photo-angles added).

Plate 15. Elephanta Cave 1, East Court; main entrance on right; East Wing on left; AAAUM 15, 126.

Plate 16. Elephanta Cave 1, Interior, looking east from shrine (extreme wide-angle view causing distortion); AAAUM 1701/71.

Plate 17. Elephanta Cave 1, Interior, south wall, Mahādeva with Ardhanārīśvara (left) and Gaṅgādhara (right); (extreme wide-angle view causing distortion); AAAUM 1699/71

Plate 18. Elephanta Cave 1, Interior, East portal, south side, Umāmaheśvara panel; AAAUM 15,244.

Plate 19. Elephanta Cave 1, Interior, East portal, south side, Umāmaheśvara (det.); AAAUM 15,245.

Plate 20. Elephanta Cave 1, Interior, shrine, east face; AAAUM 938/66.

Plate 21. Ajantā Cave 1, interior, rear wall at left of shrine antechamber, bodhisattva Padmapāṇi, *c.* 478 A.D.; copyright ASI.

Plate 22. Ajantā Cave 17, porch, rear wall at left, celestials above crowned bodhisattva, c. 469 A.D.; copyright ASI.

Plate 23. Ajantā Cave 9, facade, right rear, standing Buddha, added *c.* 479 A.D.; AAAUM TH 24.

Plate 24. Kaṇheri Cave 3, porch, left end, standing Buddha, added *c.* 494 A.D.; AAAUM 577/66.

ELURÂ.

PLAN OF DUMÂR LENÂ OR SITÂ'S NÂNI.

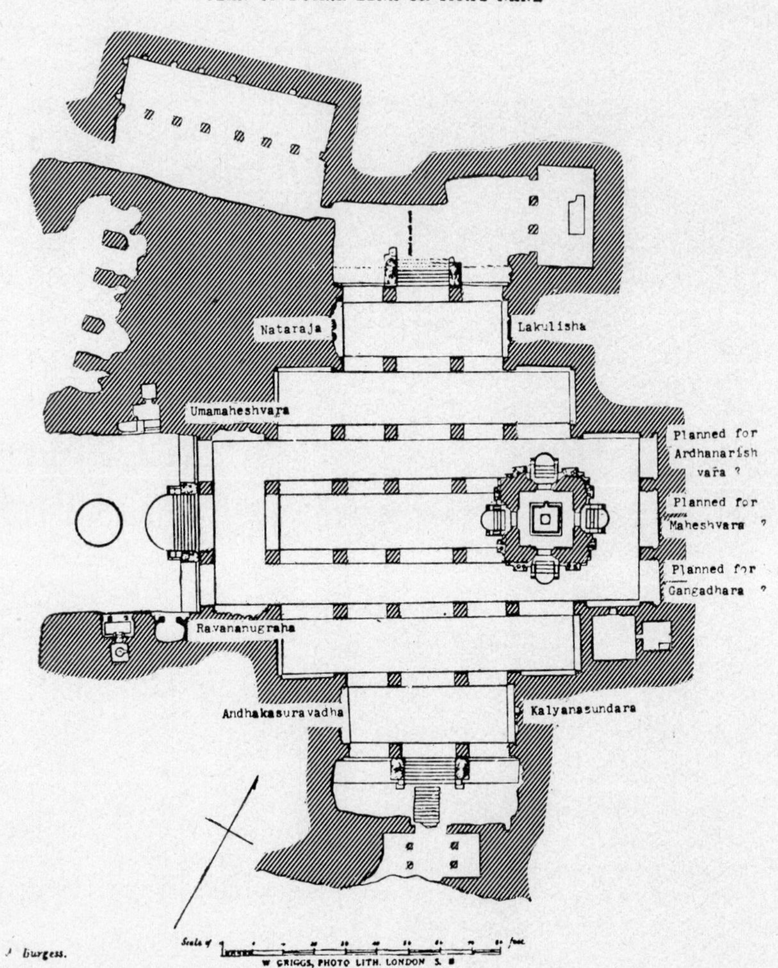

Plate 25. Ellora Cave 29 (Dhumar Lena), ground plan. Based on J. Fergusson and J. Burgess, *Cave Temples of India* (London, 1880) Plate LXXX. Date of cave *c.* 465-475 A.D. (identifications and photo-angles added).

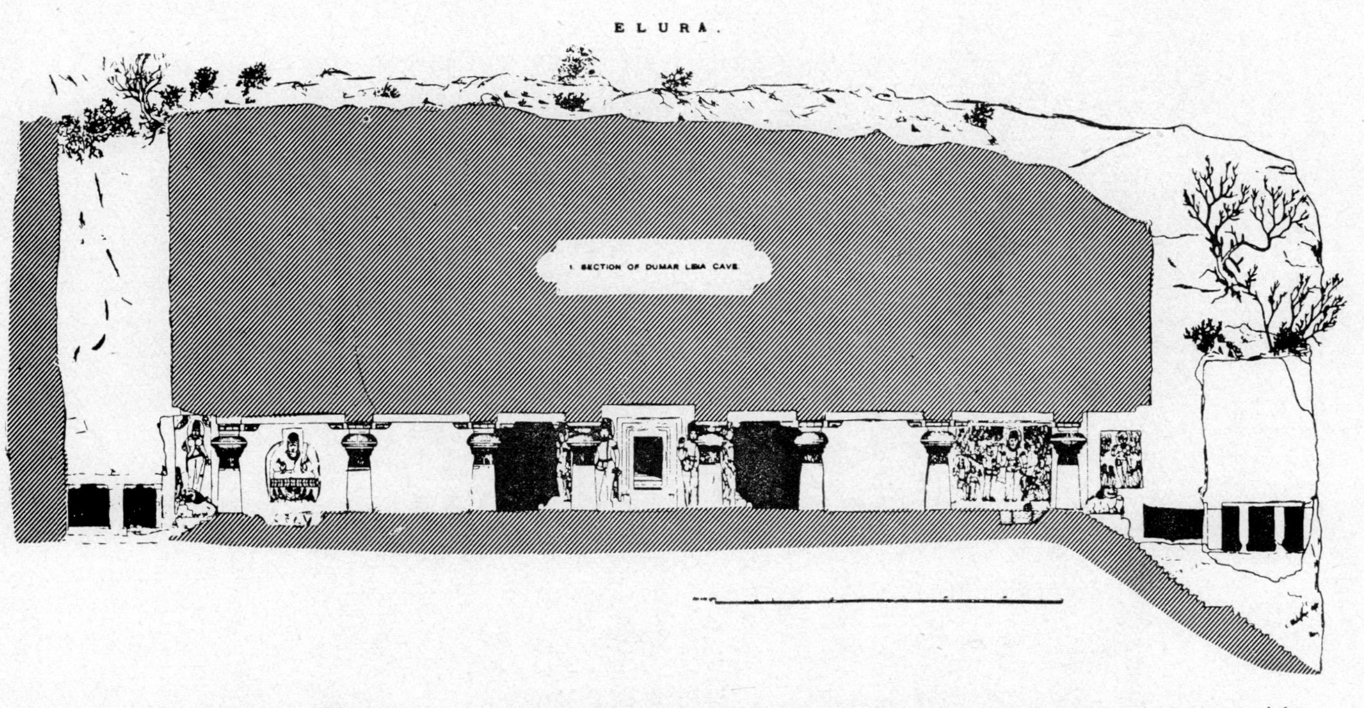

Plate 25a. Ellora Cave 29 (Dhumar Lena), section, showing light well above left court, at left of plan; total height about eighty feet. From J. Burgess, *Report on the Elura Cave Temples* (London, 1882), Plate LLLVII.

Plate 26. Ellora, Cave 29, left court, showing deep light well (about eighty feet from top to floor of court); AAAUM 11,021.

Plate 27. Ellora Cave 29, left court, from left rear; view into main hall; AAAUM 16,065.

Plate 28. Ellora Cave 29, Shrine, from front right, showing rear wall niche (presumably for Gaṅgādhara) at right of photograph; AAAUM WR 6.

Plate 29. Ellora Cave 29, interior, rear wall with niches (presumably for Mahādeva and Ardhanārīśvara, the latter at the left); AAAUM 15,023.

Plate 30. Ellora Cave 29, wall at right of front portal, Rāvaṇa shaking Kailāsa; AAAUM 15,008.

Plate 31. Ellora Cave 16 (Kailāsa Temple), Rāvaṇa Shaking Kailāsa, below south porch; AAAUM WR 18.

Plate 32 Kanheri Cave 3, stambha at right of court, showing early Buddha and attendants; AAAUM 409/73

Plate 33. Kaṇherī Cave 3, stambha at right of court, general view, showing standing Buddha at base and seated Buddha above, both second century A.D.; AAAUM 547/72.

PART IV

BIBLIOGRAPHICAL MATERIALS

11

GUPTA HISTORY AND LITERATURE: A BIBLIOGRAPHIC ESSAY

ELEANOR ZELLIOT*

I. HISTORY : GENERAL

THE Gupta period has been dealt with as a separate entity by a number of writers, but it must also be seen in the perspective of the overall history of ancient and classical India. A very brief list of histories of the pre-Muslim period follows, as well as notes on the major collections of articles dealing with the entire period thematically. First, however, are notes on two essays which offer help in sorting out the attitudes and biases of both Western and Indian historians of ancient India.

A. L. Basham's chapter, "Modern Historians of Ancient India," in C. H. Philips, ed., *Historians of India, Pakistan and Ceylon* (London : Oxford University Press, 1961), deals at length with three Europeans of different periods and nations (Christian Lassen of Norway, Vincent Smith of England, Louis de la Vallée Poussin of France), mentions the nationalist historian K. P. Jayaswal, and notes the objective, fact-based school of R. G. Bhandarkar, R. C. Majumdar, H. C. Raychaudhuri and others who avoid both the Western bias of Vincent Smith and the ultra-Indianist view of Jayaswal. S. R. Goyal goes over the discovery of Gupta history in his *History of the Imperial Guptas* (Allahabad : Central Book Depot, 1967) in an even more detailed way, offering considerable help in dealing with both attitudes and methodology of Western and Indian historians.

*Written with the assistance of Ann Whitfield.

Earliest of the overall histories still in use is Vincent A. Smith's *Early History of India : from* 600 B.C. *to the Muhammadan Conquest*, first published by Oxford at the Clarendon Press in 1906 and still in print. Smith exhibits his Western bias (such as overstressing foreign influence and dramatizing Samudra Gupta as an Indian Napoleon) so clearly that the reader can easily set this aside and appreciate Smith's pioneering reconstruction of Gupta history from coins and his readable narrative. A collection of essays by S. Krishnaswami Aiyangar published in 1911 forms a fairly complete history and adds a strong element of South Indian history to the total picture [*Ancient India and South Indian History and Culture*, vol. 1, rev. ed. (Poona : Oriental Book Agency, 1941)]. The standard overall dynastic history now, however, is H. C. Raychaudhuri, *Political History of Ancient India*, first published in 1923 and still in print (New York : AMS, 1973). Louis de la Vallée Poussin's *Dynasties et histoire de L'Inde depuis Kaniska jusqu'aux invasions Musalmans* (Paris : E. de Bocard, 1935) begins at a later date than Raychaudhuri's work and carries the history beyond the Gupta period, whereas Raychaudhuri ends with a brief section on the Gupta decline.

More recent overall histories which are very useful for undergraduates are Romila Thapar's *A History of India*, vol. 1 (Baltimore : Penguin Books, 1966); D. D. Kosambi's *Ancient India : A History of Its Culture and Civilization* (New York : Pantheon, 1966), a brilliant, idiosyncratic, Marxist approach; and A. L. Basham's *The Wonder That Was India* (New York : Grove Press, 1969), which combines a short chronological history with a broad, sweeping thematic approach to the entire period. Another simple thematic approach may be found in K. C. Chakravarty's *Ancient Indian Culture and Civilization*, 2nd ed., (Bombay : Vora, 1961). A brief clear essay linking India's two greatest periods is Romila Thapar's "Asokan India and the Gupta Age," in A. L. Basham, ed., *A Cultural History of India* (London : Oxford University Press, 1975).

Basham's *Cultural History* is perhaps the most useful and scholarly as well as the most recent of four collections of articles on various facets of Indian civilization. It replaces Geoffrey T. Garrett, ed., *The Legacy of India* (London : Oxford University Press, 1937, republished in 1962 and now out of print), although

Garrett's collection is somewhat easier to read. On the Indian side, the Sri Ramakrishna Centenary Committee and the Ramakrishna Mission of Calcutta have published two multi-volume collections, both entitled *The Cultural Heritage of India*, the first edited in 1936, the second from 1958 to 1962. These contain excellent background material, with extensive coverage of themes by many noted Indian scholars, but the first edition lacks bibliographies and indices.

Three studies on the writing of history in ancient times should be noted here. R. C. Majumdar deals with "The Idea of History in Sanskrit Literature", in C. H. Philips, *op. cit.* V. S. Pathak looks at biographical and other material in *Ancient Historians of India : A Study in Historical Biographies* (Bombay : Asia Publishing House, 1966). A. K. Warder discusses such relevant matters as Jaina historiography and the legend of Vikramāditya and Bāṇa's medieval biography in his *An Introduction to Indian Historiography* (Bombay : Popular Prakashan, 1972).

II. HISTORY : THE GUPTA AGE

While the broad histories of ancient India come from a variety of hands, specific studies of the Gupta period are all by Indian scholars. Aside from the somewhat nationalist approach of R. D. Banerji, all the studies belong to the "objective" school of scholarship; all are agreed on the designation of the Gupta period as the "Golden Age" of the Indian past. The main distinctions among them that will be made here are in terms of readability and of the balance of dynastic and cultural history. In addition to these monographs, there are innumerable articles on specific problems of the Gupta period. The interested reader will find references to these in the bibliographies of works by R. C. Majumdar, S. K. Maity, and S. R. Goyal, with a few mentioned in this and later sections of this bibliography.

The two most inclusive works are *The Vākāṭaka-Gupta Age (ca.* 200-550 A.D.), edited by R. C. Majumdar and A. S. Altekar in 1946 and reprinted by Motilal Banarsidass in 1960; and *The Classical Age,* vol. III of the *History and Culture of the Indian People*, edited by R. C. Majumdar and others, published by Bharatiya Vidya Bhavan, Bombay in 1954. Both volumes include the South, the expansion of Indian culture to other lands, literature, art, religion and administration, and are equipped with complete indices and bibliographies. *The Classical Age* has the advantage of more varying articles by a greater number of first-class scholars. The Majumdar-Altekar volume has the advantage of a political overview of much greater length and a more cohesive viewpoint.

Another work which attempts to cover both cultural and political history is S. K. Maity, *The Imperial Guptas and Their Times, ca.* A.D. 300-550 (New Delhi : Munshiram Manoharlal, 1975). This is a very good introduction, much easier to read than the compilations mentioned above, and the reader is introduced to almost every possible phase of the period one may wish to investigate. The volume has the disadvantage of being more a compilation than an analytical work. Maity's own original scholarship is in the field of economic history (see Section IV). In addition to these volumes, Maity has also written a brief, popular introduction entitled *Gupta Civilization* (Calcutta : Sanskrit Pustak, 1974). An earlier attempt at a similar breadth is R. D. Banerji, *The Age of the Imperial Guptas*, given as lectures in 1924 and published by Banaras Hindu University in 1933. It is illustrated with 41 plates and totally lacking in pedantry, but somewhat inaccurate.

For the serious student of political history, S. R. Goyal's imaginative and well-written *History of the Imperial Guptas* (Allahabad : Central Book Depot, 1967) is essential. His approach is not "what happened ?" but "why did it happen ?"; and he boldly enters into every scholarly controversy on the period, sorting out evidence and opinions in a lively manner. His work is also helpful in noting the contributions of various scholars before his time, and the opening chapters on "Method and Approach" are a model of historiography. Other monographs that concentrate on the dynastic history of the Guptas are, in chronological order of publication : S. Krishnaswami Aiyangar's *Studies in Gupta History* (Madras University, 1928); R. N. Dandekar's *A History of the Guptas* (Poona : Oriental Book Agency, 1941), which is useful but probably not available; and Radha Kumud Mookerji's textbook, *The Gupta Empire* Delhi: Motilal Banarsidass 1969, 4th ed.; first published in 1947).

The book which A. L. Basham ranks as the most thorough and up-to-date monograph on the Guptas is in Hindi, but its author has translated the first part into English; see Parameśvari Lal

Gupta, *The Imperial Guptas : Sources, Historiography and Political History*, vol. I (Varanasi : Vishwavidyalaya Prakashan, 1974). Gupta's enumeration and evaluation of source material, which includes a long section on literature, is invaluable.

Two Indian scholars have published volumes of essays which include detailed studies of aspects of the Gupta period. Udai Narain Roy's *Studies in Ancient Indian History and Culture*, vol. I (Allahabad : Lokbharti Publications, 1969), contains material on aesthetics and literature as he investigates the cities of Pāṭaliputra, Ujjayinī and Prayāga, as well as other matters. Buddha Prakash's *Studies in Indian History and Civilization* (Agra : Shiva Lal Agarwala, 1962) looks at the Vikramāditya tradition, Kālidāsa and the Hūṇas, the age of the *Mṛcchakaṭika*, and other subjects in an extremely thorough fashion.

Among the many articles on the perennial problems of the Gupta political center and Gupta lineage, some of the most provocative are B. Bhattacharyya's "New Light on the History of the Imperial Gupta Dynasty," *Journal of the Bihar Research Society*, XXX (1944), 1-46, which makes use of a neglected Purāṇa (the "Kaliyuga-rāja-vṛttānta" chapter of the Bhaviṣyottara Purāṇa); M. S. Pandey's "Original Home of the Imperial Guptas," *Journal of the Bihar Research Society*, LIV (1968), 141-45, which places that home near Magadha; Basudeva Upadhyaya's "Prayaga—the Capital of the Guptas," *Journal of the Bihar Research Society*, LVII (1971), 11-20, which stresses the Allahābād area; and Parameśvari Lal Gupta's "The Gupta Era : A Re-assessment," *Journal of the Bihar Research Society*, XLIX (1963), 71-87, which attempts to determine the initial date of the era used in Gupta inscriptions.

A number of works relate the Gupta period to other areas and problems in Indian history. Sudhakar Chattopadhyaya's *Early History of North India—*200 B.C.-659 A.D. (Calcutta : Academic Publications, 1968, rev. ed.) pays particular attention to Central Asian affairs in relationship to India. A review of this volume in the *Quarterly Review of Historical Studies*, XII (1972-73), 227-35, by B. P. Sinha commends it highly but raises interesting historical questions. Dinesh Chandra Sircar's *Studies in the Geography of Ancient and Medieval India* (Delhi : Motilal Banarsidass, 1971, rev. ed.) covers every conceivable geographic matter mentioned in Purāṇic and inscriptional place names, and his

Ancient Mālwā and the Vikramaditya Tradition (Delhi : Munshiram Manoharlal, 1969) investigates the history of Mālwā as the font of the name Vikramāditya which Candra Gupta II adopted to signify his universal overlordship. Radhagovinda Basak's *History of Northeast India from the Founding of the Gupta Empire to the Rise of the Pala Dynasty of Bengal,* 320-760 A.D. (Calcutta : Sambodhi Publications, 1967, reprint of 1934 London edition) devotes a hundred pages to the Gupta Empire in that area.

Specific articles on the Gupta's neighbor and colleague to the south include A. S. Altekar's "The Vakatakas," in *The Early History of the Deccan*, Parts I-VI, edited by G. Yazdani (London : Oxford University Press, 1960), which is very different and more readable than the political material in R. C. Majumdar and A. S. Altekar, *op. cit.*; H. Heras, "Relations between Guptas, Kadambas and Vakatakas," *Journal of the Bihar and Orissa Research Society*, XII (1926), 455-65; and M. Govind Pai, "Genealogy and Chronology of the Vakatakas," *Journal of Indian History*, XIV (1935), 1-26, 165-204.

The decline of the Guptas has been a subject of great speculation. B. P. Sinha deals with this in the Magadha area in *The Decline of the Kingdom of Magadha* (*cir*. 455-1000 A.D.) (Patna : Motilal Banarsidass, 1954). Hem Chandra Raychaudhuri discusses the waning days of the Guptas in "The Gupta Empire in the Sixth and Seventh Centuries A.D.," *Journal of the Asiatic Society of Bengal*, N. S., XVI (1920), 313-26. The greatest attention is paid to the Hūṇa invasion as the most important factor in the weakening of the dynasty; an early article on this by K. B. Pathak, "New Light on Gupta Era and Mihirakula" appeared in *The Indian Antiquary*, XLVI (1917), 287-96, and XLVII (1918), 16-22. Two more recent specialized studies of the Hūṇas contain material relating to the latter days of the Guptas : Upendra Thakur, *Hunas in India* (Varanasi : Chowkhamba, 1967) and Atreyi Biswas, *The Political History of the Hunas in India* (New Delhi : Munshiram Manoharlal, 1973). An interesting and provocative article analyzing the invasion in terms of world culture is Hermann Goetz' "The Crisis of the Migration Period and Other Key Problems of Indian History," in his *Studies in the History, Religion and Art of Classical and Medieval India,* edited by Hermann Kulke (Wiesbaden : Steiner, 1974).

A section entitled "The Imperial Guptas and the Classical

Age" in *A Historical Atlas of South Asia*, edited by Joseph E. Schwartzberg (Chicago : University of Chicago Press, 1979), is of invaluable aid in a number of matters. There are plates and text on the geography of the various empires together with chronologies, art work, a chart on Gupta organization, and maps of Purāṇic sites, cultural sites and the routes of the Chinese travellers.

III. HISTORY : BIOGRAPHY

Although Gupta inscriptions allow unusual attention to be paid to individual Gupta kings, only Samudra Gupta has received scholarly attention in the form of a full biography. Samudra Gupta's accession was the subject of a long and informative inscription engraved on the Aśokan pillar at Allahābād. This record, according to Majumdar and Altekar, *op. cit.*, p. 136, "describes the political condition of India and the achievements and personality of Samudra Gupta with such fullness of details as is not to be found in the record of any other king of Northern India, with the single exception of Aśoka." B. G. Gokhale's *Samudra Gupta : Life and Times* (Bombay : Asia Publishing House, 1962) is a short but solid monograph on this Gupta king, whose dates are estimated as 322-375 A.D. The Government of India's National Book Trust has published Lallanji Gopal's *Samudragupta* (translated by O. P. Tandon, New Delhi, 1962) in its series of readable brief biographies, written for the lay reader and without scholarly apparatus.

The problem of Vikramāditya, whose court at Ujjain produced the "Nine Jewels" of the Gupta literary height, has occupied many historians, including D. C. Sircar, *op. cit.* Article literature includes K. B. Vyas, "The Vikramaditya Problem : A Fresh Approach," in the *Annals of the Bhandarkar Oriental Research Institute*, XXVII (1946), 209-36; and S. K. Dikshit, "Candra-Gupta II, Sāhasāṁka alias Vikramāditya and the Nine Jewels," *Indian Culture*, VI (1939), 191-210.

A controversial article by A. S. Altekar used a new-found play, *Devīchandraguptam*, as support of the hypothesis that Rāma Gupta, not Candra Gupta II, was the successor to Samudra Gupta [see "A New Gupta King," *Journal of the Bihar and Orissa Research Society*, XIV (1928), 223-53]. Altekar answered criticism of his article in "Further Discussion about Ramagupta" in the same journal, XV (1929), 134-41, but recent scholarship tends to see Rāma Gupta as a curious and cowardly legendary figure who probably was killed before Candra Gupta II came to the throne. Other minor figures are dealt with by B. P. Sinha in "Kumāra Gupta III," *Journal of the Bihar Research Society*, XXXVI (1950), 57-68, and in the same journal, by S. V. Sohoni in "Govindagupta," LV (1969), 90-96.

The seventh century king Harṣa is so often considered a post-Gupta extension of the Gupta Golden age that a note on the many works about him and his rule may not be out of place here. The *Harṣacarita* (Story of Harṣa) by Bāṇabhaṭṭa, a sort of historical novel, and the notes of the Chinese traveller Hsüan-Tsang offer unusual opportunities for the role of the king to be studied. The full range of the literature of Harṣa's period will not be discussed in this essay, however.

Bāṇa's *Harṣacarita* has been translated by E. B. Cowell and F. W. Thomas (London : Royal Asiatic Society, 1929, originally published in 1897), and both translated and extensively annotated by S. Viswanathan (Madras : Sri Balamanorama Press, 2nd ed., 1964). P. V. Kane's *The Harsha Carita of Bānabhata* (Delhi : Motilal Banarsidass, 1965) includes the text in Sanskrit but also contains over 250 pages of notes in English.

Harṣa : A Political Study, by D. Devahuti (Oxford : The Clarendon Press, 1970) is a first-class piece of scholarship that is also extremely readable. The development of Harṣa's relationship to Nālandā and that of the State to religion is a useful analysis for the whole Classical period. Vasudeva Sharana Agrawala's *The Deeds of Harsha* (Varanasi : Prithivi Prakashan, 1969) uses Gupta art to throw light on words or passages in the *Harṣacarita.* Other biographies include a short essay in the Government of India's National Book Trust Series by V. D. Gangal (New Delhi, 1968); a huge volume, *Harsa and His Times* by Baijnath Sharma (Varanasi : Sushma Prakashan, 1970); R. K. Mookerji's *Harsha* in the old Rulers of India Series (London : Oxford, 1926); and K. M Panikkar's brief, simple *Sri Harsha of Kanauj* (Bombay : Taraporevala, 1922).

IV. SOCIAL AND ECONOMIC HISTORY: POLITY

Perhaps the best place to begin in this complex field is with Ram Sharan Sharma's "Historiography of the Ancient Indian

Social Order," in C. H. Philips, ed., *op. cit.*, which outlines approaches and attitudes in a most helpful way. Sharma himself has been the most innovative of all historians in dealing with the social and economic aspects of classical India. It is impossible, of course, to separate this field from the political, and Sharma's *Aspects of Political Ideas and Institutions* (Delhi: Motilal Banarsidass, 1959) indicates the involvement.

The basic work needed to reconstruct a creditable picture of Gupta economic life is S. K. Maity's *Economic Life in Northern India in the Gupta Period* (Delhi : Motilal Banarsidass, 1970, repr. of 1957 edition), which uses literary, epigraphic, architectural and archeological sources in his path-breaking effort to delineate the economic life of a specific period, something not done before by economic historians of India. The only weakness of Maity's book was pointed out by R. S. Sharma in an otherwise very favorable review, which has been reprinted in R. S. Sharma, ed., *Light on Early Indian Society and Economy* (Bombay : Manaktalas, 1966); it is that Maity does not develop the differences between the Gupta period and the periods before and after.

R. S. Sharma's *Indian Feudalism, c.* A.D. 300-1200 (Calcutta : University of Calcutta, 1965) was a pioneering attempt to analyze the socio-economic changes brought about during the Gupta period. A synopsis of his feudalism thesis may be found in "A Survey of the Land System in India from c. 200 B.C.-A.D. 650," *Journal of the Bihar Research Society*, XLIV (1958), 225-34. An important response to Sharma's book was a symposium at the University of Calcutta, and the papers from that meeting, some of them very critical, have been edited by D. C. Sircar as *Land System and Feudalism in Ancient India*, published by the University in 1966. Another view is in Lallanji Gopal's "On Some Problems of Feudalism in Ancient India", *Annals of the Bhandarkar Oriental Research Institute*, XLIV (1963), 1-32.

Other works which deal with land and revenue are two by U. N. Ghosal : *Contributions to the History of the Hindu Revenue System* (Calcutta : Saraswat Library, 1972, originally published in 1929), which contains fifty pages of material on the Gupta system; and *The Agrarian System in Ancient India* (Calcutta : Saraswat Library, 1973, originally published in 1929). Radhakrishna Choudhary's view on the "Ownership of Land in Ancient

India" appears in the *Journal of the Bihar Research Society*, LIII (1967), 27-52. Dwijendra Narayan Jha's "Assessment of Land Revenue in Post-Maurya and Gupta Times" appears in the same journal, XLVI (1960), 228-33. Dipakranja Das adds the picture of the southern empires during the period from the first to the sixth century in *Economic History of the Deccan* (Delhi : Munshiram Manoharlal, 1969).

Material on other aspects of economic life which contains matter relevant to the Guptas may be found in the following volumes : R. C. Majumdar, *Corporate Life in Ancient India* (Calcutta : University of Calcutta, 1969, 3rd rev. ed., originally published in 1918), which deals with guilds and economic organization; Radha Kumud Mookerji, *Indian Shipping* (Allahabad : Kitab Mahal, 1962, rev. ed., first published in 1912); R. A. Jairajbhoy, *Foreign Influence in Ancient India* (Bombay : Asia Publishing House, 1963); Om Prakash, *Food and Drinks in Ancient India* (Delhi : Munshiram Manoharlal, 1961), which contains a chapter specifically on the Gupta period; and R. N. Saletore's *Early Indian Economic History* (London : Curzon Press, 1975), which covers, in 859 pages, everything from medicinal plants to sea routes and banks.

R. S. Sharma's *Light on Early Indian Society and Economy* (Bombay : Manaktalas, 1966) contains a number of essays on social matters, i.e., caste and women, as well as material on irrigation and usury. His *Sudras in Ancient India* (Delhi : Motilal Banarsidass, 1958) devotes a section to the 200-500 A.D. period called "'Phase of Transformation," in which he notes the advancement of the Śūdras toward peasant status, independent artisan and trading positions, and more religious rites during that age. Rajindra Nath Sharma's *Brahmins Through the Ages* (Delhi : Ajanta Publications, 1977) devotes one of its four sections to Brāhmaṇas in the post-Maurya period. Time periods are not delineated so well in A. S. Altekar's *The Position of Women in Hindu Civilization from Prehistoric Times to the Present Day* (Banaras : Motilal Banarsidass, 1956), but it is still worth looking at. Sasanka Sekhar Parui has a specific article on "Life of Widows in the Gupta Period" in the *Journal of Ancient Indian History*, IX (1975-76), 79-96. J. Auboyer's *Daily Life in Ancient India* 200 B.C.-700 A.D., translated by Simon Watson Taylor (New York : Macmillan, 1965), makes an attempt to put the reader back in the period but is difficult to use for an understanding of historical development. R. N. Saletore has also written a book on *Life in the Gupta Age* (Bombay : Popular Book Depot, 1943), but Saletore's work seems not to be taken very seriously by other scholars.

An exceptionally valuable work for students is Sudhakar Chattopadhyaya's *Social Life in Ancient India* (*in the Background of the Yājñavalkya-smriti*), published in 1965 by Academic Publishers in Calcutta. He draws out information on caste, education, marriage, occupations, women, untouchability, etc. from that early Gupta period text and compares it with the *Manu-smṛti* so that differences can be clearly seen. (Other scholars place this *smṛti* in an earlier period, but it has been noted here because it offers a rare opportunity to study change.) The text of the *Yājñavalkya-smṛti* in part in English translation has been recently reprinted by AMS Press in New York : Book 1, translated by Srisa Chandra Vidyarnava was first published as Volume 21 in the Sacred Books of the Hindus Series in Allahābād in 1918; Part I (The Sources of Hindu Law and the Duties of a Student) was translated by Srisa Chandra Vasu, and originally appeared as Volume II, Part 1, in the Sacred Books of the Hindus Series, published in Allahābād in 1909.

Education during the Gupta period receives some attention in A. S. Altekar's *Education in Ancient India* (Varanasi : Nand Kishore & Bros., 1965) and in Radha Kumud Mookerji's *Ancient Indian Education : Brahmanical and Buddhist* (Delhi : Motilal Banarsidass, 1960, 3rd ed.). H. D. Sankalia deals specifically with the great Buddhist educational center of the Gupta period in *The University of Nalanda* (Delhi : Oriental Publishers, 1972).

Changes in the Indian village and in the Indian city over time have been dealt with minimally by scholars. Some material is available on the village in A. S. Altekar's *A History of Village Community in Western India* (Bombay : Oxford University Press, 1969, first published in 1927). Brief notes on some of the important cities during Gupta times appear in Kanwar Lal, *Holy Cities of India* (Delhi : Asia Press, 1961) and Stuart Piggott, *Some Ancient Cities of India* (London : Oxford University Press, 1945). Binode Behari Dutt deals with textual evidence on cities in *Town Planning in Ancient India* (Calcutta : Thacker, Spink & Co., 1925). A. C. Mittal includes five pages on the Gupta period in his study of the city of "Mandsaur" in the *Journal of the Oriental Institute of Baroda*, XIII (1946), 260-80. The most imaginative articles on the city are R. N. Dandekar's essay on "Some Aspects of the Gupta Civilization : Economic Conditions (Growth of Cities)" in the *Bulletin of the Deccan College Post-Graduate and Research Institute*, XX (1960), 107-15; and a graceful essay on the contrast of ideas about the city in Sanskrit and Tamil literature during the Classical period by A. K. Ramanujan, "Toward an Anthology of City Images," in *Urban India : Society, Space and Image*, edited by Richard Fox (Durham : Duke University Program in Comparative Studies on Southern Asia, 1970).

The issues of polity and kingship are dealt with in much of the material above, but specific mention of works dealing with political ideas in the Gupta period and general works on law and kingship in the ancient period which include some Gupta material is in order here. V. R. Ramachandra Dikshitar's *The Gupta Polity* (Madras : University of Madras, 1952) is a major contribution. An essential volume on polity is K. P. Jayaswal's *Hindu Polity*, first published in 1918 and reprinted by Bangalore Printing and Publishing Co. in 1943. U. N. Ghoshal's *A History of Indian Political Ideas—the Ancient Period and the Period of Transition to the Middle Ages* (Bombay : Oxford University Press, 1959) includes Jain and Buddhist as well as Hindu material in a hundred-page section devoted to the Guptas. A. S. Altekar covers the Guptas more briefly in *State and Government in Ancient India* (Delhi : Motilal Banarsidass, 1958, 3rd ed.), as does R. S. Sharma in *Aspects of Political Life and Institutions in Ancient India* (Delhi : Motilal Banarsidass, 1959). D. C. Sircar's *Studies in the Society and Administration of Ancient and Medieval India* (Calcutta : Firma K. L. Mukhopadhyay, 1967) is another general work on the subject.

Works on kingship which offer ideas applicable to the Gupta period are the articles by J. C. Heesterman and Ronald Inden in *Kingship and Authority in South Asia*, edited by J. R. Richards University of Wisconsin-Madison, (South Asia Studies 4, 1978); Charles Drekmeier's *Kingship and Community in Early India* (Stanford : Stanford University Press, 1962); and J. Gonda's *Ancient Indian Kingship from the Religious Point of View* (Leiden : E. J. Brill, 1966). A brief article by E. Washburn

Hopkins on "The Divinity of Kings," *Journal of the American Oriental Society*, LI (1931), 309-16, outlines in clear fashion the ritual, not hereditary, basis of divine Indian kingship.

For various aspects of law during this period, see the *Yājña-valkya Smṛti* translations noted above, and the relevant sections in J. Duncan M. Derrett, *Religion, Law and the State of India*, (New York : Free Press, 1968) and in Robert Lingat, *The Classical Law of India* translated by J. D. M. Derrett (Berkeley : University of California, 1973). Pandurang Vaman Kane's monumental *History of Dharmashastra*, 5 volumes in 7 tomes (Poona : Bhandarkar Oriental Research Institute, 1930-62, re-printed in 1968), should be consulted. J. Duncan M. Derrett's *Dharmasastra and Juridical Literature*, vol. 5, part 1 in the History of Indian Literature Series (Wiesbaden : Harrassowitz, 1973) is an essential source of information; this work includes critical evaluations of the limitations of Kane and other writers.

A new trend in this whole field of social, economic and political history may be seen in four recent articles which explore religious issues in historical context. An imaginative study of the effect of Northern Brāhmaṇical influence in the South may be found in Burton Stein's "Brahman and Peasant in Early South Indian History," *Brahmavidya—the Adyar Library Bulletin*, XXXI and XXXII (1967-68), 229-69. R. S. Sharma and A. K. Warder explore religion and economics in articles entitled, respectively, "Material Milieu of Tantricism" and "Feudalism and Mahayana Buddhism," in *Indian Society : Historical Probings in Memory of D. D. Kosambi*, edited by R. S. Sharma and V. Jha (New Delhi : Peoples Publishing House, 1974). Ian Proudfoot has also probed this issue in "Economic and Social Background to Changes in Indian Religion," in *Modern Review*, CXXI (1967), 337-46.

V. INSCRIPTIONS AND COINS

The heart of Gupta historiography is its extensive epigraphic material. Some of the inscriptions are of such high literary quality and give such a sense of immediacy to life in the Gupta period that they can be read with delight by students at the beginning level : for instance, the Mandasor inscription of the silk weavers, the Allahābād inscription of Samudra Gupta, the Mathurā inscription of Candra Gupta II, and the Junagadh inscription of

Skanda Gupta. All of these may be found in John F. Fleet's *Inscriptions of the Early Gupta Kings and Their Successors*, published as volume III of the *Corpus Inscriptionum Indicarum* in 1888 and fortunately reprinted in 1970 by the Indological Book House at Vārānasī with notes by A. K. Narain. However, Fleet's pioneering work needs to be supplemented by reference to numerous other inscriptions not known at the time when Fleet published his work. D. C. Sircar's *Select Inscriptions Bearing on Indian History and Civilisation*, vol. I (Calcutta : University of Calcutta, 1965, 2nd ed.) contains all the important inscriptions and includes notes, but not translations from the Sanskrit, so that its value to the non-specialist is limited. Other interpretations and longer notes than Fleet's appear in various issues of the periodical *Epigraphia Indica*, such as D. R. Bhandarkar's "Mathura Pillar Inscription of Chandragupta II : G. E. 61," vol. XXI (1931), 1-8.

Haripada Chakraborti has interpreted the inscriptional material, although without full texts, in *India as Reflected in the Inscriptions of the Gupta Period* (New Delhi : Munshiram Manoharlal, 1978). There are many interpretations of single texts or groups of texts at one site, and the *Memoirs of the Archaeological Survey of India* should be checked for these. See, for instance, Hirananda Sastri's work on the inscriptions of the Buddhist university of Nālandā, founded during Gupta times, in "Nālandā and its Epigraphic Material," *Memoirs of the Archaeological Survey*, No. 66 (1942). D. C. Sircar has also dealt with the university in "Evidence of the Nālandā Seals," *Indian Historical Quarterly*, XIX (1944), 272-81. Another interesting site of inscriptions is from Andhra Pradesh, indicating the nature of Gupta marches to the South; see G. Jawaharlal, "Rāmāpuram Stone Inscriptions of Vikramāditya I," *Journal of the Oriental Institute of Baroda*, XXIII (1974), 316-23.

Edward Joseph Thomas' *Records of the Gupta Dynasty*, first published in 1874-75, contains odd bits of inscriptional material and is now outdated, but has been republished in 1973 by the Indological Book House in Vārāṇasī.

Gupta coins also offer the student invaluable evidence as well as examples in miniature of Gupta art. The two basic collections are: John Allan, *Catalogue of the Coins of the Gupta Dynasties...* (London : British Museum, 1914), and A. S. Altekar, *Coinage of the Gupta Empire and Its Imitations* (Corpus of Indian Coins, vol. IV) (Varanasi : Numismatic Society of India, 1957). A. S. Altekar also has a book on the historic find of gold coins in Afghanistan : *The Gupta Gold Coins in the Bayana Hoard* (Bombay : Numismatic Society of India, 1954). Vincent A. Smith's very early *Catalogue of the Coins of Ancient India in the Indian Museum, Calcutta*, vol. I : The Early Foreign Dynasties and the Guptas, was reprinted in 1972 in Delhi by the Indological Book House.

Coinage in Ancient India : A Numismatic, Archaeochemical and Metallurgical Study of Ancient Indian Coins by Satya Prakash and Rajendra Singh (New Delhi : The Research Institute of Ancient Scientific Studies, 1968) contains over forty pages on the coinage of the Gupta Empire. The bibliography of this volume and those of the major histories offer some help in sorting out the hundreds of short articles on the coins of the Guptas which appear in two numismatic journals, the *Numismatic Society of India Journal*, begun in 1939, and the *Indian Numismatic Chronicle*, begun in 1960, and in a number of other periodicals such as the *Journal of the Bihar Research Society*. Two articles in the latter journal which indicate the kind of historical interpretation which can be made from coins are B. P. Sinha, "Bearing of Numismatics on the History of the Later Imperial Guptas," XXXIV (1948), 18-26; and S.V. Sohoni, "Eagle on Gupta Coins and Seals," XLII (1956), 152-56, in which he makes a case for that device as "good art and good politics".

Two of the most important scholars in the field have written on the use of this kind of material for history : A. K. Narain has a short chapter on "Numismatics and Historical Writing," in C. H. Philips, *op. cit.*; D. C. Sircar's *Indian Epigraphy* (Delhi : Motilal Banarsidass, 1965) is filled with information, has a useful index, and contains some illustrations.

VI. SCIENCE IN THE GUPTA AGE

The Gupta period is noted for its mathematics and astronomy, and it also seems to have produced an unusual technological development in the famed rustless iron pillar near the Qutub Mīnār at Delhi. Material on the history of science in India is available in some quantity, but translations on texts of the period are somewhat disappointing and there remains much work to be done in the field. The most recent work may be the best place to begin. *A Concise History of Science in India*, with D. M. Bose as chief editor and S. N. Sen and B. V. Subbarayappa as editors (New Delhi : Indian National Science Academy, 1971), contains material on all the sciences as well as "The Physical World : Views and Concepts." For the Gupta period, the most important chapters are those on source materials, S. N. Sen on astronomy and astronomers, and a resumé of the "Classical Age and Later" by B. V. Subbarayappa. Another overall volume is the *Symposium on the History of Sciences in India : Proceedings* (New Delhi : National Institute of Sciences, 1963), which has several essays relating to the Gupta period. Chapters on science in general may be found in A. L. Basham, ed., *The Cultural History of India* (Oxford at the Clarendon Press, 1975) by H. J. J. Winter; and in G. T. Garrett, ed., *The Legacy of India* (London : Oxford University Press, 1962) by Walter Eugene Clark. A book by Benoy Kumar Sarkar entitled *Hindu Achievements in the Exact Sciences* (New York : Longmans, Green and Co. 1918) covers all the sciences but is not very satisfactory. A long section entitled "The Pursuit of Science" in volume III of the Ramakrishna Centenary Committee's *Cultural Heritage of India* (Calcutta, 1936) deals with various aspects of this field.

Mathematics as it developed in India may be studied in G. R. Kaye's *Indian Mathematics* (Calcutta : Thacker, Spink and Co., 1915) and in the *History of Hindu Mathematics* : *A Source Book* by Bibhutibhusan Datta and Avadesh Narayan Singh (Bombay : Asia Publishing House, 1962, reprinted from the 1935 edition), which contains divergent views on the origin of the decimal place value system, a concept which is thought to have developed during the Gupta period.

There are a few translations of texts compiled during the Gupta age. The *Āryabhaṭīyam of Āryabhaṭa*, a fifth century mathematician and astronomer, was translated by Walter Eugene Clark (Chicago : University of Chicago, 1930). The *Sūrya Siddhānta* was translated by E. Burgess in 1860 and appeared in a Calcutta University Reprint with an introduction by P. C. Sen Gupta in 1936. An article by Dilip Kumar Biswas, "The Maga Ancestry of Varahamihira," *Indian Historical Quarterly*, XXV (1949), 175-83, adds an interesting note by linking astronomy to sun worship through an Iranian cult.

Indian medicine during the Gupta period is difficult to deal with directly. An article by A. L. Basham, "The Practice of Medicine in Ancient and Medieval India," in *Asian Medical Systems : A Comparative Study*, edited by Charles Leslie (Berkeley : University of California 1976), pays attention to time periods and includes a full bibliography of sources and secondary works.

VII. LITERATURE : GENERAL

Classical Sanskrit literature was at its height in the Gupta Age. Not only Kālidāsa, but also Śūdraka, Viśākhadatta, and a host of dramatists whose works are no longer extant brought classical drama to an apex. The poetry written then marked Sanskrit poetry for succeeding centuries. The stories and tales and the manuals on the art of love established patterns of aesthetics and eroticism. The literature of the period is vast and the translations vary from Victorian pedantry to ultra-modern syntax. Much of the literature of the Gupta period may be read for simple aesthetic enjoyment. Since it is such an integral part of the Gupta ethos, however, the reader will find that historians make much more use of the literature for both fact and atmosphere than is usual in other periods of Indian history.

The older general studies of Sanskrit literature are still very useful. Arthur A. MacDonell's *A History of Sanskrit Literature*, published first in 1899 and reprinted in 1965 by Motilal Banarsidass, Delhi, is much appreciated by undergraduates. A. Berriedale Keith's *History of Sanskrit Literature* was first published in 1920 and has been reprinted in 1966 by Oxford University Press, London. Krishna Chaitanya's *A New History of Sanskrit Literature* (Bombay : Asia Publishing House, 1962) attempts to take into account what Keith and MacDonell have done and to round out their work. Madabhushi Krishnamachariar's *History of Classical Sanskrit Literature*, all thousand pages of it, has been reprinted in 1970 by Motilal Banarsidass. The classic *History of Sanskrit Literature* by S. N. Dasgupta and S. K. De was reprinted by the University of Calcutta in 1977, and is better on the social background of the literature than any other history.

The Literature of India : An Introduction, by Edward C. Dimock Jr., *et. al.* (Chicago : University of Chicago, 1974), contains excellent essays on many facets of literature that relate to the Gupta period. Edwin Gerow's work on Poetics in this volume is an aid to the layman, and Gerow has also contributed notes to S. K. De's *Sanskrit Poetics as a Study of Aesthetics* (Berkeley : University of California, 1963). De's other work includes *A History of Sanskrit Poetics,* reprinted by Firma K. L. Mukhopadhyay in Calcutta in 1976, and *Aspects of Sanskrit Literature,* published by that firm in 1959. De has also written brief essays on *Ancient Indian Erotics and Erotic Literature* (Calcutta : Firma K. L. Mukhopadhyay, 1959). Gerow's other work includes the volume on *Indian Poetics* in the History of Indian Literature Series (Wiesbaden : Otto Harrassowitz, 1977). A delightful addition to our understanding of the period is Kapila Vatsyayan's *Classical Indian Dance in Literature and the Arts* (New Delhi : Sangeet Natak Akademi, 1968) which contains fifty pages relevant to the Gupta period.

VIII. LITERATURE : DRAMA

A work in French by Sylvain Levi, *Le Theatre Indien* (Paris : Bouillon, 1890), may still be the most classic treatment of Indian theatre. A. Berriedale Keith's *The Sanskrit Drama in its Origin, Development, Theory and Practice,* first published by Oxford University Press in London in 1924 and reprinted in 1964, exhibits Keith's usual thorough scholarly work. A newer study, Henry Willis Wells' *The Classical Drama of India* (Bombay : Asia Publishing House, 1963), is the work of a man who, while not a Sanskritist, has immersed himself in Indian classical theater and in India. All these general works must of necessity dwell on the dramatists of the Gupta period.

No precise date can be assigned to the *Nāṭyaśāstra*; this treatise on drama probably was chiefly written just before the Gupta period, but it certainly offers light on dramatic theory in evidence in the classical drama of that age. Chapters I-XXVII of the *Nāṭyaśāstra* ascribed to Bharata-Muni have been translated by Manomohan Ghosh (Calcutta : Manisha, 1967, 2nd rev. ed.,), and a selection is available in G. K. Bhat's translation under the title *Bharata-Nāṭya Mañjari* (Poona : Bhandarkar Oriental Institute, 1975). Pramod Kale interprets the text in *The Theatric Universe* (Bombay : Popular Prakashan, 1974).

Discussions of the element of *rasa* (taste, essence, mood), which sets off Sanskrit theater from other classical drama, may be found in Adya Rangacharya, *Drama in Sanskrit Literature*

(Bombay : Popular Prakashan, 1947; revised in 1967), although that work is colored by the author's intense nationalism; and in V. Raghavan, "Sanskrit Drama : Theory and Performance," in *Comparative Drama*, I (1967), pp. 36-48. Hari Ram Mishra's *The Theory of Rasa in Sanskrit Drama* (Bhopal : Vindhyachal Prakashan, 1964) discusses the subject thoroughly but is without an index or a bibliography. M. Christopher Byrski discusses the philosophy of theater in *Concept of Ancient Indian Theatre* (New Delhi : Munshiram Manoharlal, 1974). G. K. Bhat of necessity dwells on the earlier Bhāsa rather than Gupta dramatists in his *Tragedy and Śanskrit Drama* (Bombay : Popular Prakashan, 1974), but does deal with Kālidāsa's lack of the tragic sense. Ratnamavidevi Dikshit discusses *Women in Sanskrit Dramas* (Delhi : Mehar Chand Lachhman Das, 1964), focusing on Kālidāsa. Rameshchandra Sunderji Betai goes against most other scholarship as he criticizes the rigidity of the dramatic tradition in "Some Peculiarities of Sanskrit Drama and Their Results," *Journal of the University of Bombay*, N. S., XXIX (1960), 58-69.

J. A. B. van Buitenen discusses "Classical Drama" and gives synopses of three Gupta period plays in his article in *The Literatures of India* (University of Chicago, 1974). He characterizes Kālidāsa as a "mythographer," Śūdraka as a "social satirist," and Viśākhadatta as a "political scientist" to point up the variety of classical theater. Kālidāsa must receive a separate section in this essay, since his extant work is the most extensive and has received the most attention.

Van Buitenen has translated two Gupta period plays in *Two Plays of Ancient India* (New York : Columbia University Press, 1968) : Śūdraka, "The Little Clay Cart" (Mṛcchakaṭika), and Viśākhadatta, "The Minister's Seal" (Mudrārākṣasa). A collection of *Great Sanskrit Plays*, translated by P. Lal in a swinging modern style, was published by New Directions in New York in 1964 and also includes Śūdraka's play, here called "The Toy Cart," and Viśākhadatta's play, titled "The Signet Ring of Rakshasa." Lal also includes "Śakuntalā" by Kālidāsa, a play by Bhāsa, and ones by Bhavabhūti and Harṣa, who do not strictly come in the Gupta period. Henry W. Wells has edited *Six Sanskrit Plays* (Bombay : Asia Publishing House, 1964), in which he uses translations by Revilo Pendle Oliver of the "Little Clay Cart"; by A. Hjalmar Edgren of "Śakuntalā," and by

Sri Aurobindo of' 'Vikramorvaśīya" (Kālidāsa), as well as works by Bhāsa, Bhavabhūti and Harṣa. Wells himself has worked on translations of three of the same plays in his *Classical Triptych* (Mysore : University of Mysore, 1970), "Śakuntalā" by Kālidāsa, "Little Clay Cart" by Śūdraka, and Harṣa's play.

Individual volumes of translation of Śūdraka's *Mṛcchakaṭika* include a meticulous translation with copious notes by Revilo Pendle Oliver (Urbana : University of Illinois Press, 1938); a highly literary translation by Arthur W. Ryder, vol. 9 in the Harvard Oriental Series (Cambridge : Harvard University Press, 1905); and M. R. Kale's competent translation, published originally in 1924 (Bombay : Booksellers' Publishers Company, 1962). Radhagovinda Basak has written on "Indian Society as pictured in the Mṛcchakaṭika," *Indian Historical Quarterly*, V (1929), 299-325, but without attention to either the humor or the irony in the play.

Viśākhadatta's *Mudrārākṣasa* has been translated in a single volume by M. R. Kale (Delhi : Motilal Banarsidass, 1965) and by K. H. Dhruva (Poona : Oriental Book Supplying Agency, 1923), and is often discussed in the volumes on political theory (see especially the Appendix of Drekmeier, *op. cit.*).

IX. LITERATURE : POETRY

The general literature on Sanskrit literature and poetics should be consulted on this subject, along with the third volume, *Ornate Poetry*, of M. Winternitz, *A History of Indian Literature*, translated by H. Kohn (Calcutta : University of Calcutta, 1959). A. K. Warder has written an all-encompassing three-volume work on *Indian Kavya Literature* (Delhi : Motilal Banarsidass, 1972-77). Th. Stcherbatsky's "Theory of Poetry in India" has been translated from the Russian by Harish C. Gupta in *Indian Studies Past and Present*, X (1969), 289-314.

Although Kālidāsa has received the better part of scholarly attention (see Section XI), the epic poet Bhāravi's *Kirātārjunīya* has been translated twice. Cantos I-III are in Moreshwar Ramchandra Kale's version (Delhi : Motilal Banarsidass, 1966, 4th ed.). Kaisher Bahadur's translation was published by Ratna Pustak in Kathmandu (Nepal) in 1972 and includes good notes. A poet who falls in a considerably later period, the seventh century A.D., is often classed with the Gupta poets as an exponent of both the ascetic and erotic moods, namely, Bhartṛhari. The most recent translation is a delight to read. See Barbara Stoler Miller's *Bhartrihari : Poems* (New York : Columbia University Press, 1967).

Three anthologies of Sanskrit poetry offer a considerable body of excellent translations from the Gupta and later poets. The most recent is *Sanskrit Love Poetry*, translated by W. S. Merwin and J. Moussaieff Masson (New York : Columbia University Press, 1977); John Brough's slight and graceful *Poems from the Sanskrit* (Baltimore : Penguin, 1968) also includes Kālidāsa's work; Daniel H. H. Ingalls' monumental *An Anthology of Sanskrit Court Poetry* (Cambridge : Harvard University Press, 1965) is drawn from two later anthologies but certainly must be used in any study of classical poetry. Critical notes may be found in the introductions to these translations and anthologies and also in Edwin Gerow's "Sanskrit Lyric" in *The Literatures of India*, by Edward C. Dimock, *et. al* (University of Chicago, 1974).

X. LITERATURE : STORIES, TALES AND THE BOOK ON LOVE

All this material is extremely difficult to date. It adds such a human touch to the Gupta period, however, and was either so fully formed or in the process of formation during that age that a few references should be included. J. A. B. van Buitenen's *Tales of Ancient India* (Chicago : University of Chicago, 1959; New York : Bantam Books, 1961) is taken from two anthologies of a later period, but the risque tales are accredited vaguely to the "Golden Age". The *Pañcatantra*, on the other hand, may have received its final form in an earlier age, but, since the first foreign translation (into the Persian in A.D. 570) came immediately following the Gupta period, these highly influential moralistic tales should be noted. Franklin Edgerton's *The Panchatantra Reconstructed*, vol. II (New Haven : American Oriental Society, 1924) includes forty pages of translation. Arthur Ryder's translation of *The Panchatantra* was republished by the University of Chicago Press in 1964. Alfred Williams' translation was published in Oxford by Blackwell in 1930. The most recent translations seem to be that by G. L. Chandiramani and S. B. Hudlikar (Bombay : Chandiramani Publishing House, 1970).

The *Daśa-kumāra-carita*, a set of interlocking tales by Daṇḍin which is credited to the south and often used to note classical age wit, humor and morality, may not be of the Gupta period, but an article by Dharmendra Kumar Gupta, "The Historical Background of Daṇḍin's Prose Romances," *Journal of Indian History*, LIX (1976), 305-18, notes the linkage to the Gupta heritage in the north. Arthur W. Ryder's translation, *The Ten Princes*, first published in 1927, has been reprinted by the University of Chicago in 1960. A novel from the south, Prince Ilango Adigal's *Shilappadikaram* (The Ankle Bracelet) has been translated by Alain Danielou (New York : New Directions, 1965). If this is a fifth century work, as A. K. Ramanujan believes, it adds a picture of southern city life and religious and societal values to our image of the Gupta age. Van Buitenen has given us a section on "Story Literature" which illuminates this narrative material in *Literatures of India*, published by Chicago in 1974. Vātsyāyana's *Kāma Sūtra* on the art of love—or sex—is probably from a slightly earlier period, but represents the urbane Gupta view of a sophisticated life. A recent translation is by S. C. Upadhyaya (Bombay : D. B. Taraporevala, 1961).

XI. LITERATURE : KĀLIDĀSA

It is well to end this essay with the work on and by Kālidāsa, who dominates the Gupta age. The anthologies of classical drama, the collections of Sanskrit poetry, and the political as well as the cultural histories of the age draw from his work. One of the "Nine Jewels" of Vikramāditya in Ujjain, Kālidāsa wrote light poetry, epic poetry and drama. Seven works are extant : two short poems, two epic poems, and three dramas.

Daniel H. H. Ingalls' "Kālidāsa and the Attitudes of the Golden Age," in the *Journal of the American Oriental Society*, 96:1 (1976), 15-26, is a stimulating but controversial approach to this study. K. Krishnamoorthy's *Kalidasa* (New York : Twayne, 1972) tends to rhapsodize and as a biography is without much firm factual support. The rhapsody continues in the title of Sri Ram V. Bakshi's essay, "Kalidasa's Plays : Rituals of Human Perfection," in *Journal of South Asian Literature*, X:2, 3, 4 (1975), 45-49. S. A. Sabnis' *Kalidasa* : *His Style and His Times* (Bombay : N. M. Tripathi, 1966) offers an impressive example of the use of literature in cultural analysis, with chapters on female psychology, architecture, superstition, etc.

B. S. Upadhyaya also looks at the Gupta age in all its aspects through the work of Kālidāsa in *India in Kalidasa* (Delhi : S. Chand, 1968, first published in 1947). V. V. Mirashi and N. R. Navlekar discuss the known facts and the speculation about him in *Kālidāsa : Date, Life and Works* (Bombay : Popular Prakashan 1969). J. Tilakasira analyzes "Kālidāsa's Poetic Art and Erotic Traits" in the *Annals of the Bhandarkar Oriental Research Institute*, LVIII-LIX (1977-78), 365-74. Sivaprasad Bhattacharyya discusses in a scholarly and sensitive way the "old epic nucleus" of Kālidāsa's poetic work in "Kalidasa and the Harivamsa," *Journal of the Oriental Institute of Baroda*, V (1956), 182-95, and Walter Ruben links "Valmiki and Kalidasa" in the same journal, VI(1957), 223-45. Richard Robinson contrasts Kālidāsa with an earlier Buddhist dramatist, using Kālidāsa's *Kumārasambhava* as evidence in "Humanism versus Asceticism in Asvagosha and Kalidasa," *Journal of South Asian Literature*, XII: 3-4 (1977), 1-10. Wendy Doniger O'Flaherty uses the same epic in "A New Approach to Sanskrit Translation," *Mahfil*, VII: 3-4 (1971), 129-41, which includes translation from the Eighth Canto. In "Kālidāsa : An Assessment by Ānandavardhana," *Bulletin of the Deccan College Post-Graduate and Research Institute*, Silver Jubilee Volume (1966), 95-133, P. K. Narayana Pillai attempts to evaluate the dramatist in the light of Dhvani critical theory. S. V. Sohoni has written on "Kālidāsa's Description of Ujjayini" in the *Journal of the Bihar Research Society*, LVI (1970), 67-106, and on "Kālidāsa's Description of Vidiśā and Its Environs" in the same journal, LIX (1974), 41-58.

John Brough, in his article on Kālidāsa in the *Dictionary of Oriental Literatures*, vol. II, edited by Jaroslav Prusek and Dusan Zbavitel (Delhi : Vikas, 1975), refuses to cite any translations of Kālidāsa's works since they are "disappointing" and refers his readers to A. B. Keith, *op. cit.* (1924 and 1928), and to S. N. Dasgupta and S. K. De, *op. cit.* (1947) instead. Nevertheless, a good many students have enjoyed Kālidāsa in English, particularly *Śakuntalā* and *Meghadūta*, even though perfection in capturing his spirit may not yet be achieved.

A convenient way to begin, and an enjoyable one, is with Arthur W. Ryder's *Shakuntala and Other Writings* by Kālidāsa

(New York : E. P. Dutton, 1959, first published in 1912). M. Monier-Williams' translation of *Sakoontala : or The Lost Ring*, first published in 1855, can also be found in *A Treasury of Asian Literature*, edited by John D. Yohannan (New York : New American Library, 1960). Kedar Nath Das Gupta has prepared a version of the play for the English stage (London : Macmillan, 1920). M. B. Emeneau has given us an accurate literal translation from the Bengali recension in *Abhijnanasakuntala* (Barkeley : University of California Press, 1965). M. R. Kale provides a good introduction in his *The Abhijnasakuntala of Kalidasa* [Bombay : Booksellers' Publishers Company, 1961 (1898)].

Other translations of *Śakuntalā* appear in collections previously cited : P. Lal's *Great Sanskrit Plays*; Henry W. Wells' *Six Sanskrit Plays* (translated by A. Hjalmar Edgren), and Henry W. Wells' *Classical Triptych*. John D. Mitchell discusses how the setting, production and appreciation of the play differ from western standards in "A Sanskrit Classic : Shakuntala," in *Approaches to the Oriental Classics*, edited by William Theodore de Bary (New York : Columbia University Press, 1959).

Kālidāsa's other dramas have received much less attention. Henry W. Wells has included *Vikramorvaśiya* as translated by Sri Aurobindo in the *Six Sanskrit Plays* previously cited, and his own rendering in *Sanskrit Plays from Epic Sources* (Baroda : Maharaja Sayajirao University, 1968). Edwin Gerow has given us a translation of *Mālavikā and Agnimitra* in the Sanskrit Issue of *Mahfil*, VII: 3-4 (1971), 67-127. S. V. Sohoni discusses that play in relationship to Bhāsa in "The Plot and Title of Mālavikāgnimitram—a Reevaluation," *Journal of the Bihar Research Society*, LVI (1970), 113-23.

The Cloud Messenger (*Meghadūta*), Kālidāsa's poem of love and nature description, is easily available in a bilingual edition by Franklin and Eleanor Edgerton (Ann Arbor : University of Michigan Press, 1964). Leonard Nathan has given us an elegant bilingual edition in *The Transport of Love : The Meghaduta of Kalidasa* (Berkeley : Center for South and Southeast Asian Studies of the University of California, 1976), and provides extensive notes and a long introduction. There is also a translation by M. R. Kale, *The Meghadūta of Kālidāsa* (Delhi : Motilal Banarsidass, 1974, 8th ed.).

Material on Kālidāsa in both Western and Indian languages has been noted in the *Kālidāsa Bibliography* prepared by Satya Pal Narang (New Delhi : Heritage Publishers, 1976). The four-hundred pages of this bibliography indicate the importance of this literary figure to an appreciation of India's classical age.

12

RELIGION AND ART IN THE GUPTA AGE : A BIBLIOGRAPHIC ESSAY*

BARDWELL L. SMITH

FOR specialists on the Gupta period of Indian history, source materials in Sanskrit, Pāli, Tamil, and other Indian languages remain central for serious research. For the non-specialist studying this important period, yet untrained in these languages, as well as for the specialist, there is a wealth of material written in English and an increasing number of translations of original sources such as inscriptions, texts, historical works, and literature. While dozens of bibliographies include entries on Gupta life, culture, and institutional history, yet none supplies the reader with a carefully selected, annotated, and at the same time reasonably comprehensive sample. This bibliographic essay and the preceding one by Eleanor Zelliot are an attempt to provide such a selective sample of the most important materials available. Inevitably, there is some overlap between these two essays since the sources pertinent to history, social life, and belles-lettres are frequently as crucial to the understanding of religious phenomena and the realms of architecture, sculpture and painting. The essays complement each other, therefore, and are intended to be used together.

*While a few materials pertinent to Indian philosophy will be mentioned, this area of Gupta culture is not covered in the present essay. Also, this essay is largely restricted to materials available in English. A more exhaustive treatment would have to include studies done in French, German, Russian, Japanese, etc.

I. RELIGION

On a scope covering the full range of Indian history, a new series of volumes designed as scholarly guides to resources for the study of Indian philosophies and religions is scheduled to begin publication in 1980 by G. K. Hall & Co., Boston. Of the seven volumes in this series, four annotate books and articles on Gupta culture as well as materials on other periods : Frank E. Reynolds, et al., *Guide to Buddhist Religion;* Kenneth Inada, et al., *Guide to Buddhist Philosophy*; Karl Potter, et al., *Guide to Hindu Philosophy*; and David Dell, Thomas Hopkins, et al., *Guide to Hindu Religion.* One may also consult three essays which are similar to these in scope in the volume edited by Charles J. Adams entitled *A Reader's Guide to the Great Religions* (New York and London : The Free Press, second edition, 1977) : Norvin J. Hein, "Hinduism", 106-155; Frank E. Reynolds, "Buddhism", 156-222; and Kendall W. Folkert, "The Jainas", pp. 231-246. More specifically focused on the Gupta period, though also of assistance in identifying a broad range of materials, is the fifty-page bibliography in R. C. Majumdar and A. D. Pusalker, eds., *The Classical Age* (Bombay : Bharatiya Vidya Bhavan, 1954), 656-706, which is a thorough listing of original sources and modern works dealing with all regions of India during the period 320-740 A.D.

More specialized in nature yet crucial for a sophisticated understanding of Gupta inscriptions, seals, and coins are several publications which deal, among other things, with subject matter of a religious and artistic nature. Among the standard sources are the following : J. F. Fleet, *Corpus Inscriptionum Indicarum*, Vol. III, *Inscriptions of the Early Gupta Kings and their Successors* (London, 1888, reprinted in Varanasi, 1963); John Allan, *Catalogue of the Coins of the Gupta Dynasties and of Śaśāṅka, king of Gauḍa (in the British Museum)*, London, 1914; A. S. Altekar, *Catalogue of the Gupta Gold Coins in the Bāyānā Hoard* (Bombay, 1956); and A. S. Altekar, *Corpus of Indian Coins*, Vol. IV, *The Coinage of the Gupta Empire* (Varanasi : The Numismatic Society of India, 1957). One of the most useful discussions of sources on the Gupta period is the two-volume study by Parameśvari Lal Gupta entitled *The Imperial Guptas* (Varanasi : Vishvavidyalaya Prakashan, 1974). Volume I of this monumental work has three sections : the first is on sources, with chapters on inscriptions, seals and sealings, coins, and literary materials; the second section is on historiography, with chapters on genealogy and chronology and on the Gupta era; the third is on political history, with a separate chapter for each ruler of the dynasty. Volume II is devoted to cultural history, with chapters on polity and administration, social life, agriculture, commerce, currency, religion and philosophy, literature, science, and arts and crafts. The second volume concludes with a comprehensive bibliography. As a whole, this work is, in the words of A. L. Basham, "the most detailed, thorough and comprehensive study of the political history of the Guptas ever to have been produced."

Another valuable recent discussion of Gupta inscriptions is by Haripada Chakraborti in his book *India as Reflected in the Inscriptions of the Gupta Period* (New Delhi: Munshiram Manoharlal Publishers, 1978), in which he examines the four areas of social, economic, religious, and administrative history. The chapter on religious history, pages 112-178, provides an excellent detailing of inscriptions pertinent to all forms of religious life during this period. Another helpful publication with a comparable analysis of seals during the Gupta era is Kiran Kumar Thaplyal's *Studies in Ancient Indian Seals : A Study of North Indian Seals and Sealings from 'circa' Third Century* B.C. *to Mid-Seventh Century* A.D. (Lucknow : Akhila Bharatiya Sanskrit Parishad, 1972), which contains a chapter on "Religion and Iconography", 136-222, and one on "Art and Art Motifs", 265-281, as well as six others dealing with several aspects of Gupta society and culture. Another recent work dealing primarily with the pre-Gupta periods but providing important background analysis for students of the Gupta age is Bhaskar Chattopadhyay, *Coins and Icons : A Study of Myths and Symbols in Indian Numismatic Art* (Calcutta : Punthi Pustak, 1977), with chapters on religious symbolism, Greek divinities on Indian coins, Iranian deities, Brāhmaṇical deities and their emblems, and numismatics as a source of religious history.

Among the many discussions of Gupta source material two of the more cogent are those by S. R. Goyal in his work *A History of the Imperial Guptas* (Allahabad : Central Book Depot, 1967), 1-40; and Suvira Jaiswal, *The Origin and Development of Vaiṣṇavism* (*Vaiṣṇavism* 200 B.C. *to* A.D. 500) (Delhi : Munshiram Manoharlal, 1967), 8-31. Another work which is useful in bringing together facts and data from various literary, epigraphic and numismatic sources and in providing a discussion of the social, economic, administrative and religious aspects of the Gupta reigns is Radha Kumud Mookerji's *The Gupta Empire* (Delhi : Motilal Banarsidass, 1969). Other general histories of the Gupta period include chapters on religion : Sachindra Kumar Maity, *The Imperial Guptas and their Times* (*cir.* A.D. 300-550) (New *Delhi* : Munshiram Manoharlal, 1975), 170-192; A. S. Altekar, "Religion and Philosophy", in Ramesh Chandra Majumdar and Anal Sadashiv Altekar, eds., *The Vākāṭaka-Gupta Age* (*Circa* 200-550 A.D.) (Delhi : Motilal Banarsidass, 1967), 363-395; V. R. Ramachandra Dikshitar, *The Gupta Polity* (Madras : University of Madras, 1952), 279-333, which makes the claim that sectarianism did not exist in the Gupta period; and Rajaram Narayan Saletore, *Life in the Gupta Age* (Bombay : The Popular Book Depot, 1943), 489-599, whose views on that issue are quite different from those of Dikshitar. By far the most comprehensive chapter of this sort is the long one on religion and philosophy by several authors of the various sections in the Majumdar and Pusalker volume mentioned earlier, *The Classical Age*, pages 370-470. An interesting late Gupta text providing perspective on religious cults is analyzed in Ajay Mitra Shastri, *India as Seen in the 'Bṛhatsaṁhitā' of Varāhamihira* (Delhi : Motilal Banarsidass, 1969).

1. *Dharmaśāstras and Rājadharma*

Among the most essential source materials for an understanding of political and social norms, purported to be the revealed law or word of Brahmā, is the vast corpus of dharmaśāstra literature. While much of this antedates the Gupta period, it is necessary to see the various strands in continuity with each other. Though controversy remains about the dating of these, P. V. Kane has set them in this order: *Manu-smṛti* (*c.* 200 B.C.-100 A.D.); *Yājñavalkya-smṛti* (*c.* 100-300 A.D.); *Nārada-smṛti* (*c.* 100-400 A.D.); *Viṣṇu-smṛti* or *Viṣṇudharmasūtra* (*c.* 100-300 A.D.); *Bṛhaspati-smṛti* (*c.* 300-500 A.D.); and *Kātyāyana-smṛti* (*c.* 400-600 A.D.). This literature continued to be produced until the ninth or tenth century. In these treatises one finds considerable attention given to civil and criminal law as well as to the duties one has in one's station in society, with particular emphasis upon rājadharma or the responsibilities of the king. That latter aspect is tied inevitably to the tradition of arthaśāstra material in which the science of governing is spelled out in detail. While the *Arthaśāstra* of Kauṭilya (*c.* 300 B.C.-100 A.D.) was by no means the first in this tradition, it became the classic expression of this genre. As one investigates the role of kingship in Gupta society, the various rituals connected with it, and the intentional way in which the Gupta monarchs and their advisors sought for legitimation of power, one can appreciate the importance of the dharmaśāstras given the necessity of balancing pragmatic power considerations with normative precepts, of giving due weight to both daṇḍa and dharma.

In their English translations the principal texts are the following : George Bühler, translation and with a lengthy introduction, *The Laws of Manu* (*Manu-smṛti*), Sacred Books of the East Series, Vol. XXV (Delhi : Motilal Banarsidass, 1967; reprint of the 1886 Oxford edition); J. R. Gharpure, tr., *Yājñavalkya-smṛti*, Parts I-VI (Bombay, 1936-44), as well as the translation by Rai Bahadur Śriśa Chandra Vidyārṇava, in the Sacred Books of the Hindus Series, XX (New York : AMS Press, 1974; reprint of the 1918 Allahabad edition); Julius Jolly, tr., *The Minor Law-Books* (Part I : *Nārada-smṛti* and *Bṛhaspati-smṛti*), in the Sacred Books of the East Series, XXXIII (Oxford : The Clarendon Press, 1889); Julius Jolly, tr., *The Institute of Vishnu* (*Viṣṇu-smṛti* or *Vaiṣṇava Dharmaśāstra*), Sacred Books of the East Series, VII (Oxford : The Clarendon Press, 1880), which combines an old core back to the early dharmasūtra era around the sixth century B.C. with a much later redaction, making it Vaiṣṇavite in tone; P. V. Kane, ed. and tr., *Kātyāyana-smṛti* (Poona, 1933); and M. N. Dutt, tr., *Kāmandakīya Nītisāra* (Calcutta, 1896), which belongs to the fourth or fifth century A.D. and is essentially a summary of the *Arthaśāstra* of Kauṭilya. For the latter one may consult the translation by R. Shama Sastri, 5th edition, Mysore, 1956.

The secondary material on this tradition is also rich. By far the most extensive scholarship has been done by P. V. Kane. His *History of Dharmaśāstra : Ancient and Mediaeval Religious and Civil Law in India*, 5 volumes, (Poona : Bhandarkar Oriental Research Institute, 1930-62) is an authoritative and encyclopedic treatment of this subject. Volume I, Part I (revised and enlarged, 1968), considers in great detail each treatise in the dharmaśāstra tradition; Volume I, Part II, discusses the evolution of the various schools in this tradition; Volume II, Parts I and II (second edition, 1974), investigates the Vedic background, including the emergence of ritual connected with kingship; Volume III (second edition, 1973) explores the areas of rājadharma, 1-241, vyavahāra (law and the administration of justice), 242-824, and sadācāra (customs and customary law), 825-973; Volume IV (second edition, 1973) has long sections on śrāddha, tīrthayātrā (pilgrimage to holy places), among other subjects; and Volume V, Parts I and II, is an exhaustive discussion of the dharmaśāstra literature's relationship to Vedic, Epic, Purāṇic, and other materials.

Among the many other works besides that of Kane, a few may be mentioned : (1) U. N. Ghoshal, *A History of Indian Political Ideas* (London : Oxford University Press, 1966), 80-187, 307-325, 370-403; (2) Charles Drekmeier, *Kingship and Community in Early India* (Stanford : Stanford University Press, 1962), 129-164, 189-281; (3) Robert Lingat, *The Classical Law of India*, translated and with additions by J. Duncan M. Derrett (Berkeley : University of California Press, 1973); (4) H. N. Sinha, *The Development of Indian Polity* (Bombay : Asia Publishing House, 1963), 95-223; (5) J. Gonda, *Ancient Indian Kingship from the Religious Point of View* (Leiden : E. J. Brill, 1969); (6) H. C. Raychaudhuri, *Political History of Ancient India* (New York : AMS Press, 1973, originally published in 1923)); (7) John W. Spellman, *Political Theory of Ancient India* (London : Oxford University Press, 1964); (8) Ram Charitra Prasad Singh, *Kingship in Northern India* (Delhi : Motilal Banarsidass, 1968); (9) Wendy Doniger O'Flaherty and J. Duncan M. Derrett, eds., *The Concept of Duty in South Asia* (South Asia Books, 1978), 3-106; (10) J. C. Heesterman, "The Conundrum of the King's Authority", in J. F. Richards, *Kingship and Authority in South Asia* (University of Wisconsin, Madison : South Asian Studies, Series #3,1978), 1-27; (11) Ronald Indien, "Ritual, Authority and Cyclic Time in Hindu Kingship", *ibid.*, 28-73; (12) Parts IV and V, pages 301-677, in Vol. II, *Itihāsas, Purāṇas, Dharma and Other Śāstras* (Calcutta : The Ramakrishna Mission Institute of Culture, second edition, revised and enlarged, 1958), with articles by several authors; (13) Narendra Nath Bhattacharyya, *Ancient Indian Rituals and Their Social Contents* (London : Curzon Press, 1975); (14) Richard S. Kennedy, "The King in Early South India, as Chieftain and Emperor", *Indian Historical Review*, III, 1 (July 1976), 1-15; (15) Nicholas B. Dirks, "Political Authority and Structural Change in Early South Indian History", *The Indian Economic and Social History Review*, XIII (1976), 125-157; (16) Dines Chandra Sircar, *Studies in the Religious Life of Ancient and Medieval India* (Delhi : Motilal Banarsidass, 1971), 167-180, which identifies performances of the Aśvamedha in the Gupta and other periods, providing further evidence of the use of Vedic rituals to advance and confirm royal legitimacy; and (17) J. Michael McKnight, Jr., "Kingship and Religion in India's Gupta Age : An Analysis of the Role of Vaiṣṇavism in the Lives and Ideology of the Gupta Kings", *Journals of the American Academy of Religion*, XLV, 2 Supplement (June, 1977), 677-701, which discusses how the Guptas were successful in blending together the Vedic and bhakti elements in establishing the basis of their authority.

2. *Epics, Purāṇas and Classical Sanskrit Literature*

While the Mahābhārata and the Rāmāyaṇa were probably both in their final form by the fourth century A.D., there is continuity between their worlds and those of the early Purāṇas, whose origins were in the Gupta period. It is thus possible to see the epics as a gradual transformation of popular secular material into sacred literature and the Purāṇic literature as an increasingly sectarian re-fashioning of older texts with their myths and legends into elaborate forms of mythology, cosmology, festivals and ceremonies, religious devotionalism, ethics, etc. Of the various translations of the epics, the following are to be recommended : Hari Prasad Shastri, tr., *Rāmāyaṇa of Vālmīki* (London, 1962), 3 vols.; Pratap Chandra Roy, tr., *Mahābhārata* (Calcutta, 1927-32), 11 vols.; J. A. B. van Buitenen, tr., *Mahābhārata* (Chicago : University of Chicago Press, 1974—), Vols. I-III. Two of the most helpful discussions of the relationships between the epics and the Purāṇic literature may be found in Maurice Winternitz, *A History of Indian Literature*, Vol. I (New Delhi : Oriental Books Reprint Corporation, second edition, 1972), 311-586; and also in P. V. Kane, *op. cit*., Vol. I, Part I, 349-421, and Vol. V, Part II, 815-1002. Related to the social order is U. N. Ghoshal's discussion of the epics and the Purāṇas in his *History of Indian Political Ideas*, 188-286, 326-336. An important detailed study of the

Purāṇas as a whole, even though it received considerable criticism when first published in 1940, is R. C. Hazra's *Studies in the Purāṇic Records on Hindu Rites and Customs* (Delhi : Motilal Banarsidass, second edition, 1975). See also Hazra's *Studies in the Upapurāṇas* (Calcutta : University of Calcutta Press, Vol. I, 1958, Vol. II, 1963), with its sound synopses of texts and detailed discussion of dates; Willibald Kirfel, *Das Purāṇa Pañcalaksaṇa* (Bonn, 1927), an essential work; and F. E. Pargiter, *The Purāṇa Text of the Dynasties of the Kali Age* (Oxford, 1913, reprinted in Varanasi, 1962). Also, Ludo Rocher has recently completed *Purāṇas*, a volume for Professor Gonda's multi-volume series (Leiden : E. J. Brill, forthcoming).

Among the Purāṇas which made their appearance during the Gupta age there are several which have been translated into English and some which have been analyzed in detail in terms of what they reveal about the culture. An anthology of material on origins, on Viṣṇu, on Kṛṣṇa, on Śiva, on the Goddess, and on Seers, Kings and Supernaturals has been edited and translated by Cornelia Dimmitt and J. A. B. van Buitenen, *Classical Hindu Mythology : A Reader in the Sanskrit Purāṇas* (Philadelphia : Temple University Press, 1978). The following works, especially the translations, are of central importance : (1) F. E. Pargiter, translated with notes, *Mārkaṇḍeya Purāṇa* (Varanasi : Indological Book House, 1969, reprint of the 1904 Calcutta edition); (2) Nileshvari Y. Desai, *Ancient Indian Society, Religion and Mythology as Depicted in the Mārkaṇḍeya-Purāṇa (A Critical Study)* (Baroda : University of Baroda, 1968); (3) A Taluqdār of Oudh, tr., *The Matsya Puranam*, Sacred Books of the Hindus Series, XVII, Part I (New York : AMS Press, 1974, reprint of the two-volume 1916 Allahabad edition); (4) V. R. Ramachandra Dikshitar, *Matsya Purāṇa, a Study* (Madras, 1935); (5) Vasudeva S. Agrawala, *Matsya-Purāṇa : A Study* (Varanasi : All-India Kashiraj Trust, 1963); (6) S. G. Kantawala, *Cultural History from the Matsya Purāṇa* (Baroda, 1964); (7) Anand Swarup Gupta, tr., *Vāmana Purāṇa* (Varanasi, 1968), (8) Vasudeva S. Agrawala, *Vāmana Purāṇa : A Study* (Varanasi : Prithivi Prakashan, 1964); (9) V. R. Ramachandra Dikshitar, *Some Aspects of the Vāyu Purāṇa* (Madras, 1933) : (10) D. R. Patil, *Cultural History from the Vāyu Purāṇa* (Delhi : Motilal Banarsidass, 1973, reprint of the 1946 Poona edition); (11) H. H. Wilson, tr., *The Vishṇu*

Purāṇa : A System of Hindu Mythology and Tradition, 5 vols. (third edition, Calcutta, 1961, reprint of 1864-70 London edition); (12) M. N. Dutt, tr., *Viṣṇu Purāṇa* (Calcutta, 1894); (13) M. N. Dutt, tr., *Agni Purāṇam* (reprinted ed., Varanasi : Chowkhamba Sanskrit Series, 1967), 2 vols., reprint of 1903-04 edition; and (14) B. B. Mishra, *Polity in the Agni Purāṇa* (Calcutta : Punthi Pustak, 1965). Further studies of Purāṇic literature more broadly include these : A. D. Pusalker, *Studies in the Epics and Purāṇas of India* (Bombay : Bharatiya Vidya Bhavan, 1955); Jagadish Lal Shastri, *Political Thought in the Purāṇas* (Lahore, 1944); and Part III, pages 223-298, in Vol. II, *Itihāsas, Purāṇas, Dharma and Other Śāstras, op. cit.*, with articles by several authors. For a more complete listing of Purāṇas, see pp. 306-309 of Wendy Doniger O'Flaherty, *Hindu Myths* (Baltimore : Penguin Books, 1975).

Since the classical Sanskrit literature of the Gupta period has been commented on in the bibliographic essay by Eleanor Zelliot, attention here needs only to be drawn to the fact that one can derive a good deal about religious ideas and practices from the works of the great poets, dramatists and authors of prose romance who wrote during this age. For students of religious phenomena this is an area which could profit from further analysis. Among the scholarly attention given to this subject one may mention several writings : Bhagwat Saran Upadhyaya, *India in Kālidāsa* (New Delhi : S. Chand ., second edition, 1968), 296-351, on religion and philosophy; S. A. Sabnis, *Kālidāsa : His Style and His Times* (Bombay : N. M. Tripathi., 1966), 250-261, 289-305; U. N. Ghoshal, *op. cit.*, 352-369; G. K. Bhat, "Religion and Sanskrit Drama", *Journal of the Karnatak University* (*Humanities Section*), XX (1976), 112-122; B. S. Agnihotri, "Theism in Kālidāsa's Literature", *Journal of the Oriental Institute of Baroda*, X, 4 (June, 1961), 374-380; J. Bruce Long, "Śiva as Promulgator of Traditional Learning and Patron Deity of the Fine Arts", *Annals of the Bhandarkar Oriental Research Institute*, LII (1971), 67-80; U. Venkatakrishna Rao, "The Devātamaṇḍala in Bhāsa and Kālidāsa", *Journal of Indian History*, XIX, 2 (August, 1951), 183-198; Daniel H. H. Ingalls, "Kālidāsa and the Attitudes of the Golden Age", *Journal of the American Oriental Society*, 96:1 (1976), 15-26; Sivaprasad Bhattacharyya, "Kalidasa and the Harivamsa", *Journal of the Oriental Institute of Baroda*, VI,

3 (March, 1956), 182-195; Radhagovinda Basak, "Indian Society as pictured in the Mṛcchakaṭika", *Indian Historical Quarterly*, V, 2 (June, 1929), 299-325; and R. N. Dandekar, "Literature and Sciences in the Age of the Guptas", *Journal of the University of Poona* (*Humanities Section*), XIX (1964), 1-36, which, together with the same author's article entitled "Post-Vedic Literature", *op. cit.*, 23 (1966), 1-37, provides a helpful survey of the whole field of classical Sanskrit literature.

3. *Evolution of Hindu Mythology and Sectarianism*

As the world of the epics and the Purāṇas unfolds, the Hindu pantheon becomes increasingly rich, as does the institutional life and devotional practice of the bhaktas. Of some help to an understanding of this phenomenon, though it must be used with caution, is Alain Daniélou's *Hindu Polytheism* (New York : Pantheon Books, Bollingen Series LXXIII, 1964); see pages 149-249 (on the "Trinity"), 253-288 (on "The Divine Power or Śakti as the Goddess"), 291-327 (on "Secondary Gods"), and 331-383 (on "The Representation and the Worship of Deities"). Among the various overviews of this terrain, while somewhat misleading, is P. Thomas' *Epics, Myths and Legends of India : A Comprehensive Survey of the Hindus, Buddhists and Jains* (Bombay: D. B. Taraporevala, 13th edition, 1973). Of considerable use, in a more detailed sense, is Gösta Liebert's *Iconographic Dictionary of the Indian Religions : Hinduism-Buddhism-Jainism* (Leiden : E. J. Brill, 1976). A useful anthology, incorporating Vedic, epic and Purāṇic materials, is the one edited by Wendy Doniger O'Flaherty, *Hindu Myths : A Sourcebook Translated from the Sanskrit* (Baltimore : Penguin Books, 1975), with sections on Prajāpati and Brahmā; Indra; Agni; Rudra and Śiva; Viṣṇu; Devī, the Goddess; and Gods and Demons.

Two other recent publications by Wendy O'Flaherty are of major importance in dealing with the vital problems of theodicy and the conflict between spiritual aspirations and human desires respectively : *The Origins of Evil in Hindu Mythology* (Berkeley : University of California Press, 1976), and *Asceticism and Eroticism in the Mythology of Śiva* (London : Oxford University Press, 1973). Another work worthy of note is Sukumari Bhattacharji's *The Indian Theogony : A Comparative Study of Indian Mythology from the Vedas to the Purāṇas* (Cambridge :

Cambridge University Press, 1970), which deals with the historical development of Indian mythology and its connection with parallel mythologies elsewhere and focuses on gods from the Śiva, Viṣṇu and Brahmā groups. A basic study of the chronology, texts, and major sectarian movements is Part II (*L'Hindouisme Récent*) of Jan Gonda's *Les Religions de l'Inde* (Paris : Payot, 1975), with sections on Gupta and post-Gupta periods. Two other helpful discussions of the rise of Hindu sectarianism and of various sectarian developments among the Vaiṣṇavas, the Śaivas, the Śāktas, and the Sauras may be found in Sudhakar Chattopadhyaya, *Evolution of Hindu Sects* (New Delhi : Munshiram Manoharlal, 1970) and in Jitendra Nath Banerjea, *Paurāṇic and Tantric Religion* (*Early Phase*) (Calcutta : University of Calcutta Press, 1966). One may also consult Majumdar and Pusalker, *op. cit*, 419-454, as well as various chapters in Volume IV, *The Religions,* of the Cultural Heritage of India four-volume series, *op. cit.*, though the essays in that work are of uneven value. On the Saura sect especially, see V. C. Srivastava, *Sun-Worship in Ancient India* (Allahabad : Indological Publications, 1972) and Lalta Prasad Panday, *Sun-Worship in Ancient India* (Delhi : Motilal Banarsidass, 1971), pages 79-176.

With respect to Vaiṣṇavism specifically there are several books and articles to consult. One of the most thorough studies is by Suvira Jaiswal entitled *The Origin and Development of Vaiṣṇavism* (Delhi : Munshiram Manoharlal, 1967), which explores this subject in the post-Maurya and Gupta periods and looks primarily at the Vaiṣṇava pantheon, the doctrines of the Vaiṣṇavas, their rituals and observances, and the extent of their influence within the various regions of India. Beyond the immense amount of mythic material about Viṣṇu in Vedic, epic and Purāṇic sources, one may also examine the *Harivaṃśa,* translated into French by Simon Alexandre Langlois (London, 1834-5), a principal source for the myths of Vāsudeva-Kṛṣṇa and a supplement to the *Mahābhārata,* whose present form was attained about 400 A.D. Another work, while only of limited use for the Gupta period, is helpful on the full sweep of Vaiṣṇavism, its origins and development, namely, Hem Chandra Raychaudhuri, *Materials for the Study of the Early History of the Vaishnava Sect* (New Delhi : Oriental Books Reprint Corporation, second edition, 1975, originally published in Calcutta, 1920). A somewhat dated but still useful volume is R. G. Bhandarkar, *Vaiṣṇavism, Śaivism and Minor Religious Systems* (Strasbourg, 1913). An important monograph is J. Gonda's *Aspects of Early Viṣṇuism* (Delhi : Motilal Banarsidass, second edition, 1969), which considers all the textual sources about Viṣṇu from the Vedas to the Purāṇas. Of comparable value, though a different sort of study is Professor Gonda's work, *Viṣṇuism and Śivaism : A Comparison* (New Delhi : Munshiram Manoharlal, 1976), which deals first with the character of both deities in the Vedas and the *Mahābhārata*, then traces their rise to superiority over other gods, as well as the theology, ritual and mutual relations of the two religions, and finally the appearance of Śiva and Viṣṇu in folklore, myth and literature. Several chapters on the Vaiṣṇava movement, including during the Gupta period, are of interest in D. C. Sircar's *Studies in the Religious Life of Ancient and Medieval India* (Delhi : Motilal Banarsidass, 1971), a volume with essays on a broad spectrum of Indian religious life. Finally two articles may be cited : R. Champakalakshmi, "Vaiṣṇava Concepts in Early Tamil Nadu", *Journal of Indian History*, L, 3 (December, 1972), 723-754, which traces the development of Vaiṣṇava iconographic concepts in Tamil Nāḍu before 600 A.D.; and Kunja Govinda Goswami, "Vaiṣṇavism", *Indian Historical Quarterly*, XXX, 2 (June, 1955), 109-133, which looks at this phenomenon in several Indian regions.

Another feature of religious life and mythology of importance during the Gupta period is the development of Śaiva and Śākta Hinduism. While one needs to pursue this in Tantric materials which post-date the Gupta, one can see how the Gupta age contributed in many ways to the development of this process. Aside from the several works already mentioned which examine various aspects of Śaiva cult and myth, others are pertinent : S. C. Nandimath, "Śaivism in the Vedic, Epic and Pauranika Periods", *Journal of the Karnatak University (Humanities)*, 12 (1968), 1-21; Vasudeva S. Agrawala, *Śiva Mahādeva : The Great God (an Exposition of the Symbolism of Śiva)* (Varanasi : Veda Academy, 1966); Prithvi Kumar Agrawala, *Skanda-Kārttikeya : A Study in the Origin and Development* (Varanasi : Banaras Hindu University, 1967), which examines both textual evidence and archeological materials from Vedic, epic, and Purāṇic times and sources; Alice Getty, *Gaṇeśa* (Oxford :

Clarendon Press, 1936); Mahesh Chandra Prasad Shrivastava, *Gaṇeśa* and Jyeṣṭhā : A Comparative Study", *Journal of the Bihar Research Society*, LVIII (1972), 165-170; and Baij Nath Puri, "Gaṇeśa and the Gaṇapati Cult in India and South-east Asia," *Journal of Indian History*, XLVIII, 2 (August, 1970), 405-413.

Among those focusing primarily on Śākta forms of Hinduism which apply at all to the Gupta period one may consult the following : Wendell Charles Beane, *Myth, Cult and Symbols in Śākta Hinduism* (Leiden : E. J. Brill, 1977), a study of its historical and traditional origins and the cosmological, ritualistic, and eschatological features present in the phenomenon of the Goddess Durgā-Kālī as a religious symbol of "multi-structural integration". The following works are of even more importance: Wendy Doniger O'Flaherty, *Women, Androgynes and Other Mythical Beasts* (Chicago : University of Chicago Press, 1980); David Kinsley, *The Sword and the Flute* (Berkeley : University of California Press, 1975); John S. Hawley and Donna Wulff, eds., *The Divine Consort : Rādhā and the Goddesses of India* (Berkeley : Asian Humanities Press, 1982), and Gerald James Larson, Pratapaditya Pal, and Rebecca P. Gowen, eds., *In Her Image* (Santa Barbara : University of California in Santa Barbara Press, 1980), which is a catalogue of text and plates, with a very good introduction by Larson. Of major importance is Vasudeva S. Agrawala's translation of *Devī-māhātmyam : The Glorification of the Great Goddess* (Varanasi : All-India Kashiraj Trust, 1963), with introduction and annotations, of an important late Gupta text (*c.* 550 A.D.) which constitutes chapters 81-93 of the *Mārkaṇḍeya Purāṇa*. See also David Kinsley, "The Portrait of the Goddess in the *Devī-māhātmya", Journal of the American Academy of Religion*, XLVI, 4 (December, 1978), 489-506, which is an astute analysis of this text in relationship to the various goddess traditions; V. S. Agrawala, "The Devi-Mahatmya", *Journal of Indian History*, XLII, 3 (December, 1964), 823-832; Moti Chandra, "Studies in the Cult of the Mother Goddess in Ancient India", *Bulletin of the Prince of Wales Museum of Western India* (*Bombay*), XII (1973), 1-47, which examines many features of the cult of Śrī-Lakshmī in archeological materials and in evidence from later Vedic literature, the epics, the Purāṇas, and technical texts on iconography.

4. *Buddhism and Jainism*

Compared with the resurgence of the Hindu tradition and of classical Sanskrit literature neither Buddhism nor Jainism grew as much in the Gupta age, in part because of diminished royal patronage. Due to the small amount of epigraphic and literary evidence about Jainism, the picture is very incomplete. Buddhism, on the other hand, was in many ways flourishing in its artistic, philosophical and devotional modes, arising primarily but not exclusively out of the Mahāyāna tradition. Several different sorts of works shed light on the condition of these two heterodox sects. A broad survey may be found in P. V. Bapat, ed., 2500 *Years of Buddhism* (New Delhi : Government of India, 1956), several chapters of which relate to the Gupta period. Again, for both Buddhism and Jainism, one may refer to the chapter on "Religion and Philosophy" in Majumdar and Pusalker, *op. cit.*, 370-419. Among the most crucial sources for this period are the writings of the Chinese scholar-monks. A general view is provided in Prabodh Chandra Bagchi, *India and China : A Thousand Years of Cultural Relations* (New York : Philosophical Library, 1951, second edition), whose focus is on the period from the third century B.C. to the eleventh century A.D. The most basic materials are the following : H. A. Giles, tr., *The Travels of Fa-hien* (399-414 A.D.); *or Record of Buddhistic Kingdoms* (London: Routledge and Paul, 1956); James Legge, tr., *A Record of Buddhistic Kingdoms : Being An Account by the Chinese Monk Fā-hien of His Travels in India and Ceylon* (A.D. 399-414) *in Search of the Buddhist Books of Discipline* (New York : Paragon Book Reprint Corporation, 1965, first published in 1886); Samuel Beal, tr., *Si-yu-ki. Buddhist Records of the Western World*, translated from the Chinese of Hiuen-Tsang (A.D. 629), 2 volumes (Delhi : Motilal Banarsidass, Reprint 1981, first published in 1884); Thomas Watters, tr., *On Yuan Chwang's Travels in India,* 629-645 A.D., 2 volumes (New York : AMS Press, 1971, reprint of the 1904-05 London edition); Samuel Beal, tr., *The Life of Hiuen Tsang by Shaman Hwui Li. With an Introduction Containing an Account of the Works of I-tsing* (London : Kegan Paul, Trench, Trubner and Co., 1911); Hui-li, compiler, *The Life of Hsuan-tsang* (Peking : The Chinese Buddhist Association, 1959); and J. A. Takakusu, tr., *A Record of the Buddhist Religion as Practiced in India and the Malay Archipelago* (A.D. 671-695) (New

Delhi, 1966, reprint of 1896 Oxford edition). Though the writings of Hsüan-tsang and I-tsing are after the fall of the Imperial Guptas, they provide considerable insight into the nature of Buddhism in the following century. Réné Grousset's excellent depiction of the world encountered by these seventh century monks is entitled *In the Footsteps of the Buddha* (New York : Grossman Publishers, 1971). Another important account is that of the Tibetan monk Tāranātha, completed in 1607, entitled *History of Buddhism in India,* translated into English by U. N. Ghoshal and Nalinaksha Dutt, and appearing in the *Indian Historical Quarterly*, III, 60-68, 508-9, 803-7; IV, 530-3; V, 715-21; VI, 334-44; VII, 150-60; VIII, 247-252; X, 551-7; XXVII, 239-49; XXVIII, 41-50. A more recent translation is by Lama Chimpa and Alaka Chattopadhyaya, *Tāranātha's History of Buddhism in India* (Simla : Indian Institute of Advanced Study, 1970).

A great deal has been written about the sectarian movement within Buddhism and especially about the development and expansion of Mahāyāna, its philosophical schools, its greatly expanding literature, its impact upon artistic expression, and the emergence of great universities at places such as Nālandā, Valabhī, and later elsewhere. One needs also to perceive developments within the Hīnayāna tradition, in India as well as Ceylon and Southeast Asia, in the appearance of non-canonical Pāli literature and in its institutional existence alongside the schools of Mahāyāna. Among the many works to be consulted about these subjects the following are of considerable help: Maurice Winternitz, *History of Indian Literature*, Vol. II (New Delhi : Oriental Books Reprint Corporation, second edition, 1972), of which pages 174-375 are germane to the Gupta period, with discussion of a great variety of Buddhist literature; B. C. Law, *History of Pali Literature*, Vol. II (London : Kegan Paul, Trench, Trubner and Co., Ltd., 1933), with its special focus on non-canonical Pāli literature in such works as the chronicles of Ceylon and the writings of Buddhaghoṣa in the fourth and fifth centuries A.D.; A. K. Warder, *Indian Buddhism* (Delhi : Motilal Banarsidass, 1970,) pages 352-518 of which supply an excellent account of Mahāyāna schools and the thought produced by them; Nalinaksha Dutt, *Mahāyāna Buddhism* (Delhi: Motilal Banarsidass, Reprint 1979), with chapters on its political and cultural background, its pre-Bodhisattva stage, and its concepts of trikāya, nirvāṇa, paramārthasatya (truth), and tathatā; and Har Dayal, *The Bodhisattva Doctrine in Buddhist Sanskrit Literature* (Delhi : Motilal Banarsidass, 1970, reprint of the 1932 London edition), long regarded as a definitive study on this subject. Several of the above examine in detail the most prominent Mahāyāna sūtras which emerged during the Gupta age and just before, writings which had tremendous influence on the thinking, the artistic expression, and the devotional practice of Buddhists in India and beyond. The Yogācāra-Vijñānavāda school of Mahāyāna reached its peak in this period, a time producing such figures as Asaṅga, Vasubandhu, Diṅnāga, Bhāvaviveka, Āryadeva, followed by the emergence of Vajrayāna in the fifth and sixth centuries. The immediate post-Gupta developments are thoroughly discussed by Lalmani Joshi in *Studies in the Buddhistic Culture of India* (*During the 7th and 8th Centuries* A.D.) (Delhi : Motilal Banarsidass, 1967), in both their intellectual and institutional dimensions.

A sizeable number of studies help to portray the historical, religious, artistic and institutional aspects of Buddhism in various regions of India. Among the best is Sukumar Dutt's *Buddhist Monks and Monasteries of India* (London : George Allen and Unwin Ltd., 1962), much of which pertains to the Gupta age and immediately thereafter. The most extensive work of its kind is Radha Kumud Mookerji's *Ancient Indian Education* (*Brahmanical and Buddhist*) (Delhi : Motilal Banarsidass, 1969, fourth edition), pages 492-586 of which portray Buddhist forms of education in the fifth and seventh centuries based upon the Chinese pilgrims' reports. Among the various regional studies the most noteworthy are : B. G. Gokhale, *Buddhism in Maharashtra: A History* (Bombay : Popular Prakashan, 1976); Nalinaksha Dutt and Krishna Datta Bajpai, *Development of Buddhism in Uttar Pradesh* (Lucknow : Publication Bureau, Government of Uttar Pradesh, 1956), pages 308-405 especially; S. M. Pahadiya, *Buddhism in Malwa* (New Delhi : K. B. Publications, 1976), with about forty pages on the Gupta period; C. Minakshi, *Administration and Social Life under the Pallavas* (Madras : University of Madras, 1938), pages 213-238 on Buddhist and Jaina seats of learning; T. N. Vasudeva Rao, "Buddhism and Kāñcī", *Journal of Indian History*, LIII (April, 1975), 17-24; Pushpa Niyogi, "Dynastic and Regional Affiliations of Buddhism in Ancient Bengal", *Journal of Ancient Indian History*, IX (1975-76), 120-167 (124-138 on the Gupta period);

Pushpa Niyogi, "Organisation of Buddhist Monasteries in Ancient Bengal and Bihar", *Journal of Indian History*, LI, 3 (December, 1973), 531-557; Pushpa Niyogi, "Some Buddhist Monasteries in Ancient Bengal and Bihar", *Journal of Indian History,* LIV (August 1976), 273-298; Hasmukh D. Sankalia, *The University of Nālandā* (Madras : B. G. Paul and Co. 1934); R. N. Saletore, *Life in the Gupta Age,* see above, with pages 556-599 on Jaina and Buddhist institutions; Ramendra Nath Nandi, *Religious Institutions and Cults in the Deccan* (*c.* A.D. 600-A.D. 1000) (Delhi : Motilal Banarsidass, 1973), during which period epigraphic records reveal important changes occurring in the rituals, doctrines, and monastic organization of Jaina sects; Upendra Thakur, "A Historical Survey of Jainism in North Bihar", *Journal of the Bihar Research Society*, XLV, 1-4 (1959), 188-203; and B. J. Sandesara, "Cultural Data in the Vasudeva-Hiṇḍi, a Prākrit Story-book by Saṅghadāsagaṇi (circa 5th Century A.D.)", *Journal of the Oriental Institute of Baroda*, X, 1 (September, 1960), 7-17, which is the earliest extant story-book in non-canonical Jaina literature and is important in revealing social conditions of the time.

II. ART

As with all aspects of Gupta life and culture the same sources, discussed earlier, are basic to understanding this era and its richness, namely, inscriptions, seals, coins, primary literature, as well as the more recent scholarly analysis of these sources. To these must naturally be added the artistic products of the Gupta period (primarily architecture, sculpture and painting), as these help to portray why the Gupta period was called the golden or classical age and also shed light on many other aspects of culture (especially the religious). As in the case with religious life and thought during the Gupta age where no first-rate overall study exists, albeit many excellent studies of a more limited scope, so in the area of Gupta art there is yet no magnum opus which does for this period what Gordon H. Luce has, for instance, done for the Pagān period in his three-volume work, *Old-Burma—Early Pagán* (Locust Valley, New York : J. J. Augustin Publisher 1969-70). The reasons for this are not hard to find; the Gupta realm was much more extensive, included a great deal more diversity, and related to influences far broader. And yet the time may now be ripe for studies which, as with Luce's, are both rich in detail and also comprehensive. Joanna Williams' forthcoming work, *Art of Gupta India*, mentioned later, may fill this notable lacuna. The work on Gupta art that has already been done is considerable, however, as this section will suggest.

1. *Surveys of Indian Art*

A large number of books exist which devote some attention to art during the Gupta period. Among those works mentioned above which deal, *in passim*, with Gupta art are the following: R. D. Banerji, *Age of the Imperial Guptas* (Banaras: Banaras Hindu University, 1933), see the section on art; R. C. Majumdar and A. S. Altekar, eds., *The Vākāṭaka-Gupta Age*, 423-471; S. K. Maity, *The Imperial Guptas and their Times*, 228-245; R. C. Majumdar and A. D. Pusalker, eds., *The Classical Age*, 471-559, which is the best of these. Among the host of surveys of Indian art, dealing in part with the Gupta period, are these : Hermann Goetz, *India : Five Thousand Years of Indian Art* (New York : McGraw-Hill, second edition, 1964), 87-123; Mario Bussagli and Calembus Sivaramamurti, 5000 *Years of the Art of India* (New York : Harry N. Abrams, 1978), 105-156, with excellent plates; Louis Frédéric, *Indian Temples and Sculptures* (London : Thames and Hudson, 1959), 123-238, principally for the plates; Calembus Sivaramamurti, *The Art of India* (New York : Harry N. Abrams, 1977), a lavish photographic study; Pierre Rambach and Vitold DeGolish, *The Golden Age of Indian Art, Vth-XIIIth Century* (London : Thames and Hudson, 1955), principally photographs; Ananda Coomaraswamy, *History of Indian and Indonesian Art* (New York : Dover Publications, 1965), 71-91; Benjamin Rowland, *The Art and Architecture of India* : *Buddhist, Hindu, Jain* (Baltimore : Penguin Books, second edition, 1956), 121-142; Dietrich Seckel, *The Art of Buddhism* (London : Methuen, 1964), *in passim*; Vincent A. Smith, *A History of Fine Art in India and Ceylon* (Oxford : The Clarendon Press, second edition, revised by K. de B. Codrington, 1930), 77-112; and Heinrich Zimmer, *The Art of Indian Asia : Its Mythology and Transformations,* 2 volumes (New York : Pantheon Books, 1955, completed and edited by Joseph Campbell), a classical overview of Indian art with chapters on Indian ideals of beauty, symbolism of the lotus, Indian architecture, and Indian sculpture. Also summary in nature but dealing largely with themes and motifs and of varying pertinence to a study of Gupta art are the following : Radhakamal Mukerjee, *The Flowering of Indian Art* (Bombay : Asia Publishing House, 1964); Radhakamal Mukeriee, *The Cosmic Art of India : Symbol ('Murti'), Sentiment ('Rasa') and Silence* (*'Yoga'*) (Bombay : Allied Publishers Private Ltd., 1965); E. B. Havell, *The Art Heritage of India* (Bombay : D. B. Taraporevala, revised edition, 1964, a reprint combining two earlier books); and Niharranjan Ray, *Idea and Image in Indian Art* (New Delhi : Munshiram Manoharlal Publishers, 1973), which deals in part with Sārnāth and Elephanta.

2. *Gupta Architecture and Painting*

As architecture and sculpture are typically found together at specific sites, it is only for reasons of convenience that one considers them in separate sections here. Even so, there will inevitably be overlap. In general, this section and the next on sculpture differ from the previous one in their more direct focusing on the Gupta period. One helpful resource for a number of articles is the *Encyclopedia of World Art,* 15 volumes ((New York : McGraw-Hill, 1958-1968), Volume VII of which has an essay by Hermann Goetz on "The Gupta School", and other volumes have articles on Ajantā, Bāgh, Sārnāth, Bodh Gayā, etc. Though somewhat dated, there is historic interest in E. B. Havell's *The Ancient and Medieval Architecture of India* (New Delhi : S. Chand, 1972, reprint of the 1915 London edition), with sections on the Gupta empire, Ajantā, and Elephanta. A brief discussion of iconography, terracottas, sculptures, architecture and painting may be found in Vasudeva Sharan Agrawala, *Gupta Art : A History of Indian Art in the Gupta Period* (Calcutta : K. P. Bagchi, 1977, reprint of 1948 edition). See also the same author's *Studies in Indian Art* (Varanasi : Vishvavidyalaya Prakashan, 1965), pages 197-254 of which discuss several very interesting aspects of Gupta art. More directly on architecture is Prithivi Kumar Agrawala's *Gupta Temple Architecture* (Varanasi : Prithivi Prakashan, 1968), which is a useful, brief survey of this subject. Beyond these, a number of standard surveys devote some attention to the Gupta period and provide extensive illustrations : James Burgess, *Ancient Monuments, Temples and Sculpture of India* (London : W. Griggs, n.d.); Percy Brown, *Indian Architecture* (*Buddhist and*

Hindu Periods) (Bombay : D. B. Taraporevala, 1965, fifth edition), 36-61; and James Fergusson, *History of Indian and Eastern Architecture*, Vol. 1 (London : John Murray, 1910, second edition, revised and edited with additions by James Burgess). A genuine introduction to the subject is George Mitchell's *The Hindu Temple : An Introduction to Its Form and Meaning* (London : Paul Elek, 1977). Finally, among those which cover Indian architecture broadly there are several whose consideration of principles of architecture are important. The work by Stella Kramrisch entitled *The Hindu Temple*, 2 volumes (Delhi : Motilal Banarsidass, 1976, reprint of 1946 edition), has long been regarded as a classical treatment in this area. Tarapada Bhattacharyya, *A Study on Vāstuvidyā, or Canons of Indian Architecture* (Calcutta : Firma K. L. Mukhopadhyay, second edition, 1963, originally published in 1948), discusses the development of vāstuvidyā (the science of architecture) from the first through the sixth century A.D. on pages 125-153. In a collection edited by him entitled *Studies in Indian Temple Architecture* (New Delhi : American Institute of Indian Studies, 1975) Pramod Chandra has an important essay on "The Study of Indian Temple Architecture" over the past century and a half in which he discusses and evaluates the work of Ram Raz, James Fergusson, Alexander Cunningham, James Burgess, Henry Cousens, A. Foucher, G. Jouveau-Dubreuil, E. B. Havell, Ananda Coomaraswamy, Stella Kramrisch, Prabhasankar Somapura, Alice Boner, M. A. Dhaky, among others. One may also consult Andreas Volwahsen *Living Architecture*: *Indian* (New York : Grosset and Dunlap, 1974), regarding the geometric principles underlying Indian architecture, with an analysis of several sites, including Ajantā; and K.V. Soundara Rajan, *Indian Temple Styles : The Personality of Indian Architecture* (New Delhi : Munshiram Manoharlal, 1972), some portions of which deal with structural temple styles in the Gupta period.

The more detailed the studies become, the more invaluable are the *Archaeological Survey of India Reports* (A.S.I.R.), edited by Sir Alexander Cunningham between 1862 and 1884, published in 23 volumes plus an index volume, and recently reprinted by the Indological Book House, Varanasi, between 1966 and 1972. The following are among the articles and basic reports about temple architecture in this period : Sarasi Kumar Saraswati, "Temple Architecture in the Gupta Age", *Journal of the Indian Society of*

Oriental Art, VIII (1940), 146-158; G. Yazdani, "The Fine Arts of the Deccan : Architecture, Sculpture, and Painting", in G. Yazdani, ed., *The Early History of the Deccan* (London : Oxford University Press, 1960), 715-782; R. D. Banerji, *The Temple of Śiva at Bhumara,* Memoirs of the Archaeological Survey of India, No. 16 (Calcutta : Superintendent of Government Printing, 1924); Pramod Chandra, "A Vāmana Temple of Maṛhiā and Some Reflections on Gupta Architecture", *Artibus Asiae,* 32 (1970), 125-145; Michael W. Meister, "A Note on the Superstructure of the Maṛhiā Temple", *Artibus Asiae,* 36 (1974-75), 81-88; Madho Sarup Vats, *The Gupta Temple at Deogarh,* Memoirs of the Archaeological Survey of India, No. 70 (Delhi : Manager of Publications, 1952); N. R. Banerjee, "New Light on the Gupta Temples at Deogarh", *Journal of the Asiatic Society*, 1 and 2 (1963), 37-49; Walter Spink, "Monuments of the Early Kalachuri Period", *Journal of Indian History*, XLVI, 2 (August, 1967), 263-270, an article which may be seen as complementary to his essay in this volume; K. V. Soundra Rajan, "Architectural Affiliations of Early Saurashtra Temples", *Indian Historical Quarterly,* XXXVII, 1 (March, 1961), 1-7, showing the relationship between these post-Gupta temples and the Gupta ones at Deogarh and Bhitargaon; Hermann Goetz, "The Last Masterpiece of Gupta Art : The Great Temple of Yaśovarman of Kanauj ('Telī-kā-Mandir') at Gwālior" in a collection of his essays entitled *Studies in the History, Religion and Art of Classical and Mediaeval India,* edited by Herman Kulke (Wiesbaden : Franz Steiner Verlag, 1974), 49-63; and J. C. Harle, "The Post-Gupta Style in Indian Temple Architecture and Sculpture", *Journal of the Royal Society of Arts* (August, 1977), 570-589, in which he compares Gupta with post-Gupta style, a style flourishing over much of India from *c.* 550 to *c.* 950 A.D. Two systematic studies by Odette Viennot on the development of architectural forms from the fifth through the tenth centuries need to be mentioned; both greatly clarify the sequence of Gupta temples : "Le problème des temples à toit plat dans l'Inde du Nord", *Arts Asiatiques,* XVIII (1968), 23-84; and *Temples de l'Inde centrale et iccudentale* (Paris : Publications de l'École Française d'Extrême-Orient, Memoires Archéologiques, XI, 1976).

In contrast to the relative paucity of scholarship on Hindu temple architecture during the Gupta period, there is a wealth of materials on Buddhist monuments and cave temples. Among the general works are the following : (1) James Fergusson and James Burgess, *The Cave Temples of India* (Delhi : Oriental Books Reprint Corporation, 1969, reprint of 1880 edition), part II of which is by Burgess, with pages 165-398 on Buddhist cave temples in Western India, pages 399-484 on principally post-Gupta Brāhmaṇical caves (Aihole, Bādāmī, Ellorā, Elephanta), and pages 485-512 on Jaina cave temples at Ellorā; (2) James Burgess, *Report on the Buddhist Cave Temples and Their Inscriptions,* Archaeological Survey of Western India, Vol. IV (Varanasi : Indological Book House, 1964), which is supplementary to *The Cave Temples of India* and deals with Bhājā, Piṭalkhorā, Nāsik, Ajantā and Kaṇherī; (3) Krishna Deva, "Buddhist Architecture in India", *Bulletin of Tibetology*, XI, 3 (1974), 12-28, a general survey dealing with stūpas, cave architecture, temples and monasteries; (4) M. K. Dhavalikar, "Evolution of the Buddhist Rockcut Shrines of Western India", *Journal of the Asiatic Society of Bombay*, Vols. 45-46, N. S. (1970-71), 50-61, which explores the mystery of the gap between the late Hīnayāna caves and the emergence of the Mahāyāna construction in the fifth century A.D.; (5) H. Sarkar, *Studies in Early Buddhist Architecture of India* (Delhi : Munshiram Manoharlal, 1966), basically pre-Gupta in focus; (6) Owen C. Kail, *Buddhist Cave Temples of India* (Bombay: D. B. Taraporevala, 1975), with some attention to Ajantā and Auraṅgābād; (7) Debala Mitra, *Buddhist Monuments* (Calcutta : Sahitya Samsad, 1971), which deals with sites in Madhya Pradesh, pages 91-106, and in Mahārāshtra and Āndhra Pradesh on pages 149-222; (B) Vidya Dehejia, *Early Buddhist Rock Temples : A Chronology* (Ithaca, N. Y.: Cornell University Press, 1972), one of the best recent surveys of pre-Mahāyāna period; (9) R. S. Gupte and B. D. Mahajan, *Ajanta, Ellora and Aurangabad Caves* (Bombay : D. B. Taraporevala, 1962), whose focus is primarily on the Mahāyāna phase at Ajantā, 32-106; the post-Gupta Buddhist, Śaivite, and Jaina caves at Ellorā, 107-224; and on Auraṅgābād, 225-236; (10) Walter Spink, "Bāgh : A Study", *Archives of Asian Art*, XXX (1976-77), 53-84, which is an excellent analysis of this site (its cultural and political factors, its pillar forms, and its iconographic features), which he dates *c.* 465 and *c.* 480 A.D.; (11) James Burgess, *The Rock-temples of Elephanta or Ghārāpūri* (Bombay : Thacker, Vining and Co., 1871), principally on the Great Temple there, (12) R. S. Gupte, "The Dating of the Elephanta Caves", *Journal of Indian History*, XLIII, 1 (August, 1965), 513-530, whose chronology is in great contrast to that of Walter Spink's; (13) Ratan Parimoo, "Elephanta in the Context of Evolution and Significance of Śaiva Sculpture", *Journal of the Oriental Institute of Baroda*, XXVI, 3 (March, 1977), 282-305, whose chronology accords with that of Spink and who discusses both architecture and iconography; and (14) Walter M. Spink, "Ellora's Earliest Phase", *Bulletin of the American Academy of Benares*, I (1967), 11-22, in which he discusses how this phase of Hindu patronage, beginning about 550 A.D., was strongly influenced by developments at Elephanta and other monuments in the Konkan region for two or three generations.

One of the most thoroughly researched sites is that of Ajantā, whose Mahāyāna phase was in the later part of the fifth century A.D. (according to the "short chronology" of Walter Spink). One may call this a Gupta site only in terms of sphere of influence, as it was actually in territory ruled by the Vākāṭakas, who were allied to the Guptas. Several of the following references deal with all aspects of art in these cave temples, as the site is as renowned for its painting as for its architecture and sculpture. An interesting introduction is Mukul Dey's account, *My Pilgrimages to Ajanta and Bagh* (London : Oxford University Press, second edition, 1950), as a young artist who spent two years at Ajantā copying the frescoes there. An early, almost definitive work is James Burgess' *The Rock Temples of Ajanta* (New York : Susil Gupta, Publisher, second edition, 1970, originally published in 1879), which is a highly technical and detailed description of the caves and their paintings. The most detailed recent study is by Sheila L. Weiner entitled *Ajaṇṭā : Its Place in Buddhist Art* (Berkeley : University of California Press, 1977), whose three principal chapters deal with the historical setting, iconographic developments, and stylistic trends and developments. While primarily concerned with sculpture, it bears mentioning in this section as well. Walter Spink's article, "Ajanta to Ellora", *Mārg*, XX, 2 (1967), later reprinted in book form by Marg Publications, deals with historical background, architectural features, and sculptural images of various sorts. The on-going debate about the chronology of the Mahāyāna caves at Ajantā is important for its influence on the dating of many other sites. This debate may be followed in a number of articles and longer works : Wayne Edison Begley, *The Chronology of Mahāyāna Buddhist Architecture and Painting at Ajaṇṭā* (Ann Arbor, Michigan : University Microfilms, Inc., 1967); see also Begley's review of Sheila Weiner's book in the *Journal of Asian Studies*, XXXVII, 3 (May, 1978), 570-572; Walter Spink; "Ajantā and Ghaṭotkacha : A Preliminary Analysis", *Ars Orientalis,* VI (1966), 135-155; Walter Spink, "The Splendours at Indra's Crown : A Study of Mahāyāna Developments of Ajantā, *Journal of the Royal Society of Arts* (October, 1974), 743-767; Walter M. Spink, "Ajanta's Chronology : The Crucial Cave", *Ars Orientalis,* X (1975), 143-169; and Sobhna Gokhale, "Epigraphical Evidence for the Chronology of Ajanta", *Journal of Indian History*, LI, 3 (1973), 479-484.

Besides the above which deal in passing with the paintings in the Ajantā caves, there are other works focusing primarily on this feature : Madanjeet Singh, *Ajanta* (Lausanne, Switzerland: Edita, 1965), includes approximately sixty pages of text tracing the history, the social conditions, and the evolution of painting styles, along with exceptional plates; Mulk Raj Anand, *Ajanta* (Bombay : Marg Publications, 1971), provides a short presentation of technical developments as traced in the wall-paintings of several caves, as well as discussion of specific plates with extensive notes regarding style, iconography and corresponding Jātaka tale where appropriate; G. Yazdani, *Ajanta,* 4 volumes (London : Oxford University Press, 1930-55), with descriptions of each plate and several appendices explaining the inscriptions; Osamu Takata, *Ajanta Cave-Temples and Murals* (Tokyo : Heibonsha, 1971), with superlative color plates descriptions in Japanese and identifications in English; A. Ghosh, ed., *Ajanta Murals* (New Delhi : Archaeological Survey of India, 1967), an important work, with color plates, line drawings, and several essays discussing many aspects of the caves and their murals; M. K. Dhavalikar, *Ajanta : A Cultural Study* (Poona : University of Poona, 1973), which shows how the world of Ajantā helps to depict features of Indian architecture, costumes and textiles, coiffures and head-dresses, personal ornaments, household articles and furniture, arms and armour, musical instruments, flora and fauna, etc.; Dieter Schlingoff, "Kalyāṇakārin's Adventures : The Identification of an Ajanta Painting", *Artibus Asiae*, XXXVIII, 1 (1976), 5-28; and M. K. Dhavalikar,

"Śrī Yugadhara—A Master-Artist of Ajanta", *Artibus Asiae*, XXXI (1969-70), 301-308. The Ajantā scene may be put in perspective by viewing painting on a broader canvas. For this purpose, these works are useful : Krishna Chaitanya, *A History of Indian Painting : The Mural Tradition* (New Delhi : Abhinav Publications, 1976), a capable, brief summary, with discussions of Ajantā, Bāgh, Bādāmī, among other sites; Moti Chandra, *Studies in Early Indian Painting* (New York : Asia Publishing House, 1970), with an essay on the "Transformation of the Gupta-Vākāṭaka Tradition", 9-36; and Stella Kramrisch, *A Survey of Painting in the Deccan* (London : The India Society, 1937), which discusses both Ajantā and Ellorā, as well as other locations. On the nearby Bāgh caves, two works may be mentioned : Sir John Marshall, et al., *The Bagh Caves in the Gwalior State* (London : The India Society, 1927), with a chapter on its sculptures and painting by J. Ph. Vogel, 27-63; and the long essay by Walter Spink, "Bāgh : A Study", *op. cit.*

3. *Gupta Sculpture*

As with previous sections of this essay it is appropriate at the beginning to note a few general works which both provide a survey of Indian sculpture and devote some attention to the Gupta period. Among numerous volumes of this sort one of the more useful is S. K. Saraswati, *A Survey of Indian Sculpture* (New Delhi : Munshiram Manoharlal Publishers, second revised edition, 1975), with pages 123-180 on Gupta works. Mentioned earlier was P. Thomas' *Epics, Myths and Legends of India* (Bombay, 1973), which combines a discussion of traditional literature with iconographic forms, dealing with Hindu, Buddhist and Jain traditions. Another helpful survey is by Charu Chandra Das Gupta, *Origin and Evolution of Indian Clay Sculpture* (Calcutta : University of Calcutta Press, 1961), covering pre-historic, proto-historic (Indus valley civilization), and historic periods.

Two recent publications, dealing entirely with Gupta sculpture, are welcome additions to the field. One of these, by Pratapaditya Pal, is entitled *The Ideal Image : The Gupta Sculptural Tradition and Its Influence* (New York : The Asia Society, Inc., 1978). This volume treats sculpture emerging from various Indian sites during the Gupta period and also sculpture directly influenced by this period elsewhere in Asia. The book includes 96 plates of works on display in an American exhibition, extended commentary, and a substantive Introduction which discusses Gupta India, Nepal and Southeast Asia in the age of the Guptas, religious development in Gupta India (Hindu, Buddhist, Jain), and the artistic milieu of this era. The other book is J. C. Harle's *Gupta Sculpture : Indian Sculpture of the Fourth to the Sixth Centuries* A.D. (Oxford : Clarendon Press, 1974), with 149 examples of sculpture in both stone and terracotta and with extensive discussion of each. The author's Introduction describes the historical and social background of Gupta art and the direction of stylistic development in Mathurā, eastern Mālwā, Central India, and the eastern part of Madhyadeśa and Sārnāth, along with the peripheral areas of Ajantā and Western India. Joanna Williams' review of Harle's book in the *Art Bulletin*, LIX, 1 (March, 1977), 119-121, should also be consulted as an appropriate commentary on the lack of "middle-ground" scholarship on Gupta sculpture between specialized studies and generalized interpretations of the spirit of the Gupta period. The two books by Pal and Harle are capable introductions to Gupta sculpture, being both comprehensible to the layman and with extensive plate captions of use to advanced students in this field. Joanna Williams' forthcoming *Art of Gupta India : Empire and Province* (Princeton University Press, 1982) deals with both sculpture and architecture and focuses on issues of the geographical and chronological definition of artistic forms. A number of articles may be cited as helpful to an overall view of Gupta scultpure : J. C. Harle, "Late Kushan, Early Gupta : A Reverse Approach", in Norman Hammond, ed., *South Asian Archaeology*, Papers from the First International Conference of South Asian Archaeologists held at the University of Cambridge, 1971 (Park Ridge, New Jersey : Noyes Press, 1973), 231-240; U. P. Shah, "Western Indian Sculpture and the So-called Gupta Influence", in Pratapaditya Pal, ed., *Aspects of Indian Art* (Leiden : E. J. Brill, 1972), 44-48; Joanna Williams, "A Recut Aśokan Capital and the Gupta Attitude towards the Past", *Artibus Asiae*, XXXV (1974), 225-240; V. S. Agrawala, "A Survey of Gupta Art and Some Sculptures from Nachna Kuthara and Khoh", *Lalit Kalā*, IX (April, 1961), 16-26; and Sheila L. Weiner, "From Gupta to Pāla Sculpture", *Artibus Asiae*, XXV, 2-3 (1962), 167-182.

Of importance as resource materials are catalogues from various museums, especially ones in North India, which depict holdings from the Gupta period, *inter alia* : R. C. Sharma, *Mathura Museum Introduction* (Mathura : Archaeological Museum, 1971); N. P. Joshi, *Catalogue of the Brahmanical Sculptures in the State Museum, Lucknow,* Part I (Lucknow : State Museum, 1972); Pramod Chandra, *Stone Sculpture in the Allahabad Museum: A Descriptive Catalogue* (Poona : American Institute of Indian Studies, 1970); Daya Ram Sahni, *Catalogue of the Museum of Archaeology at Sarnath* (Calcutta : Superintendent of Government Printing, 1914); Parameśvari Lal Gupta, ed., *Patna Museum Catalogue of Antiquities* (*Stone, Sculptures, Metal Images, Terracottas and Minor Antiquities*) (Patna : Patna Museum, 1965); Nalini Kanta Bhattasali, *Iconography of Buddhist and Brahmanical Sculptures in the Dacca Museum* (Dacca : Dacca City Museum, 1929), containing no Gupta works but useful for iconography; and Stella Kramarisch. *Indian Sculpture in the Philadelphia Museum of Art* (Philadelphia : University of Pennsylvania Press, 1960), a useful discussion of aesthetic principles and motifs though not primarily dealing with the Gupta period.

The two most indispensable works in the area of Hindu sculpture are those by T. A. Gopinatha Rao, *Elements of Hindu Iconography*, Volumes I and II (New York : Paragon Book, Reprint Corporation, 1968, second edition, reprint of Madras 1914 edition) and Jitendra Nath Banerjea, *The Development of Hindu Iconography* (Calcutta : University of Calcutta Press, 1956, second edition). Both are comprehensive and monumental works, drawing on Sanskrit texts as well as varied sculptural types. Rao's two-volume study has lengthy sections on Viṣṇu and Śiva, with all their major and minor forms, plus extensive treatment of Devī, Gaṇapati, Subrahmaṇya (Kārttikeya), and many secondary figures, drawing considerably upon South Indian sculptures but without discussing at length the development of individual iconographic types. Banerjea's work deals principally with the general principles of Hindu iconography and remains the most important work of this kind. It includes sculptures of the Gupta age, as well as other periods particularly in North India, and provides a systematic discussion of ancient Indian coins and seals of the same periods. The importance of this volume cannot be overestimated. Two other works mentioned earlier are also pertinent here : Bhaskar Chattopadhyay, *Coins and Icons : A Study of*

Myths and Symbols in Indian Numismatic Art (Calcutta : Punthi Pustak, 1977), with a focus mainly on the pre-Gupta eras; and Kiran Kumar Thaplyal, *Studies in Ancient Indian Seals : A Study of North Indian Seals and Sealings from 'circa' Third Century* B.C. *to Mid-Seventh Century* A.D. (Lucknow : Akhila Bharatiya Sanskrit Parishad, 1972), a detailed and advanced study with an extensive chapter on religious iconography.

Another work dealing with iconographical principles is Alice Boner's *Principles of Composition in Hindu Sculpture* (*Cave Temple Period*) (Leiden : E. J. Brill, 1962), which examines the Brāhmaṇical sculptures at Bādāmī (sixth century A.D.) Mahābalipuram (seventh century A.D.), and Elūrā (eighth and ninth centuries A.D.) and argues for a form of composition based on a concentric space-organization. While a stimulating work, it is post-Gupta and also has been questioned seriously today. A more important volume is Marie-Thérèse de Mallmann's *Les enseignements iconographiques de l'Agni Purāṇa* (Paris: Presses Universitaires de France, 1963). Another study of composition in Indian sculpture is M. M. Hallade's *La Composition Plastique dans les Reliefs de l'Inde* (Paris : Librarie d'Amerique et d'Orient, 1942), which examines the parallel evolution of Buddhist and Hindu sculpture in pre-Guptan and Guptan art. One may consult also an article of Thomas S. Maxwell entitled "The Deogarh Viśvarūpa : A Structural Analysis," *Art and Archeology Research Papers*, VIII (1975), 8-23, which explores the meaning of a late sixth century stele that demonstrates a sculptural tradition based upon syncretised layers of archaic structural symbolism. An encyclopedic two-volume work compiled between the sixth and eighth centuries, the *Viṣṇudharmottara Purāṇa,* translated and edited with commentary by Priyabala Shah (Baroda : Oriental Institute, 1958-61), has as its Part III "A Treatise on Indian Painting and Image-Making", translated by Stella Kramrisch (Calcutta : Calcutta University Press, 1928, second revised and enlarged edition). Several chapters in this are of important iconographic interest. For articles on certain aspects of this, see two by Pratapaditya Pal : "Dhanada-Kubera of the *Vishṇudharmottara Purāṇa* and Some Images from North-west India", *Lalit Kalā* XVIII (1977), 13-26, and "The *Aiḍūka* of the *Viṣṇudharmottarapurāṇa* and Certain Aspects of Stūpa Symbolism", *Journal of the Indian Society of Oriental Art*, New Series, IV

(1971-72), 49-62. Three other works are worth consulting : Brindavan C. Bhattacharya, *Indian Images*, Part I. *The Brahmanic Iconography Based on Genetic, Comparative and Synthetic Principles* (Calcutta : Thacker, Spink and Co., 1921), now somewhat dated; E. B. Havell, *The Ideals of Indian Art* (London : John Murray, 1920), a capable early discussion; and Niharranjan Ray, *An Approach to Indian Art* (Chandigarh : Panjab University, 1974), which shows how the *alaṁkāra* texts have relevance to the visual plastic arts as well as to Sanskrit poetics and Indian aesthetics more broadly.

Dealing with non-Brāhmaṇic traditions also are two recent works. One, by R. S. Gupte entitled *Iconography of the Hindus, Buddhists, and Jains* (Bombay : D. B. Taraporevala, 1972), is a detailed examination of iconographic features, with discussion of each illustration. The other, by Bhagwant Sahai, *Iconography of Minor Hindu and Buddhist Deities* (New Delhi : Abhinav Publications, 1975), has much on the Gupta period. A survey of some importance has recently been published under the general editorship of David L. Snellgrove entitled *The Image of The Buddha* (Tokyo and New York : Kodansha International, 1978), with articles by major scholars such as Jean Boisselier, Niharranjan Ray, Osamu Takata, Dietrich Seckel, Alexander Soper, et al., which place the development of the Buddha image into chronological and geographic perspective and treats those of the Gupta period accordingly. By far the most extensive work of its kind is by Benoytosh Bhattacharyya entitled *The Indian Buddhist Iconography* (Calcutta : Firma K. L. Mukhopadhyay, 1968, second edition, published originally in 1924), an advanced and detailed study of this subject which draws its information almost entirely from the *Saddhanamala*, a post-Gupta text, although the ideas may originate in Gupta times. His introduction to the translation of the *Guhyasamāja Tantra or Tathāgataguhyaka* (Baroda : Oriental Institute, 1967, reprint edition, Vol. 53 of Gaekwad's Oriental Series) more closely reflects Gupta concepts.

An exhaustive study of the Bodhisattva Avalokiteśvara is provided by Marie-Thérèse de Mallmann in her work entitled *Introduction à l'étude d'Avalokiteçvara* (Paris : Civilisations due Sud, 1948); see also her *Étude iconographique sur Mañjuśrī*, Vol. LV, Publications de l'École Française d'Extrême-Orient (Paris : École Française d'Extrême-Orient, 1964). Also on Avalokiteśvara are articles by Ajit Ghose, "An Image of Ārya Avalokiteśvara of the Time of Vainyagupta", *Journal of the Indian Society of Oriental Art*, XIII (1945), 49-54, and Krishna Kumar, "Some Gupta Caurī-Bearers", *Journal of the Indian Society of Oriental Art*, New Series, VI (1974-75), 9-13, which discusses Vajrapāṇi also as two attendant figures at Sārnāth in 477 A.D. For an introduction to Jain art during the Gupta era, see A. Ghosh, *Jaina Art and Architecture* (New Delhi : Bharatiya Jnanpith, 1974-75, 3 volumes), Vol. I, Part III, pages 107-140, on monuments and sculpture from 300 to 600 A.D.

More specific studies of Hindu deities important during the Gupta period, especially of Viṣṇu, may be found in a large number of writings. The following are representative, beyond those already mentioned. Kalpana S. Desai's *Iconography of Viṣṇu* (*in Northern India, up to the Mediaeval Period*) ((New Delhi : Abhinav Publications, 1973) is a careful discussion of the origins of Viṣṇu worship and Viṣṇu images, with separate chapters on fifteen major iconographic forms of Viṣṇu from the first century B.C. to the fourteenth century A.D. (many in the Gupta era). Another significant work is Wayne E. Begley's *Viṣṇu's Flaming Wheel : The Iconography of the 'Sudarśana-Cakra'* (New York : New York University Press, 1973). This explores both the literary and iconographic traditions in ancient, classical and medieval history. These articles are also germane : Chitta Ranjan Prasad Sinha, "Varāha-Viṣṇu in Art and Epigraph of Bihar", *Journal of the Bihar Research Society*, LVI (1970), 54-60; Debala Mitra, "Varāha-Cave of Udayagiri—An Iconographic Study", *Journal of the Asiatic Society* (*Calcutta*), 3 & 4 (1963), 99-104; S. V. Sohoni, "Varāha Avatāra Panel at Udayagiri, Vidiśā", *Journal of the Bihar Research Society*, LVII (1971), 49-56; R. C. Agrawala, "Nṛsiṁha-Varāha-Vishṇu Images and Some Allied Problems", *Lalit Kalā*, XVI (1974), 11-21; C. Sivaramamurti, "The Weapons of Vishṇu", *Artibus Asiae*, XVIII (1930), 128-136; B. Ch. Shastri, "Identification of a Relief belonging to the Gupta-Temple of Deogaṛh". *Acta Orientalia*, XII (1963), 117-125; B. Ch. Chhabra, "Garuda of Vishnu", *Journal of Indian History*, XXXXIII, 2 (August, 1965), 387-390; and Prithivi Kumar Agrawala, "Gupta Pillars at Bhitari, Ghazipur, *Journal of the Indian Society of Oriental Art*, New Series, VI (1974-75), 14-18. Śaivite sculpture during the Gupta, though nowhere near as extensive as that of Viṣṇu, is still considerable.

While many works mentioned above devote attention to this, one may also cite these : Bhagwant Sahai, "Ardhanārīśvara in North Indian Art", *Journal of the Bihar Research Society,* LX, 1-4 (January-December, 1974), 14-27; K. S. Ramachandran and C. Krishnamurthy, "Ardhanārīśvara in Mediaeval Sculpture", *Journal of Indian History*, XXXIX, 3 (December, 1961), 467-471; and Krishna Chandra Panigrahi, "Sculptural Representations of Lakulīśa and other Pāśupata Teachers", *Journal of Indian History,* XXXVIII, 3 (December, 1960), 635-43.

Gupta sculpture abounds in figures of secondary, though important function. Again, these too are treated in many works listed above, but one may find further discussion in the following : M. C. Joshi, "Two Interesting Sun Images from Nachna", *Journal of Indian History*, XLVIII, 1 (April, 1970), 80-87; Odette Viennot, *Les divinités fluviales Gaṅgā et Yamunā aux portes des sanctuaires de l'Inde* (Paris : Presses Universitaires de France, 1964); K. Bharatha Iyer, "An Early Gupta Seal of the Mahiṣāsuramandinī", *Artibus Asiae*, XXXI, 2/3 (1969), 179-184; Ananda K. Coomaraswamy, *Yakṣas* (New Delhi : Munshiram Manoharlal, 1971); G. Yazdani, "Woman in the Sculpture of the Deccan, An Artistic Study", *Annals of the Bhandarkar Oriental Research Institute*, XXIII (1942), 678-686; Asis Sen, *Animal Motifs in Ancient Indian Art* (Calcutta : Firma K. L. Mukhopadhyay, 1972), which depicts the evolution, symbolically, of the elephant, Gaṇeśa, and the makara, snake, bull, lion, horse, and bird; James Fergusson, *Tree and Serpent Worship* (Delhi : Oriental Publishers, 1971, reprint of 1868 edition), with special attention to sculpture from Sāñchī and Amarāvatī in the first and fourth centuries A.D.; and M. S. Randhawa, "The Cult of Trees and Tree Worship, in Buddhist-Hindu Sculpture", *Roopa-Lekha,* XXXIII, (1-2 1967), 1-42.

A final and essential way to investigate sculpture during the Gupta period is to focus on the various regions of North India, as well as contiguous areas. An excellent recent study by Frederick M. Asher entitled *The Art of Eastern India*, 300-800 (Minneapolis: University of Minnesota, 1980) examines Hindu and Buddhist sculpture (bronze, terracotta and stone) from what is presently Bihār, West Bengal, and Bangladesh during the Gupta and pre-Pāla periods, with an important chapter on "The Gupta Age", pages 13-34. Another work of significance is S. K. Saraswati's *Early Sculpture of Bengal*

(Calcutta : Sambodhi Publications, second edition, 1962), with pages 17-36 on the Gupta period. See also D. K. Chakravarty, "On the Survival of Some Typical Gupta Decorative Motifs on the Temples of Purulia District, West Bengal", *Journal of Indian History*, LIII, 7 (August, 1975), 233-241. On the temple at Bodh Gayā and its sculpture many works exist : Rajendralala Mitra, *Buddha Gaya : The Great Buddhist Temple* (Delhi : Indological Book House, 1972, originally published in 1878); Alexander Cunningham, *Mahābodhi; or the Great Buddhist Temple Under the Bodhi Tree at Buddha-Gayā* (London : W. H. Allen, 1892); Benimadhab Barua, *Gayā and Buddha-Gayā* (Calcutta : Indian Research Institute, 1943); Ananda Coomaraswamy, *La sculpture de Bodhgayā, Ars Asiatica*, Vol. XVIII (Paris : Editions d'Art et d'histoire, 1935); Tarapada Bhattacharyya, *The Bodhgaya Temple* (Calcutta : Firma K. L. Mukhopadhyay, second edition, 1966); and Prudence R. Myer's meticulous and comprehensive article entitled "The Great Temple at Bodh-Gaya", *Art Bulletin*, XL, 4 (December, 1958), 277-299. Several articles on Gupta sculpture in the Sārnāth area are noteworthy : Adris Banerji, "Gupta Sculptures of Benares : A Study", in D. R. Bhandarkar, ed., *B. C. Law Volume*, Part I (1945), 504-518; John M. Rosenfield, "On the Dated Carvings of Sārnāth", *Artibus Asiae*, XXVI (1963), 10-26; and Joanna Williams, "Sārnāth Gupta Steles of the Buddha's Life", *Ars Orientalis*, X (1975), 171-192. Two important publications on *Nepal* by Pratapaditya Pal show, among other things, how Vaiṣṇava Gupta sculpture in Central and Western India influenced certain iconic types in Nepal. Pal's *Vaiṣṇava Iconology in Nepal : A Study in Art and Religion* (Calcutta : The Asiatic Society, 1970) deals with the Gupta period and with post-Gupta tantric forms; his work *The Arts of Nepal*, Part I, *Sculpture* (Leiden : E. J. Brill, 1974), is a major study, to be followed by others on painting and on architecture.

While one of the earliest Buddhist sites outside its region of origin, Sāñchī was also a place where one can trace architectural and sculptural additions up through the Gupta period. The classic work on this site is that of John Marshall and Alfred Foucher entitled *The Monuments of Sanchi*, 3 vols. (Calcutta : Government of India Press, n.d.). A brief volume by Vasudeva S. Agrawala, *Masterpieces of Mathura Sculpture* (Varanasi :

Prithivi Prakashan, 1965) recounts the synthesis of Indian, Iranian, and Hellenistic influences which created this school of art. See also V. S. Agrawala, "Catalogue of the Mathura Museum", *Journal of the Uttar Pradesh Historical Society*, XXI-XXIV (1948-51), which, while not illustrated, is invaluable; and the article in *Lalit Kalā*, XIX, on the finds at Govindanagar, including the first dated Buddha image (434 A.D.) of the Gupta period known from Mathurā. Other articles of interest are as follows : Gritli von Mitterwallner, "Two Stūpa Basements of Mathurā of the 4th and 5th Centuries A.D.", in Anna Libera Dallapiccola, ed., *The Stūpa : Its Religious, Historical and Architectual Significance* (Wiesbaden : Franz Steiner Verlag, 1980) 72-89; Joanna Williams, "A Mathura Gupta Buddha Reconsidered", *Lalit Kalā*, XVII (1974), 28-31; V.S. Agrawala, "The Terracottas of Ahichchhatra", *Ancient India,* IV (January, 1948), 104-179, and "Pottery Designs from Ahichchhatra", *Lalit Kalā*, III (April, 1956), 74-78. A valuable article by Joanna Williams entitled "The Sculpture of Mandasor", *Archives of Asian Art*, XXVI (1972-73), 50-66, makes the case that the Mandasor images of 525 A.D. are a strong indication of a beginning of a distinct regionalism, of a Western India style whose carvings draw upon the Gupta heritage but whose aesthetic was transitional between the classical decorum and the "medieval canons which subordinated the figure to the larger religious purpose".

Along with the works which discuss Ajantā, Ellorā, and Auraṅgābād there are separate treatments of the latter site : Deborah Brown Levine, "Aurangabad : A Stylistic Analysis", *Artibus Asiae*, XXVIII (1967), 175-204; Amita Ray, "Sculptures in Aurangabad", *Mārg*, XVI, 3 (June, 1963), 34-54; and Amita Ray, *Aurangabad Sculptures* (Calcutta : Firma K. L. Mukhopadhyay, 1966), which elaborates on his article in *Mārg* and discusses the three historical periods at this site. Recent archeological exploration and research in Western India, especially at Devanī Morī in Rājasthān, have been of major import in terms of knowing more about culture in this region during the Gupta empire. The following help to provide a picture of these developments : Pratapaditya Pal, "Some Rajasthani Sculptures of the Gupta Period", *Bulletin of the Dudley Peter Allen Memorial Art Museum*, Oberlin College, XXVIII (1971), 104-118; R. C. Agrawala, "Rājaputānā through the Ages (Śaka-Kuṣāṇa and Gupta Periods)", *Journal of the Bihar Research Society*, XLI (September, 1955), 292-326; Umakant Premanand Shah, "Gupta Sculptures from Iḍar State (Gujarāt)", *Journal of Indian Museums*, X (1953), 90-103; and U. P. Shah, "Sculpture from Samlaji and Roda", *Bulletin of the Baroda Museum and Picture Gallery*, XIII (special number, 1960).

CONTRIBUTORS

Frederick M. Asher is Associate Professor of Art History and South Asian Studies at the University of Minnesota and currently Chairman of the Art History Department. He received his B.A. from Dartmouth College and his M.A. and Ph. D. from the University of Chicago. He is author of *The Art of Eastern India, 300-800* (University of Minnesota Press, 1980) and several article-length studies based on field work in India and Bangladesh.

A. L. Basham was recently the Distinguished Visiting Professor at the University of New Mexico in Albuquerque (1980-81). He is the recipient of the B.A., Ph.D., and D. Litt. degrees. His teaching career has principally been at the School of Oriental and African Studies, University of London (1947-65) and at the Australian National University in Canberra, where he was Professor and Head of the Department of Asian Civilizations (1965-79). His chief publications include : *History and Doctrines of the Ājīvikas; The Wonder that was India; Studies in Ancient Indian History and Culture; Papers on the Date of Kaniṣka* (Editor); and *A Cultural History of India* (Editor). He has given courses at several universities and colleges in the United States, including the University of Pennsylvania, Columbia University, the University of Wisconsin, the University of Minnesota, and Carleton College. He has also lectured at numerous institutions in the Indian subcontinent, and in Australia, the United Kingdom, Sweden, Germany, Malaysia, the United States, Mexico, Costa Rica, Argentina and Peru.

Norman Cutler is Assistant Professor of Tamil in the Department of South Asian Languages and Civilizations at the University of Chicago. He completed his Ph. D. in the same department in 1980 after spending two years in South India pursuing research for his dissertation on the poetry of the Tamil saints. He received his B.A. from the University of Michigan (1971) and his M.A. from the University of Washington (1975). One of his primary interests is translation of Tamil poetry, and he is the author of *Consider Our Vow : An English Translation of Tiruppāvai and Tiruvempāvai* (Madurai, 1979).

Balkrishna Govind Gokhale is Professor of History and Director, Asian Studies Program at Wake Forest University, Winston-Salem, North Carolina. He is the author of nine books and numerous papers on Indian history and culture and Buddhism, which include *Buddhism and Asoka* (1949), *Indian Thought Through the Ages* (1960) *Samudra Gupta* (1962), *Asoka Maurya* (1966), *Buddhism in Maharashtra* (1976) and *Surat in the XVIIth Century* (1979).

Barbara Stoler Miller is Professor of Oriental Studies at Barnard College, Columbia University. She received her B.A. in Philosophy from Barnard, then her M..A. in Sanskrit from Columbia and her Ph.D. in Indic Studies from the University of Pennsylvania. She has traveled widely throughout the Indian subcontinent and lived there to study Sanskrit and Indian art. Her books include *Phantasies of a Love-Thief : The Caurapañcāśikā Attributed to Bilhaṇa* (1971); *Love Song of the Dark Lord : Jayadeva's Gītagovinda* (1977); and *The Hermit and the Love-Thief : Poems of Bhartrihari and Bilhaṇa* (1978). She is currently at work on critical studies and translations of various Indian classical dramas.

A. K. Narain was born in Gaya (Bihar), India. His B.A. and M.A. degrees are from Banaras Hindu University and his Ph.D. from London University. His teaching career has been at Banaras Hindu University (1947-71) and the University of Wisconsin in Madison since 1971. He has served as an Editor of the *Journal of the Numismatic Society of India* since 1955 and was its Chief Editor from 1964 to 1974. Also, he was Editor of *Bharati, Bulletin of Indological Studies* (formerly *Bulletin of College*

Indology), 1963-70, and of *Puratattva, Bulletin of the Indian Archaeological Society of India*, 1967-70, and is currently Editor-in Chief of the *Journal of the International Association of Buddhist Studies*. Among his many publications are the following : *The Coin Types of Indo-Greek Kings* (1954); *The Indo-Greeks* (1957); *The Chronology of Punch-Marked Coins* (1966); *Alexander to Kanishka* (1967); *Excavations at Rajghat* (Parts I-IV, 1976-78), with T. N. Roy, P. Singh, and P. K. Agrawala; *Studies in Pali and Buddhism* (Editor, 1978); and *History of Buddhism* (Editor, 1979).

Wendy Doniger O'Flaherty received doctorates from Harvard University and Oxford University; she is Professor of History of Religions in the Divinity School, the Department of South Asian Languages and Civilizations, the Committee on Social Thought and the College in the University of Chicago. Among her publications are *Asceticism and Eroticism in the Mythology of Siva* (1973); *Hindu Myths* (1975); *The Origins of Evil in Hindu Mythology* (1976); and *Women, Androgynes, and Other Mythical Beasts* (1980). She has also edited *The Concept of Duty in South Asia* (1978); *The Critical Study of Sacred Texts* (1979); and *Karma and Rebirth in Classical Indian Tradition* (1980), and has just completed a translation of selections from the Rig Veda.

A. K. Ramanujan was born in South India and has degrees in English and in Linguistics. He is Professor in the Departments of Linguistics, Anthropology, and South Asian Languages and Civilizations at the University of Chicago. He has held teaching appointments at the Universities of Baroda (India), Wisconsin, Berkeley, Michigan, and Carleton College and is a Fellow of the School of Letters at Indiana University. He has contributed articles in linguistics, folklore, and Indian literature to many journals and books; his poetry and translations (from Kannada, Tamil, and Malayalam) have been widely published in India, the United States, and Great Britain. His publications include *Proverbs* (in Kannada, 1955), *The Striders* (Poetry Book Society Recommendation, 1966), *The Interior Landscape* (translations from Classical Tamil, 1970), *Hokkulalli Hūvilla* (Kannada poems, 1969), *Relations* (poems, 1971), *Speaking of Siva* (translations from Medieval Kannada,

1972), *Selected Poems* (1977), *Samskara : A Rite for a Dead Man* (translation of a Kannada novel, 1978, revised edition), and *Hymns for the Drowning* (translations from Nammālvār, 1981).

Bardwell L. Smith is the John W. Nason Professor of Asian Studies at Carleton College, Northfield, Minnesota. He also served as Dean of the College, 1967-72. He has received his B.A., B.D., M.A., and Ph.D. from Yale University and was a member of the Yale University Council, 1969-74. During 1972-73 he did research at the School of Oriental and African Studies, University of London, on a grant from the American Council of Learned Societies. He has edited a number of books, among them : *The Two Wheels of Dhamma : Essays on the Theravada Tradition in India and Ceylon.* (American Academy of Religion, 1972); *Tradition and Change in Theravada Buddhism : Essays on Ceylon and Thailand in the 19th and 20th Centuries* (Leiden : E. J. Brill, 1973); *Unsui : A Diary of Zen Monastic Life* (Honolulu : University Press of Hawaii, 1973); *Hinduism : New Essays in the History of Religions* (Leiden : E. J. Brill 1976); *Religion and Social Conflict in South Asia* (Leiden : E. J. Brill, 1976); *Essays on T'ang Society : The Interplay of Social, Political and Economic Forces* (Leiden : E. J. Brill, 1976), co-edited with John Curtis Perry; *Religion and Legitimation of Power in Sri Lanka* (Anima Books, 1978); and *Warlords, Artists and Commoners : Japan in the Sixteenth Century* (Honolulu : University Press of Hawaii, 1981), co-edited with George Elison.

Walter M. Spink is Professor of Indian Art at the University of Michigan, in Ann Arbor. He received his B.A. from Amherst College in 1949, and his M.A. and Ph. D. from Harvard University in 1950 and 1954. He taught at Brandeis University 1956-1961, and thereafter at the University of Michigan. He first studied in India in 1952-3 as a Fulbright Fellow, and since then has made various trips to India and Europe on research grants from the American Institute of Indian Studies, the Smithsonian Institution, National Endowment for the Humanities, American Council of Learned Societies, etc. He has served as President of the American Committee for South Asian Art, as Trustee of the American

Institute of Indian Studies, as an editor of *Ars Orientalis*, and as Director of the Asian Art Archives of the University of Michigan., He has written *Ajanta to Ellora* (1967), *Krishnamandala* (1971), *The Axis of Eros* (1973), and is currently writing a series of volumes on Ajanta and related cave sites.

Burton Stein is Professor of History at the University of Hawaii. Following completion of his doctorate at the University of Chicago in 1958, he taught at the University of Minnesota and has held visiting professorships at the University of California, Berkeley, the University of Washington, Seattle, and the Universities of Chicago and Pennsylvania. During the past twenty years, he has conducted research in India and in the United Kingdom and published on a variety of aspects of medieval South India, including two edited volumes (*Essays on South India*, 1975, and *South Indian Temples*; *An Analytical Study*, 1978) and a monograph entitled : *Peasant State and Society in Medieval South India*, Oxford University Press (New Delhi), 1980. He is presently engaged in preparation of a biography of Sir Thomas Munro (1761-1827).

Joanna G. Williams received her B.A. from Swarthmore college (1960) and her Ph.D. from Harvard University (1969, on Khotanese Painting). She is Professor of the History of Art at the University of California at Berkeley. She has worked in India during 1969 and 1974-5 (on Gupta art, as a Fellow of the American Institute of Indian Studies) and during 1978-9 (on Orissan pictorial arts, as a Guggenheim Fellow). She is the editor of *Kalādarśana : American Studies on the Art of India* (American Institute of Indian Studies, New Delhi, 1980). Her book, *The Art of Gupta India : Empire and Province,* will be published by Princeton University Press in 1982.

Eleanor Zelliot is Professor of History and Asian Studies at Carleton College, Northfield, Minnesota. Her degrees are from William Penn College (B.A.), Bryn Mawr College (M.A.), and the University of Pennsylvania (Ph.D. in South Asian Studies).

Her primary published research is on the history of the movement led by Dr. B. R. Ambedkar in India in this century and on the 16th century Bhakti saint-poet Eknath. She has also produced one other bibliographic essay, "The Medieval Bhakti Movement in History—an Essay on the Literature in English" in *Hinduism: New Essays in the History of Religions,* edited by Bardwell L. Smith (Leiden : E. J. Brill, 1976), and two comphrehensive bibliographies : "Bibliography on Untouchability" in *The Untouchables in Contemporary India,* edited by J. Michael Mahar (Tucson : University of Arizona, 1972), and "Bibliography of Modern Marathi Literature in English" in *A Marathi Sampler : Varied Voices in Contemporary Marathi Short Stories and Poetry,* edited by Eleanor Zelliot and Philip Engblom for the *Journal of South Asian Literature* (forthcoming).

GENERAL INDEX

AUTHOR INDEX FOR BIBLIOGRAPHICAL ESSAYS